2,000

FAMOUS LEGAL QUOTATIONS

by M. Frances McNamara

Member of the New York Bar
Librarian, New York State Department of Law

AQUEDUCT BOOKS

A division of The Lawyers Co-operative Publishing Co.
Rochester, New York

1967

Subject Headings

A

Abuse
Accord and Satisfaction
Accuracy
Achievement
Act
Actions
Act of God
Administration of Justice
Administrative Law
Admiralty
Admissions
Adverse Possession
Advertising
Advice
Advisory Opinions
Advocacy
Age
Agreement
Aliens
Ambiguity
Ambition
Ambulance Chasing
Amendment
Analogy
Analysis
Animals
Anomaly

Answer
Appeal
Apportionment
Arabiniana
Arbitration
Argument
Assumption of the Risk
Attack
Attempt
Attorney and Client
Authority
Average
Avoidance

B

Banking
Bankruptcy
Bench and Bar
Biography
Black Monday
Blackstone's Commentaries
Books
Books (Law)
Boundaries
Brain
Breach of Promise
Brevity
Bribery

iii

Brief ("Brandeis")
Brotherhood
Burke, Sir Edmund

C

Cases
Cases (Complex)
Cases (Popular Names)
Cause
Certainty
Chance
Chancery
Change
Charity
Children
Choice
Christianity
Church and State
Circumstances
Citations
Citizens
Civil Rights
Civil Service
Clarity
Clerk
Code
Coke, Sir Edward
Commendation (Self)
Commerce
Common Employment
Common Law
Communism

Concurrence
Confessions
Conflict of Interest
Conflict of Laws
Confrontation
Congressional Record
Consequence
Conservatism
Consistency
Conspiracy
Constitution
Constitution (Amendments)
Constitution (English)
Constitutional Law
Constitutionality
Consumer Fraud
Contemporaneous
Contempt of Court
Contracts
Convenience
Conveyancing
Copyright and Patent
Coram Nobis
Corporations
Costs
Courage
Court Packing
Court Packing (Nine Old Men)
Courts
Courts (Small Claims)
Crime
Criminal Justice

vi

x

Acknowledgments

Grateful acknowledgment is made to the publishers, authors and authors' representatives for permission to use selections from the publications as indicated below.

Appleton-Century-Crofts, Inc.
    in respect to: Frederick Trevor Hill, *Lincoln, The Lawyer,* 1906.

The Association of the Bar of the City of New York
    in respect to: Learned Hand, *Deficiencies of Trials to Reach the Heart of the Matter,* 3 Lectures on Legal Topics, Assn Bar City of N. Y.; James Garrett Wallace, *Wallace's Third Party,* from a minstrel show produced by the Assn Bar of City of N. Y.

Benet, *The Devil and Daniel Webster.*
    from: *The Selected Works of Stephen Vincent Benet,* Holt, Rinehart and Winston, Inc., Copyright 1936 by The Curtis Publishing Co. Reprinted by permission of Brandt & Brandt.

Bureau of National Affairs, Inc.
    in respect to: Frederick Bernays Wiener, *Briefing and Arguing Federal Appeals,* c. 1961.

Butterworths, London
    in respect to: *All England Law Reports* and *Law Times Reports.*

Callaghan & Co.
    in respect to: Rudolph von Jhering, *Struggle for Law,* 2nd ed (trans. Lalor), 1915.

Cambridge University Press
    in respect to: Helen Cam, *Selected Historical Essays of F. W. Maitland,* 1957; Maitland, *Collected Legal Papers* (ed. H. A. L. Fisher), 1911; Lord Macmillan, *Law and Other Things,* 1937; Roscoe Pound, *Interpretations of Legal History,* 1923; Lord Wright (of Durley), *Legal Essays and Addresses.*

Cassell & Co., Ltd.
    in respect to: Frederick E. S. Birkenhead, *Fourteen English Judges.*

ACKNOWLEDGMENTS

Henry Cecil
in respect to: Henry Cecil, *Friends at Court,* published by Michael Joseph, Ltd.

Clarendon Press, Oxford
in respect to: Harpsfield, *Life and Death of Sir Thomas More,* 1932. Reprinted by permission.

Columbia University Press
in respect to: Charles Evans Hughes, *Supreme Court of the United States,* c. 1928; Frederick Pollock, *Genius of the Common Law,* c. 1912; Woodrow Wilson, *Constitutional Government in the United States,* 1908 ed.

Doubleday & Company
in respect to: Drew Pearson and Robert S. Allen, *Nine Old Men.*

Farrar, Straus & Giroux, Inc.
in respect to: Quentin Reynolds, *Courtroom,* 1950.

Fortune and the Hon. Earl Warren
in respect to: Warren, *The Law and the Future,* Fortune, Nov. 1955.

Fortune and Mark Woolsey
in respect to: *The Supreme Court,* Fortune, Oct. 1949.

Foundation Press, Inc.
in respect to: Henry T. Lummus, *The Trial Judge,* 1937.

Erle Stanley Gardner
in respect ot: A. A. Fair (pseud.) *Some Women Won't Wait.*

K. Frederick Gross
in respect to: Fred L. Gross, *What is the Verdict?* Macmillan, 1944.

Harcourt, Brace & World, Inc.
in respect to: *The Just and the Unjust,* copyright, 1942, by James Gould Cozzens. Reprinted by permission of Harcourt, Brace & World, Inc.
in respect to: *Law and Literature* by Benjamin Cardozo, copyright, 1931, by Harcourt, Brace & World, Inc.; renewed, 1959, by First National City Trust Company. Reprinted by permission of the publisher.
in respect to: *Collected Legal Papers* by Oliver Wendell Holmes, copyright, 1920, by Harcourt, Brace & World, Inc.; renewed, 1948, by Edward J. Holmes. Reprinted by permission of the publisher.
in respect to: *Of Law and Men,* copyright, 1956, by Felix Frankfurter. Reprinted by permission of Harcourt, Brace & World, Inc.

Harper & Row, Publishers, Inc.
   in respect to: Finley Peter Dunne, *Dissertations by Mr. Dooley,*
   c. 1906; Dorothy L. Sayers, *Unnatural Death,* c. 1927.

Harrison Company
   in respect to: James M. Beck, *May It Please the Court,* c. 1930.

Harvard University Press, The President and Fellows of Harvard College; reprinted by permission of the publishers from:
   Alexander M. Bickel, *The Unpublished Opinions of Mr. Justice Brandeis,* Cambridge, Mass.: The Belknap Press of Harvard University Press, Copyright 1957 by the President and Fellows of Harvard College.
   Eugen Ehrlich, *Fundamental Principles of the Sociology of Law,* Cambridge, Mass.: Harvard University Press, Copyright 1936 by the President and Fellows of Harvard College, 1964 by Walter Lewis Moll.
   Felix Frankfurter, *Mr. Justice Holmes and the Supreme Court,* Cambridge, Mass.: The Belknap Press of Harvard University Press, Copyright 1938, 1961, by the President and Fellows of Harvard College, 1966 by Marion A. Denman Frankfurter.
   Learned Hand, *The Bill of Rights,* Cambridge, Mass.: Harvard University Press, Copyright 1958 by the President and Fellows of Harvard College.
   Mark DeWolfe Howe, editor, *Holmes-Pollock Letters,* Cambridge, Mass.: The Belknap Press of Harvard University Press, Copyright 1941, 1961, by the President and Fellows of Harvard College.
   Mark DeWolfe Howe, editor, *Holmes-Laski Letters,* Cambridge, Mass.: Harvard University Press, Copyright 1953 by the President and Fellows of Harvard College.
   Robert H. Jackson, *The Supreme Court in the American System of Government,* Cambridge, Mass.: Harvard University Press, Copyright 1955 by the President and Fellows of Harvard College.

Sir Alan Herbert, The Proprietors of Punch, and Methuen & Co. Ltd.
   in respect to: A. P. Herbert, *Uncommon Law,* 1935.

B. Herder Book Co.
   in respect to: Heinrich Rommen, *Natural Law* (trans. Hanley), 1947.

Mrs. Reginald Hine
   in respect to: Reginald L. Hine, *Confessions of an Un-Common Attorney,* Macmillan Co., 1945.

Houghton Mifflin Co.
   in respect to: Albert J. Beveridge, *Life of John Marshall,* 4v. 1916–19; Calvin Coolidge, *Have Faith in Massachusetts,* 1919; Arthur

ACKNOWLEDGMENTS

Schlesinger, *Politics of Upheaval*, 1960; *Autobiography of Will Rogers* (ed. by Donald Day), 1940.

Hutchinson Publishing Group Ltd.
in respect to: Lord Hewart, *Not Without Prejudice.*

Incorporated Council of Law Reporting for England and Wales
in respect to: *The Law Reports.*

Johns Hopkins Press
in respect to: H. L. Mencken, *A Carnival of Buncombe* (ed. by Malcolm Moos), 1956.

Alfred A. Knopf, Inc.
in respect to: Curtis Bok, *I, Too, Nicodemus*, 1946; Learned Hand, *Spirit of Liberty*, ed. by Irving Dilliard, 1952; Robert H. Jackson, *Struggle for Judicial Supremacy*, 1941.

Little, Brown & Co.
in respect to: Oliver Wendell Holmes, *Speeches*, 1913; Karl Llewellyn, *The Common Law Tradition Deciding Appeals*, 1960; Charles Warren, *The Supreme Court in United States History*, 1922.

Little, Brown & Co. and Atlantic Monthly Press
in respect to: Catherine Drinker Bowen, *Yankee From Olympus*, 1944.

Louisiana State University Press
in respect to: Alpheus T. Mason, *The Supreme Court From Taft to Warren*, 1958.

Macmillan Co., New York
in respect to: John Chipman Gray, *Nature and Sources of the Law*, 2nd ed., 1921; Edward Marjoribanks, *For the Defence*, 1929; Merlo Pusey, *Charles Evans Hughes*, 1952.

Hon. Miles F. McDonald, in respect to his *Prayer for Lawyers.*

David McKay Co., Inc.
in respect to: George M. Trevelyan, *Lord Grey of the Reform Bill*, 1920, pub. N.Y. by Longmans, Green & Co., Inc. Used by permission of David McKay Company, Inc.

Michie Company
in respect to: Edward J. Bander, ed., *Mr. Dooley on the Choice of Law*, c. 1963.

New York University Press
in respect to: Pound, *A Hundred Years of American Law*, in Law a Century of Progress, c. 1937; Albert T. Vanderbilt, *Cases and Other Materials on Modern Procedure*, c. 1952.

The New Yorker
in respect to: Howard Brubaker, *Of All Things,* April 10, 1937,
p. 34 and June 19, 1937, p. 30; *The Talk of the Town,* Mar. 6,
1937, p. 13.

The New Yorker and Albert Hirschfeld
in respect to: *The Talk of the Town,* Dec. 6, 1958, p. 43.

Princeton University Press
in respect to: Piero Calamandrei, *Eulogy of Judges* (trans. Adams
and Phillips) 1942; Alpheus T. Mason, *Brandeis, Lawyer and Judge
in the Modern State,* 1933; Jerome Frank, *Courts on Trial,* 1949,
William O. Douglas, *America Challenged,* 1960.

Publishers' Weekly, issue of March 24, 1958, p. 15
in respect to remark of Catherine Drinker Bowen.

Putnam's . Coward-McCann . John Day
in respect to: Jerome Frank, *Law and the Modern Mind,* 1949.

Random House, Inc.
in respect to: *The Public Papers and Addresses of Franklin D.
Roosevelt* (Rosenman, ed.) c. 1938.

Random House, Inc. and Anthony Lewis
in respect to: *Gideon's Trumpet,* c. 1964.

St. Martin's Press, Inc., Macmillan & Co., Ltd.
in respect to: Lord Macmillan, *A Man of Law's Tale,* 1952.

Charles Scribner's Sons
in respect to: Finley Peter Dunne, *Mr. Dooley on Making a Will,*
1919; Finley Peter Dunne, *Mr. Dooley Says,* 1910; John Galsworthy, *In Chancery,* 1920; John Galsworthy, *Justice* and *Windows,*
from *Plays,* 1929.

William Seagle
in respect to: William Seagle, *Quest for Law,* Knopf, 1941.

Session Cases Committee of the Faculty of Advocates, Scotland
in respect to: *Session Cases.*

Sheed & Ward, Inc., New York
in respect to: G. K. Chesterton, *Tremendous Trifles,* c. 1909.

Simon & Schuster, Inc.
in respect to: Charles P. Curtis, *A Commonplace Book,* c. 1957;
Harold L. Ickes, *Secret Diary,* c. 1953–1954.

ACKNOWLEDGMENTS

Stevens & Sons, Ltd.
in respect to: JPC, *Poetic Justice,* 1947; Law Quarterly Review; Mackinnon, *Inner Temple Papers,* 1948; Morris & Leach, *Rules vs. Perpetuities,* 2nd ed.

University of Kansas Press
in respect to: Lord Evershed, *Practical and Academic Characteristics of English Law,* 1956.

University of North Carolina Press
in respect to: Felix Frankfurter, *The Commerce Clause Under Marshall,* Taney and Waite, 1937.

Viking Press, Inc.
in respect to: Alpheus Thomas Mason, *Brandeis, A Free Man's Life,* 1946, and *The Curse of Bigness,* Miscellaneous Papers of Louis D. Brandeis, ed. by Osmond K. Fraenkel as projected by Clarence M. Lewis.

Yale University Press
in respect to: Benjamin N. Cardozo, *Growth of the Law,* 1924; Benjamin N. Cardozo, *The Nature of the Judicial Process,* 1921; Felix Frankfurter, ed. *Mr. Justice Brandeis,* 1932.

LAW REVIEWS AND JOURNALS:

American Bar Association Journal (Copyright: American Bar Association).
v. 30, c. 1944; v. 32, c. 1946; v. 33, c. 1947; v. 37, c. 1951; v. 38, c. 1952; v. 39, c. 1953; v. 41, c. 1955; v. 47, c. 1961; v. 48, c. 1962.

Bar Bulletin (New York County Lawyers Assn) v. 13, 1956.

Boston University Law Review, v. 17, c. 1937.

Brief Case, v. 9, 1951 (National Legal Aid Assn).

Buffalo Law Review, v. 14, c. 1964.

California Law Review, v. 53, c. 1965 California Law Review Inc.; reprinted by permission.

Canadian Bar Review, v. 3, 1925.

Columbia Law Review (Copyright by the Directors (or Trustees) of The Columbia Law Review Assn).
v. 30, c. 1930; v. 31, c. 1931; v. 39, c. 1939; v. 41, c. 1941.

Cornell Law Quarterly, v. 14, c. 1929.

Harvard Law Review (Copyright by the Harvard Law Review Association).
v. 32, copyright 1918; v. 41, copyright 1927; v. 43, copyright 1930; v. 44, copyright 1931; v. 45, copyright 1932; v. 48, copyright 1934; v. 50, copyright 1936; v. 56, copyright 1942; v. 71, copyright 1957.

Illinois Law Review, v. 10, c. 1915–16, Northwestern University Press.

Journal of the American Judicature Society, v. 32, 1948, v. 39, 1955–56.

Journal of Legal Education, v. 1, 1948–49, c. Assn American Law Schools.

Law and Contemporary Problems, v 14, 1949. Reprinted by permission from symposium issue, *Religion and the State.* Published by Duke University School of Law, c. 1949 by Duke University, Durham, N.C.

Massachusetts Law Quarterly, v. 3, 1917.

New York Law Forum, v. 2, c. 1956 by New York Law School.

New York State Bar Association:
New York State Bar Bulletin, vols. 1, 3, 4, 5, 7.
New York State Bar Journal, v. 36.

New York University Law Review, v. 35, c. N.Y. University, 1960
in respect to: Black, *The Bill of Rights* (First James Madison Lecture given at the New York University Law Center).

New Zealand Law Journal, v. 36, 1960.

Notre Dame Lawyer, v. 19, c. 1943–44.

The Record (Assn of the Bar of the City of New York) v. 18, 1963; v. 20, 1965.

St. John's Law Review, v. 13, c. 1939.

University of Chicago Law Review, v. 9, 1941.

University of Pennsylvania Law Review, v. 79, c. 1930, v. 105, c. 1957.

Virginia Law Review, v. 39, c. 1953.

Yale Law Review, v. 57, c. 1947; v. 60, c. 1951 by Yale Law Journal Co., Inc.

Credit is also given for brief quotations from the following publications:

John F. Blair, Winston-Salem
in respect to: George W. Dalzell, *Benefit of Clergy in America,* 1955.

Boston Book Co.
in respect to: James Bradley Thayer, *Legal Essays,* 1908; Eugen Ehrlich, *Freedom of Decision,* in Science of Legal Method, v. 9 Modern Legal Philosophy Series (trans. Bruncken); and Rudolph von Jhering, *Law as a Means to an End* (trans. Husik), 1913.

Doubleday & Co. Inc.
in respect to: H. G. Wells, *Work, Wealth and Happiness of Mankind,* 1931.

Houghton Mifflin Co.
in respect to: John Buchan, *Homilies and Recreations,* 1926.

ACKNOWLEDGMENTS

Incorporated Council of Law Reporting for Ireland
in respect to: Irish Reports.

Selden Society Publications, England

Southern Publishers, Inc.
in respect to: McDaniel, *The Saga of Judge Roy Bean,* c. McDaniel,
1936.

Survey Graphic
in respect to: December, 1933, issue.

Times Law Reports, London

———

*I also wish to express my appreciation of the facilities of the New
York State Library and the courtesies extended to me by the entire staff.
I am particularly indebted to Mr. Ernest H. Breuer, the Law Librarian,
and his staff.*

2,000 FAMOUS LEGAL QUOTATIONS

Abuse

I like a clamour whenever there is an abuse. The fire-bell at midnight disturbs your sleep, but it keeps you from being burned in your bed.

> EDMUND BURKE, *Speech: Powers of Juries in Prosecutions for Libel.*

Accord and Satisfaction

And it was resolved by the whole court, thát payment of a lesser sum on the day in satisfaction of a greater, cannot be any satisfaction for the whole, because it appears to the judges that by no possibility a lesser sum can be a satisfaction to the plaintiff for a greater sum: but the gift of a horse, hawk, or robe, etc., in satisfaction is good. For it shall be intended that a horse, hawk or robe, etc., might be more beneficial to the plaintiff than the money, in respect of some circumstance, or otherwise the plaintiff would not have accepted of it in satisfaction.

COKE, *Pinnel's Case* (1602) 5 Rep. 117 a.

A creditor might accept anything in satisfaction of his debt except a less amount of money. He might take a horse, or a canary, or a tomtit if he chose, and that was accord and satisfaction; but, by a most extraordinary peculiarity of the English Common Law, he could not take 19s. 6d. in the pound; that was *nudum pactum*. . . . That was one of the mysteries of English Common Law.

JESSEL, M.R., *Couldery v Bartrum* (1881) 19 Ch. D. 394, 399.

Accuracy

There is an accuracy that defeats itself by the overemphasis of details. . . . The sentence may be so overloaded with all its possible qualifications that it will tumble down of its own weight.

BENJAMIN N. CARDOZO, *Law and Literature* 7 (1931).

Delusive exactness is a source of fallacy throughout the law.

HOLMES, J., *Truax v Corrigan* (1921) 257 US 312, 342, 66 L ed 254, 267, 42 S Ct 124, 27 ALR 375.

Achievement

One cannot be pulled up a great height. Only a short distance can you be lifted by your arms. But by climbing with your feet and stepping on the solid ground below, you can climb mountains.

> LOUIS D. BRANDEIS, *Notebook, November 12, 1880.*
> See MASON, *Brandeis, — A Free Man's Life* 61 (1946).

Act

An act which, in itself, is merely a voluntary muscular contraction, derives all its character from the consequences which will follow it under the circumstances in which it is done.

> HOLMES, J., *Aikens v Wisconsin* (1904) 195 US 194, 205, 49 L ed 154, 159, 25 S Ct 3.

Act of God

The act of God shall prejudice no man; as, where the law prescribeth means to perfect or settle any right or estate, if by the act of God the means, in some circumstances, become impossible, no party shall receive any damage thereby.

> COKE, *First Institute* 123.

Actions

He [Hippodamus] maintained that there are three subjects of lawsuits—insult, injury and homicide.

> ARISTOTLE, *Politics,* bk. 2, ch. 8 (Jowett trans.).

There was made also another law for peace in general, and repressing of murders and manslaughters, and was in

amendment of the common laws of the realm; being this:
That whereas by the common law the King's suit, in case
of homicide, did expect the year and the day, allowed to
the party's suit by way of appeal; and that it was found by
experience that the party was many times compounded
with, and many times wearied with the suit, so that in the
end such suit was let fall; and by that time the matter
was in a manner forgotten, and thereby prosecution at the
King's suit by indictment (which is ever best *flagrante
crimine*) neglected; it was ordained that the suit by indictment might be taken as well at any time within the year
and the day as after; not prejudicing nevertheless the party's
suit.

> BACON, *History of King Henry VII.* The wife and heir of the
> man killed had the right to prosecute in their own name. The
> statute is 3 Henry 7, c. 3.

The forms of actions we have buried, but they still rule
us from their graves.

> FREDERIC WM. MAITLAND, *Forms of Actions at Common Law,*
> Lecture 1 (1909).

I am a great friend to the action for money had and
received; and therefore I am not for stretching, lest I should
endanger it.

> LORD MANSFIELD, C.J., *Weston v Downes* (1778) 1 Doug. 23,
> 24.

Administration of Justice

If I were to ask you, gentlemen of the jury, what is the
choicest fruit that grows upon the tree of English liberty,
you would answer, security under the law. If I were to

4

ask the whole people of England, the return they looked for at the hands of government, for the burdens under which they bend to support it, I should still be answered, security under the law; or, in other words, an impartial administration of justice.

> THOMAS ERSKINE, arguendo, *Trial of Thomas Paine* (1792) 22 How. St. Tr. 358, 417.

The sound of their voices arose, together with a scent as of neglected wells, which, mingling with the odour of the galleries, combined to form the savour, like nothing but the emanation of a refined cheese, so indissolubly connected with the administration of British justice.

> JOHN GALSWORTHY, *Man of Property,* ch. 28.

Important as it was that people should get justice, it was even more important that they should be made to feel and see that they were getting it.

> FARRER HERSCHELL, retort at Bar when Sir George Jessel attempted to cut him short in an argument. See 2 Atlay, *Victorian Chancellors* 460 (1908).

It . . . is of fundamental importance that justice should not only be done, but should manifestly and undoubtedly be seen to be done.

> LORD HEWART, C.J., *R. v Sussex Justices, ex p. McCarthy* [1924] 1 K.B. 256, 259.

That people will be happiest whose laws are best, and are best administered.

> THOMAS JEFFERSON, *Letter to Cornelius C. Blatchly, Oct. 21, 1822.*

5

Though the law itself be fair on its face and impartial in appearance, yet, if it is applied and administered by public authority with an evil eye and an unequal hand, so as practically to make unjust and illegal discriminations between persons in similar circumstances, material to their rights, the denial of equal justice is still within the prohibition of the Constitution.

> MATTHEWS, J., *Yick Wo v Hopkins* (1886) 118 US 356, 373, 30 L ed 220, 227, 6 S Ct 1064.

The most important and most constant cause of dissatisfaction with all law at all times is to be found in the necessarily mechanical operation of legal rules. This is one of the penalties of uniformity. Legal history shows an oscillation between wide judicial discretion on the one hand and strict confinement of the magistrate by minute and detailed rules upon the other hand. . . . The law has always ended in a compromise, in a middle course between wide discretion and over-minute legislation. In reaching this middle ground, some sacrifice of flexibility of application to particular cases is inevitable. In consequence, the adjustment of the relations of man and man according to these rules will of necessity appear more or less arbitrary and more or less in conflict with the ethical notions of individuals.

> ROSCOE POUND, *The Causes of Popular Dissatisfaction with the Administration of Justice*, 29 A.B.A.R. 395, 397 (1906).

The sporting theory of justice, the "instinct of giving the game fair play," as Professor Wigmore* has put it, is so rooted in the profession in America that most of us take

---

*1 Wigmore, *Evidence* 127 (1904). See also, 20 J. Am. Jud. Soc. 176 (1937) where Wigmore refers to this classic speech of Pound as "The spark that kindled the white flame of progress."

it for a fundamental legal tenet. But it is probably only a survival of the days when a lawsuit was a fight between two clans in which change of venue had been taken to the forum. So far from being a fundamental fact of jurisprudence, it is peculiar to Anglo-American law.

> ROSCOE POUND, *The Causes of Popular Dissatisfaction with the Administration of Justice,* 29 A.B.A.R. 395, 404 (1906).

The fundamental premise of the federal rules is that a trial is an orderly search for the truth in the interest of justice rather than a contest between two gladiators with surprise and technicalities as their chief weapons, an outmoded point of view that unfortunately still lingers on in all too many states.

> ARTHUR T. VANDERBILT, *Cases and Materials on Modern Procedure* 10 (1952).

Impressed with a conviction that the due administration of justice is the firmest pillar of good government, I have considered the first arrangement of the judicial department as essential to the happiness of our country and to the stability of its political system. Hence selection of the fittest characters to expound the laws, and dispense justice, has been an invariable object of my anxious concern.

> GEORGE WASHINGTON, *Letter, Sept. 27, 1789, to Edmund Randolph,* offering him the position of Attorney General. See *11 Writings (Ford ed.) 432.*

Administrative Law

I have given you my Law, and you set up commissions.

T. S. ELIOT, *The Rock.*

If however, the Commission is sustained in this case, and, accordingly, behaves similarly in future cases, then its conduct will indeed be a mystery. Its so-called "valuations" will then be acceptable, no matter how contrived. In that event, it would be desirable to abandon the word "valuation"—since that word misleadingly connotes some moderately rational judgment—and to substitute some neutral term, devoid of misleading associations, such as "aluation," or, perhaps better still, "woosh-woosh." The pertinent doctrine would then be this: "When the I.C.C. has ceremonially woosh-wooshed, judicial scrutiny is barred."

> FRANK, J., dissenting, *Old Colony Bondholders v N. Y., N. H. & H. R. Co.* (1947) 161 F2d 413, 450.

Admiralty

The sea is a strange and wondrous thing, and equally so is the law it inspires. Rules derived from it reflect not the fury of this element in its stormy mood but the gentle nature of a close harbor in the morning calm.

> HALE, J., *Sullivan v Lyon Steamship Ltd.* (1963) 63 Wash 2d 316.

Admissions

No admission of the party . . . can make that legal which is in its nature illegal.

> ASHHURST, J., *Atherfold v Beard* (1788) 2 T. R. 610, 615.

Admissions are mostly made by those who do not know their importance.

> LORD DARLING, *Scintillae Juris: Of Witnesses.*

Thy adverse party is thy advocate.

> SHAKESPEARE, *Sonnets XXXV.*

Adverse Possession

Under a claim of his own, he must raise the flag of hostile possession and, planting himself under its folds, keep it flying through such effluxion of time as ripens into a title by adverse possession.

LAMM, J., *Himmelberger-Harrison Lumber Co. v Craig* (1913) 248 Mo 319, 330.

Advertising

Johnson: Sir, it is wrong to stir up law-suits; but when once it is certain that a law-suit is to go on, there is nothing wrong in a lawyer's endeavoring that he shall have the benefit rather than another.

Boswell: You would not solicit employment, Sir, if you were a lawyer?

Johnson: No, Sir, but not because I should think it wrong, but because I should disdain it. However, I would not have a lawyer to be wanting to himself in using fair means. I would have him to inject a little hint now and then to prevent his being overlooked.

SAMUEL JOHNSON. Boswell, *Life of Johnson: 1776.*

To get his name on the title page of a useful law book has always been recognized as one of the few legitimate methods of publicity open to an aspiring member of the Bar.

LORD MACMILLAN, *Man of Law's Tale* 55 (1952).

Advice

The greatest trust between man and man is the trust of giving counsel: for in other confidences men commit the

parts of life, their lands, their goods, their children, their
credit, some particular affair; but to such as they make
their counsellors they commit the whole; by how much
more they are obliged to all faith and integrity.

> BACON, *Essays: Of Counsel.*

Your law may be perfect, your ability to apply it great,
and yet you cannot be a successful adviser unless your
advice is followed; it will not be followed unless you can
satisfy your clients, unless you impress them with your
superior knowledge, and that you cannot do unless you
know their affairs better than they do because you see them
from a fullness of knowledge. The ability to impress them
grows with your own success in advising others, with the
confidence which you yourself feel in your powers. That
confidence can never come from books; it is gained by
human intercourse.

> LOUIS D. BRANDEIS, Letter to William H. Dunbar, 1893. Mason,
> *Brandeis, A Free Man's Life* 80 (1946).

The fact that a lawyer advised such foolish conduct, does
not relieve it of its foolishness.

> EMERY, J., *Hanscom v Marston* (1890) 82 Me 288, 298.

When lawyers take, what they would give
And doctors give what they would take.

> O. W. HOLMES, SR., *Latter-Day Warnings.*

A lawyer's advice is his stock in trade.

> .   ABRAHAM LINCOLN—attributed to.

Go not for every grief to the physician, nor for every quarrel to the lawyer, nor for every thirst to the pot.

Proverb. HERBERT, *Jacula Prudentum (1651).*

Advisory Opinions

We have considered the previous question stated in a letter written by your direction to us by the Secretary of State, on the 18th of last month [regarding] the lines of separation, drawn by the Constitution between the three departments of the government. These being in certain respects checks upon each other, and our being judges of a court in the last resort, are considerations which afford strong arguments against the propriety of our extra-judicially deciding the questions alluded to, especially as the power given by the Constitution to the President, of calling on the heads of departments for opinions, seems to have been *purposely* as well as expressly united to the executive departments.

JOHN JAY, CHIEF JUSTICE, to President Washington, Aug. 8, 1793. See 3 *Correspondence and Public Papers of John Jay* (Johnston ed. 1891) 488.

We exceedingly regret every event that may cause embarrassment to your administration, but we derive consolation from the reflection that your judgment will discern what is right, and that your usual prudence, decision, and firmness will surmount every obstacle to the preservation of the rights, peace and dignity of the United States.

JOHN JAY, *ibid.*

Advocacy

He had a habit of refusing to appear in civil actions where he was not persuaded of the justice of the cause. This is not to be commended. The Bar as a profession offers its services to all litigants. Counsel supports his client's case within the limits prescribed by personal and professional honour. He is not the judge to decide the merits; his function is to present his client's case. If counsel usurps the duties of the judge, then two results follow. First, men are deprived of that legal assistance to which they are entitled. Secondly, the fact that counsel is known only to accept cases in which he personally believes may work injustice to those whom he refuses. . . . And so Hale (Sir Matthew) sometimes found that he had caused injustice in several instances where he had made up his mind on the merits and found afterwards that he had rejected the case on insufficient grounds.

LORD BIRKENHEAD, *Fourteen English Judges* 61 (1926).

A man's rights are to be determined by the Court, not by his attorney or counsel. It is for want of remembering this that foolish people object to lawyers that they will advocate a case against their own opinions. A client is entitled to say to his counsel, I want your advocacy, not your judgment; I prefer that of the Court.

BRAMWELL, B., *Johnson v Emerson* (1871) L.R. 6 Ex. 329, 367.

An advocate, by the sacred duty which he owes his client, knows, in the discharge of that office, but one person in the world, that client and none other. To save that client by all expedient means—to protect that client at all hazards and costs to all others, and among others to himself,— is the highest and most unquestioned of his duties; and he must not regard the alarm, the suffering, the torment, the destruction which he may bring upon any other. Nay, separating even the duties of a patriot from those of an advocate, and casting them, if need be, to the wind, he must go on reckless of the consequences, if his fate it should unhappily be, to involve his country in confusion for his client's protection.*

> HENRY BROUGHAM, arguendo, *Trial of Queen Caroline,* 1820.

It is a great mistake to consider the speeches we deliver before the courts as a faithful depository of our personal opinions. All these speeches emanate from the cause and the circumstances rather than the man and the orator, for if the cause could speak for itself there would be no need of counsel. We are therefore called upon not to utter our own maxims, but to bring out everything of significance that the cause can furnish.

> CICERO, *Pro Cluentio,* L.

My noble and learned friend, Lord Brougham, whose words are the words of wisdom, said that an advocate should be fearless in carrying out the interest of his client; but I couple that with this qualification and this restriction

---

* This speech has been severely criticized. Brougham in 1859 wrote to Forsyth that his statement was anything but a well considered opinion on the duties of an advocate. It was a "menace" directed to George IV to stop him from pressing the bill of divorcement beyond a certain point. It was a threat to impeach the King's own title by proving that he had forfeited the crown by marrying while heir apparent, a Roman Catholic, Mrs. Fitzherbert. See, Forsyth, *History of a Lawyer* 380 (1875).

"I never did commit adultery but once, and I have repented it ever since. It was with the husband of Mrs. Fitzherbert." Queen Caroline, in Grey family correspondence. See, Trevelyan, *Lord Grey of the Reform Bill* 191 (1920).

—that the arms which he wields are to be the arms of the warrior and not of the assassin.

LORD COCKBURN, November 8, 1864, Middle Temple Banquet in honor of Mons. Berryer.

He [the advocate] is a representative, but not a delegate. He gives to his client the benefit of his learning, his talents, and his judgment; but all through he never forgets what he owes to himself and to others. He will not knowingly misstate the law—he will not wilfully misstate the facts, though it be to gain the cause for his client. He will ever bear in mind that if he be the Advocate of an individual, and retained and remunerated (often inadequately) for his valuable services, yet he has a prior and perpetual retainer on behalf of truth and justice; and there is no Crown or other license which in any case, or for any party or purpose, can discharge him from that primary and paramount retainer.

CRAMPTON, J., *R. v O'Connell* (1844) 7 Ir. L.R. 261, 313.

He [the advocate] lends his exertions to all, himself to none. The result of the cause is to him a matter of indifference. It is for the Court to decide. It is for him to argue. He is, however he may be represented by those who understand not his true situation, merely an officer assisting in the administration of justice, and acting under the impression that truth is best discovered by powerful statements on both sides of the question.

LORD ELDON, *Ex parte Lloyd* (1822) Montagu Bankr. R., 70 n. 72.

If the advocate refuses to defend, from what he may think of the charge or of the defence, he assumes the character of the judge; nay, he assumes it before the hour of judgment; and in proportion to his rank and reputation, puts the heavy influence of perhaps a mistaken opinion into the scale against the accused.

> THOMAS ERSKINE, arguendo, *Trial of Thomas Paine* (1792) 22 How. St. Tr. 358, 412.

From the first he showed that the stuff of the advocate was in him, and . . . had fashioned himself into an accomplished practitioner of the art of persuasion.

> FELIX FRANKFURTER, *Of Law and Men (Stanley M. Silverberg)* 321 (1956).

It is a popular, but gross, mistake to suppose that a lawyer owes no fidelity to anyone except his client; and that the latter is the keeper of his professional conscience. He is expressly bound by his official oath to behave himself in his office of attorney with all due fidelity to the court as well as the client; and he violates it when he consciously presses for an unjust judgment. . . . The high and honorable office of a counsel would be degraded to that of a mercenary, were he compelled to do the biddings of his client against the dictates of his conscience.

> GIBSON, C.J., *Rush v Cavenaugh* (1845) 2 Barr(Pa.) 187, 189.

He is an ingenious counsel, who has made the most of his cause: he is not obliged to gain it.

> SAMUEL JOHNSON. Boswell, *Life of Johnson:* 1772.

Stand forth pale *Ajax,* and thy Speech repeat;
Assert thy Client's Freedom; bawl, and tear
So loud, thy Country-Judge at least may hear,

15

If not discern; and when thy Lungs are sore,
Hang up the Victor's Garland at thy Door.

> JUVENAL, *Satires,* VII (Dryden trans.) When an orator had won
> a cause, a garland was hung up before his door.

Who to poor Basilus his Cause would trust,
Tho' ne'er so full of Pity, ne'er so just?
His Clients, unregarded, claim their due;
For Eloquence in Rags was never true.
Go, Wretch, thy Pleadings into Africk send;
Or France, where Merit never needs a Friend.

> JUVENAL, *Satires,* VII (Dryden trans.) Africa and France were
> then famous for great lawyers and fat fees.

No counsel supposes himself to be the mere advocate
or agent of his client, to gain a victory, if he can, on a
particular occasion. The zeal and the arguments of every
counsel, knowing what is due to himself and his honourable
profession, are qualified not only by considerations affecting his own character as a man of honour, experience, and
learning, but also by considerations affecting the general
interests of justice.

> LORD LANGDALE, M.R., *Hutchinson v Stephens* (1837) 1 Keen
> 659, 668.

Advocacy is an enthralling vocation but an exhausting
one, and after many years of it one grows a little weary
of throwing all one's energies into other people's disputes.
It becomes increasingly difficult to keep up a head of steam
in the boiler. The unique advantage of the Bar as a profession is that it offers in their later years to those who
have succeeded in it the sanctuary of the Bench where
they may continue to serve the law in a serener atmosphere

and turn to useful account the garnered stores of their experience.

> LORD MACMILLAN, *Man of Law's Tale* 142 (1952).

My profession and that of an actor are somewhat akin, except that I have no scenes to help me, and no words are written for me to say. There is no black-cloth to increase the illusion. There is no curtain. But, out of the vivid, living dream of somebody else's life, I have to create an atmosphere,—for that is advocacy.

> SIR EDWARD MARSHALL HALL. Marjoribanks, *For the Defence* 1 (1929).

I always said, I will be my client's advocate, not his agent. To hire himself to any particular course, is a position in which no member of the profession ought to place himself.

> POLLOCK, C.B., *Swinfen v Lord Chelmsford* (1860) 2 L.T. (N.S.) 406, 413.

An advocate will not defend all persons indiscriminately, nor will he throw open the harbor of his eloquence as a port of refuge to pirates; and he will be influenced to advocate any cause chiefly by the good opinion which he forms of the nature of it.

> QUINTILIAN, *Inst. of Oratory,* bk 12, 7, 4.

Age

Men of age object too much, consult too long, adventure too little, repent too soon, and seldom drive business home to the full period, but content themselves with a mediocrity of success.

> BACON, *Essays: Of Youth and Age.*

[Legal Quotations]—2

17

There is not a man in England who can rightly adjudge her of age or under age.   Some women who are thirty years old will seem eighteen.

CAVENDISH, C. J., 6 Y.B. 50 Edw. III (1375) 6, 12.

Agreement

That what is agreed to be done, must be considered as done.

LORD HARDWICKE, L.C., *Guidot v Guidot* (1745) 3 Atk. 254, 256.

That is to be looked upon as done which ought to be done.

JEKYLL, M.R., *Banks v Sutton* (1732) 2 P. Wms. 700, 715.

Be at agreement with thy adversary betimes, whilst thou are in the way with him.

Matthew 5:25.

Agree for the law is costly.

Proverb. CAMDEN, *Remains Concerning Britain: Proverbs* (1674).

An ill agreement is better than a good judgment.

Proverb. HERBERT, *Jacula Prudentum* (1651).

Aliens

Their law of keeping out strangers is a law of pusillanimity and fear.

BACON, *New Atlantis.*

Let there be equal judgment among you, whether he be a stranger, or a native.

Leviticus 24:22.

Hear them, and judge that which is just; whether he be one of your country or a stranger.

Deuteronomy 1:16.

I have never discovered that disregard of the Nation's liquor taxes excluded a citizen from our best society and I see no reason why it should banish an alien from our worst.

JACKSON, J., *Jordan v DeGeorge* (1951) 341 US 223, 241, 95 L ed 886, 897, 71 S Ct 703.

Ambiguity

The great sophism of all sophisms being equivocation or ambiguity of words and phrase.

BACON, *Advancement of Learning,* bk 2.

Ambiguity may disappear in the context in which the word is used.

LORD KEITH of Avonholm, *Hamilton v National Coal Bd.* [1960] 2 W.L.R. 313, 323.

Ambition

Ambition which ever rideth without reines.

COKE, *Second Institute: Proeme.*

19

No man has earned the right to intellectual ambition until he has learned to lay his course by a star which he has never seen,—to dig by the divining rod for springs which he may never reach.

> OLIVER WENDELL HOLMES, *Profession of the Law, Speeches* 24 (1913); Coll. Leg. Pap. 31.

Ambulance Chasing

In New York City there is a style of lawyers known to the profession as "ambulance chasers" because they are on hand wherever there is a railway wreck or a street car collision or a gasoline explosion . . . with their offers of professional service.

> 1897 *Congressional Record,* July 24, 2961. This is the first use of the phrase, according to Mathews, *Dictionary of Americanisms* (1951).

Amendment

A state without the means of some change is without the means of its conservation. Without such means it might even risk the loss of that part of the constitution which it wished the most religiously to preserve.

> EDMUND BURKE, *Reflections on the French Revolution.*

Blessed be the amending hand.

> EDMUND PLOWDEN. See Coke, *Fourth Institute: Epilogue.*

It is between the stirrup and the ground, Brother; but you may amend by replying.

> TINDAL, C.J., *Spincer v Spincer* (1841) 5 Jur. (O.S.) 100, 102. Alluding to the gentleman who fell from his horse and broke his neck—"Betwixt the stirrup and the ground, Mercy I askt, mercy I found." Camden, *Remains Concerning Britain: Epitaph* (1674).

Analogy

If any new and unwonted circumstances, hitherto unprecedented in the realm shall arise, then if anything analogous has happened before, let the case be adjudged in like manner, since it is a good opportunity for proceeding *a similibus ad similia*.

> BRACTON, *De Legibus et Consuetudinibus Angliae*, f. 1b.

When things are called by the same name it is easy for the mind to slide into an assumption that the verbal identity is accompanied in all its sequences by identity of meaning.

> CARDOZO, J., *Lowden v Northwestern Nat. Bank & T. Co.* (1936) 298 US 160, 165, 80 L ed 1114, 1119, 56 S Ct 706.

For like reason doth make like law.

> COKE, *First Institute* 10.

Analysis

Dismemberment may be necessary in aid of the process of analysis, but in the end there must be a synthesis that will bring the severed parts together.

> CARDOZO, C.J., *Marchant v Mead-Morrison M. Co.* (1929) 252 NY 284, 299.

21

Animals

If a person wakes up in the middle of the night and finds an escaping tiger on top of his bed and suffers a heart attack, it would be nothing to the point that the intentions of the tiger were quite amiable.

> DEVLIN, L.J., *Behrens v Bertram Mills Circus, Ltd.* [1957] 2 K.B. 1, 17. (A "tame" circus elephant "Buffa" was snapped at by plaintiff's manager's unauthorized dog and in going after the dog knocked down a stall in which a midget was seriously injured by flying timbers. Defendant argued that his elephant was not of a savage disposition and therefore not an animal ferae naturae. Held: as a matter of law all elephants are dangerous).

THE PLAINTIFF

O where, O where is my leetle hound's tail
    That you've made of no worth to be,
From a hound of fame, and Dutch Oven his name,
    To a dog of low degree?
Mit your negligent shove-car trundling around,
    You trod on his tail full sore;
Dutch Oven was worth to me sixty pound,
    And he never will course no more.

THE RAILWAY COMPANY

The tail and the claim they are both cut short,
    You paid us a common dog's fee;
Two pounds you may have, and they lie in Court,
    For the balance you signed us free.
And if more you meant, it was five per cent.
    You'd have paid on our special scale
('Twould make shillings threescore and other four)
    To insure that little hound's tail.

> SIR FREDERICK POLLOCK, *Leading Cases Done Into English: The Hound's Tail's Case* 52 (1892). For reported case see *Dickson v Great Northern Ry. Co.,* 18 Q.B.D. 176.

THE COURT OF APPEAL

Now here, O here's an unanimous voice
    Against this proud Company;
They takes your money and gives no choice
    In reason, that we can see;
But will break, steal, kill at their servants' will,
    Or a monstrous rate will fix—
Eighteenth of the Queen,* it shall well be seen,
    Was made for to stop such tricks.

THE REPORTER

But where, O where is the tailless hound,
    And what shall be done with he?
Shall a place for him in the Court be found,
    The Lords Justices' dog to be?
With glory increased, a reported beast,
    Though he course no more on ground,
He shall hunt like a spectre the grasping Director,
    Dutch Oven the tailless hound.

SIR FREDERICK POLLOCK, *ibid.*

Every dog is entitled to one bite.

Proverb.

That if a dog has once bit a man, and the owner having
notice thereof keeps the dog, and lets him go about, or
lie at his door; an action will be against him at the suit
of a person who is bit, though it happened by such person's treading on the dog's toes, for it was owing to his
not hanging the dog on the first notice.

LEE, C.J., *Smith v Pelah* (1746) 2 Stra. 1265.

* The Railway and Canal Traffic Act, 17 & 18 Vict. c. 31.

It seems agreed that where the owner of a dog has no reason to suppose that it is ferocious the mere fact that it has turned out to be so would not make him liable for anything it has done; the dog has in fact the privilege of one worry.

> LORD MONCRIEFF, *Burton v Moorhead* (1881) 8 S.C. 4th ser. 892, 895.

Anomaly

Anomalies in the law . . . sometimes arise from blindly following the hasty decision of a distinguished judge.

> COWEN, J., *Waydell v Luer* (1843) 5 Hill (NY) 448, 453.

Answer

In law also the right answer usually depends on putting the right question.

> FRANKFURTER, J., *Rogers v Commissioner* (1943) 320 US 410, 413, 88 L ed 134, 137, 64 S Ct 172.

Appeal

But Paul said, "I am standing at the tribunal of Caesar; there I ought to be tried. To Jews I have done no wrong, as thou thyself very well knowest. For if I have done any wrong or committed a crime deserving of death, I do not refuse to die. But if there is no ground to their charges against me, no one can give me up to them; I appeal to Caesar." Then Festus, after conferring with the council, answered, "Thou hast appealed to Caesar; to Caesar thou shalt go."

> Acts 25:10–12. When a Roman citizen under trial appealed to the emperor, the case passed out of the jurisdiction of all other magistrates.

In law, to put the dice into the box for another throw.

> AMBROSE BIERCE, *Devil's Dictionary.*

The point appears here in its virgin state, wearing all its maiden blushes, and is therefore out of place.

> BLECKLEY, J., *Cleveland v Chambliss* (1879) 64 Ga 352, 359.

Supposing fishes had the gift of speech, who would listen to a fisherman's weary discourse on flycasting, the shape and color of the fly, the size of the tackle, the length of the line, the merit of different rod makers and all the other tiresome stuff that fishermen talk about, if the fish himself could be induced to give his views on the most effective methods of approach.

> JOHN W. DAVIS, *The Argument of an Appeal.* Address October 1940, Assn Bar N.Y.C. In *Jurisprudence in Action.*

An appeal, Hinnissy, is where ye ask wan coort to show its contempt f'r another coort.

> FINLEY PETER DUNNE, *Mr. Dooley Says: The Big Fine.*

Back here, I continued to paint, began to do caricatures for the *Times,* and sued *Variety* on behalf of my beard, which I'd just grown. *Variety* ran a page-one story about people who weren't able to get any work growing beards in order to get work, elevator boys growing beards to give

them stature, and so forth.   My name was the only one
in the whole story.   My lawyer, David Schenker, advised
me to sue, and after a three-year delay the case came up
before Judge Peter Schmuck.   Schenker tried the case
as though it was murder.   The jury brought in a verdict
of six cents against *Variety,* plus costs.   My lawyer wanted
compensatory as well as punitive damages, and urged me
to appeal.   I had discussed the difference between humor
and satire at great length on the witness stand, and found
that the appeal would have cost four thousand dollars,
much of it going toward printing my remarks, double-spaced,
on handmade paper.   You have to do this for an appeal.
It's as though you were Max Beerbohm!   Well, I wouldn't
do it.

> ALBERT HIRSCHFELD, *Talk of the Town,* 34 New Yorker, Dec.
> 6, 1958, p. 43.   (Many courts now permit typewritten papers
> on appeal).

We granted certiorari, and in this Court the parties
changed positions as nimbly as if dancing a quadrille.

> JACKSON, J., *Orloff v Willoughby* (1953) 345 US 83, 87, 97 L ed
> 842, 846, 73 S Ct 534.

It had been publicly asserted that appeals in the House
of Lords were nothing more than appeals from the Lord
Chancellor in one place to the Lord Chancellor in another.

> TWISS, 2 *Life of Lord Eldon* 477 (1844).

Appeal from Philip drunk to Philip sober.

> Proverb. See Valerius Maximus, bk 6, ch. 2.

Philip, Alexander's father, gave sentence against a prisoner, what time he was drowsy, and seemed to give small

attention.   The prisoner, after sentence was pronounced, said: *I Appeal.*   The king somewhat stirred, said; *To whom do you appeal?*   The prisoner answered; *From Philip when he gave no ear, to Philip when he shall give ear.*

BACON, *Apothegms New and Old*, no. 158.

Apportionment

The discrimination here does not fit any pattern—as I have said, it is but a crazy quilt.

CLARK, J., concurring, *Baker v Carr* (1962) 369 US 186, 258, 7 L ed 2d 663, 709, 82 S Ct 691.

The conception of political equality from the Declaration of Independence, to Lincoln's Gettysburg Address, to the Fifteenth, Seventeenth, and the Nineteenth Amendments can mean only one thing—one person, one vote.

DOUGLAS, J., *Gray v Sanders* (1963) 372 US 368, 381, 9 L ed 2d 821, 830, 83 S Ct 801.

Courts ought not to enter this political thicket.   The remedy for unfairness in districting is to secure State legislatures that will apportion properly, or to invoke the ample powers of Congress.

FRANKFURTER, J., *Colegrove v Green* (1949) 328 US 549, 556, 90 L ed 1432, 1436, 66 S Ct 1198.

To the extent that *Baker v Carr,* expressly or by implication, went beyond a discussion of jurisdictional doctrines independent of the substantive issues involved here, it

27

should be limited to what it in fact was: an experiment in venturesome constitutionalism.

> HARLAN, J., dissenting, *Reynolds v Sims* (1964) 377 US 533, 625, 12 L ed 2d 506, 563, 84 S Ct 1362.

Equal representation is so fundamental a principle in a true republic that no prejudice can justify its violation because the prejudices themselves cannot be justified.

> THOMAS JEFFERSON, *Letter to William King, 1819,* Jefferson Papers, Library of Congress, v. 216, p. 38616.

The apportionment of representation in our Legislatures and (to a lesser extent) in Congress has been either deliberately rigged or shamefully ignored so as to deny the cities and the voters that full and proportionate voice in government to which they are entitled.

> JOHN F. KENNEDY (when U. S. Senator), *The Shame of the States, N. Y. Times Magazine 12 (May 18, 1958).*

It often comes to pass, that in Governments, where part of the Legislative consists of Representatives chosen by the People, that in tract of time this Representation becomes very *unequal* and disproportionate to the reasons it was at first establish'd upon. To what gross absurdities the following of Custom, when Reason has left it, may lead, we may be satisfied when we see the bare Name of a Town, of which there remains not so much as the ruines, where scarce so much Housing as a Sheep-cote or more Inhabitants than a Shepherd is to be found, sends as many Representatives to the grand Assembly of Law-makers, as a whole County numerous in People, and powerful in riches. This Strangers stand amazed at, and every one must confess needs a remedy.

> JOHN LOCKE, *Second Treatise of Government,* sec. 157. See Laslett ed. (1960) 390.

The yokels hang on because old apportionments give them unfair advantages. The vote of a malarious peasant on the lower Eastern Shore counts as much as the votes of twelve Baltimoreans. But that can't last. It is not only unjust and undemocratic; it is absurd. For the lowest city proletarian, even though he may be farm-bred, is at least superior to the yokel. He has had enterprise enough to escape from the cow and the plow. . . . In the long run he is bound to revolt against being governed from the dung-hill.

> H. L. MENCKEN, *A Carnival of Buncombe* 160 (Moos, ed., 1956) reprinted from Baltimore Evening Sun, July 23, 1928.

Gerrymander.

> Proverb, applied to politically maneuvered apportionment. The expression was coined in 1812 in reference to the grotesque shape of the map of Essex County, Massachusetts, drawn in accordance with a proposed plan for redistricting. Elbridge Gerry was Governor. The map appeared in several newspapers and caused much comment. Attribution of the phrase varies. One version is that Elkanah Tisdale, sketched in some wings and someone suggested naming it a Salamander but Richard Alsop's suggestion of Gerrymander was accepted by those present. Another version is that Gilbert Stuart, the famous painter, sketched in the wings and said, "That will do for a Salamander", and Benjamin Russell exclaimed, "Salamander! call it a Gerrymander." See JOHN WARD DEAN, *The Gerrymander,* 1892 New England Historical and Genealogical Reg. 374–83.

Constitutionally Republican.

> ALFRED E. SMITH, Governor of New York; a frequent expression referring to the State Legislature. See *Politics of Reapportionment* (Jewell ed. 1962) ch. 13.

The right to vote freely for the candidate of one's choice is of the essence of a democratic society, and any restrictions on that right strike at the heart of representative government. And the right of suffrage can be denied by a debasement or dilution of the weight of a citizen's vote just as effectively as by wholly prohibiting the free exercise of the franchise.

> WARREN, C.J., *Reynolds v Sims* (1964) 377 US 533, 555, 12
> L ed 2d 506, 523, 84 S Ct 1362.

Legislators represent people, not trees or acres. Legislators are elected by voters, not farms or cities or economic interests.

> WARREN, C.J., *Reynolds v Sims* (1964) 377 US 533, 562, 12
> L ed 2d 506, 527, 84 S Ct 1362.

Arabiniana

The Court: If ever there was a case of clearer evidence than this of persons acting in concert together, this is that case.

> ARABIN, J. The dicta and charges of Judge Wm. St. Julien
> Arabin were collected by H.B.C. (H. Blencowe Churchill) and
> privately printed in 1843. Arabin has been described as a
> "quaint little man who enunciated absurdities with the most
> perfect innocence." He was "not wanting in mother wit, but
> very much so in the faculty of expressing himself rationally."

The Court, in charge: I cannot suggest a doubt: she goes into a shop, and looks at several things, and purchases nothing: that always indicates some guilt.

> ARABIN, *ibid.*

The Court, in charge (speaking of the inhabitants of Uxbridge): They will steal the very teeth out of your mouth as you walk through the streets.   I know it from experience.

ARABIN, *ibid.*

The Court, to prisoner: I have no doubt of your guilt; you go into a public house, and break bulk, and drink beer; and that's what in the law is called embezzlement.

ARABIN, *ibid.*

The Court, to prisoner: If you are in distress, you must apply to the proper authorities, and not take the law into your own hands, and steal.

ARABIN, *ibid.*

Arbitration

The arbitrator looks to what is equitable, the judge to what is law; and it was for this purpose that arbitration was introduced, namely, that equity might prevail.

ARISTOTLE, *Rhetoric,* bk 1, ch. 13.

Argument

The gentleman puts me in mind of an old hen which persists in setting after her eggs are taken away.

FISHER AMES. Referring to opposing counsel, Ben. Whitman, who continued to argue after points were ruled against him. See Parsons, *Memoir of Theophilus Parsons* (1859) 171.

They said, when he stood up to speak, stars and stripes came right out in the sky, and once he spoke against a

31

river and made it sink into the ground. They said, when
he walked the woods with his fishing rod, Killall the trout
would jump out of the streams right into his pockets, for
they knew it was no use putting up a fight against him;
and, when he argued a case, he could turn on the harps
of the blessed and the shaking of the earth underground.
That was the kind of man he was.

> STEPHEN VINCENT BENET, *The Devil and Daniel Webster.*

The distinguished counsel who argued this case before
us have I think, drawn three red herrings across the path
of the Court, in the hope that we should be drawn off the
scent.

> LORD BOWEN, *Re Blackburn & District Benefit Bldg. Soc.* (1883)
> 24 Ch.D. 421, 436.

Expediency may tip the scales when arguments are nicely
balanced.

> CARDOZO, J., *Woolford Realty Co. v Rose* (1932) 286 US 319,
> 330, 76 L ed 1128, 1134, 52 S Ct 568.

"In my youth," said his father, "I took to the law,
And argued each case with my wife;
And the muscular strength which it gave to my jaw
Has lasted the rest of my life."

> LEWIS CARROLL, *Alice in Wonderland*, ch. 5.

The Judge left the Court, looking deeply disgusted:
But the Snark, though a little aghast,
As the lawyer to whom the defence was intrusted,
Went bellowing on to the last.

> LEWIS CARROLL, *The Hunting of the Snark: Barrister's Dream.*
> When sentence was imposed "the pig had been dead for some
> years".

When the defendants had failed in satisfying him that the plaintiff was wrong, the plaintiff's counsel often succeeded in doing so.

LORD ELDON. See 129 Edinburgh Rev. 48, per Lord Kingsdown

Much cry and little wool.

SIR JOHN FORTESCUE, *Governance of England,* ch. 10.

He respected the traditions of the Supreme Court as a tribunal not designed as a dozing audience for the reading of soliloquies but as a questioning body, utilizing oral arguments as a means for exposing the difficulties of a case with a view to meeting them.

FELIX FRANKFURTER, *Of Law and Men (Stanley M. Silverberg)* 321 (1956).

After all, advocates, including advocates for States, are like managers of pugilistic and election contestants in that they have a propensity for claiming everything.

FRANKFURTER, J., *First Iowa Hydro-Electric Co-op. v Federal Power Com.* (1946) 328 US 152, 187, 90 L ed 1143, 1162, 66 S Ct 906.

Do not think it beneath you to rehearse for an argument. Not even Caruso, at the height of his artistic career, felt above rehearsing for a hundredth performance, although he and the whole cast were guided and confined by a libretto and a score.

ROBERT H. JACKSON, *Advocacy Before the Supreme Court; Suggestions for Effective Case Presentations,* 37 A.B.A.J. 801, 861 (1951).

I used to say that, as Solicitor General, I made three
arguments of every case.   First came the one that I planned
—as I thought, logical, coherent, complete.   Second was
the one actually presented—interrupted, incoherent, dis-
jointed, disappointing.   The third was the utterly devastat-
ing argument that I thought of after going to bed that night.

> ROBERT H. JACKSON, *ibid.,* 803.

Counsel searching for authority for lack of argument.

> JESSEL, M.R. (a frequent phrase) See, Goodhart, *Five Jewish
> Lawyers* 22.

Nay, Sir, argument is argument.   You cannot help paying regard to their arguments if they are good.

> SAMUEL JOHNSON.   Boswell, *Life of Johnson: 1784.*   Reply to
> Sir James Johnston's remark that he paid no regard to the
> arguments of counsel at the bar of the House of Commons,
> because they were paid for speaking.

It is unjust, Sir, to censure lawyers for multiplying words
when they argue; it is often necessary for them to multiply
words.

> SAMUEL JOHNSON.   Boswell, *Life of Johnson:* 1781.

We have listened to an ingenious argument by Mr.
Schiller.   That argument persuaded me of one thing—
namely, that this case was arguable—but it did not persuade
me of anything further.   As the charm of his rhetoric
fades away I believe that I shall revert to the belief that
this case was really unarguable.

> MACKINNON, L.J., *Gowers v Lloyds & National Provincial For-
> eign Bank, Ltd.* (1938) 54 T.L.R. 550, 554.

This is not a case of murder nor assault nor poison. It's a case involving three goats. I claim that my neighbor stole them and the court wants the accusation proved. You keep telling us about the battle of Cannae, the war with Mithridates, the furious struggle with the perfidious Carthaginian, about Sulla, Marius and the like. And all with a roar and a waving of hands. Don't you think it's about time, Postumus, that you talked about those three goats.

MARTIAL, *Epigrams,* VI, 19.

The last point is perfectly new, and it is so startling that I do not apprehend it will ever become old.

MAULE, J., *Whitaker v Wisbey* (1852) 12 C.B. 44, 58.

He was a bad lawyer, said O'Connell, but he was the most sensible looking man talking nonsense he ever saw.

DANIEL O'CONNELL, referring to Lord Manners. Burke, *History of Lord Chancellors of Ireland* (1879) 203.

He that has the worst cause makes the most noise.

Proverb. THOMAS FULLER, *Proverbs* (1732).

No case, abuse the plaintiff's attorney.

Proverb.

Am I then to attack the man when there is no room for argument. *(In hominem dicendum est igitur, quum oratio argumentationem non habet.)*

CICERO, *Pro Flacco* 10. Actually Cicero was protesting that the witnesses were under the control of the prosecutor.

35

I well remember that on one occasion, when he was speaking in the Basilica Julia before the first tribunal, and the four companies of judges, as is usual, were assembled, while the whole place resounded with noise, he was not only heard and understood, but was applauded from all the four tribunals, to the great prejudice of those who were speaking at the same time.

QUINTILLIAN, *Inst. of Oratory*, bk 12, 5, 6 (trans. Watson). Referring to the stentorian voice of the advocate Trachalus.

Spare me quotations, which though learn'd are long,
On points remote at best, and rarely strong.

JOSEPH STORY, *Lines on Hearing Argument in Court.* See 1 Story, Life and Letters (1851) 413.

I was with you, Mr. Scott—till I heard your argument.

LORD THURLOW. Scott (Lord Eldon) often related this. See 1 Twiss, *Life of Lord Eldon* (1844 ed) 135.

Still another method is to talk into a recording device and to play it back. If you own such a device, this method has many obvious advantages—although its use may be somewhat disconcerting, for it is probably correct to say that the most unsettling experiences anyone can have are the first glimpse of one's own profile and the first time one really hears one's own voice.

FREDERICK BERNAYS WIENER, *Briefing and Arguing Federal Appeals* (1961) 309. Discussing preparation for oral argument.

Then, if at any time you find you have the worst end of the staff, leave off your cause and fall upon the person of your adversary.

JOHN WILSON, *The Cheats,* I, 4 (1664).

Bluster, sputter, question, cavil; but be sure your argument be intricate enough to confound the court.

> WILLIAM WYCHERLEY, *The Plain Dealer*, Act 3, scene 1.

This argument has indeed a captivating sound; it strikes the passions with a winning address: but it will be found as fallacious as the rest, and equally begs the very question in dispute.

> YATES, J., *Millar v Taylor* (1769) 4 Burr. 2303, 2359.

Assumption of the Risk

If you cannot see where you are going, you must not go.

> BARON BRAMWELL. See Scrutton, L.J., in *Evans v Downer & Co.* (1933) 102 L.J.K.B. 568 n.

The antics of the clown are not the paces of the cloistered cleric. The rough and boisterous joke, the horseplay of the crowd, evokes its own guffaws, but they are not the pleasures of tranquillity. The plaintiff was not seeking a retreat for meditation. Visitors were tumbling about the belt to the merriment of onlookers when he made his choice to join them. He took the chance of a like fate, with whatever damages to his body might ensue from such a fall. The timorous may stay at home.

> CARDOZO, C.J., *Murphy v Steeplechase Amusement Co.*, 250 NY 479, 483 (1929).

His poverty, not his will, consented to incur the danger.

> HAWKINS, J., *Thrussell v Handyside & Co.* (1888) 20 Q.B.D. 359, 364. Mr. Justice Hawkins may have had in mind the scene in Romeo and Juliet in which Romeo is trying to buy poison, and the apothecary says, reluctantly, "My poverty but not my will consents".

37

Attack

He has peculiar powers as an assailant, and almost always, even when attacked, gets himself into that attitude, by making war upon his accuser; and he has, withal, an instinct for the jugular and the carotid artery, as unerring as that of any carnivorous animal.

RUFUS CHOATE, referring to John Quincy Adams. 1 Brown, *Works of Choate* 293 (1862).

Attempt

The stage of fulfillment has been reached, and that of promise left behind.

CARDOZO, J., *People v Werblow,* 241 NY 55, 62 (1925).

Attorney and Client

Petitioner tried his own case. He introduced no evidence, except to make a formal statement which, unfortunately, we find far from clear. This perhaps illustrates the fact that a party who tries his own case is like a man cutting his own hair—in a poor position to appraise what he is doing.

ALDRICH, J., *Carr v F.T.C.,* 302 F2d 688, 689 (1962).

Webster, fortunately for Philadelphia and for the orphan children, lost his case, and indeed it may be here noted that Webster lost more than one-half of all the cases he argued. It was with him, as later with John G. Johnson,

38

his very fame at times made him a coroner for the dead rather than a physician for the living.

> JAMES M. BECK, *May It Please The Court* 19 (1930). Referring to the Girard Will Case.

I would rather have clients than be somebody's lawyer.

> LOUIS D. BRANDEIS, *Interview,* by Ernest Poole, 71 Amer. Mag. 492 (1911).

To this brave man the Knight repairs
For counsel in his law-affairs,
And found him mounted in his pew,
With books and money plac'd for shew,
Like nest-eggs to make clients lay,
And for his false opinion pay.

> SAMUEL BUTLER, *Hudibras,* Pt. III, Canto III, 1. 621.

Certain clients come to a lawyer, confide their troubles to him, and then go home light-hearted, feeling that they have rid themselves of all their problems. They go to bed and fall fast asleep like innocent children, in the belief that the lawyer has assumed the professional duty to lie awake and worry on their account. One evening I met a client of mine at the theater. He had been in that day to tell me he was on the brink of bankruptcy. He showed surprise and annoyance at finding me in a place of diversion, and throughout the performance he shot disapproving glances in my direction, as if to let me know that with ruin facing him I should be home bemoaning his fate and that it was, to say the least, indelicate of me to go out seeking entertainment.

> PIERO CALAMANDREI, *Eulogy of Judges* 60 (1942) trans. Adams and Phillips.

"I suppose," said Roger quite calmly, "that your idea is that we should invent a good story for you to tell."

"What else is a lawyer for?   When truth is good, what need have I of a lawyer?   I go to a lawyer when the truth is—how do you say?—inconvenient."

"Well," said Roger, "there may be some countries where lawyers behave like that.   And there may be one or two over here who'd do it for you, but not many, and they'd be kicked out pretty quick if they were found out."

"There are not many such?" asked Mr. Glacier.

"Very few," said Roger.

"You have their addresses perhaps?" said Mr. Glacier.

"I have not," said Roger.

HENRY CECIL, *Friends at Court,* ch. 5 (1956).

Who calls a lawyer rogue, may find, too late,
On one of these depends his whole estate.

GEORGE CRABBE, *Tales—The Gentleman Farmer.*

Here   .   .   .   Mr. Tulkinghorn has at once his house and office.   He keeps no staff; only one middle aged man. .   .   .   who sits in a high Pew in the hall.   .   .   .   He wants no clerks.   He is a great reservoir of confidences, not to be so tapped.   His clients want HIM.   He is all in all.

CHARLES DICKENS, *Bleak House,* ch. 10.

If there were no bad people there would be no good lawyers.

CHARLES DICKENS, *Old Curiosity Shop,* ch. 56.

Whene'er he heard a tale of woe
    From client A or client B,

His grief would overcome him so,
He'd scarce have strength to take his fee.

WILLIAM S. GILBERT, *The Bab Ballads: Baines Carew, Gentleman.*

This litigation owes its origin to the manner in which a series of professional gentlemen in the north of England permitted themselves to transact, or in more accurate phrase to entangle and perplex, some legal business entrusted to their care. These licensed pilots undertook to steer a post-captain through certain not very narrow straits of the law, and with abundance of sea room ran him aground on every shoal they could make.

KNIGHT BRUCE, L. J., *Walker v Armstrong* (1856) 8 DeG.M.&G. 531, 538.

You state your case to a lawyer, simply. He answers you doubtfully, hesitatingly. You feel that it's quite indifferent to him which side he would take. But once you have retained him and paid him to bite into it, he begins to be interested and his will becomes warmed up to it. His reasoning and his learning warm up more and more. A manifest and indubitable truth presents itself. He discovers a wholly new light, and he honestly believes it. He is convinced. Indeed, I do not know if the zeal that is born of despite and obstinacy in an encounter with the violence of a magistrate and with danger, or a concern for reputation, has not driven a man to be burned at the stake for an opinion for which among his friends and at ease he would not have been willing to singe the tip of his finger.

MONTAIGNE, *Essays: Apology for Raymond Sebond* bk 2, ch. 12.

41

The end and aim of a lawyer is duplex, first, to know, and second to appear to know—the latter brings in clients and the former holds them.

  ROGER NORTH, *On the Study of Laws* 28.

Good men have no need of an advocate.

  PLUTARCH, *Lives: Phocion,* ch. 10.

Deceive not thy physician, confessor, nor **lawyer.**

  Proverb. HERBERT, *Jacula Prudentum* (1651).

He who is his own lawyer has a fool for a **client.**

  Proverb.

Ah! Mr. Cleave, don't you mind that adage: it was framed by the lawyers.

  LORD LYNDHURST, to a defendant who was arguing his own
    case. 1 Grant, *Bench and Bar* 151 (1838).

Lawyers' gowns are lined with the willfulness of their clients.

  Proverb. HAZLITT, *Poverbs* (1869).

It is not uncommon for the litigant to demand a base and inhuman gratification of his rancor, thinking more of revenge than the defense of his cause. But in this, as in many other things, it is the duty of the advocate to refuse to comply with his client's desires.

  QUINTILIAN, *Inst. of Oratory,* bk 12, 9, 10.

Good counsellors lack no clients.

> SHAKESPEARE, *Measure for Measure,* Act 1, scene 2.

Authority

I accede to the authority of that case, although I think it a very strong decision. It does not convince me; it overcomes me.

> ALDERSON, B., *Mearing v Hellings* (1845) 14 M. & W. 711, 712.

The fact is, Lord Coke had no authority for what he states, but I am afraid we should get rid of a good deal of what is considered law in Westminster hall, if what Lord Coke says without authority is not law.

> BEST, C.J., *Garland v Jekyll* (1824) 2 Bing. 273, 296.

A legal proposition may be nearly as well established by its general acceptance and the failure of anyone to question it as it can be by a series of judicial decisions.

> CULLEN, C.J., *Glennan v Rochester Trust & S. D. Co.,* 209 NY 12, 19 (1913).

The mere repetition of the *cantilena* of lawyers, cannot make it law, unless it can be traced to some competent authority, and if it be irreconcilable to some clear legal principle.

> LORD DENMAN, C.J., *O'Connell v R.* (1844) 11 Cl. & F. 155, 373.

The ABC of the law is generally not questioned before your Lordships, just because it is the ABC.

> LORD DUNEDIN, *Johnston v O'Neill* [1911] A.C. 552, 592.

Decisions of this Court do not have equal intrinsic authority.

> FRANKFURTER, J., *Adamson v California* (1947) 332 US 46, 59, 91 L ed 1903, 1913, 61 S Ct 1672.

A judge, like an executive adviser, may be surprised at the poverty of really useful and unambiguous authority applicable to concrete problems of executive power as they actually present themselves. Just what our forefathers did envision, or would have envisioned had they foreseen modern conditions, must be divined from materials almost as enigmatic as the dreams Joseph was called upon to interpret for Pharaoh. A century and a half of partisan debate and scholarly speculations yields no net result but only supplies more or less apt quotations from respected sources on each side of any question. They largely cancel each other.

> JACKSON, J., concurring, *Youngstown Sheet & Tube Co. v Sawyer* (1952) 343 US 579, 634, 96 L ed 1153, 1198, 72 S Ct 863, 26 ALR2d 1378.

The clearer a thing is, the more difficult it is to find any express authority or any dictum exactly to the point.

> JAMES, L.J., *Panama & So. Pacific Tel. Co. v India Rubber, Gutta Percha & Tel. W. Co.* (1875) 10 Ch. App. 515, 526.

There is nothing too absurd but what authority can be found for it.

> MANISTY, J., *Henderson v Preston* (1888) 4 T.L.R. 633.

If no reason had been given, the authority might have had more weight: but, to be sure, the reason is a false one.

> LORD MANSFIELD, C.J., *Ingle v Wordsworth* (1762) 3 Burr. 1284, 1286.

I have arranged all the cases that have been determined in Westminster Hall, in order of time; and when I come to state them, you will be surprised to see they stand so little in the way, as binding authorities against justice, reason, and common sense.

> LORD MANSFIELD, C.J., *Pugh v Duke of Leeds* (1777) 2 Cowp. 714, 718.

On these two commandments depend the whole Law and the Prophets.

> Matthew 22:40.

In that case the Bench was divided, and the decision was not relished. A decision in an arbitrary question is of great authority; not so when pronounced on wrong principles. The cause was not fully pleaded at first; and some Judges are like the old Bishop, who, having begun to eat the asparagus at the wrong end, did not choose to alter.

> LORD PITFOUR, *Sinclair v Sinclair* (1768) 1 Hailes Dec. 247, 248.

Great men in judicial places will never want authority.

> Proverb. See COKE, *Second Institute* 553.

Every direct authority known to us is against us. Nevertheless, we are right, and these authorities are all wrong, as time and further judicial study of the subject will manifest.

> SIMMONS, C.J., *Green v Coast Line Railroad Co.,* 97 Ga. 15, 36 (1895).

45

The matter is very clearly stated in a work, fortunately not a work of authority, but to which we are all as lawyers indebted, Sir Frederick Pollock's Law of Torts.

> LORD WRIGHT, M.R., *Nicholls v Ely Beet Sugar Factory Ltd.*
> [1936] Ch. 343, 349. Referring to the English rule that the
> words of living authors are not considered as authority.

Average

I abhor averages. I like the individual case. A man may have six meals one day and none the next, making an average of three meals per day, but that is not a good way to live.

> LOUIS D. BRANDEIS. Fraenkel, *Curse of Bigness, An Interview*
> 41.

All loss which arises in consequence of extraordinary sacrifices made, or expences incurred, for the preservation of the ship and cargo come within general average, and must be borne proportionably by all who are interested.

> LAWRENCE, J., *Birkley v Presgrave* (1801) 1 East 220, 228.

Avoidance

The retort courteous . . . the quip modest . . . the reply churlish . . . the reproof valiant . . . the countercheck quarrelsome . . . the lie with circumstance . . . the lie direct. All these you may avoid but the lie direct; and you may avoid that too, with an "if." I knew when seven justices could not take up a quarrel; but then the parties were met themselves, one of them thought but of an "if," as "If you said so, then I said so;" and they

46

shook hands and swore brothers. Your "if" is the only peace-maker; much virtue in "if."

> SHAKESPEARE, *As You Like It,* Act 5, scene 4.

Banking

If in 1815 the common law halted outside the bankers' door, by 1879 equity had had the courage to lift the latch, walk in and examine the books.

> ATKIN, L.J., *Banque Belge Pour l'Etranger v Hambrouck* [1921] 1 K.B. 321, 335.

That is hardly a practical suggestion. A banker so very careful to avoid risk would soon have no risk to avoid.

> LORD MACNAGHTEN, *Bank of England v Vagliano Brothers* [1891] A.C. 107, 157. One of the judges suggested that banks should not pay until satisfied by inquiry and investigation that all endorsements were genuine.

Bankruptcy

For it is among the duties of society, to enforce the rights of humanity.

> JOHNSON, J., *Ogden v Saunders* (1827, US) 12 Wheat 213, 283, 6 L ed 606, 630. Upholding a state bankruptcy act.

I will be their vassal for life, and dig in the mine of my imagination to find diamonds (or what may sell for such) to make good my engagements, not to enrich myself. And this from no reluctance to allow myself to be called the Insolvent, which I probably am, but because I will not put out of the power of my creditors the resources, mental or literary, which yet remain to me.

> SIR WALTER SCOTT, *Journal, January 24, 1826.* At the time bankruptcy was suggested to him and his debts were more than one hundred thousand pounds.

Bench and Bar

It is no grace to a judge first to find that which he might have heard in due time from the bar; or to show quickness of conceit in cutting off evidence or counsel too short; or to prevent information by questions, though pertinent.

> BACON, *Essays: Of Judicature.*

There is due from the judge to the advocate some commendation and gracing, where causes are well handled and fair pleaded; especially towards the side which obtaineth not; for that upholds in the client the reputation of his counsel, and beats down in him the conceit of his cause.

> BACON, *ibid.*

And let not the counsel at the bar chop with the judge, nor wind himself into the handling of the cause anew after the judge hath declared his sentence; but on the other side, let not the judge meet the cause half way, nor give occasion for the party to say his counsel or proofs were not heard.

> BACON, *ibid.*

It was said that when one of the equity judges, in reference to some application made to the Court, made answer that he would turn the matter over in his mind, Bethell turning round to his junior with a smile, said, loud enough so to be heard by the bar "Take a note of that; his Lordship says that he will turn it over in what he is pleased to call his mind."

> Referring to Richard Bethell (Lord Westbury). See, 1 Nash, *Life of Lord Westbury* (1888) 158.

It is not, of course, in cases of complication possible for their Lordships to be aware of all the authorities, statutory or otherwise, which may be relevant to the issues which in the particular case require decision. Their Lordships are therefore very much in the hands of counsel, and those who instruct counsel, in these matters, and this House expects, and indeed insists, that authorities which bear one way or the other upon matters under debate shall be brought to the attention of their Lordships by those who are aware of those authorities. This observation is quite irrespective of whether or not the particular authority assists the party which is so aware of it. It is an obligation of confidence between their Lordships and all those who assist in the debates in this House in the capacity of counsel.

> BIRKENHEAD, L.C., *Glebe Sugar Refining Co., Ltd. v Greenock Harbour Trustees,* 1921 S.C. (H.L.) 72, 73.

A suppressed speech may occasion more mental torture than a lost case.

> BLECKLEY, J., *Early v Oliver,* 63 Ga 11, 18 (1879).

A judge rarely performs his functions adequately unless the case before him is adequately presented.

> LOUIS D. BRANDEIS, *Living Law,* 10 Ill. L.R. 461, 470 (1916).

This Court in which we sit is a temple of justice; and the Advocate at the Bar, as well as the Judge upon the Bench, are equally ministers in that temple.   The object of all equally should be the attainment of justice.

> CRAMPTON, J., *R. v O'Connell* (1844) 7 Ir. L.R. 261, 312.

I do not like to appear in the character of a drill-sergeant with my cane rapping the knuckles of a private, when I become a colonel from the ranks.

> JOHN P. CURRAN, when reproached for too much forbearance on becoming Master of the Rolls.   2 Townsend, *Lives of Twelve Eminent Judges* 261 (1846).

Lord Mansfield treated me, not with contempt indeed, for of that his nature was incapable, but he put me aside with indulgence, as you do a child, when it is lisping its prattle out of season.

> THOMAS ERSKINE, referring to his argument in the Dean of St. Asaph libel trial.   1 Townsend, *Lives of Twelve Eminent Judges* 422 (1846).

A judge who observes the demeanour of the witnesses while they are being examined by counsel has from his detached position a much more favourable opportunity of forming a just appreciation than a judge who himself conducts the examination.   If he takes the latter course he, so to speak, descends into the arena and is liable to have his vision clouded by the dust of the conflict.

> GREENE, M.R., *Yuill v Yuill* [1945] P. 15, 20.

Proceed.   You have my biased attention.

> JUDGE LEARNED HAND. To counsel who demanded the right to reargue a motion already heard extensively.   See, Clark, *Learned Hand,* 18 *Record* (Assn Bar N.Y.C.) 498, 502 (1963).

Shall I ask what a court would be, unaided? The law is made by the Bar, even more than by the Bench.

> OLIVER WENDELL HOLMES, *The Law—Speeches* 16 (1913).

It is the duty of a Judge to make it disagreeable to counsel to talk nonsense.

> LORD CHANCELLOR LYNDHURST, Campbell, *Lives of Lord Chancellors: Lyndhurst, ch. 5.*

When my Father became a Judge I said to him, "Be kind to the *young* lawyers." When I became a Judge, he said to me, "Be kind to the *old* lawyers."

> CLAUDE McCOLLOCH, *Notes of a District Judge,* Pt. II, 25. (Privately printed, Portland, Ore., 1948.)

The acme of judicial distinction means the ability to look a lawyer straight in the eyes for two hours and not to hear a damned word he says.

> JOHN MARSHALL, retort to young lawyer who sought to flatter him by saying that the Chief Justice had reached the "acme of judicial distinction." 4 Beveridge, *Life of Marshall,* ch. 2.

A judge has nothing to do with the getting up of a case.

> MOULTON, L. J., *Enoch and Zaretzky, Bock & Co.* [1910] 1 K.B. 327, 332.

James II: I am determined to have twelve lawyers for judges who will be all of my mind as to this matter.
Chief Justice Thomas Jones: Your Majesty may find twelve *judges* of your mind, but hardly twelve *lawyers.*

> Referring to the dispensing power of the King, i.e., that the King could by proclamation dispense with Acts of Parliament. See Campbell, *Lives of the Chief Justices: Edward Herbert.*

Biography

His Life (Lord Lyndhurst) has been written by Lord Campbell, and fully justified what he himself said when he heard that it was contemplated, that the prospect added another pang to death.

> SERJEANT BALLANTINE, *Some Experiences of a Barrister's Life* 145 (1882).

His Life, unlike the Lives of those whose history he has written, has been delivered to posterity by himself, and he escaped the death-pang that others, not without reason, apprehended from his undertaking their biography.

> SERJEANT BALLANTINE, *Some Experiences of a Barrister's Life* 185 (1882), referring to Lord Campbell, author of the *Lives of the Chancellors.*

He would not cut off his claws, nor make a tiger a cat, to please anybody.

> JAMES BOSWELL. Reply to Hannah More who asked him to mitigate some of Samuel Johnson's asperities in his *Life.* 1 Memoirs H. More 228 (N.Y. 1834).

Mortuary estimates.

> FELIX FRANKFURTER, *Mr. Justice Brandeis* 50 (1932). Referring to the inadequacy of biographies of supreme court justices.

Death is now attended with a fresh terror.

> SIR CHARLES WETHERELL, referring to the *Lives of the Lord Chancellors,* by Lord Campbell. See 2 *Life of Lord Campbell,* 219 (1881). (Arbuthnot had called the printer, Curll, "one of the new terrors of death" from his habit of publishing trashy obituaries on the death of any eminent man.)

Black Monday

On Monday, May 27, 1935, the United States Supreme Court in three unanimous decisions invalidated the National Industrial Recovery Act *(A.L.A. Schechter Poultry Corp. v United States,* 295 US 495, 79 L ed 1570, 55 S Ct 837, 97 ALR 947) and the Frazier-Lemke Act *(Louisville Joint Stock Land Bank v Radford,* 295 US 555, 79 L ed 1593, 55 S Ct 854, 97 ALR 1106), and denied the right of the President to remove members of independent regulatory commissions *(Humphrey v United States,* 295 US 602, 79 L ed 1611, 55 S Ct 869).

Blackstone's Commentaries

He it was who first gave to the law the air of a science. He found it a skeleton, and clothed it with life, colour and complexion: he embraced the cold statue, and by his touch it grew into youth, health and beauty.

LORD AVONMORE.

He it is, in short, who, first of all institutional writers, has taught Jurisprudence to speak the language of the Scholar and the Gentleman: put a polish upon that rugged science: cleansed her from the dust and cobwebs of the office: and if he has not enriched her with that precision that is drawn only from the sterling treasury of the sciences, has decked her out, however, to advantage, from the toilette of classic erudition: enlivened her with metaphors and allusions: and sent her abroad in some measure to instruct, and in still greater measure to entertain, the most miscellaneous and even the most fastidious societies.

JEREMY BENTHAM, *Fragment on Government: Preface,* par. 46.

It was not so much his learning that made the book
as it was the book that made him learned.

LORD ELLENBOROUGH.

It is a good gentleman's law book, clear but not deep.

HORNE TOOKE.

The prose epic of the common law.

UNKNOWN.

Books

I have not got as much from books as I have from tackling
concrete problems. I have generally run up against a
problem, have painfully tried to think it out, with a measure
of success, and have then read a book and found to my
surprise that some other chap was before me.

LOUIS D. BRANDEIS, *Interview,* by Ernest Poole, 71 Amer. Mag.
482 (1911).

It deserves not to be read in schools,
But to be freighted in the Ship of Fools.

COKE, when Sir Francis Bacon presented him with a copy of his
Novum Organum, on the title page of which appeared the device
of a ship sailing through the Pillars of Hercules.

Though backward in accounting, they seemed to be
practised in book-keeping.

LORD ELDON, referring to book borrowers, after having lost
two volumes of precedents copied by him. 1 Twiss, *Life of
Eldon* 98 (1844).

First, there's the Bible,
And then the Koran
Odgers on Libel,
Pope's Essay on Man.

> MOSTYN PIGOTT, *The Hundred Best Books.*

He is like a book in breeches.

> SYDNEY SMITH. 1 Holland, *Memoir of Smith* 320 (The reference is to Thomas Macaulay).

Books (Law)

Almost any law book that is more than twenty-one years of age, like a single lady who has attained that climacter, is said to be too old for much devotion.

> HORACE BINNEY, *Leaders of the Old Bar of Philadelphia.*

A masterpiece upon a masterpiece.

> Referring to Coke, *on Littleton.*

"I am improving my legal knowledge, Master Copperfield," said Uriah. "I am going through Tidd's Practice. Oh, what a writer Mr. Tidd is, Master Copperfield!"

> CHARLES DICKENS, *David Copperfield,* ch. 16.

That underdone-pie-crust-coloured cover, which is technically known as "law-calf".

> CHARLES DICKENS, *Pickwick Papers,* ch. 34.

It will some day seem a wonderful thing that men once thought that they could write the history of medieval

England without using the Year Books. . . . They come
to us from life.   Some day they will return to life once
more at the touch of some great historian.

> FREDERIC WM. MAITLAND, *1 Year Book Series, Selden Society:
> Introduction* XX (1903).

He (Serjeant Maynard) had such a relish of the old year-
books, that he carried one in his coach to divert his time
in travel and said he chose it before any comedy.

> ROGER NORTH, 1 *Life of Lord Keeper Guilford* 27 (1826).

Every Christmas, during all the time of his practice he
read Littleton all over.   And this he enjoined himself for
a task: for that book having gained an authority, as a
tract of law, and the foundation of conveyancing, he judged
it necessary to be punctually remembered, without giving
time the advantage to obliterate, or corrupt any part of
it from his just thoughts.

> ROGER NORTH, 1 *Life of Lord Keeper Guilford* 104 (1826).

Boundaries

Love thy neighbour, but cut not up thy hedge for him.

> Proverb. FULLER, *Proverbs* (1732).

Good fences make good neighbors.

> ROBERT FROST, *Mending Wall* (1914).

Brain

The brain is like the hand. It grows with using.

> LOUIS D. BRANDEIS, in *Filene Cooperative Assn. Echo,* May
> 1905. See, Mason, *Brandeis, Lawyer and Judge in Modern
> State* 84 (1933).

Breach of Promise

When she found he wouldn't wed her,
In a river, in a meadder,
Took a header, and a deader
            Was Ophelia!
Ophelia to her sex was a disgrace,
   Whom nobody could feel compassion tor.
Ophelia should have gone to Ely Place
   To consult an eminent solicitor.
       When such promises as these
          Breaks a suitor, rich and regal,
       Why, substantial damages
         Is the panacea legal.

> WILLIAM S. GILBERT, *The Montebanks,* Act 2.

Judge:
   At length I became as rich as the Gurneys—
      An incubus then I thought her,
  So I threw over that rich attorney's
      Elderly, ugly daughter.
  The rich attorney my character high
      Tried vainly to disparage—
  And now, if you please, I'm ready to try
      This Breach of Promise of Marriage!

> WILLIAM S. GILBERT, *Trial by Jury.*

Counsel:
　　Picture, then, my client naming,
　　　　And insisting on the day:
　　Picture him excuses framing—
　　　　Going from her far away;
　　Doubly criminal to do so,
　　For the maid had bought her *trousseau!*

　　WILLIAM S. GILBERT, *ibid.*

Brevity

Praised be he who can state a cause in a clear, simple and succinct manner, and then stop.

　　BELT, J., *Jungwirth v Jungwirth,* 115 Ore 668, 672 (1925).

There is no need for the purposes of this case to plot it on the legal map.

　　CARDOZO, J., *W. B. Worthen Co. v Kavanaugh* (1935) 295 US 56, 60, 79 L ed 1298, 1301, 55 S Ct 555, 97 ALR 905.

Nothing conduces to brevity like a caving in of the knees.

　　OLIVER WENDELL HOLMES. Bowen, *Yankee From Olympus,* ch. 30. Holmes sometimes wrote his opinions standing up.

With as little bewordling and as few reasons as possible.

　　HUTCHESON, J., *Commissioner Int. Rev. v McLean,* 127 F2d 942, 944 (1942).

Bribery

Though the bribe be small, yet the fault is great.

　　COKE, *Third Institute* 147.

They that buy will sell.

> COKE, *Third Institute* 148.

Men are more often bribed by their loyalties and ambitions than by money.

> JACKSON, J., *United States v Wunderlich* (1951) 342 US 98, 103, 96 L ed 113, 117, 72 S Ct 123.

A basket justice, a jill justice, a good forenoon justice.

> Proverb. RAY, *Proverbs* (1678).

He that buyeth magistracy will sell justice.

> Proverb. RAY, *Proverbs* (1678).

Brief ("Brandeis")

In patent cases counsel are apt to open the argument with a discussion of the state of the art. It may not be amiss, in the present case, before examining the constitutional question, to notice the course of legislation as well as expressions of opinion from other than judicial sources. In the brief filed by Mr. Louis D. Brandeis, for the defendant in error, is a very copious collection of all these matters, an epitome of which is found in the margin.

> BREWER, J., *Muller v Oregon* (1908) 208 US 412, 419, 52 L ed 551, 555, 28 S Ct 324.

By a series of arguments and briefs he created practically a new technique in the presentation of constitutional questions. Until his famous brief in *Muller v. Oregon,* social legislation was supported before the courts largely *in vacuo*

—as an abstract dialectic between "liberty" and "police power" unrelated to a world of trusts and unions, of large-scale industry and all its implications. In the *Oregon* case, the facts of modern industry which provoke regulatory legislation were, for the first time, adequately marshalled before the Court. It marks an epoch in the disposition of cases presenting the most important present-day constitutional issues.

> FELIX FRANKFURTER, *Mr. Justice Brandeis and the Constitution*, 45 Harv. L. Rev. 33, 37.

Brotherhood

Right knows no boundaries, and justice no frontiers; the brotherhood of man is not a domestic institution.

> LEARNED HAND, second *"I Am an American Day"* address, Central Park, New York City, May 20, 1945. See Hand, *Spirit of Liberty* (Dilliard, ed.) 193.

Even in our own interest we must have an eye to the interests of others; a nation which lives only to itself will in the end perish; false to the faith, it will shrivel and pass to that oblivion which is its proper receptacle. We may not stop until we have done our part to fashion a world in which there shall be some share of fellowship; which shall be better than a den of thieves. Let us not disguise the difficulties; and above all, let us not content ourselves with noble aspirations, counsels of perfection, and self-righteous advice to others.

> LEARNED HAND, *ibid.*

Burke, Sir Edmund

Oft have we wonder'd that on Irish ground,
No poisonous reptile has e'er been found;
Reveal'd the secret stands of Nature's work—
She saved her venom to produce her Burke.

ROBERT DALLAS, counsel for the defense in the trial of Warren
Hastings. Burke was one of the Managers of the impeachment.

Cases

But a more scandalous transaction,
Paltry, vexatious cause of action,
Or a more lame, more flat, more stale,
Dull and unprofitable tale,
I never met in all my reading,
In the whole course of law-proceeding,
Than this same woful trumpt-up story,
My learned brother has just laid before **ye.**

JOHN ANSTEY, *Pleader's Guide,* bk 2 (1802).

It is a sound precept not to take the law from the rules,
but to make the rule from the existing law. For the proof
is not to be sought from the words of the rule, as if it
were the text of law. The rule, like the magnetic needle
points at the law, but does not settle it.

BACON, *De Augmentis Scientiarum,* bk 8, c. 3, Aph. 85.

The hardship of the particular case is no reason for
melting down the law. For the sake of fixedness and uniformity, law must be treated as a solid, not as a fluid. It
must have, and always retain, a certain degree of hardness,
to keep its outlines firm and constant. Water changes

shape with every vessel into which it is poured; and a liquid law would vary with the mental conformation of judges, and become a synonym for vagueness and instability.

> BLECKLEY, J., *Southern Star Lightning Rod Co. v Duvall,* 64 Ga. 262, 268 (1879).

Some cases tax the anxious diligence of a court not by their difficulty but their simplicity.

> BLECKLEY, C.J., *Wells v Savannah,* 87 Ga. 397, 398 (1891).

In the ornithology of litigation this case is a tomtit, furnished with a garb of feathers ample enough for a turkey.

> BLECKLEY, C.J., *Lukens v Ford,* 87 Ga. 541, 542 (1891).

I have, of course, as often a bad case as a good one; and what with disagreeable and formidable opponents and imbecile judges, I lead a life worse than a convict in the treadmill.

> LORD CAMPBELL, letter to his brother, December 19, 1835. 2 *Life of Lord Campbell* 76 (1881).

Many questions are raised rather out of the weight of the matter than the difficulty of the case.

> COKE, 10 Rep., *Preface.*

I often wished in after-life that all the causes were apple-pie causes.

> LORD ELDON. When a senior fellow at University College, two undergraduates complained to him that the cook had sent them an apple-pie that could not be eaten. He ordered the pie to be produced but in the meanwhile other students had consumed it. So Eldon found it impossible to decide "that that was not eatable, which was actually eaten". 1 Twiss, *Life of Lord Eldon* 92 (1844).

Of a nature worthy the judicature of a Roman senate rather than of a single judge.

> LORD HARDWICKE, L.C., *Penn v Lord Baltimore* (1750) 1 Ves. Sr. 444, 446.

Neither law nor equity consists merely of cases and precedents, but of general rules and principles by the reason of which, the several cases coming before the courts of justice are to be governed.

> LORD HARDWICKE, L.C., *Gorton v Hancock* (1744) Harg. Mss. 383, f. 122 (as cited in 2 Yorke, *Life of Lord Hardwicke* 492).

Great cases like hard cases make bad law. For great cases are called great, not by reason of their real importance in shaping the law of the future, but because of some accident of immediate overwhelming interest which appeals to the feelings and distorts the judgment.

> HOLMES, J., *Northern Secur. Co. v United States* (1904) 193 US 197, 400, 48 L ed 679, 726, 24 S Ct 436.

My keenest interest is excited, not by what are called great questions and great cases, but by little decisions which the common run of selectors would pass by because they did not deal with the Constitution or a telephone company, yet which have in them the germ of some wider theory, and therefore of some profound interstitial change in the very tissue of the law.

> OLIVER WENDELL HOLMES, *John Marshall, Speeches* (1913) 87; Coll. Leg. Pap. 269.

General propositions do not decide concrete cases.

> HOLMES, J., *Lochner v New York* (1905) 198 US 45, 76, 49 L ed 937, 949, 25 S Ct 539.

If a man keeps a case six months, it is supposed to be decided on "great consideration". It seems to me that intensity is the only thing. A day's impact is better than a month of dead pull.

    OLIVER WENDELL HOLMES, 1 *Holmes-Pollock Letters* 154.

I long have said there is no such thing as a hard case. I am frightened weekly, but always when you walk up to the lion and lay hold the hide comes off and the same old donkey of a question of law is underneath.

    OLIVER WENDELL HOLMES, 1 *Holmes-Pollock Letters* 156.

Some litigants find that on leaving the Courts
They have found themselves fame in the legal Reports.
For reasons they never will quite understand
They have added a bit to the law of the land.
Their case has decided some interesting law,
Which maybe their barristers never foresaw—
Thus litigant laymen acquire legal fame
Whose lawyers may never accomplish the same.

    J.P.C., *Poetic Justice* 4 (1947).

This case reminds me of one in which I likened the Plaintiff's case to a colander, because it was so full of holes.

    JESSEL, M.R., *Ex parte Hall* (1882) 19 Ch.D. 580, 584.

Tibullus: How now, Ovid! Law-cases in verse? . . .
Ovid: Troth, if I live, I will new dress the Law
In sprightly Poesy's habiliments.

    BEN JONSON, *Poetaster*, Act 1, scene 3.

The law does not consist in particular cases; but in general principles, which run through the cases, and govern the decision of them.

> LORD MANSFIELD, C.J., *Rust v Cooper* (1777) 2 Cowp. 629, 632.

Hard cases make bad law.

> Proverb. 3 LEAN, *Collect.* 479 (1902). Ram, *Legal Judgment* 116 (1871), attributes to Lord Tenterden.

Points more than all the lawyers in Bohemia can learnedly handle.

> SHAKESPEARE, *Winter's Tale,* Act 4, scene 4.

I am sure none of us [judges] ought to make the parties' case better than the law has made it.

> SOMERS, L.K., *The Bankers' Case* (1699) 14 How. St. Tr. 39, 45.

Hard cases, it has been frequently observed, are apt to introduce bad law.

> WOLFE, B., *Winterbottom v Wright* (1842) 10 M. & W. 116.

Cases (Complex)

And in this question, if the parties demurred in our judgment, we might ask advyce further of learned men and judges. We might, quod he, by suite to be sure of ye matter make it a chequer chamber case.

> SIR THOMAS MORE, *Heresies,* bk 3 (Works 1557) 216.

Where if in the lawe the case seeme to the judges that sittee doubtfull, it is called a checker chamber case and all the judges will meet together and what they shall pronounce to be the lawe, that is helde for right, and the other partie looseth his action or lande forever.

THOMAS SMITH, *De Republica Anglorum* (1583; 1906 ed. 73).

Make a Federal Case out of it.

Saying.
1. To overemphasize the importance of something or to render complicated something that is really very simple. See, Wentworth and Flexner, eds. *Dictionary of American Slang* (1960) 179.
2. The expression . . . is frequently encountered, generally in public performances of entertainment media—one notable recent example was the judge's query in *Anatomy of Murder*—and pre-eminently, among the shrewd but semi-educated. . . . Despite research . . . despite repeated inquiries among the learned, philological and legal both, I have been unable to trace the source. . . . Some persons surmise that it originated early in the prohibition era . . . another guess is that it is contemporary with the Mann Act's interdiction of interstate romancing; and one suggestion . . . is that it may be found in the works of Mark Twain. See Wiener, *Wanna Make a Federal Case Out of It?* 48 A.B.A.J. 59 (1962).

Shallow: Sir Hugh, persuade me not; I will make a Star chamber matter of it; if he were twenty Sir John Falstaffs he shall not abuse Robert Shallow, esquire.

SHAKESPEARE, *Merry Wives of Windsor,* Act 1, scene 1.

Cases (Popular Names)

Dog and the Potman: Or "Go It, Bob". *Baker v Snell* [1908] 2 K. B. 352.

SIR FREDERICK POLLOCK'S designation. See, 25 L.Q.R. 317.

The Paternoster case. *Kerr v Kerr,* 134 App. Div. (N. Y.) 141 (1909).

I once convinced three of my four associates when I was a Justice of the Appellate Division of the Supreme Court by citing Burton's *Anatomy of Melancholy* as an authority. It was a divorce case against a man. The proof showed that he met the woman at the railroad station, that they came together in a hack with their baggage to the hotel, that the man registered them as man and wife, and that they went to the bedroom assigned to them. One of the judges wrote an opinion that this evidence was not sufficient. I wrote an opinion that legal inference of misconduct could and should be drawn from it, that they did not go there to say their prayers, and cited that passage of the *Anatomy of Melancholy* which says of a man under such conditions, "It is presumed he saith not a paternoster."

WILLIAM J. GAYNOR, *Letters and Speeches* (1912).

The sick chicken case. *A. L. A. Schechter Poultry Corp. v United States,* 295 US 495, 79 L ed 1570, 55 S Ct 837, 97 ALR 947.

Snail in the Bottle. *Donoghue v Stevenson* [1932] A. C. 562.

SIR FREDERICK POLLOCK'S designation. See 49 L.Q.R. 22 (1933).

Cause

Men serve causes because of their devotion to them.

HARLAN F. STONE, *The Public Influence of the Bar,* 48 Harv. L. Rev. 1, 14 (1934).

Certainty

If a man will begin with certainties, he shall end in doubts; but if he will be content to begin with doubts, he shall end in certainties.

> BACON, *Advancement of Learning*, bk 1.

The power of the lawyer is in the uncertainty of the law.

> JEREMY BENTHAM, *Correspondence, Letter to Sir James Macintosh* (1808). See 10 *Works* (1843 Bowring ed.) 429.

I was much troubled in spirit, in my first years upon the bench, to find how trackless was the ocean on which I had embarked. I sought for certainty. I was oppressed and disheartened when I found that the quest for it was futile. I was trying to reach land, the solid land of fixed and settled rules, the paradise of a justice that would declare itself by tokens plainer and more commanding than its pale and glimmering reflections in my own vacillating mind and conscience. I found with the voyager in Browning's *Paracelsus* that "the real heaven was always beyond."

> BENJAMIN N. CARDOZO, *Nature of the Judicial Process* 166 (1921).

Law, like other branches of social science, must be satisfied to test the validity of its conclusions by the logic of probabilities rather than the logic of certainty.

> BENJAMIN N. CARDOZO, *Growth of the Law* 33 (1924).

They do things better with logarithms.

> BENJAMIN N. CARDOZO, *Paradoxes of Legal Science* 1 (1928).

Certainty is the mother of quietness and repose, and uncertainty the cause of variance and contentions.

COKE, *First Institute* 212.

I cannot avoid noticing an error into which they fall who complain of the uncertainty of law as though it were a weakness. Rather should it be considered the chiefest of all sanctions . . . Many would dare to do wrong, did they know for certain what would follow.

LORD DARLING, *Scintillae Juris: Of Laws.*

It is better the law should be certain, than that every Judge should speculate upon improvements in it.

LORD ELDON, *Sheddon v Goodrich* (1803) 8 Ves. 481, 497.

The tendency of the law must always be to narrow the field of uncertainty.

OLIVER WENDELL HOLMES, *Common Law* 127 (1881).

Certainty generally is illusion, and repose is not the destiny of man.

OLIVER WENDELL HOLMES, *Path of the Law,* 10 Harv. L. Rev. 457, 465 (1897).

The law is a sort of hocus-pocus science, that smiles in yeer face while it picks yeer pocket; and the glorious uncertainty of it is of mair use to the professors than the justice of it.

CHARLES MACKLIN, *Love a la Mode* [1759] Act 2, scene 1.

It would be very hard upon the profession, if the law was so certain, that every body knew it: the misfortune is that it is so uncertain, that it costs much money to know what it is, even in the last resort.

> LORD MANSFIELD, C.J., *Jones v Randall* (1774) 1 Cowp. 37, 40. This was in reply to counsel, Dunning, who in arguing this case stated: "The laws of this country are clear, evident, and certain: all the judges know the laws, and knowing them, administer justice with uprightness and integrity."

Mr. Boswell has attempted a new and ingenious limitation of literary property, by entering *separately* in Stationers Hall, two valuable articles in his life of Dr. Johnson, viz., the Conversation with the King, and the Letter to Lord Chesterfield; both of which were advertised some time ago, price half a guinea each.–And then having thus *secured* them, as he would maintain, has introduced them into his great work. How far this will be *effectual,* must be left to the *glorious uncertainty of the Law.*

> *The Public Advertiser,* Tuesday, 17 May, 1791 (no. 17,741). See 195 *Notes and Queries* 296.

Chance

Curious results sometimes happen by chance, but when those results happen so largely along the lines of the purposes of those who have control of the supposed chance, it is not strange that outsiders are apt to feel that purpose, and not chance determined the result.

> BREWER, J., *Taylor v Beckham* (1900) 178 US 548, 584, 44 L ed 1187, 1203, 20 S Ct 890.

Chancery

The Chancery is ordained to supply the law, and not to subvert the law.

> BACON, *Speech,* May 7, 1617, on taking his seat in Chancery as Lord Keeper.

Chancery, the Pretorian power for mitigating the rigour of law, in case of extremity, by the conscience of a good man.

> BACON, *History of King Henry VII.*

This Court is not a Court of conscience.

> BUCKLEY, J., *Re Telescriptor Syndicate Ltd.* [1903] 2 Ch. 174, 195.

The raw afternoon is rawest, and the dense fog is densest, and the muddy streets are muddiest, near that leaden-headed old obstruction, appropriate ornament for the threshold of a leaden-headed old corporation: Temple Bar. And hard by Temple Bar, in Lincoln's Inn Hall, at the very heart of the fog, sits the Lord High Chancellor in his High Court of Chancery.

> CHARLES DICKENS, *Bleak House,* ch. 1.

The Lord High Chancellor ought to be sitting here— as here he is—with a foggy glory round his head, softly fenced in with crimson cloth and curtains, addressed by a large advocate with great whiskers, a little voice, and an interminable brief, and outwardly directing his contemplation to the lantern in the roof, where he can see nothing but fog. On such an afternoon, some score of members of the High Court of Chancery bar ought to be—as here they are—mistily engaged in one of the ten thousand stages of an endless cause, tripping one another up on slippery precedents, groping kneedeep in technicalities, running their goat-hair and horse-hair warded heads against walls of words, and making a pretence of equity with serious faces, as players might.

CHARLES DICKENS, *Bleak House,* ch. 1.

Your chancery lawyers
Whose subtilty thrives
In spinning out suits
To the length of three lives;
Such suits as the clients
Do wear out in slavery
Whilst pleader makes conscience
A cloak for his knavery.

English Drinking Song (18th Cent.)

Chancery mends no man's bargain, though it sometimes mends his assurance.

LORD FINCH, L.C., *Maynard v Moseley* (1676) 3 Swanst. 653, 655.

Full oft within the spatious walls
When he had fifty winters o'er him,
My grave Lord Keeper led the Brawls:
The Seal and Maces, danc'd before him.
His bushy beard and shoe-strings green
His high-crown'd hat and sattin doublet,
Mov'd the stout heart of England's Queen,
Tho' Pope and Spaniard could not trouble it.

THOMAS GRAY, *A Long Story.* Sir Christopher Hatton, Lord
Chancellor under Elizabeth, was called the "dancing chancellor".

Three things are helped in conscience
Fraud, accident, and confidence.

SIR THOMAS MORE. See Coke, 4 Inst. 84.

Hell and Chancery are always open.

Proverb. THOMAS FULLER, *Proverbs* (1732).

It is always term time in the court of conscience.

Proverb. THOMAS FULLER, *Proverbs* (1732).

Change

New laws are like the apothecaries' drugs: though
they remedy the disease, yet they trouble the body.

BACON, *Reading on the Statute of Uses.*

Until the advent of the Warren Court, we judges were
too often content to sit on our status quo. That highest
court moved out of the traditional bind with decisions
bearing on confessions and counsel for the indigent.

BERNARD BOTEIN. See Samuels, *A Judge With Disciplined In-
dignation*, N. Y. Times Mag., Jan. 15, 1967.

Modification implies growth. It is the life of the law.

BRANDEIS, J., *Washington v W. C. Dawson & Co.* (1924) 264 US
219, 236, 68 L ed 646, 656, 44 S Ct 302.

Justice is not to be taken by storm. She is to be wooed
by slow advances. Substitute statute for decision, and

you shift the center of authority, but add no quota of inspired wisdom.

> BENJAMIN N. CARDOZO, *Growth of the Law* 133 (1924).

Existing rules and principles can give us our present location, our bearings, our latitude and longitude. The inn that shelters for the night is not the journey's end. The law, like the traveler, must be ready for the morrow. It must have the principle of growth.

> BENJAMIN N. CARDOZO, *Growth of the Law* 20 (1924).

Law grows, and though the principles of law remain unchanged, yet (and it is one of the advantages of the common law) their application is to be changed with the changing circumstances of the times. Some persons may call this retrogression, I call it progression of human opinion.

> COLERIDGE, C.J., *R. v Ramsey* (1883) 1 C. & E. 126, 135.

The law is like apparel, which alters with the time. (*Le ley est come apparel, que alter ove le temps.*)

> DODDRIDGE, J., *Jones v Powell* (1628) Palm. 536, 538.

Lawes were not made for their own sakes, but for the sake of those who were to be guided by them; and though it is true they are and ought to be sacred, yet, if they be or are become unusefull for their end, they must either be amended if it may be, or new lawes be substituted.

> SIR MATTHEW HALE, *Considerations Touching the Amendments of Lawes* (In Hargrave, *Law Tracts* 269).

He that thinks a state can be exactly steered by the same lawes in every kind, as it was two or three hundred years since, may as well imagine, that the cloaths that fitted him when he was a child should serve him when he is grown a man. The matter changeth the custom, the contracts the commerce; the dispositions, educations and tempers of men and societies change in a long tract of time; and so must their lawes in some measure be changed, or they will not be usefull for their state and condition. And besides all this, as I before said, time is the wisest thing under heaven.

> SIR MATTHEW HALE, *Considerations Touching the Amendment of Lawes* (In Hargrave, *Law Tracts* 269).

I set out on this ground which I suppose to be self-evident, "that the earth belongs in usufruct to the living," that the dead have neither powers nor rights over it. . . . On similar ground it may be proved that no society can make a perpetual constitution, or even a perpetual law. The earth belongs always to the living generation. They may manage it then, and what proceeds from it, as they please, during their usufruct. They are masters too of their own persons, and consequently may govern them as they please. But persons and property make the sum of the objects of government. The constitution and the laws of their predecessors extinguished them, in their natural course, with those whose will gave them being. This could preserve that being till it ceased to be itself, and no longer. Every constitution, then, and every law, naturally expires at the end of nineteen years.

> THOMAS JEFFERSON, *Letter to James Madison, September 6, 1789.*

I tell this tale, which is strictly true,
Just by way of convincing you,
How very little since things were made
They have altered in the lawyers' trade.

RUDYARD KIPLING, *A Truthful Song.*

It is a well settled rule that the law varies with the varying reasons on which it is founded. This is expressed by the maxim, *"cessante ratione, cesset ipsa lex."* This means that no law can survive the reasons on which it is founded. It needs no statute to change it; it abrogates itself. If the reasons on which a law rests are overborne by opposing reasons, which in the progress of society gain a controlling force, the old law, though still good as an abstract principle, and good in its application to some circumstances, must cease to apply as a controllig principle to the new circumstances.

LOOMIS, J., *Beardsley v City of Hartford,* 50 Conn. 529, 541 (1883).

Time works changes, brings into existence new conditions and purposes. Therefore a principle to be vital must be capable of wider application than the mischief which gave it birth. This is particularly true of constitutions. They are not ephemeral enactments, designed to meet passing occasion.

McKENNA, J., *Weems v United States* (1910) 217 US 349, 373, 54 L ed 793, 801, 30 S Ct 544.

Every age should be mistress of its own law.

FREDERIC WM. MAITLAND, *Collected Papers* (1911) 487.

As the usages of society alter, the law must adapt itself to the various situations of mankind.

> LORD MANSFIELD, C.J., *Barwell v Brooks* (1784) 3 Doug. 371, 373.

The law of each age is ultimately what that age thinks should be the law.

> POUND, J., *People ex rel. Durham Realty Corp. v La Fetra*, 230 N. Y. 429, 450 (1921).

We have been relegated to the horse-and-buggy definition of interstate commerce.

> FRANKLIN D. ROOSEVELT, *Press Conference, May 31, 1935.* After the decision in *A. L. A. Schechter Poultry Corp. v United States* (1935) 295 US 495, 79 L ed 1570, 55 S Ct 837, 97 ALR 947, which invalidated the N.I.R.A. See Schlesinger, *Politics of Upheaval* (1960) 286.

The Constitution was not meant to hold the government back to the time of horses and wagons, the time when postboys carried every communication that passed from merchant to merchant, when trade had few long routes within the nation and did not venture in bulk beyond neighborhood transactions.

> WOODROW WILSON, *Constitutional Government in the United States* (1908) 16.

Charity

Secret charities are often, if not uniformly, a genuine index of the real character of the donor.

> BAUGH, J., *Applegate v McFadin*, 20 SW2d 396, 398 (Tex. Ct. Civ. App., 1929).

I readily assume that the motive which leads old women to make bequests to this society is concern for the welfare of the dear dogs.   As one who has more than once experienced the grief of losing a beloved spaniel, I can respect and applaud that motive: though I do not think my respect and applause can be expected when it becomes a matter of the dear guinea-pigs and the dear rats.   .   .   . On the reasoning and assumption of Chitty, J., I conceive that a society, whose object was to secure legislation making illegal the manufacture and sale of rat-traps and rat poisons, would have to be held established for charitable purposes; and that the more readily if the tribunal insisted on "standing neutral" on the question whether rats are, or are not, vermin that are a menace to mankind.

> MacKINNON, L.J., *Commissioners of Inland Rev. v National Anti-Vivisection Soc.* [1946] K.B. 185, 211.

Children

There are no illegitimate children, only illegitimate parents.

> YANKWICH, J.   In a child custody case in Superior Court of Los Angeles, 1928.   See biography of Judge Yankwich in *Who's Who in America.*

Choice

In reality, the carrier is given no choice, except a choice between the rock and the whirlpool,—an option to forego a privilege which may be vital to his livelihood or submit to a requirement which may constitute an intolerable burden.

> SUTHERLAND, J., *Frost & F. Trucking Co. v Railroad Com.* (1926) 271 US 583, 593, 70 L ed 1101, 1104, 76 S Ct 605, 47 ALR 605.

Christianity

There is no act which Christianity forbids, that the law will not reach: if it were otherwise, Christianity would not be, as it has always been held to be, part of the law of England.

> BEST, C.J., *Bird v Holbrook* (1828) 4 Bing. 628, 641.

Christianity is part of the law of England.

> LORD ELDON, *In Re Bedford Charity* (1819) 2 Swans. 470, 527.

My Lords, with all respect for the great names of the lawyers who have used it, the phrase "Christianity is part of the law of England" is really not law; it is rhetoric.

> LORD SUMNER, *Bowman v Secular Soc. Ltd.* [1917] A.C. 406, 464.

Church and State

The "establishment of religion" clause of the First Amendment means at least this: Neither a state nor the Federal Government can set up a church. Neither can pass laws which aid one religion, aid all religions, or prefer one religion over another. . . . In the words of Jefferson, the clause against establishment of religion by law was intended to erect "a wall of separation between church and State."

> BLACK, J., *Everson v Board of Education* (1947) 330 US 1, 15, 91 L ed 711, 723, 67 S Ct 504, 168 ALR 1392.

That Amendment [First] requires the state to be a neutral in its relations with groups of religious believers and non-believers; it does not require the state to be their adversary.   State power is no more to be used so as to handicap religions than it is to favor them.

> BLACK, J., *Everson v Board of Education* (1947) 330 US 1, 18, 91 L ed 711, 724, 67 S Ct 504, 168 ALR 1392.

The First Amendment does not select any one group or any one type of religion for preferred treatment.   It puts them all in that position.

> DOUGLAS, J., *United States v Ballard* (1944) 322 US 78, 87, 88 L ed 1148, 1154, 64 S Ct 882.

We are a religious people whose institutions presuppose a Supreme Being.

> DOUGLAS, J., *Zorach v Clauson* (1952) 343 US 306, 313, 96 L ed 954, 962, 72 S Ct 679.

We find no constitutional requirement which makes it necessary for government to be hostile to religion and to throw its weight against efforts to widen the effective scope of religious influence.

> DOUGLAS, J., *Zorach v Clauson* (1952) 343 US 306, 314, 96 L ed 954, 962, 72 S Ct 679.

The laws of the realm do admit nothing against the law of God.

> HOBART, C. J., *Colt and Glover* (1617) Hobart 140, 149.

Our civil rights have no dependence on our religious opinions.

> THOMAS JEFFERSON, *A Bill for Establishing Religious Freedom* (1786).

Believing with you that religion is a matter which lies solely between man and his God, that he owes account to none other for his faith or his worship, that the legislative powers of government reach actions only, and not opinions, I contemplate with sovereign reverence that act of the whole American people which declared that their legislature should "make no law respecting an establishment of religion, or prohibiting the free exercise thereof," thus building a wall of separation between Church and State.

> THOMAS JEFFERSON (when President), Reply to Greetings from Committee of the Danbury Baptist Assn. of Connecticut, January 1, 1802.

I cannot think . . . that it was a brilliant day in our legal annals when the affairs of the Free Church of Scotland were brought before the House of Lords, and the dead hand fell with a resounding slap upon the living body.

> FREDERIC WM. MAITLAND, *Moral Personality and Legal Personality* in 3 Coll. Papers 319. In the case of *The Free Church of Scotland v Overtoun* [1904] A. C. 515, involving a church dissolution, the House of Lords refused to sanction the use of funds for purposes other than according to the terms of the trust, although the religious views of a large number of the members had changed. This decision was immediately displaced by legislation — 5 Edw. VII, ch. 12.

Sir Richard Rich (King's Solicitor): Admit there were an act of Parliament that the realme should take me for king, would you not, Mr. More take me for king?

Sir Thomas More: That would I.

Sir Richard Rich: Were there an act of Parliament that all the realme should take me for Pope, would you not then Mr. More, take me for Pope?

[Legal Quotations]—6   *81*

Sir Thomas More: Suppose the Parliament would make a law that God should not be God, would you then, Mr. Rich, say that God were not God?

Sir Richard Rich: That I would not since no Parliament may make any such law.

Sir Thomas More: No more could the Parliament make the King the Supreme Head of the Church.

SIR THOMAS MORE. Roper, *Life of More.*

We cannot conceive that cursing a public officer is the exercise of religion in any sense of the term.

MURPHY, J., *Chaplinsky v New Hampshire* (1942) 315 US 568, 571, 86 L ed 1031, 1035, 62 S Ct 766.

The "wall of separation between church and State" that Mr. Jefferson built at the University which he founded did not exclude religious education from that school. The difference between the generality of his statements on the separation of church and state and the specificity of his conclusions on education are considerable. A rule of law should not be drawn from a figure of speech.

REED, J., *Illinois ex rel. McCollum v Board of Education* (1948) 333 US 203, 247, 92 L ed 649, 677, 68 S Ct 461, 2 ALR2d 1338.

Congress shall make no law respecting an establishment of religion, or prohibiting the free exercise thereof; or abridging the freedom of speech, or of the press; or the right of the people peaceably to assemble, and to petition the government for a redress of grievances.

United States Constitution, First Amendment (1791).

             [Legal Quotations]

Circumstances

Circumstances alter cases.

> THOMAS C. HALIBURTON, *The Old Judge,* ch. 15 (1843).

The character of every act depends upon the circumstances in which it is done.

> HOLMES, J., *Schenck v United States* (1919) 249 US 47, 52, 63 L ed 470, 473, 39 S Ct 247.

The case is altered, quoth Plowden.

This became a proverbial saying when a case broke down on the facts. Sir Edmund Plowden was a devout Catholic. To assist at mass in his day was a crime. Summoned for his attendance but feeling that he had been entrapped he cross examined the celebrant and demanded of him if he would swear that he was a "priest". The answer was "no" and Plowden retorted: "The case is altered, no priest, no mass, no mass, no violation of the law."

> See, 1 WOOLRYCH, *Lives of the Serjeants* 117, citing MS. Cooper's *Athenae Cantab.* I, 502.

Citations

Stanton J.: Where have you seen a gentleman vouch on a writ of dower?

Miggely (Of Counsel): Sir, in Trinity term last, past, and of that I vouch the record.

Stanton J.: If you find it, I will give you my hat. (Jeo vous dorra mon chaperon.)

> See Anon. Y.B. 4 Edw. II (Seld. Soc. VI) 168 (1311).

Court: What say you to the cases quoted?
Counsellor Bore'um:
My Lord, these cases I have noted;
Mere *nisi prius* cases, loose,
Loose law, my Lord, quite out of use—
My learned friend is fond of citing
Old cases, which he's seldom right in?
Settling the law as some great men do,
On points reported arguendo.

JOHN ANSTEY, *Pleader's Guide,* bk 2 (1802).

Counsel Randle Jackson: In the book of nature, my Lords, it is written—
Lord Ellenborough: Will you have the goodness to mention the page, Sir, if you please?

LORD CAMPBELL, 3 *Lives of the Chief Justices* 239 (1857).

It will be observed, that I have cited no cases in support of this opinion; not that I have not read, and considered, and puzzled myself with the multitude that were commented on in the argument; but because, finding them like the Swiss troops, fighting on both sides, I have laid them aside and gone upon what seems to me the true spirit of the law.

CARR, J., *Watkins v Crouch,* 5 Leigh (32 Va.) 530 (1834).

In those days few cases in law were cited, but very pithy and pertinent to the purpose, and those ever pinch most; and now in so long arguments with such a farrago of authorities, it cannot be but there is much refuse, which ever doth weaken or lessen the weight of argument.

COKE, 10 Rep., *Preface* (1826 ed. pp. xxi–xxii).

Does anyone doubt the old saw, that the Devil (being a layman) quotes Scripture for his own ends?

CHARLES DICKENS, *Martin Chuzzlewit,* ch. 11.

Antonio: The devil can cite Scripture for his purpose.

SHAKESPEARE, *Merchant of Venice,* Act 1, scene 3.

Citizens

I should think myself a weak reasoner and a bad citizen, were I not, though a royalist in London, a republican in Paris. I should deem it a fair consequence of my being a royalist in London, that I should become a republican in Paris. Thus doing, I should alike respect the rights and follow the example of my sovereign, who while an Anglican in England, is a Presbyterian in Scotland, and a Lutheran in Hanover.

> JEREMY BENTHAM, *Letter to the Minister of the Interior of the French Republic,* 10 Works 282. On August 26, 1792, Bentham was one of a number of foreigners who were honored with the title of Citizen of France, by the National Assembly.

If cats were born in an oven wud they be biscuits?

> FINLEY PETER DUNNE. The Supreme Court held in *United States v Wong Kim Ark* (1898) 169 US 649, 42 L ed 890, 18 S Ct 456, that all Chinese who were born in the United States were citizens. See King, *Life of Fuller* 237.

We should say now, and in no uncertain terms, that a man's mere property status, without more, cannot be used by a state to test, qualify, or limit his rights as a citizen of the United States. "Indigence" in itself is neither a

source of rights nor a basis for denying them. The mere
state of being without funds is a neutral fact—constitutionally an irrelevance, like race, creed or color.

> JACKSON, J., concurring, *Edwards v California* (1941) 314 US
> 160, 185, 86 L ed 119, 131, 62 S Ct 164.

Unless this Court is willing to say that citizenship of the
United States means at least this much to the citizen, then
our heritage of constitutional privileges and immunities is
only a promise to the ear to be broken to the hope, a
teasing illusion like a munificent bequest in a pauper's
will.

> JACKSON, J., concurring, *Edwards v California* (1941) 314 US
> 160, 186, 86 L ed 119, 132, 62 S Ct 164. California's "anti-
> okie" law made it a misdemeanor to bring into the state a
> non-resident indigent person.

I think that before the marriage, it should be love. So
if I will love this country and this country will love me,
then the marriage will be settled.

> SVETLANA (STALIN) ALLILUYEVA, Reply at TV press con-
> ference May 1, when asked if she would apply for United
> States citizenship. See Newsweek, May 8, 1967, p. 40.

Civil Rights

The rights of the person may be again divided into three;
the right of security, by which a man has a right to be locked
up in the station-house, if found drunk and incapable of
taking care of himself; the right of personal liberty, by
which a person may go wherever he pleases, if he has
only the money necessary to pay the fare; and the right of

private property, enabling every man to keep what he has got, when the Government has helped itself, through the medium of taxation, to all that it requires.

> GILBERT ABBOTT à BECKETT, *The Comic Blackstone,* Pt. 1, ch. 1 (1866).

Civil liberty, which is that of a member of society, is no other than natural liberty, so far restrained by human laws, and no farther, as is necessary and expedient for the general advantage of the public.

> BLACKSTONE, *Commentaries,* bk 1, 125.

For repeated and unredressed attacks on the constitutional liberties of the humble will tend to destroy the foundations supporting the constitutional liberties of everyone. The test of the moral quality of a civilization is its treatment of the weak and powerless.

> FRANK, J., *United States ex rel. Caminito v Murphy,* 222 F.2d 698, 706 (1955).

The history of liberty has largely been the history of observance of procedural safeguards.

> FRANKFURTER, J., *McNabb v United States* (1943) 318 US 332, 347, 87 L ed 819, 827, 63 S Ct 608.

It is a fair summary of history to say that the safeguards of liberty have frequently been forged in controversies involving not very nice people.

> FRANKFURTER, J., dissenting, *United States v Rabinowitz* (1950) 339 US 56, 69, 94 L ed 653, 662, 70 S Ct 430.

The hope is that the sanctions of law will not be forever required to curb discrimination; that in due course after civil rights will come civility.

PAUL A. FREUND, *Civil Rights and the Limits of Law*, 14 Buff. L. Rev. 199 (1964).

Ancient Right unnoticed as the breath we draw—
Leave to live by no man's leave underneath the law.

KIPLING, *The Old Issue*, stanza 6.

In a free government, the security for civil rights must be the same as for religious rights. It consists in the one case in the multiplicity of interests, and in the other, in the multiplicity of sects.

JAMES MADISON, *The Federalist No. 51* (1788).

The heart of any constitution consists of its bill of rights, those provisions that secure to the people their liberty of conscience, of speech, of the press, of lawful assembly, and the right to uniform application of the laws and to due process.

GOVERNOR EARL WARREN, *Address to the Legislative Joint Interim Committee on Constitutional Revision and its Advisory Committee*, Santa Barbara, Calif., Oct. 29, 1947.

Civil Service

Peers shall teem in Christendom,
And a Duke's exalted station
Be attainable by com-
Petitive examination!

WILLIAM S. GILBERT, *Iolanthe*, Act 1.

Clarity

Accepting the risk of obscuring the obvious by discussing it, and without splitting hairs as to where the naked legal title to the coal would be when in transit, we may be sure that it was mined and produced under the same "authority" that transported it over the railroad.

> CLARKE, J., *United States v Reading Co.* (1920) 253 US 26, 61, 64 L ed 760, 780, 40 S Ct 425.

His conspicuous defect was obscurity of judicial speech. . . . "He speaks as if he were an Act of Parliament."

> HENRY COCKBURN, *Memorials of His Time,* ch. 5 (N.Y. ed. 1856) p. 282. Referring to William Adam, Scottish Lord Chief Commissioner of the Jury Court (1816) and quoting Lord Glenlee.

The power of clear statement is the great power at the bar.

> DANIEL WEBSTER, *Letter to R.M. Blatchford,* 1849. See Harvey, *Reminiscences of Daniel Webster* 118.

Clerk

An ancient clerk, skilful in precedents, wary in proceeding, and understanding in the business of the court, is an excellent finger of a court; and doth many times point the way to the judge himself.

> BACON, *Essays: Of Judicature.*

His clerk, assistant, housekeeper, secretary, confidential plotter, adviser, intriguer, and bill of costs increaser, Miss Brass—a kind of amazon at common law.

> CHARLES DICKENS, *Old Curiosity Shop,* ch. 33.

It is the justice's clerk that makes the justice.

> Proverb. FULLER, *Proverbs* (1732).

Code

Exceptions excepted, let the masculine singular comprehend both genders and numbers.

> JEREMY BENTHAM, *Nomography*. See 3 *Works* (Bowring ed.) 265.

Justinian's Pandects only make precise,
What simply sparkled in men's eyes before,
Twitched in their brow or quivered on their lip,
Waited the speech they called but would not come.

> ROBERT BROWNING, *Ring and the Books: Count Guido Franceschini.*

No one ever supposed that a system complete in all its parts, could be struck out at a heat, by the most able lawgiver that ever lived.

> GIBSON, J., *Pennock v Hart,* 8 *Serg.* & Rawle 369, 378 (Pa. 1822).

It has been frequently remarked with great propriety, that a voluminous code of laws is one of the inconveniences necessarily connected with the advantages of a free government.

> ALEXANDER HAMILTON, *The Federalist No. 78 (1788).*

The most celebrated system of jurisprudence known to the world begins, as it ends, with a Code.

> SIR HENRY MAINE, *Ancient Law* 1. Referring to the Twelve Tables and the Code of Justinian.

My true glory is not in having won forty battles; . . .
Waterloo will blot out the memory of those victories. . . .
But nothing can blot out my Civil Code.   That will live
forever.

> NAPOLEON. 1 De Montholon, *Recits de la Captivite de Napoleon*
> 401.

My code is lost.

> NAPOLEON, when he first heard that a commentary on his code
> had been published.

I will go down to posterity with the Code in my hand.

> NAPOLEON. Butler, *Reminiscences* 43 (Amer. ed. 1824).

Mr. Prin . . . did discourse with me . . . about
the laws of England, telling me the many faults in them; and
among others, their obscurity through multitude of long
statutes, which he is about to abstract out of all of a sort;
and as he lives, and Parliaments come, get them put into
laws, and the other statutes repealed, and then it will be
a short work to know the law, which appears a very noble
good thing.

> SAMUEL PEPYS, *Diary, April 25, 1666.*

Coke, Sir Edward

When the play called *Ignoramus* (made by one Ruggle
of Clare-hall) was acted with great applause before King
James, they dressed Sir Ignoramus like Chief Justice Coke
and cutt his beard like him and feigned his voyce.   Mr.
Peyton, our vicar of Chalke, was then a scholar at Kings
College and sawe it.   This drollery did *ducere in seria*

mala: it sett all the lawyers against the clergie, and shortly upon this Mr. Seldon wrote of Tythes not *jure divine.*

> JOHN AUBREY, *Brief Lives: Coke.* The play performed before James I in 1615 ridiculed lawyers on the occasion of the dispute (1611–12) as to precedence between the mayor of Cambridge and the vice-chancellor of the University.

The common speech is that fowre Ps have overthrown and put him down, that is, Pride, Prohibitions, Praemunire and Prerogative.

> JOHN CHAMBERLAIN, *Letter to Dudley Carleton, November 14, 1616.*

He is held too great an oracle amongst the people, and they may be mislead by anything that carries such an authority as all things do that he either speaks or writes.

> CHARLES I. (The King in 1631 ordered that all papers of Coke be seized immediately upon his death.)

The jewel of his mind was put into a fair case, a beautiful body with a comely countenance, a case which he did wipe and keep clean, delighting in good clothes well worn; being wont to say that the outward neatness of our bodies might be a monitor of purity to our souls.

> THOMAS FULLER, *Worthies: Norfolk.*

I do wish the Devil had old Cooke [Coke], for I am sure I never was so tired of an old dull scoundrel in my life.

> THOMAS JEFFERSON, *Letter to John Page, Dec. 25, 1762.*

A sounder whig never wrote, nor of profounder learning in the orthodox doctrines of the British constitution, or in what were called English liberties. . . . Our lawyers were then all whigs. But when his black-letter text, and uncouth but cunning learning got out of fashion, and the honied Mansfieldism of Blackstone became the student's hornbook, from that moment, that profession (the nursery of our Congress) began to slide into Toryism, and nearly all the young brood of lawyers now are of that hue. They suppose themselves, indeed, to be whigs because they no longer know what whigism or republicanism means.

THOMAS JEFFERSON, *Letter to James Madison, Feb. 17, 1826.*

He that should search all glories of the gown,
And steps of all raised servants of the crown,
He could not find than thee, of all that store,
Whom fortune aided less, or virtue more.

Ben JONSON, *Underwoods.*

That wonderful Edward Coke was loose—masterful, masterless man.

FREDERIC WM. MAITLAND, *English Law and the Renaissance.* Rede Lecture (1901).

The founder of our legal storehouse, and, which his rivals must confess, though their spleen should burst by reason of it, the head of our jurisprudence.

SIR HENRY SPELMAN. See Woolrych, *Life of Sir Edward Coke* (1826) 210.

Commendation (Self)

I thank God for three things: That I never gave my body to physic, my heart to cruelty, nor my hand to corrup-

tion; and I commend myself for three things: Obtaining
so fair a fortune with my first wife, my successful study
of the law, and the independent manner in which I obtained all my public employments, *nec prece, nec pretio,*
without either prayers or pence.

> COKE. Seward's *Anecdotes* 211.

Commerce

The Court admits that the commerce involved in this
case is foreign commerce, but subjects it to the state police
power on the ground that it is not very foreign.

> JACKSON, J., *Bob-Lo Excursion Co. v Michigan* (1948) 333 US
> 28, 44, 92 L ed 455, 467, 68 S Ct 358.

If it is interstate commerce that feels the pinch, it does
not matter how local the operation which applies the
squeeze.

> JACKSON, J., *United States v Women's Sportswear Mfrs. Asso.*
> (1949) 336 US 460, 464, 93 L ed 805, 811, 69 S Ct 714.

It is the power to regulate; that is, to prescribe the rule
by which commerce is to be governed. This power, like
all others vested in Congress, is complete in itself, may be
exercised to its utmost extent, and acknowledges no limitations, other than are prescribed in the Constitution. . . .
If, as has always been understood, the sovereignty of Congress, though limited to specified objects, is plenary as to
those objects, the power over commerce with foreign nations, and among the several States, is vested in Congress
as absolutely as it would be in a single government, having
in its constitution the same restrictions on the exercise of

the power as are found in the constitution of the United States. The wisdom and the discretion of Congress, their identity with the people, and the influence which their constituents possess at elections, are, in this, as in many other instances, as that, for example, of declaring war, the sole restraints on which they have relied, to secure them from its abuse. They are the restraints on which the people must often rely solely, in all representative governments.

> MARSHALL, C. J., *Gibbons v Ogden* (1824, US) 9 Wheat 1, 196, 6 L ed 23, 70.

Commerce, undoubtedly, is traffic, but it is something more: it is intercourse. It describes the commercial intercourse between nations, and parts of nations, in all its branches, and is regulated by prescribing rules for carrying on that intercourse.

> MARSHALL, C. J., *Gibbons v Ogden* (1824, US) 9 Wheat 1, 189, 6 L ed 23, 68.

Common Employment

Lord Abinger planted it,* Baron Alderson watered it** and the Devil gave it increase.

> Source unknown. This doctrine was abrogated by statute in 1948, 11 and 12 Geo. 6, c. 41.

Common Law

This unwritten or common law is properly distinguishable into three kinds: 1. General customs; which are the

---

* Priestley v Fowler (1837) 3 M. & W. 1.
** Hutchinson v The York (1850) 5 Exch. 343.

universal rule of the whole kingdom, and form the common law, in its stricter and more usual signification. 2. Particular customs; which for the most part affect only the inhabitants of particular districts. 3. Certain particular laws; which by custom are adopted and used by some particular courts, of pretty general and extensive jurisdiction.

BLACKSTONE, *Commentaries,* bk 1, 67.

In many cases, the common law will control Acts of Parliament, and sometimes adjudge them to be utterly void: for when an Act of Parliament is against common right and reason, or repugnant, or impossible to be performed, the common law will control it, and adjudge such Act to be void.

COKE, *Bonham's Case,* 8 Rep. 118 (1610).

Any proposition the result of which would be to shew that the Common Law of England is wholly unreasonable and unjust, cannot be part of the Common Law of England.

LORD ESHER, M.R., *Emmens v Pottle* (1885) 16 Q.B.D. 354, 357.

Its origin . . . is as undiscoverable as the Head of the Nile.

SIR MATTHEW HALE, *History of the Common Law,* ch. 3.

That confusing forest of learned judgments which constitutes the Common Law of England.

A. P. HERBERT, *Uncommon Law: Fardell v. Potts.*

The statute is like a tyrant; where he comes he makes all void; but the common law is like a nursing father, makes void only that part where the fault is, and preserves the rest.

> CHIEF JUSTICE HOBART. See Twisden, C.J. in the case of *Maleverer v Redshaw* (1669) 1 Mod. 35.

The common law is not a brooding omnipresence in the sky but the articulate voice of some sovereign or quasi-sovereign that can be identified.

> HOLMES, J., *Southern Pacific Co. v Jensen* (1917) 244 US 205, 222, 61 L ed 1086, 1101, 37 S Ct 524.

A statute very seldom can take in all cases, therefore the common law, that works itself pure by rules drawn from the fountain of justice, is for this reason superior to an act of parliament.

> MURRAY (LORD MANSFIELD), *arguendo* as Sol. Gen., *Omychund v Barker* (1744) 1 Atk. 21, 33.

Penn: I desire you would let me know by what law it is you prosecute me, and upon what law you ground my indictment.

Rec.: Upon the common-law.

Penn: Where is that common-law?

Rec.: You must not think that I am able to run up so many years, and over so many adjudged cases, which we call common-law, to answer your curiosity.

Penn: This answer I am sure is very short of my question, for if it be common, it should not be so hard to produce.

* * *

Rec.: The question is, whether you are Guilty of this Indictment?

Penn: The question is not, whether I am Guilty of this Indictment, but whether this Indictment be legal. It is too general and imperfect an answer, to say it is the common-law, unless we knew both where and what it is. For where there is no law, there is no transgression; and that law which is not in being, is so far from being common, that it is no law at all.

Rec.: You are an impertinent fellow, will you teach the court what law is? It is "Lex non scripta," that which many have studied 30 or 40 years to know, and would you have me tell you in a moment?

Penn: Certainly, if the common-law be so hard to understand it is far from being common.

> *Trial of William Penn.* 6 How. St. Trials (1670) 951, 958. Penn was refused admittance to the Quaker Meeting Hall and in protest began to preach in the street. He was indicted under the common law for taking part in an unlawful and tumultuous assembly. The jury refused to render a verdict of guilty and were taken into custody.

For if there is any virtue in the Common Law whereby she stands for more than intellectual excellence in a special kind of learning, it is that Freedom is her sister, and in the spirit of freedom her greatest work has ever been done. By that spirit our lady has emboldened her servants to speak the truth before kings, to restrain the tyranny of usurping license, and to carry her ideal of equal public justice and ordered right into every quarter of the world.

> SIR FREDERICK POLLOCK, *The Genius of the Common Law* 124 (1912).

Mastering the lawless science of our law,
That codeless myriad of precedent,

That wilderness of single instances,
Through which a few, by wit or fortune led,
May beat a pathway out to wealth and fame.

> TENNYSON, *Aylmer's Field.*

The common law is nothing else but statutes worn out
by time; all our law began by consent of the Legislature,
and whether it is now law by usage or writing, it is the same
thing.

> WILMOT, C.J., *Collins v Blantern* (1767) 2 Wils, K. B., 341, 348.

Communism

Courts should give to a Communist every right and
advantage that they give to any defendant. But it is in-
conceivable that being a Communist can entitle a defendant
to more.

> JACKSON, J., concurring, *Dennis v United States* (1950) 339 US
> 162, 174, 94 L ed 734, 744, 70 S Ct 519.

The Communist Party is a conspiratorial and revolu-
tionary junta, organized to reach ends and to use methods
which are incompatible with our constitutional system.

> JACKSON, J., *American Communications Asso., C. I. O. v Douds*
> (1950) 339 US 382, 424, 94 L ed 925, 957, 70 S Ct 674.

Your crime is worse than murder. . . . Who knows
but that millions more of innocent people may pay the
price of your treason. Indeed by your betrayal you undoubtedly altered the course of history to the disadvantage
of our country.

> KAUFMAN, J., sentencing to death the atom spies, Julius and Ethel
> Rosenberg, New York Times, April 6, 1951, p. 10.

I should suspect that quite a few members of the Charles' Law Faculty are still what the citizens of Prague call "radishes"—red on the outside and white inside.

> JAROSLAV MAYDA, *Lawyers Under Communism*, 39 A.B.A.J. 1071 (1953).

Concurrence

Having listened all day to things which I do not think I ever heard of before, I can safely say I am of the same opinion, and for the same reasons.

> BARON BRAMWELL. (When first sitting as Lord Justice on the Chancery side of the Court.)

To reach a conclusion on this matter involved the court in wading through a monstrous legislative morass, staggering from stone to stone and ignoring the marsh gas exhaling from the forest of schedules lining the way on each side. I regarded it at one time, I must confess, as a slough of despond through which the court would never drag its feet, but I have, by leaping from tussock to tussock as best I might, eventually, pale and exhausted, reached the other side where I find myself, I am glad to say, at the same point as that arrived at with more agility by my Lord.

> HARMAN, L.J., *Davy v Leeds Corporation* [1964] 1 W.L.R. 1218, 1224. (On the question of compensation for property taken for slum clearance.)

I heartily join the court's opinion. But I derive no pleasure from implying, contrary to the views of my Brothers in the minority, that there was such complete want of evidence of negligence by respondent that "reasonable men"

100

could not differ about it, for, at the very least, I regard
my Brothers who dissent as reasonable men.

> WHITTAKER, J., concurring, *Inman v Baltimore & O. R. Co.*
> (1959) 361 US 138, 141, 4 L ed 2d 198, 202, 80 S Ct 242.

Confessions

I beseech your Lordships, be merciful to a broken reed.

> BACON, acknowledging his confession (1621).

I do plainly and ingenuously confess that I am guilty
of corruption; and do renounce all defence, and put myself
upon the grace and mercy of your Lordships.

> BACON, *Confession and Submission to Parliament* (1621).

Conflict of Interest

Complaints are every where heard from our most considerate and virtuous citizens, equally the friends of public
and private faith, and of public and personal liberty; that
our governments are too unstable; that the public good is
disregarded in the conflicts of rival parties; and that measures are too often decided, not according to the rules of
justice, and the rights of the minor party; but by the superior
force of an interested and over-bearing majority.

> JAMES MADISON, *The Federalist No. 10* (1787).

But the most common and durable source of factions, has
been the various and unequal distribution of property.
Those who hold, and those who are without property, have
ever formed distinct interests in society.   Those who are

101

creditors, and those who are debtors, fall under a like discrimination. A landed interest, a manufacturing interest, a mercantile interest, a monied interest, with many lesser interests, grow up of necessity in civilized nations, and divide them into different classes, actuated by different sentiments and views. The regulation of these various and interfering interests forms the principal task of modern Legislation, and involves the spirit of party and faction in the necessary and ordinary operations of Government.

> JAMES MADISON, *The Federalist No. 10* (1787).

Conflict of Laws

The question is not what we think but what we think the New York Court of Appeals would think the Supreme Court of Ohio would think. . . . With the Ohio authorities in this indeterminate state, I suspect the New York Court of Appeals would think the Supreme Court of Ohio would think what it would think.

> FRIENDLY, J., dissenting, *Cooke v E. F. Drew & Co.,* 319 F.2d 498, 503, 504 (1963).

Confrontation

Festus laid Paul's case before the king, saying, "There is a certain man left a prisoner by Felix, and when I was at Jerusalem, the chief priests and elders of the Jews presented their case against him, and asked for his conviction. But I told them that Romans are not accustomed to give any man up before the accused has met his accusers face to face and has been given a chance to defend himself against the charges."

> *Acts of the Apostles* 25: 14–16.

King:

Then call them to our presence: face to face,
And frowning brow to brow, ourselves will hear
The accuser and the accused freely speak:
High-stomach'd are they both, and full of ire,
In rage deaf as the sea, hasty as fire.

> SHAKESPEARE, *Richard II,* Act 1, scene 1.

Cranmer:

I do beseech your lordships,
That, in this case of justice, my accusers
Be what they will, may stand forth face to face,
And freely urge against me.

> SHAKESPEARE, *Henry VIII,* Act 5, scene 3.

Congressional Record

The Congressional Record is not the United States Code.

> CHARLES P. CURTIS, *A Better Theory of Legal Interpretation,* in *Jurisprudence in Action* 143.

Consequence

Consequences cannot alter statutes, but may help to fix their meaning.

> CARDOZO, J., *Matter of Rouss,* 221 N. Y. 81, 91 (1917).

Conservatism

We have a maxim in the House of Commons, and written on the walls of our house, that old ways are the safest and surest ways.

> COKE, *Speech, May 8, 1628.*

Consistency

The law is always approaching, and never reaching, consistency. It is forever adopting new principles from life at one end, and it always retains old ones from history at the other, which have not yet been absorbed or sloughed off. It will become entirely consistent only when it ceases to grow.

> OLIVER WENDELL HOLMES, *Common Law* 36 (1881).

Conspiracy

Incitement and execution are touched with equal guilt.

> CARDOZO, J., *People v Emieleta,* 238 N. Y. 158, 163 (1924).

Conspiracy, that darling of the modern prosecutor's nursery.

> L. HAND, J., *Harrison v United States,* 7 F.2d 259, 263 (1925).

The Constitution does not make conspiracy a civil right.

> JACKSON, J., *Dennis v United States* (1951) 341 US 494, 572, 95 L ed 1137, 1185, 71 S Ct 857.

She kept the nest that hatched the egg.

> PRESIDENT ANDREW JOHNSON—to Rev. J. G. Butler, St.
> Paul's Church, Washington, D.C. on July 7, 1865, a few hours
> after the execution of Mrs. Surratt for conspiracy in the assassi-
> nation of Lincoln. See Judge Advocate General Joseph Holt,
> *Vindication* 9 (1873).

Constitution

The Constitution itself had been extorted from the grinding necessity of a reluctant nation.

> JOHN QUINCY ADAMS, *Jubilee Discourse on the Constitution*
> 55 (1839).

It is, after all, a national Constitution we are expounding.

> BRENNAN, J., *Jacobellis v Ohio* (1964) 378 US 184, 195, 12 L ed
> 2d 793, 802, 84 S Ct 1676.

A *constitution* states or ought to state not rules for the
passing hour, but principles for an expanding future.   In
so far as it deviates from that standard, and descends into
details and particulars it loses its flexibility, the scope of
interpretation contracts, the meaning hardens.

> BENJAMIN N. CARDOZO, *Nature of the Judicial Process* 83
> (1921).

The Constitution, in all its provisions, looks to an indestructible Union, composed of indestructible States.

> CHASE, C.J., *Texas v White* (1868, US) 7 Wall 700, 725, 19 L ed
> 227, 237.

105

Now the opinion of Cato becomes more certain, that the constitution of the republic is the work of no single time or of no single man. (*Nunc fit illud Catonis certius, nec temporis unius nec hominis esse constitutionem rei publicae; perspicuum est enim, quanta in singulos reges rerum bonarum et utilium fiat accessio.*)

> CICERO, *De Re Publica*, II, 21 (37).
> McIlwain, *Constitutionalism, Ancient and Modern* (1940) 27 attributes to Cicero the first use of the word "constitution" in its accepted modern sense.

The Constitution of the United States is a law for rulers and people, equally in war and in peace, and covers with the shield of its protection all classes of men, at all times, and under all circumstances.

> DAVIS, J., *Ex parte Milligan* (1866, US) 4 Wall 2, 120, 18 L ed 281, 295.

The Constitution is a compact between sovereigns.

> DOUGLAS, J., dissenting, *New York v United States* (1946) 326 US 572, 595, 90 L ed 326, 340, 66 S Ct 310.

Our Constitution is in actual operation; everything appears to promise that it will last; but in this world nothing is certain but death and taxes.

> BENJAMIN FRANKLIN, *Letter to Jean Baptiste Le Roy, Nov. 13, 1789.*

The American Constitution is, so far as I can see, the most wonderful work ever struck off at a given time by the brain and purpose of man. It has had a century of trial, under the pressure of exigencies caused by an expansion unexampled in point of rapidity and range; and its exemption from formal change, though not entire, has certainly proved the sagacity of the constructors, and the stubborn strength of the fabric.

> W. E. GLADSTONE, *Kin Beyond Sea,* 127 No. Amer. Rev. 185 (1878).

A constitution is not intended to embody a particular economic theory, whether of paternalism and the organic relation of the citizen to the State or of *laissez-faire.* It is made for people of fundamentally differing views.

> HOLMES, J., *Lochner v New York* (1905) 198 US 45, 75, 49 L ed 937, 949, 25 S Ct 539.

Our constitution . . . is an experiment, as all life is an experiment.

> HOLMES, J., dissenting, *Abrams v United States* (1919) 250 US 616, 630, 63 L ed 1173, 1180, 40 S Ct 17.

I have the highest regard for the courts. My whole life has been spent in work conditioned upon respect for the courts. I reckon him one of the worst enemies of the community who will talk lightly of the dignity of the bench. We are under a Constitution, but the Constitution is what the judges say it is, and the judiciary is the safeguard of our liberty and of our property under the Constitution.

> CHARLES EVANS HUGHES, *Speech, Elmira Chamber of Commerce, May 3, 1907.*

It is a good canvas, on which some strokes only want retouching.

> THOMAS JEFFERSON, *Letter to James Madison, July 31, 1788.*

107

In questions of power, then, let no more be heard of confidence in man, but bind him down from mischief by the chains of the Constitution.

THOMAS JEFFERSON, *Kentucky Resolutions,* November 1798.

Some men look at constitutions with sanctimonious reverence, and deem them like the ark of the covenant, too sacred to be touched.   They ascribe to the men of the preceding age a wisdom more than human, and suppose what they did to be beyond amendment.

THOMAS JEFFERSON, *Letter to Samuel Kercheval, July 12, 1816.*

Your Constitution is all sail and no anchor.

MACAULAY, *Letter to H. S. Randall, May 23, 1857.*   See 2 *Life & Letters* 409 (Trevelyan ed).

A constitution, to contain an accurate detail of all the subdivisions of which its great powers will admit, and of all the means by which they may be carried into execution, would partake of the prolixity of a legal code, and could scarcely be embraced by the human mind.   It would probably never be understood by the public.   Its nature, therefore, requires, that only its great outlines should be marked, its important objects designated, and the minor ingredients which compose those objects, be deduced from the nature of the objects themselves.   That this idea was entertained by the framers of the American constitution, is not only to be inferred from the nature of the instrument, but from the language. . . .   In considering this question, then, we must never forget, that it is a constitution we are expounding.

MARSHALL, C. J., *M'Culloch v Maryland* (1819, US) 4 Wheat 316, 407, 4 L ed 579, 601.

This provision is made in a constitution intended to endure for ages to come, and consequently, to be adapted to the various crises of human affairs. To have prescribed the means by which government should in all future times execute its powers would have been to change entirely the character of the instrument and to give it the properties of a legal code. It would have been an unwise attempt to provide by immutable rules for exigencies, which, if foreseen at all, must have been seen dimly and can best be provided for as they occur.

> MARSHALL, C.J., *M'Culloch v Maryland* (1819, US) 4 Wheat 316, 415, 4 L ed 579, 603.

The people made the constitution, and the people can unmake it. It is the creature of their will, and lives only by their will. But this supreme and irresistible power to make or unmake, resides only in the whole body of the people; not in any subdivision of them.

> MARSHALL, C.J., *Cohens v Virginia* (1821, US) 6 Wheat 264, 389, 5 L ed 257, 287.

I yield slowly and reluctantly to the conviction that our constitution cannot last. . . . Our opinions are incompatible with a united government even among ourselves. The union has been prolonged thus far by miracles, I fear they cannot continue.

> JOHN MARSHALL, *Letter to Joseph Story, September 22, 1832.* 4 Beveridge's *Life of Marshall* 559.

A constitution is not the act of a government, but of a people constituting a government; and government without a constitution, is power without a right.

> THOMAS PAINE, *Rights of Man,* pt 2, ch. 4.

The United States Constitution has proved itself the most marvellously elastic compilation of rules of government ever written.

> FRANKLIN D. ROOSEVELT, *Radio Address, Mar. 2, 1930.*

Our Constitution is so simple and practical that it is possible always to meet extraordinary needs by changes in emphasis and arrangement without loss of essential form.

> FRANKLIN D. ROOSEVELT, *Inaugural Address, March 4, 1933.*
> See 2 *Public Papers and Addresses* (Rosenman ed.) 14.

The Constitution cannot make itself; somebody made it, not at once but at several times. It is alterable; and by that draweth near Perfection; and without suiting itself to different Times and Circumstances, it could not live. Its Life is prolonged by changing seasonably the several Parts of it at several times.

> GEORGE SAVILE, *Works* (Raleigh ed. 1912) 211.

A constitution which will not bend will sooner or later break.

> JOHN SALMOND, *Jurisprudence* (5th ed.) 473.

There is a higher law than the Constitution.

> WILLIAM H. SEWARD, Speech in Senate, March 11, 1850, *California Union and Freedom*, Congr. Globe, v. 19 App. Pt 1, 265.

The Constitution of the United States is not a mere lawyers' document: it is a vehicle of life, and its spirit is always the spirit of the age.

> WOODROW WILSON, *Constitutional Government in the United States* 69 (1927).

Constitution (Amendments)

It is my belief that there *are* "absolutes" in our Bill of Rights, and that they were put there on purpose by men who knew what words meant, and meant their prohibitions to be "absolutes".

> HUGO BLACK, *The Bill of Rights,* 35 N. Y. Univ. L. R. 865, 867 (1960).

We reach a different plane of social and moral values when we pass to the privileges and immunities that have been taken over from the earlier articles of the federal bill of rights and brought within the Fourteenth Amendment by a process of absorption. . . . If the Fourteenth Amendment has absorbed them, the process of absorption has had its source in the belief that neither liberty nor justice would exist if they were sacrificed.

> CARDOZO, J., *Palko v Connecticut* (1937) 302 US 319, 326, 82 L ed 288, 292, 58 S Ct 149.

In these and other situations immunities that are valid as against the federal government by force of specific pledges of particular amendments have been found to be implicit in the concept of ordered liberty, and thus, through the Fourteenth Amendment, become valid as against the states.

> CARDOZO, J., *Palko v Connecticut* (1937) 302 US 319, 324, 82 L ed 288, 291, 58 S Ct 149.

Between the incorporation of the Fourteenth Amendment into the Constitution and the beginning of the present membership of the Court—a period of seventy years—the scope of that Amendment was passed upon by forty-three judges. Of all these judges, only one, who may respectfully be called an eccentric exception, ever indicated the belief

111

that the Fourteenth Amendment was a shorthand summary of the first eight Amendments theretofore limiting only the Federal Government, and that due process incorporated those eight Amendments as restrictions upon the powers of the States.

> FRANKFURTER, J., concurring, *Adamson v California* (1947) 332 US 46, 62, 91 L ed 1903, 1914, 67 S Ct 1672, 171 ALR 1223. Referring to Mr. Justice Harlan (1833–1911).

The Fourteenth Amendment does not enact Mr. Herbert Spencer's Social Statics.

> HOLMES, J., *Lochner v New York* (1905) 198 US 45, 75, 49 L ed 937, 949, 25 S Ct 539.

There is nothing that I more deprecate than the use of the Fourteenth Amendment beyond the absolute compulsion of its words to prevent the making of social experiments that an important part of the community desires, in the insulated chambers afforded by the several States, even though the experiments may seem futile or even noxious to me and to those whose judgment I most respect.

> HOLMES, J., *Truax v Corrigan* (1921) 257 US 312, 344, 66 L ed 254, 268, 42 S Ct 124, 27 ALR 375.

We cannot give some constitutional rights a preferred position without relegating others to a deferred position.

> JACKSON, J., dissenting, *Brinegar v United States* (1949) 338 US 160, 180, 93 L ed 1879, 1893, 69 S Ct 1302.

The very purpose of a Bill of Rights was to withdraw certain subjects from the vicissitudes of political controversy, to place them beyond the reach of majorities and officials and to establish them as legal principles to be applied by the courts. One's right to life, liberty, and

112

property, to free speech, a free press, freedom of worship and assembly, and other fundamental rights may not be submitted to vote; they depend on the outcome of no elections.

> JACKSON, J., *West Virginia State Board of Education v Barnette* (1943) 319 US 624, 638, 87 L ed 1628, 1638, 63 S Ct 1178, 147 ALR 674.

If they [the first ten Amendments] are incorporated into the constitution, independent tribunals of justice will consider themselves in a peculiar manner the guardians of those rights; they will be an impenetrable bulwark against every assumption of power in the legislative or executive; they will be naturally led to resist every encroachment upon rights expressly stipulated for in the constitution by the declaration of rights.

> JAMES MADISON, 1 *Annals of Congress, 1789* (Gales & Seaton, ed.) 457.

The First Amendment is not confined to safeguarding freedom of speech and freedom of religion against discriminatory attempts to wipe them out. On the contrary, the Constitution, by virtue of the First and the Fourteenth Amendments, has put those freedoms in a preferred position.

> STONE, C. J., dissenting, *Jones v Opelika* (1942) 316 US 584, 608, 86 L ed 1691, 1707, 62 S Ct 1231, 141 ALR 514.

Constitution (English)

The most subtle organism which has proceeded from progressive history.

> W. E. GLADSTONE, *Kin Beyond the Sea,* 127 No. Amer. Rev. 185 (1878).

[Legal Quotations]—8   *113*

Like the British Constitution, she owes her success in practice to her inconsistencies in principle.

THOMAS HARDY, *Hand of Ethelberta,* ch. 9.

When one scrutinizes the English Constitution, it is like looking at the nests of birds or at the curious and intricate work of beavers and insects; its strange contrivances seem not so much the ordered and foreseen result of human wisdom as a marvellous outcome of instinct, of a singular political sense and apprehension, feeling its sure way for centuries, amid all sorts of obstacles, through and around and over them, with the busy persistence of a tribe of ants.

JAMES BRADLEY THAYER, *Legal Essays* 191 (1908).

Nobody planned the British estate system, nobody planned the British aristocratic system, nobody planned the confounded constitution. It came about; it was like layer after layer wrapping round an agate, but you see it came about so happily in a way, it so suited the climate and the temperament of our people and our island, it was on the whole so cosy, that our people settled down into it. You can't help settling down into it.

H. G. WELLS, *Mr. Britling Sees It Through,* bk 1, ch. 1, sec. 11.

Constitutional Law

A great principle of constitutional law is not susceptible of comprehensive statement in an adjective.

CARDOZO, J., *Carter v Carter Coal Co.* (1936) 298 US 238, 327, 80 L ed 1160, 1197, 56 S Ct 855.

The petitioner may have a constitutional right to talk politics, but he has no constitutional right to be a policeman.

> HOLMES, J., *McAuliffe v Mayor*, 155 Mass 216, 220 (1892).

Constitutional law like other mortal contrivances has to take some chances.

> HOLMES, J., *Blinn v Nelson* (1911) 222 US 1, 7, 56 L ed 65, 68, 32 S Ct 1.

This Court is forever adding new stories to the temples of constitutional law, and the temples have a way of collapsing when one story too many is added.

> JACKSON, J., concurring, *Douglas v Jeannette* (1943) 319 US 157, 181, 87 L ed 1324, 1338, 63 S Ct 877.

Constitutionality

A statute which is ultimately declared unconstitutional is presumed to have been known by all to be a nullity from the time of its enactment, even though the fact of its nullity is not known until declared a long time afterwards by a five to four decision.

> CARSWELL, J., *Holland v Atlantic Stevedoring Co.*, 210 App Div (N.Y.) 129, 130 (1924).

If any act of Congress, or of the legislature of a state, violates those constitutional provisions, it is unquestionably void; though I admit, that as the authority to declare it void is of a delicate and awful nature, the Court will never resort to that authority, but in a clear and urgent case.

> IREDELL, J., *Calder v Bull* (1798, US) 3 Dall 386, 399, 1 L ed 648, 654.

There is no war between the Constitution and common sense.

> CLARK, J., *Mapp v Ohio* (1961) 367 US 643, 657, 6 L ed 2d
> 1081, 1091, 81 S Ct 1684, 84 ALR2d 933.

An unconstitutional act is not a law; it confers no rights; it imposes no duties; it affords no protection; it creates no office; it is, in legal contemplation, as inoperative as though it had never been passed.

> FIELD, J., *Norton v Shelby County* (1886) 118 US 425, 442, 30
> L ed 178, 186, 6 S Ct 1121.

Preoccupation by our people with the constitutionality, instead of with the wisdom of legislation or of executive action is preoccupation with a false value. . . . Focusing attention on constitutionality tends to make constitutionality synonymous with wisdom.

> FRANKFURTER, J., concurring, *Dennis v United States* (1951)
> 341 US 494, 555, 95 L ed 1137, 1176, 71 S Ct 857.

This holding seems to me to stand on its head the usual rule of governing this Court's approach to the validity of legislative enactments, state as well as federal, which is of course that they come to us with a strong presumption of regularity and constitutionality. . . . The burden of showing unconstitutionality should be left here, as in other cases, on the attacking party.

> HARLAN, J., dissenting, *Swann v Adams* (1967) 385 US 440, 447,
> 17 L ed 2d 501, 506, 87 S Ct 569.

The particular phraseology of the constitution of the United States confirms and strengthens the principle, supposed to be essential to all written constitutions, that a law repugnant to the constitution is void; and that courts, as well as other departments, are bound by that instrument.

> MARSHALL, C.J., *Marbury v Madison* (1803, US) 1 Cranch 137, 180, 2 L ed 60, 74.

Let the end be legitimate, let it be within the scope of the constitution, and all means which are appropriate, which are plainly adapted to that end, which are not prohibited, but consist with the letter and spirit of the constitution, are constitutional.

> MARSHALL, C.J., *M'Culloch v Maryland* (1819, US) 4 Wheat 316, 421, 4 L ed 579, 605.

Novelty is no argument against constitutionality.

> POUND, J., *People ex rel. Durham Realty Corp. v La Fetra,* 230 N. Y. 429, 446 (1921).

Consumer Fraud

Things are seldom what they seem,
Skim milk masquerades as cream;
Highlows pass as patent leathers;
Jackdaws strut in peacock's feathers.

> WILLIAM S. GILBERT, *H.M.S. Pinafore, Act 2.*

Contemporaneous

Great weight has always been attached, and very rightly attached to contemporaneous exposition.

> MARSHALL, C.J., *Cohens v Virginia* (1821, US) 6 Wheat 264, 418, 5 L ed 257, 294.

117

Contempt of Court

Justice is not a cloistered virtue: she must be allowed to suffer the scrutiny and respectful, even though outspoken, comments of ordinary men.

> LORD ATKIN, *Ambard v. Atty. Gen. for Trinidad* [1936] A.C. 322, 335.

An ill-disposed person may exhibit contempt of court in divers ways—for example, he may scandalize the court itself, which may be done not merely by the extreme measure of hurling missiles at the presiding judge, or loudly contemning his learning or authority, but by ostentatiously reading a newspaper in his presence, or laughing uproariously at a joke made by someone else. Such contempts, committed as they are *in facie curiae,* are criminal offences, and may be punished summarily by immediate imprisonment without the right of appeal. It speaks well both for the great good sense of the judges and for the deep-rooted legal instincts of our people that such offences are seldom heard of. It would be impossible nicely to define what measure of freedom of manners should be allowed in a court of justice, which, as we know, is neither a church nor a theatre, but, as a matter of practice, the happy mean between an awe-struck and unmanly silence and free-and-easy conversation is well preserved.

> AUGUSTINE BIRRELL, *In the Name of Bodleian: Contempt of Court.*

The object of the discipline enforced by the Court in case of contempt of Court is not to vindicate the dignity of the Court or the person of the Judge, but to prevent undue interference with the administration of justice.

> BOWEN, L.J., *Helmore v Smith* (1887) 35 Ch. D. 449, 455.

The law of contempt is not made for the protection of judges who may be sensitive to the winds of public opinion. Judges are supposed to be men of fortitude, able to thrive in a hardy climate.

> DOUGLAS, J., *Craig v Harney* (1947) 331 US 367, 376, 91 L ed 1546, 1552, 67 S Ct 1249.

Judges as persons, or courts as institutions, are entitled to no greater immunity from criticism than other persons or institutions. Just because the holders of judicial office are identified with the interests of justice they may forget their common human frailties and fallibilities. There have sometimes been martinets upon the bench as there have also been pompous wielders of authority who have used the paraphernalia of power in support of what they called their dignity. Therefore judges must be kept mindful of their limitations and of their ultimate public responsibility by a vigorous stream of criticism expressed with candor however blunt.

> FRANKFURTER, J., *Bridges v California* (1941) 314 US 252, 289, 86 L ed 192, 217, 62 S Ct 190, 159 ALR 1346.

The liberty of the press is no greater and no less than the liberty of every subject of the Queen.

> LORD RUSSELL, C.J., *Regina v Gray* [1900] 2 Q. B. 36, 40.

They are imprisoned only until they comply with the orders of the court, and this they may do at any time. They carry the keys of their prison in their own pockets.

> SANBORN, J., *In re Nevitt,* 117 Fed. 448, 461 (1902).

Henry V:
How might a prince of my great hopes forget
So great indignities you laid upon me?

119

What! rate, rebuke, and roughly send to prison
The immediate heir of England! Was this easy?
May this be wash'd in Lethe, and forgotten?

Ch. Justice:
I then did use the person of your father;
The image of his power lay then in me:
And, in the administration of his law,
Whiles I was busy for the commonwealth,
Your highness pleased to forget my place,
The majesty and power of law and justice,
The image of the king whom I presented,
And struck me in my very seat of judgment;
Whereon, as an offender to your father,
I gave bold way to my authority,
And did commit you. If the deed were ill,
Be you contented, wearing now the garland,
To have a son set your decrees at nought,
To pluck down justice from your awful bench,
To trip the course of law, and blunt the sword
That guards the peace and safety of your person.

> SHAKESPEARE, *Henry IV*, Pt. 2, Act 5, scene 2.

Henry V:
You are right, justice; and you weigh this well;
Therefore still bear the balance and the sword:
And I do wish your honours may increase
Till you do live to see a son of mine
Offend you and obey you, as I did.
So shall I live to speak my father's words:
"Happy am I, that have a man so bold
That dares do justice on my proper son;
And not less happy, having such a son,
That would deliver up his greatness so

Into the hands of justice." You did commit me:
For which, I do commit into your hand
The unstained sword that you have us'd to bear;
With this remembrance, that you use the same
With the like bold, just, and impartial spirit
As you have done 'gainst me. There is my hand.

SHAKESPEARE, *ibid.*

Contracts

The law has outgrown its primitive stage of formalism
when the precise word was the sovereign talisman, and every
slip was fatal. It takes a broader view today. A promise
may be lacking, and yet the whole writing may be "instinct
with an obligation," imperfectly expressed.

CARDOZO, J., *Wood v Duff-Gordon.* 222 N. Y. 88, 91 (1917).
The quoted phrase is from Mr. Justice Scott's opinion in *McCall
v. Wright,* 133 App. Div. (N.Y.) 62, 68 (1909).

Necessitous men are not, truly speaking, free men, but, to
answer a present exigency, will submit to any terms that
the crafty may impose upon them.

LORD HENLEY, L.C., *Vernon v Bethell* (1762) 2 Eden 110, 113.

The movement of the progressive societies has hitherto
been a movement from status to contract.

SIR HENRY MAINE, *Ancient Law,* ch. 5.

That which in any contract is left to be implied and need
not be expressed is something so obvious that it goes without saying; so that, if, while the parties were making their
bargain, an officious bystander were to suggest some express

121

provision for it in their agreement, they would testily suppress him with a common "Oh, of course!"

> MacKINNON, L.J., *Shirlaw v Southern Foundries (1926) Ltd.* [1939] 2 K.B. 206, 227.

If a man will improvidently bind himself up by a voluntary deed, and not reserve a liberty to himself by a power of revocation, this court will not loose the fetters he hath put upon himself, but he must lie down under his own folly.

> LORD NOTTINGHAM, L.C., *Villers v Beaumont* (1682) 1 Vern. 100, 101.

Convenience

Convenience is not a legal principle.

> PEARCE, L.J., *Midland Silicones Ltd. v Scruttons Ltd.* [1961] 1 Q.B. 106, 126.

Conveyancing

I, John of Gaunt
Do give and do grant
To Sir John Burgoyne
And the heirs of his loin
Both Sutton and Potton
Till the world goes rotten.

> Anon.

The science of conveyancing to sing:
A noble theme which Coke himself supposes
To be at least as old as Lawyer Moses.

> S.G.B. GRANT, *The Conveyancer's Guide* (1820).

Copyright and Patent

Half a century writes *Finis* to most authors, while in the case of the few who prove to be for all time, the feeling of mankind would be one of resentment were there now living in Paternoster Row or Madrid or Florence a capitalist who could say, "Hamlet is mine," "Sancho Panza is mine," "The 'Inferno' belongs to me." Who would not feel that this disreputable *bourgeois* was the enemy, not the friend, of the world-wide genius of Shakespeare, of Cervantes, of Dante?

> AUGUSTINE BIRRELL, *Law and History of Copyright 25* (1899).
> Argument against proposal of perpetual copyright.

Johnson: No, sir, a man's repeating it no more makes it his property than a man may sell a cow which he drives home.

Boswell: I said printing an abridgment of a work was allowed, which was only cutting the horns and tail off the cow.

Johnson: No, sir, 'tis making the cow have a calf.

> BOSWELL, *Journal of a Tour to the Hebrides with Samuel Johnson:* entry, Aug. 20, 1773. Boswell had mentioned Lord Monboddo's opinion, that if a man could get a work by heart, he might print it, as by such an act "the mind is exercised."

Books are published with an expectation, if not a desire, that they will be criticised in reviews, and if deemed valuable that parts of them will be used as affording illustrations by way of quotation, or the like—and if the quantity taken be neither substantial nor material, if, as it has been expressed by some Judges, a "fair use" only be made of the publication, no wrong is done and no action can be brought.

> LORD HATHERLEY, *Chatterton v Cave* (1878) 3 App. Cas. 483, 492.

123

The patent system . . . added the fuel of interest to the fire of genius.

> ABRAHAM LINCOLN, *Lecture on Discoveries, Inventions and Improvements*, February 11, 1859.

Ideas are free. But while the author confines them to his study, they are like birds in a cage, which none but he can have a right to let fly: for, till he thinks proper to emancipate them, they are under his own dominion.

> YATES, J., *Millar v Taylor* (1769) 4 Burr. 2303, 2378.

Coram Nobis

The wild ass of the law which the courts cannot control.

> SIMS, J., *Anderson v Buchanan*, 292 Ky 810, 822 (1943).

Corporations

An ingenious device for obtaining individual profit without individual responsibility.

> AMBROSE BIERCE, *Devil's Dictionary*.

The director is really a watch-dog, and the watch-dog has no right, without the knowledge of his master, to take a sop from a possible wolf.

> BOWEN, L.J., *In re North Australian Territory Co.* [1892] 1 Ch. 322, 341.

They cannot commit treason, nor be outlawed, nor excommunicate, for they have no souls.

> COKE, *Sutton's Hospital Case* (1612) 10 Rep. 32b.

124

The law does not permit the stockholders to create a sterilized board of directors.

COLLIN, J., *Manson v Curtis,* 223 N.Y. 313, 323 (1918).

The corporation is, and must be, the creature of the State. Into its nostrils the State must breathe the breath of a fictitious life for otherwise it would be no animated body but individualistic dust.

FREDERIC WM. MAITLAND, *Introduction,* xxx, *to Gierke, Political Theories of the Middle Ages.*

As touching corporations: that they were invisible, immortall, and that they had no soule, and therefore no subpoena lieth against them, because they have no conscience or soule; a corporation, is a body aggregate, none can create soules but God; but the King creates them, and therefore they have no soules.

MANWOOD, C.B., *Tipling v Pexall,* 2 Bulstrode 233.

One gains the distinct impression that the bankrupt held up the veils of the fourteen collateral corporations primarily, if not solely, for the benefit of the tax gatherer, but otherwise completely disregarded them. Even Salome's could not have been more diaphanous.

MOORE, J., *Soviero v Franklin Nat. Bank of L. I.,* 328 F.2d 446, 448 (1964).

You never expected justice from a company, did you? They have neither a soul to lose, nor a body to kick.

LORD THURLOW. See 1 Holland, *Memoir of Sydney Smith* 331.

A corporation cannot blush. It was a body it was true; had certainly a head—a new one every year—an annual

125

acquisition of intelligence in every new lord mayor. Arms he supposed it had, and long ones too, for it could reach at any thing. Legs, of course, when it made such long strides. A throat to swallow the rights of the community, and a stomach to digest them! But whoever yet discovered, in the anatomy of any corporation, either bowels, or a heart?

> HOWEL WALSH, in a corporation case tried at the Tralee assizes. Hone, *Table Book* 524 (1837).

Costs

There is one panacea which heals every sore in litigation, and that is costs. I have very seldom, if ever, been unfortunate enough to come across an instance, where a person has made a mistake in his pleadings which has put the other side to such a disadvantage as that it cannot be cured by the application of that healing medicine.

> BOWEN, L.J., *Cropper v Smith* (1884) 26 Ch. D. 700, 711.

Costs as between party and party are given by the law as an indemnity to the person entitled to them: they are not imposed as a punishment on the party who pays them, nor given as a bonus to the party who receives them.

> BRAMWELL, B., *Harold v Smith* (1860) 5 H. & N. 381, 385.

Courage

The heroic hours of life do not announce their presence by drum and trumpet, challenging us to be true to ourselves by appeals to the martial spirit that keeps the blood at heat. Some little, unassuming, unobtrusive choice presents itself before us slyly and craftily, glib and insinuating, in the modest garb of innocence. To yield to its blandishments is so easy. The wrong, it seems, is venial. . . . Then it is that you will be summoned to show the courage of adventurous youth.

> BENJAMIN N. CARDOZO, *Law and Literature* 170 (1931).

I thought I heard my little children plucking at my robe and crying out to me—Now, father, is the time to get us bread.

> THOMAS ERSKINE, reply when asked how, in his maiden speech at the bar in the Baillie Case, he had the courage to persist in naming Lord Sandwich, the First Lord of the Admiralty, in the face of judicial warning not to do so. See 6 Campbell, *Lives of the Lord Chancellors,* ch. 177 (1847).

Court Packing

We are told that the Supreme Court's about-face was not due to outside clamor. It seems that the new building has a soundproof room, to which justices may retire to change their minds.

> HOWARD BRUBAKER, *Of All Things,* 13 New Yorker, April 10, 1937, p. 34.

If they want me to preside over a convention, I can do it.

> CHIEF JUSTICE CHARLES EVANS HUGHES. Pusey, 2 *Charles Evans Hughes* 753. Roosevelt's court packing bill of 1937 would have given the president the power to appoint a co-adjutor judge for every federal judge who had been on the bench for ten years and had not resigned within six years after reaching the age of seventy.

127

I asked Tom [Corcoran] about the Court fight and he
said everything was in good shape. He admitted that Chief
Justice Hughes has played a bad hand perfectly while we
[F.D.R. and his advisers] have played a good hand badly.

HAROLD L. ICKES, 2 *Secret Diary* (May 22, 1937) 145.

There is much comfort to be found in the realization
that even if Congress should pass the law remodelling the
Supreme Court, the Supreme Court could always declare
the law unconstitutional. This ought not be hard, either,
with all the practice they've had lately.

The Talk of the Town, 13 New Yorker, March 6, 1937, p. 13.

In the case holding the New York Minimum Wage Law
unconstitutional, Justice Stone said that the majority were
actually reading into the Constitution their own "personal
economic predilections," and that if the legislative power is
not left free to choose the methods of solving the problems
of poverty, subsistence and health of large numbers in the
community, then "government is to be rendered impotent,"
and two other Justices agreed with him.

FRANKLIN D. ROOSEVELT, *Fireside Chat,* March 9, 1937.
(President Roosevelt adopted Mr. Justice Stone's phrase "economic predilections" as his slogan for his court packing plan).

A switch in time saves nine.

Saying. After F.D.R. sent court packing bill to Congress on February 5, 1937, the Court upheld New Deal legislation. Mr.
Justice Roberts changed his position and voted for the constitutionality of a minimum wage in *West Coast Hotel v Parrish*
(1936) 300 US 379, 81 L ed 703, 57 S Ct 578, 108 ALR 1330.
For explanation of his change see Frankfurter, *Mr. Justice
Roberts,* 104 Univ. of Pa. L. Rev. 311 (1955).

It can't be done because I've tried it and it doesn't work. Whenever you put a man on the Supreme Court, he ceases to be your friend. I'm sure of that.

> HARRY S. TRUMAN, *Lecture at Columbia University,* April 28, 1959. See N. Y. Herald Tribune, April 29, 1959, p. 18, col. 3.

Court Packing (Nine Old Men)

The issue may well simmer down to whether the judgment of the courts of the United States, the executive arm of the United States and, in fact though not in form, the apparent opinion of the great majority of the United States, considers essential this economic readjustment; or whether the nine old men of the Supreme Court are entitled to form their own opinion about it and to upset a movement of national scope solely on that opinion.

> A. A. BERLE, *Law and the Social Revolution,* Survey Graphic (December 1933) 592, 594.

"Nine million dollars!" sighed the late Huey Long, casting an appraising eye over the columns, the copper, the oak paneling. "A million dollars apiece for those Nine Old Men. And they used to be glad to sit in one room."

> PEARSON and ALLEN, *Nine Old Men* (1936) 14. Referring to new Supreme Court Building.

Courts

A swallow had built her nest under the eaves of a Court of Justice. Before her young ones could fly, a serpent gliding out of his hole ate them all up. When the poor bird returned to her nest and found it empty, she began a pitiable wailing. A neighbor suggested, by way of comfort, that she was not the first bird who had lost her young. "True," she replied, "but it is not only my little ones that I mourn, but that I should have been wronged in that very place where the injured fly for justice."

AESOP, *Fables.*

The place of justice is an hallowed place; and therefore not only the bench but the foot-pace and precincts and purprise thereof, ought to be preserved without scandal and corruption.

BACON, *Essays: Of Judicature.*

In England we had a court once, that sat in a chamber, with stars for ornaments on the roof of it. It had of course, like its fellows, a set of rules of its own. We had then star-chamber justice, in addition to equity justice, and common-law justice. Star-chamber justice has been convicted, and has abjured the realm.

JEREMY BENTHAM, *Rationale of Judicial Evidence,* bk. 8, ch. 19, sec. 4. See 7 *Works* (1843 Bowring ed.) 301.

Under our constitutional system, courts stand against any winds that blow as havens of refuge for those who might otherwise suffer because they are helpless, weak, outnumbered, or because they are non-conforming victims of prejudice and public excitement.

BLACK, J., *Chambers v Florida* (1940) 309 US 227, 241, 84 L ed 716, 724, 60 S Ct 472. (Four young Negroes had been convicted of murder on basis of what they claimed were coerced confessions.)

It is of great consequence that the public should know what takes place in Court; and the proceedings are under the control of the Judges.   The inconvenience therefore arising from the chance of injury to private character is infinitesimally small as compared to the convenience of publicity.

> LORD CAMPBELL, C.J., *Davison v Duncan* (1857) 7 E. & B. 229, 231.

It (the court as an institution) is the lengthened shadow of many men.

> FIELD, C.J., Observance of the 250th Anniversary of the Supreme Judicial Court, 312 Mass 746.

Hark the hour of ten is sounding:
Hearts with anxious fears are bounding,
Hall of Justice crowds surrounding,
    Breathing hope and fear—
For to-day in this arena,
Summoned by a stern subpoena,
Edwin sued by Angelina,
    Shortly will appear.

> WILLIAM S. GILBERT, *Trial by Jury.*

A court in our Anglo-American system is a substantially passive instrument, to be moved only by the initiative of litigants.

> ROBERT H. JACKSON, *The Supreme Court in the American System of Government* 12 (1955).

Trial courts search for truth and appellate courts search for error.

> *Saying.*

Humanity is the second virtue of courts, but undoubtedly the first is justice.

SCOTT, J., *Evans v Evans* (1790) 1 Hag. Con. 35.

Courts are not the only agency of government that must be assumed to have capacity to govern.

STONE, J., *United States v Butler* (1936) 297 US 1, 87, 80 L ed 477, 499, 56 S Ct 312, 102 ALR 914.

Courts (Small Claims)

And besides all these there must be courts for small suits about sums of a drachma up to five drachmas, or a little more, which have to be determined.

ARISTOTLE, *Politics,* bk. 4, ch. 16 (Jowett trans.).

Crime

When a felon's not engaged in his employment,
Or maturing his felonious little plans,
His capacity for innocent enjoyment
Is just as great as any honest man's.
Our feelings we with difficulty smother
When constabulary duty's to be done.
Ah, take one consideration with another,
A policeman's lot is not a happy one.

WILLIAM S. GILBERT, *Pirates of Penzance,* Act II.

When the enterprising burglar's not a-burgling,
When the cut-throat isn't occupied in crime,

He loves to hear the little brook a-gurgling,
And listen to the merry village chime.
When the coster's finished jumping on his mother,
He loves to lie a-basking in the sun.
Ah, take one consideration with another,
The policeman's lot is not a happy one.

> WILLIAM S. GILBERT, *ibid.*

Criminal Justice

If rogues did but know all the pains that the law has taken for their benefit, honest men would have nothing left they could call their own.

> JEREMY BENTHAM, *Rationale of Judicial Evidence,* 6 Works 205.

But all punishment is mischief: all punishment in itself is evil. Upon the principle of utility, if it ought at all to be admitted, it ought only to be admitted in as far as it promises to exclude some greater evil.

> JEREMY BENTHAM, *Principles of Morals and Legislation,* ch. XVI, sec. 2. See 1 *Works* (1843 Bowring ed.) 83.

Whence originated the prodigal fury with which the punishment of death has been inflicted? It is the effect of resentment which at first inclines to the greatest rigour; and of an imbecility of soul, which finds in the rapid destruction of convicts the great advantage of having no further occasion to concern one's self about them.

> JEREMY BENTHAM, *Theory of Legislation* 354.

Capital Punishment, a penalty regarding the justice and expediency of which many worthy persons—including all the assassins—entertain grave misgivings.

> AMBROSE BIERCE, *Devil's Dictionary.*

In criminal trials a state can no more discriminate on account of poverty than on account of religion, race or color.

> BLACK, J., *Griffin v Illinois* (1956) 351 US 12, 17, 100 L ed 891, 898, 76 S Ct 585, 55 ALR2d 1055.

There can be no equal justice where the kind of trial a man gets depends on the amount of money he has.

> BLACK, J., *Griffin v Illinois* (1956) 351 US 12, 19, 100 L ed 891, 899, 76 S Ct 585, 55 ALR2d 1055.

I oft have heard of Lydford law,
How, in the morn, they hang and draw,
And sit in judgment after.
At first I wonder'd at it much,
But since I find the reason's such,
As it deserves no laughter.

> WILLIAM BROWNE. See 6 Chalmers, *British Poets* 335 (1810).

No! No! Sentence first—verdict afterwards.

> LEWIS CARROLL, *Alice in Wonderland,* ch. 12.

Indeed one would rather that twenty guilty persons should escape the punishment of death, than one innocent person should be executed.

> SIR JOHN FORTESCUE, *De Laudibus Legum Angliae,* ch. 27.

134

My object all sublime
I shall achieve in time—
To let the punishment fit the crime—
The punishment fit the crime.

WILLIAM S. GILBERT, *The Mikado*, Act 2.

At the present time in this country there is more danger
that criminals will escape justice than that they will be
subjected to tyranny.

HOLMES, J., dissenting, *Kepner v United States* (1904) 195 US
100, 134, 49 L ed 114, 126, 24 S Ct 797.

For, when Man's Life is in debate,
The Judge can ne'er too long deliberate.

JUVENAL, *Satires*, VI (Dryden trans.).

I went out to Charing Cross to see Major-general Harrison hanged, drawn, and quartered; which was done there,
he looking as cheerful as any man could do in that condition.

SAMUEL PEPYS, *Diary, October 13, 1660.*

I think Sir Godfry should decide the suit;
Who sent the thief that stole the cash, **away,**
And punished him that put it in his **way.**

POPE, *Imitations of Horace*, II, ii.

First hang and draw,
Then hear the cause by Lidford law.

Proverb. FULLER, *Worthies: Devonshire* **(1662).**

135

Falstaff: Shall there be gallows standing in England when thou art king, and resolution thus fobbed as it is with the rusty curb of old father antick, the law? Do not thou, when thou art king, hang a thief.

SHAKESPEARE, *Henry IV, Pt. 1*, Act 1, Scene 2.

For lest some sturdy criminal
    False witnesses should bring—
His witnesses were not allowed
    To swear to anything.

And lest his oily advocate
    The court should overreach,
His advocate was not allowed
    The privilege of speech.

Yet such was the humanity
    And wisdom of the law,
That if in his indictment there
    Appeared to be a flaw—

The court assigned him counselors,
    To argue on the doubt,
Provided he himself had first
    Contrived to point it out.

Yet lest their mildness should perchance
    Be craftily abused,
To show him the indictment they
    Most sturdily refused.

But still that he might understand
    The nature of the charge,
The same was in the Latin tongue
    Read out to him at large.

JOHN WILLIAM SMITH. (In criminal cases the defendant had
    no right to examine witnesses until 1760 and no right to coun-
    sel until 1836. See 9 Holdsworth, *History of English Law*,
    216, 232).

136

The prisoner knew, that though his spirit was broken with guilt, and incapable of language to defend itself, all would be gathered from him which could conduce to his safety; and that his judge would wrest no law to destroy him, nor conceal any that could save him.

> STEELE, *Tatler* no. 14, May 12, 1709. Referring to Sir John Holt, Lord Chief Justice of the King's Bench.

"You're a young gentleman that doesna approve of Caapital Punishment," said Hermiston. "Weel, I'm an auld man that does."

> ROBERT L. STEVENSON, *Weir of Hermiston*, ch. 3.

At Halifax the law so sharpe doth deale
That whoso more than thirteen pence doth steals,
They have a jyn that wondrous quick and well
Sends thieves all headless into heaven or hell.

> JOHN TAYLOR ("The Water Poet") *Newes from Hell, Hull and Halifax* (1630).

There's a lot of law at the end of a nightstick.

> GROVER WHALEN (when Police Commissioner, N.Y.C. 1928–30). See Quentin Reynolds, *Courtroom*, ch. 2.

There is more law in the end of a policeman's nightstick than in a decision of the Supreme Court.

> ALEXANDER S. WILLIAMS (when Inspector of Police, N.Y.C. during 1870's). See Quentin Reynolds, *Courtroom*, ch. 2.

137

Criminal Justice (Summary)

I have had Halifax Law; to be condemned first, and inquired upon after.

> EARL OF LEICESTER, *Letter March 17, 1586 to Burghley.* See *Notes & Queries,* 8th ser. vol. 8 (1895) 368.

There is a proverb, and a prayer withal,
That we may not to three strange places fall:
From Hull, from Halifax, from Hell, 'tis thus,
From all these three, good Lord, deliver us!

> JOHN TAYLOR ("The Water Poet") *A Merry-Wherry-Ferry Voyage* (1623) line 575.

With what little scruple they accomplished their work is significantly commemorated in the Border phrase "Jeddart Justice"—hang first and try afterwards.

> P. H. BROWN, 2 *History of Scotland* (1902) 263. Sir William Cranstoun, as first Captain of a mounted police, and the Earl of Dunbar, appointed Chief Commissioner, were commissioned under James VI to put down rampant crime on the border, which followed the Union of the Crowns (1603).

We will have Jedwood justice—hang in haste and try at leasure.

> SIR WALTER SCOTT, *Fair Maid of Perth,* ch. 32.

Are you going to hang him anyhow—and try him afterwards?

> MARK TWAIN, *Capt. Blakely's View of Justice,* ch. 5.

First he punished before he heard, and when he had heard his denial, he compelled the party accused by torture to confess. (*Castigatque, auditque dolos subigitque fateri.*)

> VIRGIL, *Aeneid, VI,* 566. Referring to Radamanthus, the judge of Hell.

Cross Examination

You seem to think that the art of cross-examining is to examine crossly.

> BARON ALDERSON, to counsel cross-examining with more temper than skill. See Ballantine, *Some Experiences of a Barrister's Life* 124 (2nd ed. 1882).

Judge: Really, this is a long way from the point.

Serj. Ballantine: If I were to begin any nearer, the witness would discover my object.

> BALLANTINE, *Some Experiences of a Barrister's Life* 127 (2nd ed. 1882).

Would you be suprised to hear that—?

> LORD BOWEN. Phrase used repeatedly by Coleridge when cross-examining the "Claimant" in the famous Tichborne Case. The expression which became a byword is said to have been invented by Bowen who at the time was a junior counsel appearing with Coleridge against the claimant. The intent of the phrasing was to abstain from giving in the form of the question any indication as to whether it would be correctly answered in the affirmative or in the negative. D.N.B., Supp. 1.

More cross-examinations are suicidal than homicidal.

> EMORY R. BUCKNER. See ch. 12 in Wellman's *Art of Cross Examination.*

Battledore and shuttlecock's a wery good game, vhen you ain't the shuttlecock and two lawyers the battledores, in vich case it gets too excitin' to be pleasant.

> CHARLES DICKENS, *Pickwick Papers,* ch. 20.

Asked: Whether she kenw that she was in the grace of God,

139

Answered: If I am not, may God please to put me in it; and if I am, may God please to keep me in it;

And she said that if she knew she was not in the grace of God, she would be the most sorrowful person in the world (la plus dolente du monde);

Said also, if she was in sin, that the voice would not come to her. And wished that everyone understood it as well as she did herself.

> *Trial of Joan of Arc,* Third day, February 24, 1431.
>> Was there ever a better answer on cross-examination: If Joan had said, Yes, I am in a state of grace, it would have been a presumption of her own salvation. If she said, No, that would be a confession. . . . on this answer of hers: *"Si je n'y suis, Dieu m'y veuille mettre; et si j'y suis, Dieu m'y veuille tenir."* . . . Paul Doncoeur, who has edited the record of Joan's examination, suggests in a note that Joan's answer here is contained in a prayer which is part of the instructions of the Church. This makes Joan's answer perfect, as any lawyer will agree.
>> CHARLES CURTIS, *A Commonplace Book* (1957) 204.

If by cross-examination to credit you prove that a man's oath cannot be relied on, and he has sworn he did not go to Rome on May 1, you do not, therefore, prove that he did go to Rome on May 1; there is simply no evidence on the subject.

> SCRUTTON, L.J., *Hobbs v Tinling* [1929] 2 K.B. 1, 21.

Custom

One of the main triangles of the laws of England; those laws being divided into common law, statute law and custom.

> COKE, *First Institute* 110b.

Neglect of duty does not cease by repetition to be neglect of duty.

> LORD TOMLIN, *Bank of Montreal v Dominion Gresham Guarantee & Cas. Co.* [1930] A.C. 659, 666.

Usage is one of the great master-keys which unlocks the meaning of words.

> WILMOT, L.C.J., *Drinkwater v. Royal Exchange Assurance Co.* (1767) Wilmot 282, 287.

No degree of antiquity can give sanction to a usage bad in itself.

> YATES and ASTON, J.J., *Leach v Three of the King's Messengers* (1765) 19 Now. St. Tr. 1027.

Damages

Nominal damages are a mere peg on which to hang costs.

> MAULE, J., *Beaumont v Greathead* (1846) 2 C.B. 494, 499.

It is a common experience that there is a painful gap between profits anticipated and profits realized. Mere prospects have little pecuniary value.

> MAXEY, J., *Laureldale Cemetery Co. v Reading Co.*, 303 Pa. 315, 324 (1931).

The very definition of a good award is, that it gives dissatisfaction to both parties.

> PLUMER, M.R., *Goodman v Sayers* (1820) 2 Jac. & W. 249, 259.

141

Danger

Danger invites rescue. The cry of distress is the summons to relief.

> CARDOZO, J., *Wagner v International Ry.*, 232 N.Y. 176, 180 (1921).

Death

Old Lord Keeper Sir Nicholas Bacon had his barber rubbing and combing his head. Because it was very hot, the window was open to let in a fresh wind. The Lord Keeper fell asleep, and awaked all distempered and in great sweat. Said he to his barber, Why did you let me sleep? Why, my Lord, saith he, I durst not wake your Lordship. Why then, saith my Lord, you have killed me with kindness. So removed into his bed chamber and within a few days died.

> BACON, *Apothegms,* No. 23.

Stay friend, until I put aside my beard, for that never committed treason.

> SIR THOMAS MORE, to executioner, before placing head on block. Roper, *Life of More.*

I pray you, Master Lieutenant, see me safe up; and for my coming down let me shift for myself.

> SIR THOMAS MORE, at the steps of the scaffold. ROPER, *ibid.*

Debt

It is the policy of the law that the debtor be just before he be generous.

> FINCH, J., *Hearn 45 St. Corp. v Jano,* 283 N. Y. 139, 142 (1940).

You must know then, once more, that nobody can be arrested in Scotland for debt. . . . As a compulsitor, therefore, of payment—that being a thing to which no debtor is naturally inclined, as I have too much reason to warrant from the experience I have had with my own—we had first the letters of four forms, a sort of gentle invitation, by which our sovereign lord the king, interesting himself, as a monarch should, in the regulation of his subjects' private affairs, at first by mild exhortation, and afterwards by letters of more strict enjoyment and more hard compulsion. . . . You suppose, now, a man's committed to prison, because he cannot pay his debt? Quite otherwise; the truth is, the king is so good as to interfere at the request of the creditor, and to send the debtor his royal command to do him justice within a certain time, fifteen days, or six, as the case may be. Well, the man resists and disobeys— what follows? Why, that he be lawfully and rightfully declared a rebel to our gracious sovereign, whose command he has disobeyed, and that by three blasts of a horn at the market-place of Edinburgh, the metropolis of Scotland. And he is then legally imprisoned, not on account of any civil debt, but because of his ungrateful contempt of the royal mandate.

> SIR WALTER SCOTT, *The Antiquary,* ch. 39. This passage may be found cited in the Law Reports. See *Thom v Black* (1828) 7 Shaw 159, in which Lord Gillies said, "The law on this subject cannot be better expressed than it is by Monkbarns in a work of fiction, with which we are all well acquainted."

Deceit

The statute enjoins truth; this label exhales deceit.

> McREYNOLDS, J., *United States v Schider* (1918) 246 US 519, 522, 62 L ed 863, 866, 38 S Ct 369.

Deceive not thy physician, confessor, nor lawyer.

> Proverb. HERBERT, *Jacula Prudentum* (1651).

Decisions

Then said Paul unto him, God shall smite thee, thou whited wall: for sittest thou to judge me after the law, and commandest me to be stricken contrary to the law?

> Acts 23:3.

A judge ought to prepare his way to a just sentence, as God useth to prepare his way, by raising valleys and taking down hills: so when there appeareth on either side an high hand, violent prosecution, cunning advantages taken, combination, power, great counsel, then is the virtue of a judge seen, to make inequality equal; that he may plant his judgment as upon an even ground.

> BACON, *Essays: Of Judicature.*

Decided cases are the anchors of the law, as laws are of the state.

> BACON, *De Augmentis Scientiarum,* bk. 8, Aph. 73.

If we would guide by the light of reason, we must let our minds be bold.

> BRANDEIS, J., *Jay Burns Baking Co., v Bryan* (1924) 264 US 504, 520, 68 L ed 813, 829, 44 S Ct 412, 32 ALR 661.

144

To say of a judge that his decisions are fine in the sense
that they are exquisite essays, exposing a dazzling erudition, is not to my way of thinking a way to compliment him.
Decisions should simply be just, within the limits of human
possibility. If we bear in mind the seriousness of the function they are supposed to perform, which is that of bringing
peace to men, we cannot evaluate opinions on purely
esthetic criteria unless we hold that justice can be reduced
to the level of a literary diversion or a schoolboy's theme.

> PIERO CALAMANDREI, *Eulogy of Judges* 78 (1942) trans.
> Adams and Phillips.

Nor should it be forgotten that if style is to be prized
above all else in opinions, credit for their excellence should
be given to the lawyers, since many of the stylistic gems
which adorn the judge's opinions are culled from the lawyer's briefs. But the conscientious judge knows that whereas it may be proper for him to borrow rhetorical ornaments
and erudition from the lawyer in order to make his dia-
lectical premises more brilliant, when the time comes to
render judgment, he must forget literature and search
within himself for the unadorned word of justice which,
disdainful of beautiful phrases, is most appropriately expressed in monosyllables.

> PIERO CALAMANDREI, *Eulogy of Judges* 79 (1942) trans.
> Adams and Phillips.

In his written judgments as they appear in the law reports, he betrays an utter disregard of rhythm, and his
hereditary love of parenthesis is constantly breaking out.

> LORD CAMPBELL, 3 *Lives of the Chief Justices* (1857) 236.
> Referring to Lord Ellenborough.

Write an opinion, and read it a few years later when
it is dissected in the briefs of counsel. You will learn for

[Legal Quotations]—10   *145*

the first time the limitations of the power of speech, or, if not those of speech in general, at all events your own.

> BENJAMIN N. CARDOZO, *Law and Literature* 8 (1931).

The picture cannot be painted if the significant and the insignificant are given equal prominence. One must know how to select. All these generalities are as easy as they are obvious, but, alas! the application is an ordeal to try the souls of men.

> BENJAMIN N. CARDOZO, *ibid.*

I seem to discern six types or methods which divide themselves from one another with measurable distinctness. There is the type magisterial or imperative; the type laconic or sententious; the type conversational or homely; the type refined or artificial, smelling of the lamp, verging at times upon preciosity or euphuism; the type demonstrative or persuasive; and finally the type tonsorial or agglutinative, so called from the shears and the pastepot which are its implements and emblem.

> BENJAMIN N. CARDOZO, *Law and Literature* 10 (1931).

We have one judge even now who can vie with the best of his English brethren, past as well as present, in the art of packing within a sentence the phosphorescence of a page. If I begin to quote from the opinions of Mr. Justice Holmes, I hardly know where I shall end.

> BENJAMIN N. CARDOZO, *Law and Literature* 347 (1925).

When an issue is squarely and fully presented to the Court and its disposition is essential to the result reached in a case, the issue is decided, whether the Court says much or little, whether the opinion is didactic or elliptical.

> FRANKFURTER, J., dissenting, *Federal Maritime Board v Isbrandtsen Co.* (1958) 356 US 481, 523, 2 L ed 2d 926, 951, 78 S Ct 851.

To quote from Mr. Justice Brandeis' opinions is not to pick plums from a pudding but to pull threads from a pattern. He achieves not by epigrammatic thrust but through powerful exposition.

> FELIX FRANKFURTER, *Mr. Justice Brandeis and the Constitution,* 45 Harv. L. Rev. 33, 104 (1931).

To consider Mr. Justice Holmes' opinions is to string pearls.

> FELIX FRANKFURTER, *Mr. Justice Holmes and the Constitution,* 41 Harv. L. Rev. 121, 146 (1927).

I am hard at work . . . preparing small diamonds for people of limited intellectual means.

> OLIVER WENDELL HOLMES, 2 *Holmes-Pollock Letters* 173 (Dec. 1, 1925).

All the legal furies seize you!
No proposal seems to please you,
I can't stop up here all day,
I must shortly go away.
Barristers, and you, attorneys,
Set out on your homeward journeys;
Gentle, simple-minded Usher,
Get you, if you like, to Russher;
Put your briefs upon the shelf,
I will marry her myself!

> WILLIAM S. GILBERT, *Trial by Jury.*

Mr. Justice Brandeis is . . . the master of both microscope and telescope. Nothing of importance, however minute, escapes his microscopical examination of every problem, and through his powerful telescopic lens, his mental vision embraces distant scenes, ranging far beyond the familiar worlds of conventional thinking.

> CHARLES EVANS HUGHES. See *Mr. Justice Brandeis* (Frankfurter, ed. 1932) 3.

Then said the king. The one saith, This is my son that liveth, and thy son the dead: and the other saith, Nay; but thy son is the dead, and my son is the living.

And the king said, Bring me a sword. And they brought a sword before the king.

And the king said, Divide the living child in two, and give half to the one, and half to the other.

Then spake the woman whose the living child was unto the king, for her bowels yearned upon her son, and she said, O my lord, give her the living child, and in no wise slay it. But the other said, Let it be neither mine nor thine, but divide it.

Then the king answered and said, Give her the living child, and in no wise slay it: she is the mother thereof.

And all Israel heard of the judgment which the king had judged; and they feared the king: for they saw that the wisdom of God was in him, to do judgment.

> 1 Kings 3:23–28 (Solomon's judgment).

Solomon was a wise old king, he was so very cute;
He once thought out a clever way to settle a dispute;
He took a wretched baby, and he cut it down in half,
And he knew which one was its mother, by the one that
    didn't laugh.

> Unknown. Quoted from recollection by Sir Jocelyn Simon, *English Idioms From the Law,* 76 L.Q. Rev. 435 (1960).

John Marshall has made his decision now let him enforce it.

> ANDREW JACKSON. Attributed to the President following the decision in *Worcester v Georgia* (1832, US) 6 Pet 515, upholding the rights of the Cherokee Indians to their lands. See Sumner, *Andrew Jackson* (1882) 182.

An opinion is huddled up in conclave, perhaps by a majority of one, delivered as if unanimous, and with the silent acquiescence of lazy or timid associates, by a crafty chief judge, who sophisticates the law to his mind by the turn of his own reasoning.

> THOMAS JEFFERSON, *Letter to Thomas Ritchie, Dec. 25, 1820.*

Judicial decisions are not babies brought by constitutional storks but are born out of the travail of economic circumstance.

> MAX LERNER, *Fate of the Supreme Court,* 142 Nation 379 (1936).

A per curiam opinion is one where we agree to pool our weaknesses.

> HENRY S. MANLEY, *Nonpareil Among Judges,* 34 Corn. L.Q. 52 (1948)—quoting "a judge of the New York Court of Appeals".

Give your judgment, but give no reasons. As you are a man of integrity, sound sense, and information, it is more than an even chance that your judgments will be right; but, as you are ignorant of the law, it is ten to one that your reasons will be wrong.

> LORD MANSFIELD, advice to a new Colonial Judge. See 27 How. St. Tr. 1060.

Pray let us so resolve cases here that they may stand with the reason of mankind, when they are debated abroad. Shall that be reason here that is not reason in any part of the world besides?

> LORD NOTTINGHAM, L.C., *Duke of Norfolk's Case* (1681) 3 Ch. Cas. 14, 33.

The only mode of pronouncing a correct judgment is altogether to abstain from giving any reasons for it. Let the appeal judges find that out for themselves.

> CHARLES PHILLIPS, when unanimously reversed. Robinson, *Bench and Bar 55* (1894).

The idea that the language of a judicial opinion in one case has any peculiar sanctity as applied to another case is quite without foundation. Judicial opinions are written to guide the judge as to the law, not to standardize the language to be used in instructions to the jury.

> POUND, C.J., *People v Rutigliano,* 261 N.Y. 103, 107 (1933).

I can hardly see the use of writing judicial opinions unless they are to embody methods of analysis and of exposition which will serve the profession as a guide to the decisions of future cases. If they are not better than an excursion ticket, good for this day and trip only, they do not serve even as protective coloration for the writer of the opinions and would much better be left unsaid.

> H. F. STONE to FELIX FRANKFURTER, February 17, 1936 (The Stone Papers). See Mason, *The Supreme Court From Taft to Warren* (1958) 105.

Decisions (Overruling)

I agree that *Betts v. Brady* should be overruled but consider it entitled to a more respectful burial than has been accorded, at least on the part of those of us who were not on the Court when that case was decided.

> HARLAN, J., concurring, *Gideon v Wainwright* (1963) 372 US 335, 349, 9 L ed 2d 799, 808, 83 S Ct 792, 93 ALR2d 733.

Decisions (Seriatim)

The subject of my uneasiness is the habitual mode of making up and delivering the opinions of the Supreme Court of the United States. You know that from the earliest ages of the English law, from the date of year-books at least, to the end of the IId George, the judges of England, in all but self-evident cases, delivered their opinions seriatim with the reasons and authorities which governed their decisions. . . . Besides the light which their separate arguments threw on the subject, and the instruction communicated by their several modes of reasoning, it shewed whether the judges were unanimous or divided, and gave accordingly more or less weight to the judgment as a precedent. . . . When Ld. Mansfield came to the bench he introduced the habit of caucusing opinions. The judges met at their chambers, or elsewhere, secluded from the presence of the public, and made up what was to be delivered as the opinion of the court.

> THOMAS JEFFERSON, *Letter to William Johnson, October 27, 1822.*

I rejoice in the example you set of *seriatim* opinions. I have heard it often noticed, and always with high approbation. Some of your brethren will be encouraged to follow it occasionally, and in time, it may be felt by all as a duty, and the sound practice of the primitive court be again restored. Why should not every judge be asked his opinion, and give it from the bench, if only by yea or nay? Besides ascertaining the fact of his opinion, which the public have a right to know, in order to judge whether it is impeachable or not, it would show whether the opinions were unanimous or not, and thus settle more exactly the weight of their authority.

> THOMAS JEFFERSON, *Letter to William Johnson, June 12, 1823.*

Defense

The laws of God and man both give the party an opportunity to make his defence, if he has any. I remember to have heard it observed by a very learned man upon such an occasion, that even God himself did not pass sentence upon Adam before he was called upon to make his defence. Adam (says God) where are thou? Hast thou eaten of the tree whereof I commanded thee that thou shouldst not eat? And the same question was put to Eve also.

> FORTESCUE ALAND, J., *R. v Chancellor* (1723) 1 Stra. 557, 567.

Out of thine own mouth will I judge thee.

> Luke 19:22.

Defense (Unpopular Cause)

While I live and have my health, I must walk the mountain ranges of my profession, swept by the storms of human hate and passion. Neither self respect nor my love for you will permit me to seek obscurity and consequent shelter of deep valleys and smooth meadows.

> MATTHEW HALE CARPENTER, *Letter to his wife.* At the time of the Hayes-Tilden election contest he appeared for Tilden and was much criticized.

I will for ever, at all hazards, assert the dignity, independence, and integrity of the English Bar; without which, impartial justice, the most valuable part of the English Constitution, can have no existence. From the moment that any advocate can be permitted to say, that he will or will not stand between the Crown and the subject arraigned in the court where he daily sits to practise, from that moment the liberties of England are at an end.

> THOMAS ERSKINE, arguendo, *Trial of Thomas Paine* (1792) 22 How. St. Tr. 358, 412.

I was twice called to the council of him who was my master, when all the world coveted the honor; and I owe him the same service now, when that duty is thought dangerous by many.

> MALESHERBES, *Letter, December 11, 1792 to the National Convention,* requesting permission to defend Louis XVI. Soon after the King's trial Malesherbes was arrested, tried for treason and executed. See 23 *Nouvelle Biographie Universelle* 28 (1860).

As it once was put to me, always remember that you are in the position of a cabman on the rank, bound to answer to the first hail.

> SIR RALPH NEVILLE, *Letter to The Times (London) June 16, 1913,* p. 3 col. 1. Referring to the English rule that a barrister is bound to accept any brief in the Courts in which he professes to practice.

153

That it was easier to commit than to justify a parricide.

> PAPINIAN. Reply to the Emperor Caracalla, who caused the assassination of his own brother, who shared the throne with him, and directed Papinian, then his attorney general, to write a legal opinion in justification. See GIBBON, *Decline and Fall of the Roman Empire,* ch. 6.

Let such be told, Sir, that these criminals, charged with murder, are not yet legally proved guilty, and therefore, however criminal, are entitled, by the laws of God and man, to all legal counsel and aid; that my duty as a man obligated me to undertake; that my duty as a lawyer strengthened the obligation. . . . This and much more might be told with great truth; and I dare affirm that you and this whole people will one day rejoice that I became an advocate for the aforesaid "criminals" charged with the murder of our fellow citizens.

> JOSIAH QUINCY, JR., *Letter, March 26, 1770, to his father,* referring to his defense of the British soldiers involved in the Boston Massacre. In *Memoir of Josiah Quincy, Jr.* by his son.

No advocate without very good cause shall refuse to act for any person tendering a reasonable fee under pain of deprivation of his office of advocate.

> SCOTLAND, Rules of Court, ch. 1, s. 2, 4. (Adopted May 27, 1532).

In due time, gentlemen of the jury, when I shall have paid the debt of nature, my remains will rest here in your midst with those of my kindred and neighbors. It is very possible they may be unhonored, neglected, spurned! But perhaps years hence, when the passion and excitement which now agitate this community shall have passed away, some wandering stranger, some lone exile, some Indian, some Negro, may erect over them an humble stone, and thereon this epitaph: HE WAS FAITHFUL.

> WILLIAM H. SEWARD, arguendo, in defense of William Freeman, Auburn, N.Y., 1846. The defendant was deaf and obviously insane but his commission of double murder aroused the community. The defendant had previously been imprisoned and mistreated for a theft which he had not committed.

Definition

It is one of the maxims of the civil law, that definitions are hazardous.

> SAMUEL JOHNSON, *Rambler*, May 28, 1751.

While for the purposes of judicial decision dictionary definitions often are not controlling, they are at least persuasive that meanings which they do not embrace are not common.

> STONE, J., *Aschenbrenner v United States Fidelity & G. Co.* (1934) 292 US 80, 85, 78 L ed 1137, 1141, 54 S Ct 590.

A definition originally correct was adhered to and acted on, after it had ceased, from a change in circumstances, to be the true description.

> TANEY, C.J., *The Genesee Chief v Fitzhugh* (1851, US) 12 How 443, 13 L ed 1058.

Delay

Fresh justice is the sweetest.

> BACON, *Speech*, May 7, 1617, on taking his seat as Lord Keeper.

155

Sir Thomas Moore [More] when the counsel of the party pressed him for a longer day, said; *Take Saint Barnaby's day, which is the longest day in the year.* Now Saint Barnaby's day was with few days following.

BACON, *Apothegms New and Old,* no. 118.

He must have patience who to law will go.

ROBERT DODSLEY, *Pain and Patience* (1745).

When more business becomes concentrated in one firm than it can handle, it has two obvious remedies: to put on more legal help, or let some of the business go to offices which have time to attend to it. I doubt if any court should be a party to encouraging the accumulation of more business in one law office than it can attend to in due time.

JACKSON, J., *Knickerbocker Printing Corp. v United States* (1954, US) 99 L ed 1292, 1293, 75 S Ct 212 (Opinion in chambers).

I must with Patience all the Terms attend,
Among the common Causes that depend
Till mine is call'd; and that long look'd-for Day
Is still encumber'd with some new delay:
Perhaps the Cloth of State is only spred,
Some of the *Quorum* may be sick a-bed;
That Judge is hot, and doffs his Gown while this
O'er Night was bowsie, and goes out to piss:
So many Rubs appear, the time is gone
For hearing, and the tedious Suit goes on.

JUVENAL, *Satires,* XVI (Dryden trans.).

But Buff, and Belt-Men, never know these Cares
No Time, nor Trick of Law their Action Bars:

156

Their Cause they to an earlier Issue put;
They will be heard, or they lug out, and cut.
Another Branch of their Revenue still
Remains beyond their boundless Right to kill,
Their Father yet alive, impowr'd to make a Will.
For, what their Prowess gain'd the Law declares
Is to themselves alone, and to their Heirs:
No share of that goes back to the Begetter.

> JUVENAL, *Satires,* XVI (Dryden trans.) Under Roman law *(patria potestas)* a son could not own property except that which was acquired during military service *(peculium castrense).*

Delay of justice is injustice.

> WALTER SAVAGE LANDOR, *Imaginary Conversations: Peter Leopold and President DuPaty.*

The law is so lordly and loth to maken end.

> LANGLAND, *Piers Plowman,* Passus 4.

Suits hang half a year in Westminster Hall
At Tyburn, half an hour's hanging endeth all.

> Proverb. JOHN HEYWOOD, *Proverbs* (1546).

When More sometime had Chancellor been
No more suits did remain.
The like will never more be seen
Till More be there again.

> *Saying.*

I thought ye had some law affair of your ain to look after;
I have ane mysell—a ganging plea that my father left me,
and his father afore left to him. It's about our back yard;

ye'll maybe hae heard of it in the Parliament House, Hutchinson against MacKitchinson; it's a weel kenn'd plea—it's
been four times in afore the fifteen, and deil onything the
wisest o' them could make o't, but just to send it out again
to the outer-house.   O it's a beautiful thing to see how
lang and how carefully justice is considered in this country.

> WALTER SCOTT, *The Antiquary*, ch. 2.

The law's delay.

> SHAKESPEARE, *Hamlet*, Act 3, scene 1.

Democracy

Democracy in any sphere is a serious undertaking.   It
substitutes self-restraint for external restraint.   It is more
difficult to maintain than to achieve.   It demands continuous sacrifice by the individual and more exigent obedience
to the moral law than any other form of government.   Success in any democratic undertaking must proceed from
the individual.   It is possible only where the process of
perfecting the individual is pursued.   His development is
attained mainly in the processes of common living.   Hence
the industrial struggle is essentially an affair of the Church
and its imperative task.

> LOUIS D. BRANDEIS, *Letter to Robert W. Bruere*, February 25,
> 1922.   (As quoted by Richberg, 31 Col. L. R. 1099).

Dictum

Obiter dicta, like the proverbial chickens of destiny, come
home to roost sooner or later in a very uncomfortable way

to the Judges who have uttered them, and are a great source of embarrassment in future cases.

> BOWEN, L.J., *Cooke v New River Co.* (1888) 38 Ch. D. 56, 71.

Dicta are not always ticketed as such, and one does not recognize them always at a glance.

> BENJAMIN N. CARDOZO, *Nature of the Judicial Process* 30 (1921).

A case is only an authority for what it actually decides. I entirely deny that it can be quoted for a proposition that may seem to follow logically from it. Such a mode of reasoning assumes that the law is necessarily a logical code, whereas every lawyer must acknowledge that the law is not always logical at all.

> LORD HALSBURY, L.C., *Quinn v Leathem* [1901] A.C. 495, 506.

I recognize, of course, that the rule of stare decisis binds us to follow that court [U.S. Supreme] in respect of things decided by it. I know of no rule of stare "dictis" which binds us to follow it in respect of things merely said by it.

> HUTCHESON, J., *Hercules Gasoline Co. v Comm'r.* 147 F.2d 972, 974 (1945).

An *obiter dictum*, in the language of the law, is a gratuitous opinion, an individual impertinence, which, whether it be wise or foolish, right or wrong, bindeth none—not even the lips that utter it.

> *The Old Judge.* Quoted on title page of Birrell, *Obiter Dicta* (1885).

It is a maxim, not to be disregarded, that general expressions, in every opinion, are to be taken in connection with the case in which those expressions are used. If they go beyond the case, they may be respected, but ought not to control the judgment in a subsequent suit, when the very point is presented for decision.

> MARSHALL, C.J., *Cohens v Virginia* (1821, US) 6 Wheat 264, 399, 5 L ed 257, 290.

As this State has always permitted foreign judgments to be impeached for fraud, the preceding fifty-four pages of the opinion may be regarded as magnificent dictum, entitled to the utmost respect, but not determinative of the question.

> POUND, J., *Johnston v Compagnie Generale Transatlantique*, 242 N.Y. 381, 388 (1926). Referring to the opinion of Mr. Justice Gray in *Hilton v Guyot* (1895) 159 US 113, 40 L ed 57, 15 S Ct 1027.

There is in my opinion no justification for regarding as obiter dictum a reason given by a judge for his decision, because he has given another reason also. If it were a proper test to ask whether the decision would have been the same apart from the proposition alleged to be obiter, then a case which ex facie decided two things would decide nothing.

> LORD SIMONDS, *Jacobs v London County Council* [1950] A.C. 361, 369.

No "guidance" is more misleading, no "kindly light" is more of a will-o'-the-wisp than an obiter dictum sometimes contrives to be.

> LORD SUMNER, *Sorrell v Smith* [1925] A.C. 700, 743.

An opinion given in Court, if not necessary to the judgment given of record, but that it might have been as well

given if no such, or a contrary, opinion had been broached
is no judicial opinion, nor more than a gratis dictum.

> VAUGHAN, C.J., *Bole v Horton* (1670) Vaugh. 360, 382.

Difficulty

I sometimes even think that there is a certain advantage
in difficulties, and that one sails better with the wind on
the quarter than when it is directly astern.

> OLIVER WENDELL HOLMES, 1 *Holmes-Pollock Letters* 16
> (March 5, 1881).

Diligence

It is a reasonable presumption that a man who sleeps
upon his rights has not got much right.

> BOWEN, L.J., *Ex parte Hall, In re Wood* (1883) 23 Ch. D. 644,
> 653.

Diligence is always valuable, particularly in defending
causes. . . . It is the one virtue that contains in itself
all the rest. (*Diligentia, inquam, quae cum omnibus in
rebus tum in causis defendendis plurimum valet . . .
diligentia, qua una virtue omnes virtutes reliquae conti-
nentur.*)

> CICERO, *De Oratore*, II, 35.

Dining

Sir Edward Coke was wont to say, when a great man
came to dinner to him, and gave him no knowledge of

his coming; *Well, since you sent me no word of your coming, you shall dine with me; but if I had known of your coming, I would have dined with you.**

> BACON, *Apothegms New and Old,* no. 133.

I approve of the dining system; it puts people in good humor, and makes them agree, when they otherwise might not: a dinner lubricates business.

> LORD STOWELL. 2 Townsend, *Lives of Twelve Eminent Judges* 362 (1846).

Disclosure

Disclosure is the antidote to partiality and favor.

> CARDOZO, C.J., *People ex rel. Fordham M.R. Church v Walsh,* 244 N.Y. 280, 291 (1927).

Discovery

A common-law trial is and always should be an adversary proceeding. Discovery was hardly intended to enable a learned profession to perform its functions either without wits or on wits borrowed from the adversary.

> JACKSON, J., *Hickman v Taylor* (1947) 329 US 495, 516, 91 L ed 451, 465, 67 S Ct 385.

Discretion

"Reasonable"—that irrepressible, vague and delusive standard which at times threatens to engulf the entire law,

---

* Cf. with current Americanism: If I had known you were coming I would have baked a cake.

including the Constitution itself, in a sea of judicial discretion.

> BLACK, J., dissenting, *Green v United States* (1958) 356 US 165, 197, 2 L ed 2d 672, 695, 78 S Ct 632.

The discretion of a Judge is the law of tyrants: it is always unknown. It is different in different men. It is casual, and depends upon constitution, temper, passion. In the best it is oftentimes caprice; in the worst it is every vice, folly, and passion, to which human nature is liable.

> LORD CAMDEN, C.J., *Hindson v Kersey* (1765), cited, 8 How. St. Tr. 57 fn.

The exercise of a discretion has been characterized as odious; but where the necessity exists for its exercise, a judge is bound not to shrink from the responsibility devolving on him.

> CRAMPTON, J., *Conway v Queen* (1845) 1 Cox C.C. 210, 217.

Absolute discretion is a ruthless master. It is more destructive of freedom than any of man's other inventions.

> DOUGLAS, J., *United States v Wunderlich* (1951) 342 US 98, 101, 96 L ed 106, 113, 72 S Ct 154.

Sir John Fineux, sometime Chief Justice of the King's Bench, was often heard to say, "Who so taketh from a Justice the order of his discretion, taketh surely from him more than half his Office."

> See CAMDEN, *Remains Concerning Britain: Wise Speeches* (1674).

"Discretion" means when it is said that something is to be done within the discretion of the authorities that that

163

something is to be done according to the rules of reason and justice, not according to private opinion; according to law, and not humour. It is to be, not arbitrary, vague, and fanciful, but legal and regular. And it must be exercised within the limit, to which an honest man competent to the discharge of his office ought to confine himself.

LORD HALSBURY, L.C., *Sharp v Wakefield* [1891] A.C. 173, 179.

The reason, if reason is to be found anywhere, seems to be this—that it requires more discretion to dispose of your own property than to dispose of other people's.

JESSEL, M.R., *Re D'Angibau* (1880) 15 Ch.D. 228, 233. Referring to the fact that although an infant could not dispose of his own property, he could exercise a power.

The idea is Utopian, that government can exist without leaving the exercise of discretion somewhere. Public security against the abuse of such discretion must rest on responsibility, and stated appeals to public approbation.

JOHNSON, J., *Anderson v Dunn* (1821, US) 6 Wheat 204, 226, 5 L ed 242, 247.

The writer of this opinion has known a popular judicial officer grow quite angry with a suitor in his court, and threaten him with imprisonment, for no ostensible reason, save the fact, that he wore an overcoat made of wolf skins! Moreover, it cannot safely be denied that mere judicial discretion is sometimes very much interfered with by prejudice, which may be swayed and controlled by the merest trifles—such as the toothache, the rheumatism, the gout, or a fit of indigestion, or even through the very means by which indigestion is frequently sought to be avoided.

PETERS, J., *Ex Parte Chase,* 43 Ala 303, 310 (1869).

Discrimination

If there has been discrimination, whether accomplished ingeniously or ingenuously, the conviction cannot stand.

> BLACK, J., *Smith v Texas* (1940) 311 US 128, 132, 85 L ed 84, 87, 61 S Ct 164.

Our constitution is color-blind.

> HARLAN, J., *Plessy v Ferguson* (1896) 163 US 537, 559, 41 L ed 256, 263, 16 S Ct 1138.

By the Louisiana statute, the validity of which is here involved, all railway companies (other than street railroad companies) carrying passengers in that State are required to have separate but equal accommodations for white and colored persons.

> HARLAN, J., *Plessy v Ferguson* (1896) 163 US 537, 552, 41 L ed 256, 261, 16 S Ct 1138. The Court held that this statute did not violate constitutional provisions. Mr. Justice Harlan alone dissented. In his opinion he turned the words of the statute "equal but separate" into "separate but equal" and it is his terminology that has since prevailed.

The law knows no finer hour than when it cuts through formal concepts and transitory emotions to protect unpopular citizens against discrimination and persecution.

> MURPHY, J., dissenting, *Falbo v United States* (1944) 320 US 549, 561, 88 L ed 305, 312, 64 S Ct 346.

I dissent, therefore, from this legalization of racism. Racial discrimination in any form and in any degree has no justifiable part whatever in our democratic way of life. It is unattractive in any setting but it is utterly revolting among a free people who have embraced the principles

165

set forth in the Constitution of the United States. All residents of this nation are kin in some way by blood or culture to a foreign land. Yet they are primarily and necessarily a part of the new and distinct civilization of the United States. They must accordingly be treated at all times as the heirs of the American experiment and as entitled to all the rights and freedoms guaranteed by the Constitution.

> MURPHY, J., dissenting, *Korematsu v United States* (1944) 323 US 214, 242, 89 L ed 194, 212, 65 S Ct 193. (Japanese relocation case.)

Dispute

Coke: Mr. Bacon, if you have any tooth against me, pluck it out, for it will do you more hurt than all the teeth in your head will do you good.

Bacon: Mr. Attorney, I respect you: I fear you not: and the less you speak of your own greatness, the more I will think of it.

> Altercation in the Exchequer, 1601 (Bacon, letter to Cecil).

Dissent

Comparatively speaking at least, the dissenter is irresponsible. The spokesman of the court is cautious, timid, fearful of the vivid word, the heightened phrase. He dreams of an unworthy brood of scions, the spawn of careless *dicta,* disowned by the *ratio decidendi,* to which all legitimate offspring must be able to trace their lineage. The result is to cramp and paralyze. One fears to say anything when the peril of misunderstanding puts a warning finger to the lips. Not so, however, the dissenter. He has laid aside the role of the hierophant, which he will be only too glad to resume when the chances of war make him again the spokesman of the majority. For the moment, he is the gladiator making a last stand against the lions.

> BENJAMIN N. CARDOZO, *Law and Literature* 34 (1931).

The dissenter speaks to the future, and his voice is pitched to a key that will carry through the years. . . . The prophet and the martyr do not see the hooting throng. Their eyes are fixed on the eternities.

> BENJAMIN N. CARDOZO, *Law and Literature* 36 (1931).

The right to dissent is the only thing that makes life tolerable for a judge of an appellate court.

> WILLIAM O. DOUGLAS, *America Challenged* 4 (1960).

The law is not a series of calculating machines where definitions and answers come tumbling out when the right levers are pushed.

> WILLIAM O. DOUGLAS, *The Dissent, a Safeguard of Democracy,* 32 J. Am. Jud. Soc. 105 (1948).

In this Court dissents have gradually become majority opinions.

> FRANKFURTER, J., *Graves v New York* (1939) 306 US 466, 491, 83 L ed 927, 939, 59 S Ct 595, 120 ALR 1466.

A dissent in a court of last resort is an appeal to the brooding spirit of the law, to the intelligence of a future day.

> CHARLES EVANS HUGHES, *Supreme Court of the United States* 68 (1928).

167

Upon constitutional questions, the public have a right to know the opinion of every judge who dissents from the opinion of the court, and the reasons of his dissent.

> STORY, J., dissenting, *Briscoe v Bank of Kentucky* (1837, US) 11 Pet 257, 350, 9 L ed 709, 746.

Some states have inflicted upon their judges the cruel and inhuman punishment of prohibiting dissenting opinsions,—a crude and humiliating device of doubtful constitutionality.

> HENRY W. TAFT, 4 N.Y.S. Bar Bull. 17 (1932).

The only purpose which an elaborate dissent can accomplish, if any, is to weaken the effect of the opinion of the majority, and thus engender want of confidence in the conclusions of courts of last resort.

> WHITE, J., *Pollock v Farmers' Loan & Trust Co.* (1895) 157 US 429, 608, 39 L ed 759, 829, 15 S Ct 673.

But as Justice Frankfurter once quipped, "It is better for the Supreme Court to be divided than to be wrong."

> MARK WOOLSEY, *The Supreme Court,* Fortune, Oct. 1949, p. 167.

Dissents

I have the misfortune to differ from the Lord Justice Cotton, and I do so with a deep sense of the probability that he is right.

> BOWEN, L.J., *In re Haseldine* (1886) 31 Ch. D. 511, 517.

But on mature consideration, all I can say is that I differ on this question from those judges, and I feel bound to say that when I do differ from two such judges, I entertain much more doubt as to the propriety of my decision than of theirs.

> BRETT, L.J., *Blake v Blake* (1882) 7 P.D. 102, 114. (The judges referred to were Sir C. Cresswell and Lord Penzance.)

I ran upon a dissenting opinion not long ago, which I have been harboring in secret in the hope of using it hereafter, if provocation shall seem adequate, upon recalcitrant associates. I found it in the reports of the Supreme Court of Ohio. The dissenting judge delivered himself of this restrained comment upon the rule of the majority: "The majority opinion," he said, "to me seems a labored one, its arguments specious and its conclusions faulty." There was not much left of the majority opinion after that.

> BENJAMIN N. CARDOZO, *Address,* New York County Lawyers Yearbook 258 (1927).

The blunderbuss fashion in which the majority couches "its artillery of words" together with the morass of cases it cites as authority and the obscurity of their application to the question at hand makes it difficult to grasp the true thrust of its decision.

> CLARK, J., dissenting, *Keyishian v Board of Regents* (1967) 385 US 589, 620, 17 L ed 2d 629, 651, 87 S Ct 675.

I know that this, like every other case, will become the parent stock from which a motley progeny will spring. In those after years when this case, elevated to high authority by the cold finality of the printed page is quoted with the customary, "It has been said," perchance another Court will say, "Mayhaps the potter's hand trembled at the wheel." Possibly when that moment comes these words

169

may give that Court a chance to say, "Yea, and a workman standing hard by saw the vase as it cracked."

> CLARKSON, J., *Oliver v Raleigh*, 212 NC 465, 471 (1937).

The careful ambiguities and silences of the majority opinion.

> FRANKFURTER, J., *Bridges v California* (1941) 314 US 252, 279, 86 L ed 192, 212, 62 S Ct 190, 159 ALR 1346.

Although I think it useless and undesirable, as a rule, to express dissent, I feel bound to do so in this case and to give my reasons for it.

> HOLMES, J., *Northern Secur. Co. v United States* (1904) 193 US 197, 400, 48 L ed 679, 726, 24 S Ct 436.

My brothers differ from me in opinion, and they all differ from one another in the reasons of their opinion; but not withstanding their opinion, I think the plaintiff ought to recover.

> HOLT, C.J., *Ashby v White* (1703) 2 Ld. Raym. 938, 950.

I give up. Now I realize fully what Mark Twain meant when he said, "The more you explain it, the more I don't understand it."

> JACKSON, J., *Securities & Exch. Com. v Chenery Corp.* (1947) 332 US 194, 214, 91 L ed 1995, 2008, 67 S Ct 1575.

My object in expressing my opinion in this case, is to avoid having an ambiguous decision hereafter imputed to me, or an opinion which I would not wish to be understood to have given.

> JOHNSON, J., *Marine Ins. Co. v Young* (1809, US) 5 Cranch 187, 191, 3 L ed 74, 75.

It is impossible almost to overestimate the result of what
has been done here this day.   The Constitution as many
of us have understood it, the Constitution that has meant
so much to us has gone.   The guarantees which men and
women heretofore have supposed protected them against
arbitrary action, have been swept away.   The powers of
Congress have been enlarged to such an extent no man
can foresee their limitations, and we stand as a people
today stripped of the very fundamental guarantees which
we have heretofore supposed stood between us and arbitrary action.

> MR. JUSTICE McREYNOLDS, extemporaneous dissent, Feb. 18,
> 1935 when the Gold Clause decisions (*Norman v Baltimore &
> O. R. Co.* (1935) 294 US 240, 79 L ed 885, 55 S Ct 407, 95
> ALR 1352, and related cases) were handed down.   See *Wall
> Street Journal,* Feb. 23, 1935, p. 1.

We protest.   That never was the law, it never ought to
be the law, and the shame and the humiliation of it all
no one of us can foresee.

> MR. JUSTICE McREYNOLDS, *ibid.*

This is the first instance of a final difference of opinion
in this Court, since I sat here.   Every order, rule, judgment, and opinion, has hitherto been unanimous.   That
unanimity never could have happened, if we did not among
ourselves communicate our sentiments with great freedom;
if we did not form our judgments without any prepossess-
ion to first thoughts; if we were not always open to conviction, and ready to yield to each other's reasons.   We
have all equally endeavoured at that unanimity, upon this
occasion   .   .   .   but, in vain.   We continue to differ.
And whoever is right, each is bound to abide by and deliver

171

that opinion which he has formed upon the fullest examination.

> LORD MANSFIELD, C.J., *Millar v Taylor* (1769) 4 Burr. 2303,
> 2395.

I should now, as is my custom, when I have the misfortune to differ from this court, acquiesce silently in its
opinion, did I not believe that the judgment of the circuit
court of Virginia gave general surprise to the profession,
and was generally condemned.

> MARSHALL, C.J., *Bank of United States v Dandridge* (1827, US)
> 12 Wheat 64, 90, 6 L ed 552, 561.

It is disheartening to find so much that is right in an
opinion which seems to me so fundamentally wrong.

> MURPHY, J., dissenting, *Wolf v Colorado* (1949) 338 US 25, 41,
> 93 L ed 1782, 1792, 69 S Ct 1359.

They are his own babies, albeit often branded as illegitimates.

> JUDGE SAMUEL H. SIBLEY, attributed to. See 33 A.B.A.J. 312
> (1947).

At best, the operation of the rule which the Court
today enunciates for the first time may be expected to
confound confusion in a field already replete with com-
plexities.

> VINSON, C.J., *Trupiano v United States* (1948) 334 US 699, 716,
> 92 L ed 1663, 1675, 68 S Ct 1229.

It is an old truism that a conclusion is just as sound and
no more so than the premises upon which it is based. I

make bold to say that there is contained in this language the most beautiful bouquet of Bourbon blunders, expressed and implied, that has ever been handed to the bench and bar of Ohio.

> WANAMAKER, J., *City of Cleveland v Pub. Util. Comm.*, 100 Ohio St. 121, 147 (1919). Referring to associates' opposing opinion.

Distinction

It has been distinguished with more zest than it has been followed.

> LORD BIRKENHEAD, L.C., *Portman v Viscount Portman* [1922] 2 A.C. 473, 488. Referring to an earlier case.

He was in logic a great critic,
Profoundly skill'd in analytic;
He could distinguish, and divide
A hair 'twixt south, and south-west side.

> SAMUEL BUTLER, *Hudibras*, Pt. I, Canto I, 1. 65.

This distinction appeared to me to be too thin.

> LORD ELDON, *Ex parte Kensington* (1813) 2 V. & B. 79, 84.

Distinction without a difference.

> HENRY FIELDING, *Tom Jones*, bk 6, ch. 13.

We have not heretofore been so beguiled by changes in the scenery that we have lost sight of principle.

> FORTAS, J., dissenting, *Fortson v Morris* (1966) 385 US 231, 249, 17 L ed 2d 330, 342, 87 S Ct 446.

173

I have known gentlemen to split a hair, and I may have tried to do it myself. But I never before saw any one decimate a hair and count the pieces before the court.

> ALEXANDER HAMILTON, referring to his opponent Theophilus
> Parsons. Parsons, *Memoir of Theophilus Parsons* 160 (1859).

I have heard it suggested that the difference is one of degree. I am the last man in the world to quarrel with a distinction simply because it is one of degree. Most distinctions, in my opinion, are of that sort, and are none the worse for it.

> HOLMES, J., *Haddock v Haddock* (1906) 201 US 562, 631, 50
> L ed 867, 895, 26 S Ct 525.

No two cases are exactly alike. A young attorney found two opinions in the New York Reports where the facts seemed identical although the law was in conflict, but an older and more experienced attorney pointed out to him that the names of the parties were different.

> CUTHBERT W. POUND, 5 N.Y.S. B. Bull. 267 (1933).

Having referred to a late decision of the King's Bench, which is, in effect, a complete overruling of the case then before the Lords (Richardson v Campbell, 5 B and A 196) I said: "My learned friend will say that the cases are different. And they are different: the Lord Chief Justice, in giving judgment, says so. My Lords, since the short time that I have been in the profession, nothing has excited my admiration so much as the mingled delicacy and astuteness with which the learned Judges of one court avoid overruling the decisions of other courts. (Here Richardson, Parke, and Bailey smiled, and the Chancellor winked.) It would be indecorous in me to insinuate, even if I dared to imagine, what the opinion of the Judges of the King's Bench is; but I beg your Lordships to consider whether the reasoning of Lord Chief Justice Abbott applies to that part of the case in which it differs from the case before the House, or to that in which the cases are the same."

> HENRY CRABB ROBINSON, *Diary*, ch. 26, year 1822.

Lord Alverstone thought he had found distinctions between . . . cases and the case before him which I have not been fortunate enough to understand. I think the real truth is that he did not like the decisions; he thought they led to unreasonable results, and he declined to follow the Court of Appeal.

> SCRUTTON, L.J., *Hill v Aldershot Corporation* [1933] 1 K.B. 259, 269.

Divorce

Lord Chamberlain:
It seems the marriage with his brother's **wife**
Has crept too near his conscience.

Duke of Suffolk:
     No; his conscience
Has crept too near another lady.

> SHAKESPEARE, *Henry VIII*, Act 2, scene 2.

No choice was left his feelings or his pride,
Save death or Doctors' Commons—so he died.

> BYRON, *Don Juan*, c. 1, xxvi.

This is a use of the address of a court for its jurisdiction. . . . This was only divorce *a mensa et thoro,* equivalent to the modern judicial separation . . . but such is the fascination of matrimonial misfortune that in popular speech Doctors' Commons meant divorce and only divorce.

> SIR JOCELYN SIMON, *English Idioms From the Law,* 76 L.Q. Rev. 431 (1960).

Domicil

Whenever even a mere factory is founded in the eastern parts of the world, European persons trading under the shelter and protection of those establishments are conceived to take their national character from that association under which they live and carry on their commerce. It is a rule of the law of nations, applying peculiarly to those countries, and is different from what prevails ordinarily in Europe and western parts of the world, in which men take their present national character from the general character of the country in which they are resident; and this distinction arises from the nature and habit of the countries: In the western parts of the world alien merchants mix in the society of the natives; access and intermixture are permitted: and they become incorporated to almost the full extent. But in the East, from the oldest times, an immiscible character has been kept up; foreigners are not admitted into the general body and mass of the society of the nation; they continue strangers and sojourners as all of their fathers were—*Doris amara suam non intermiscuit undam.*

> SCOTT, J. (Lord Stowell) *The Indian Chief* (Adm. 1801) 3 C. Rob. 12, 28 (An American residing in Calcutta must be deemed to have a British commercial domicil.)

Double Jeopardy

The Court apparently takes the position that a second trial for the same act is somehow less offensive if one of the trials is conducted by the Federal Government and the other by a State. Looked at from the standpoint of the individual who is being prosecuted, this notion is too subtle for me to grasp.

> BLACK, J., dissenting, *Bartkus v Illinois* (1959) 359 US 121, 155, 3 L ed 2d 684, 707, 79 S Ct 676.

Doubt

The most learned doubteth most.

> COKE, *First Institute* 337b.

I always thought it better to allow myself to doubt before I decided, than to expose myself to the misery after I had decided, of doubting whether I had decided rightly and justly.

> LORD ELDON. See 3 Twiss, *Life of Lord Eldon* 350 (1844).

He delights to balance a straw, to see a feather turn the scale, or make it even again; and divides a scruple to the smallest fraction. He hugs indecision to his breast, and takes home a modest doubt or a nice point to solace himself with it in protracted, luxurious dalliance. Delay seems, in his mind, to be of the very essence of justice.

> WILLIAM HAZLITT, *Spirit of the Age* (1825). (Re Lord Eldon)

He had such a diffidence of himself, that he did not dare to do right for fear of doing wrong; decrees were always

[Legal Quotations]—12

extorted from him; and had he been left alone, he would never have given any suitor his due for fear of giving him what was not so.

> HERVEY, 1 *Memoirs of Reign of George II* 286 (1884), referring to Lord Chancellor King.

I may be wrong, and often am, but I never doubt.

> SIR GEORGE JESSEL, reply to Attorney General Coleridge when asked if he had any doubts in reference to the Alabama Claims. Jessel admitted that the story was true but added, "Coleridge, with his constitutional inaccuracy has told it wrong. I can never have said 'Often wrong'." See 219 Blackwood's Mag. 51 (1926).

Mr. Leach
Made a speech,
    Angry, neat but wrong:
Mr. Hart,
On the other part,
Was heavy, dull, and long:
Mr. Parker
Made the case darker,
    Which was dark enough without:
Mr. Cooke
Cited his book,
And the Chancellor, said—"I doubt."

> SIR GEORGE ROSE, when asked by a reporter to take a note of a case for him during his absence. The Chancellor was Lord Eldon. 3 Twiss, *Life of Lord Eldon* 326.

Due Process

That no man of what estate or condition, shall be put out of land or tenement, nor taken nor imprisoned, nor disinherited, nor put to death, without being brought in answer by due process of law.

> Statute of Westminster, 28 Edw. III (1354).

The due process clause and commerce clause have been used like Siamese twins in a never-ending stream of challenge to government regulation.

> BLACK, J., dissenting, *H. P. Hood & Sons, Inc. v Du Mond* (1949) 336 US 525, 562, 93 L ed 865, 887, 69 S Ct 657.

Due process is a growth too sturdy to succumb to the infection of the least ingredient of error.

> CARDOZO, J., *Roberts v New York* (1935) 295 US 264, 278, 79 L ed 1429, 1436, 55 S Ct 689.

It is of the very nature of a free society to advance in its standards of what is deemed reasonable and right. Representing as it does a living principle, due process is not confined within a permanent catalogue of what may at a given time be deemed the limits or essentials of fundamental rights.

> FRANKFURTER, J., *Wolf v Colorado* (1949) 338 US 25, 27, 93 L ed 1782, 1785, 69 S Ct 1359.

No single one of these circumstances alone would in my opinion justify a reversal. I cannot escape the conclusion, however, that in combination they bring the result below the Plimsoll line of "due process."

> FRANKFURTER, J., *Fikes v Alabama* (1957) 352 US 191, 199, 1 L ed 2d 246, 252, 77 S Ct 281.

179

The phrase is of convenient vagueness.

> CHARLES M. HOUGH, *Due Process of Law—Today*, 32 Harv. L.
> Rev. 218 (1919).

Duel

About a century since,
  The code of the duello
    To sudden death
    For want of breath
  Sent many a strapping fellow.
The then presiding Prince
  (Who useless bloodshed hated),
    He passed an Act,
    Short and compact,
  Which may be briefly stated.
Unlike the complicated laws
A Parliamentary draughtsman draws,
  It may be briefly stated.

By this ingenious law,
  If any two shall quarrel,
    They may not fight
    With falchions bright
  (Which seemed to him immoral);
But each a card shall draw,
  And he who draws the lowest
    Shall (so 'twas said)
    Be thenceforth dead—
  In fact, a legal "ghoest"
(When exigence of rhyme compels,
Orthography forgoes her spells,
  And "ghost" is written "ghoest.")

When off the loser's popped
  (By little legal fiction),
    And friend and foe
    Have wept their woe
  In counterfeit affliction,
The winner must adopt
  The loser's poor relations—
    Discharge his debts,
    Pay all his bets,
  And take his obligations.

In short, to briefly sum the case,
  The winner takes the loser's place,
    With all its obligations.

    WILLIAM S. GILBERT, *The Grand Duke,* Act 1.

Duty

The rule that you are to love your neighbour becomes in law, you must not injure your neighbour; and the lawyer's question, Who is my neighbour? receives a restricted reply. You must take reasonable care to avoid acts or omissions which you can reasonably foresee would be likely to injure your neighbour. Who, then, in law, is my neighbour? The answer seems to be—persons who are so closely and directly affected by my act that I ought reasonably to have them in contemplation as being so affected when I am directing my mind to the acts or omissions which are called in question.

    LORD ATKIN, *Donoghue v Stevenson* [1932] A.C. 562, 580.

Our country has not given us birth, or educated us under her law, as if she expected no succor from us; or that, seeking to administer to our convenience only she might afford a safe retreat for the indulgence of our ease, or a peaceful asylum for our indolence; but that she might hold in pledge the various and most exalted powers of our mind, our genius, and our judgment, for her own benefit and that she might leave for our private use such portion only, as might be spared for that purpose.

CICERO, *De Re Publica,* I, iv.

As the naturalists say, that there is no kind of bird or fowl of the wood or of the plain that doth not bring somewhat to the building and garnishing the eagle's nest, some cinnamon, and other things of price, and some juniper, and such like of lesser value, every one according to their quality, power, and ability: so ought every man, according to his power, place, and capacity, to bring somewhat, not only to the profit and adorning of our dear country (our great eagle's nest) but therein also, as much as such mean instruments can, to express their inward intention and desire, to honour the peaceable days of his Majesty's happy and blessed government to all posterity.

COKE, 8 Rep.: *Preface.*

You see how the vague circumference of the notion of duty shrinks and at the same time grows more precise when we wash it with cynical acid and expel everything except the object of our study, the operations of the law.

OLIVER WENDELL HOLMES, *Path of the Law,* 10 Harv. L.R. 457, 461 (1897).

182

Dying Declaration

If a man be robbed or wounded and he writes down a perfect description of the men whereby they are known and so dies, this will be good evidence to convict them.

> COKE, *Les Reportes del Cases* 318.

John of Gaunt:
O! but they say the tongues of dying men
Enforce attention like deep harmony:
Where words are scarce, they are seldom spent in vain,
For they breathe truth that breathe their words in pain.

> SHAKESPEARE, *Richard II*, Act 2, scene 1.

Earth

So the earth hath He appointed as the suburbs of heaven to be the habitation of man.

> COKE, *First Institute* 4a.

The earth hath in law a great extent upwards, not only of water, as hath been said, but of air and all other things even up to heaven; for *cujus est solum ejus est usque ad coelum.*

> COKE, *First Institute* 4a.

Education

The system of competitive examinations is a sad necessity. Knowledge is wooed for her dowry, not her diviner charms.

> LORD BOWEN, *Lecture on Education.* See Manson, Builders of Our Law 113 L.T. 356 (1902).

Let the soldier be abroad if he will, he can do nothing in this age. There is another personage,—a personage less imposing in the eyes of some, perhaps insignificant. The schoolmaster is abroad, and I trust to him, armed with his primer, against the soldier in full military array.

> HENRY BROUGHAM, *Speech in House of Commons,* January 29, 1828.

It is idle to pretend that this task is one for which we can find in the Constitution one word to help us as judges to decide where the secular ends and the sectarian begins in education. Nor can we find guidance in any other legal source. It is a matter on which we can find no law but our own prepossessions.

> JACKSON, J., *Illinois ex rel. McCollum v Board of Education* (1948) 333 US 203, 237, 92 L ed 649, 672, 68 S Ct 461, 2 ALR2d 1338.

The fundamental theory of liberty upon which all governments in this Union repose excludes any general power of the State to standardize its children by forcing them to accept instruction from public teachers only. The child is not the mere creature of the State.

> McREYNOLDS, J., *Pierce v Society of Sisters* (1925) 268 US 510, 535, 69 L ed 1070, 1078, 45 S Ct 571, 39 ALR 468.

A whale-ship was my Yale College and my Harvard.

> HERMAN MELVILLE, *Moby Dick,* ch. 24.

It is, Sir, as I have said, a small college. And yet, there are those who love it.

> DANIEL WEBSTER, arguendo in Dartmouth College Case, U.S. Supreme Court, 1818. See R. Choate, *Eulogy on Webster,* for account of trial by Professor Chauncey A. Goodrich.

Education (Legal)

They must pry into the secret recesses of the human heart, and become well acquainted with the whole moral world, that they may discover the abstract reason of all laws: and they must trace the laws of particular states, especially of their own, from the first rough sketches to the more perfect draughts; from the first causes or occasions that produced them, through all the effects, good and bad, that they produced.

> LORD BOLINGBROKE, *On the Study and Use of History: Letter 5* (1739).

He was bred to the law, which is, in my opinion, one of the first and noblest of human sciences; a science which does more to quicken and invigorate the understanding, than all the other kinds of learning put together; but it is not apt, except in persons very happily born, to open and liberalize the mind exactly in the same proportion.

> BURKE, *Speech on American Taxation,* April 19, 1774.

This study renders men acute, inquisitive, dextrous, prompt in attack, ready in defence, full of resources. In other countries, the people, more simple, and of a less mercurial cast, judge of an ill principle in government only by an actual grievance; here they anticipate the evil, and judge of the pressure of the grievance by the badness of the principle. They augur misgovernment at a distance, and snuff the approach of tyranny in every tainted breeze.

> BURKE, *Speech on Conciliation with America,* March 22, 1775.

No man can be a compleat Lawyer by universality of knowledge without experience in particular Cases, nor by

185

bare experience without universality of knowledge; he must be both speculative and active, for the science of the laws, I assure you, must joyn hands with experience.

COKE, *Book of Entries: Preface.*

Six hours to sleep, as many to righteous law;
Four to your prayers, and two to fill your maw;
The rest bestow upon the sacred Muses.
(Sex horas somno, totidem des legibus aequis,
Quatuor orabis, des epulisque duas;
Quod superest ultra sacris largire Camaenis.)

COKE, (translation of ancient verse) *First Institute* 64b.

Legal studies . . . sharpen, indeed, but like a grinding stone narrow whilst they sharpen.

SAMUEL T. COLERIDGE, *Table Talks: Duties and Needs of an Advocate.*

We lawyers are always curious, always inquisitive, always picking up odds and ends for our patchwork minds, since there is no knowing when and where they may fit into some corner.

CHARLES DICKENS, *Little Dorrit*, bk. 2, ch. 12.

I myself was uncommercially preparing for the Bar—which is done, as everybody knows, by having a frayed old gown put on in a pantry by an old woman in a chronic state of St. Anthony's fire and dropsey, and, so decorated, bolting a bad dinner in a party of four, whereof each individual mistrusts the other three.

CHARLES DICKENS, *Uncommercial Traveller: Chambers,* ch. 14.

Live like a hermit and work like a horse.

> LORD ELDON, reply to Wilberforce's question as to what advice
> he would give students who wanted to be young Grants in the
> law, 3 *Life of Wilberforce* 9, Journal entry, April 17, 1801.

There is nothing does a young lawyer so much good as
to be half starved: it has a fine effect.

> LORD ELDON, 1 Twiss, *Life of Eldon* 134 (1844).

Pursue the study of the law, rather than the gain of it;
pursue the gain of it enough to keep out of the briers,
but give your main attention to the study of it. The next
is, not to marry early; for an early marriage will obstruct
your improvement; and in the next place, it will involve
you in expense. Another thing is, not to keep much company, for the application of a man who aims to be a lawyer
must be incessant; his attention to his books must be constant, which is inconsistent with keeping much company.*

> JEREMIAH GRIDLEY, Advice given to John Adams in 1758,
> 2 *Works of John Adams* 46.

I can but envy the felicity of the generation to whom it
is made so easy to see their subject as a whole. When I
began, the law presented itself as a ragbag of details.

> OLIVER WENDELL HOLMES, 1 *Continental Legal History Series:
> Introduction* xlvii; *Coll Leg Pap* 301.

---

* His advice made so deep an impression on my mind, that I believe
no lawyer in America ever did so much business as I did afterwards,
in the seventeen years that I passed in practice at the bar, for so little
profit.

JOHN ADAMS. See 2 Works 46.

For the rational study of the law the black-letter man may be the man of the present, but the man of the future is the man of statistics and the master of economics.

> OLIVER WENDELL HOLMES, *Path of the Law,* 10 Harv. L. Rev. 457, 469 (1897).

Other branches of science, and especially history, are necessary to form a lawyer.

> THOMAS JEFFERSON, *Letter to John Garland Jefferson, June 11, 1790.*

I do not see why the study of the law is called dry and unpleasant; and I very much suspect that it seems so to those only who would think any study unpleasant which required a great application of the mind and exertion of the memory.

> SIR WILLIAM JONES, *Letter June 3, 1771,* to Lord Chief Justice Wilmot.

Seven hours to law, to soothing slumber seven,
Ten to the world allot, and all to Heaven.

> SIR WILLIAM JONES. See 2 Teignmouth, *Life of Jones,* ch. 11 (1804). Compare Coke, supra.

I am only a mast-fed lawyer.

> ABRAHAM LINCOLN. See Hill, *Lincoln, the Lawyer* 198 (1906).

Extemporaneous speaking should be practised and cultivated. It is the lawyer's avenue to the public. . . . And yet there is not a more fatal error to young lawyers than relying too much on speech-making. If anyone upon his

rare powers of speaking, shall claim an exemption from
the drudgery of the law, his case is a failure in advance.

ABRAHAM LINCOLN, *Notes for a Law Lecture, July 1, 1850.*

Law schools make tough law.

FREDERIC WM. MAITLAND, *English Law and the Renaissance.*
Rede Lecture (1901).

Taught law is tough law.

FREDERIC WM. MAITLAND, *ibid.*

I have heard Serjeant Maynard say the law is *ars
bablativa,* meaning that all the learning in the world will
not set a man up in bar practice without a faculty of a
ready utterance of it.

ROGER NORTH, *On the Study of the Laws* 29.

Sir Henry Finch used to say, study all the morning, and
talk all the afternoon.

ROGER NORTH, *On the Study of Laws* 8.

The schoolmaster of the American Bar.

ROSCOE POUND,—appellation bestowed upon.   See *Annual
Survey of American Law: Dedication,* 1947.

A lawyer without history or literature is a mechanic, a
mere working mason; if he possesses some knowledge of
these, he may venture to call himself an architect.

WALTER SCOTT, *Guy Mannering,* ch. 37.

189

The subject matter of law is somewhat transcendent, and too high for ordinary capacities.

WILLIAM SHEPPARD, *Touchstone: Preface* (1650).

This lawyer's preparatory education is certainly one of the most cold blooded, prejudiced pieces of invention that ever a man was slave to. . . . A fellow should do and think of nothing else than LAW.

THACKERAY, *Letter,* January 14, 1832 (to his mother).

On the other side of the third landing . . . sits Mr. Paley, who took the highest honors, and who is a fellow of his college, who will sit and read and note cases until two o'clock in the morning; who will rise at seven and be at the pleader's chambers as soon as they are open, where he will work until an hour before dinner-time. . . . He has not been throwing himself away: he has only been bringing a great intellect laboriously down to the comprehension of a mean subject, and in his fierce grasp of that, resolutely excluding from his mind all higher thoughts, all better things, all the wisdom of philosophers and historians, all the thoughts of poets; all wit, fancy, reflection, art, love, truth altogether—so that he may master that enormous legend of the law, which he proposes to gain his livelihood by expounding.

THACKERAY, *Pendennis,* ch. 29.

Law schools belong in the modern university no more than a school of fencing or dancing.

THORSTEIN VEBLEN, *Higher Learning in America* (1918) 211.

Emergency

While emergency does not create power, emergency may furnish the occasion for the exercise of power.

> HUGHES, C.J., *Home Bldg. & L. Asso. v Blaisdell* (1934) **290 US 398, 426, 78 L ed 413, 421, 54 S Ct 231, 88 ALR 1481.**

Although an emergency may not call into life a power which has never lived, nevertheless emergency may afford a reason for the exertion of a living power already enjoyed.

> WHITE, C.J., *Wilson v New* (1917) 243 US 332, 348, 61 L ed **755, 774, 37 S Ct 298.**

Entrapment

Even if inducements to commit crime could be assumed to exist in this case, the allegation of the defendant would be but the repetition of the plea as ancient as the world, and first interposed in Paradise: "The serpent beguiled me and I did eat." That defence was overruled by the great Lawgiver, and whatever estimate we may form, or whatever judgment pass upon the character or conduct of the tempter, this plea has never since availed to shield crime or give indemnity to the culprit, and it is safe to say that under any code of civilized, not to say Christian ethics, it never will.

> BACON, J., *Bd. of Commrs. Onon. Co. v Backus,* 29 **How. Pr.** (N.Y.) 33, 42 (1864).

The power of government is abused and directed to an end for which it was not constituted when employed to promote rather than detect crime and to bring about the downfall of those who, left to themselves, might well have obeyed the law. Human nature is weak enough and suffi-

191

ciently beset by temptations without government adding to them and generating crime.

> FRANKFURTER, J., concurring, *Sherman v United States* (1958) 356 US 369, 384, 2 L ed 2d 848, 858, 78 S Ct 819.

Environment

There is a plain old house in the hills of Oneida, overlooking the valley of the Mohawk, where truth and honor dwelt in my youth. When I go back, as I am about to go, to spend my declining years, I mean to go with the feeling that I can say I have not failed to speak and to act in accordance with the lessons that I learned there from the God of my fathers.

> ELIHU ROOT, *N. Y. Const. Conv. 1915*, 4 Rev. Rec. 3505.

Epitaphs

He was splendid
In an undefended.

> J.P.C., *Epitaph on a Barrister*, 116 Just. P. 640 (1952).

Here lies John Shaw,
Attorney-at-law;
And when he died,
The Devil cried,
"Give us your paw,
John Shaw
Attorney-at-law!"
"Pshaw! pshaw."

> On an attorney. See Loaring, *Epitaphs, Quaint, Curious and Eloquent* 188.

In Memory of Richard, Baron Westbury,
Lord High Chancellor of England.
He was an eminent Christian,
An energetic and successful Statesman,
And a still more eminent and successful Judge.
During his Three Years of Office he abolished
The Time-honoured Institution of the Insolvent Debtors'
     Court,
The Ancient Mode of Conveying Land and
The Eternity of Punishment.
Towards the End of his Earthly career
In the Judicial Committee of the Privy Council
He dismissed Hell with Costs,
And took away from the orthodox members of
The Church of England
Their best hope of Eternal Damnation.

> EDWARD H. PEMBER. Lord Westbury in his judgment in the
> case of *Bishop of Salisbury v Williams and Wilson,* said that
> the charge that Wilson in his *Essay* had departed from the
> teaching of the Protestant Church as to Eternal Punishment had
> not been made out.

Equal Protection

The prohibition of the Equal Protection Clause goes no
further than the invidious discrimination.

> DOUGLAS, J., *Williamson v Lee Optical of Okla., Inc.* (1955) 348
> US 483, 489, 99 L ed 563, 573, 75 S Ct 461.

Exact equality is no prerequisite of equal protection of
the laws within the meaning of the Fourteenth Amendment.

> DOUGLAS, J., *Norvell v Illinois* (1963) 373 US 420, 423, 10 L ed
> 2d 456, 459, 83 S Ct 1366.

[Legal Quotations]—13

It is the usual last resort of constitutional arguments to point out shortcomings of this sort. But the answer is that the law does all that is needed when it does all that it can, indicates a policy, applies it to all within the lines, and seeks to bring within the lines all similarly situated so far and so fast as its means allow.

> HOLMES, J., *Buck v Bell* (1927) 274 US 200, 208, 71 L ed 1000, 1002, 47 S Ct 584.

Equal protection of the laws is not achieved through indiscriminate imposition of inequalities.

> VINSON, C.J., *Shelley v Kraemer* (1948) 334 US 1, 22, 92 L ed 1161, 1185, 68 S Ct 836, 3 ALR2d 441.

Equality

When Lycurgus was to reform and alter the state of Sparta, in the consultation one advised that it should be reduced to an absolute popular equality. But Lycurgus said to him: *Sir, begin it in your own house.*

> BACON, *Apothegms New and Old,* no 29.

Therefore, since law is the bond which unites the civic association, and the justice enforced by law is the same for all, by what justice can an association of citizens be held together when there is no equality among the citizens? For if we cannot agree to equalize men's wealth, and equality of innate ability is impossible, the legal rights at least of those who are citizens of the same commonwealth ought to be equal. For what is a State except an association or partnership in justice?

> CICERO, *De Re Publica De Legibus,* I, xxxii, 49 (trans. Keyes).

Equality may be as much as anything else equality of misery.

> RUDOLPH VON JHERING, *Law as a Means to an End,* ch. 8, sec. 11 (5 Mod. Leg. Phil. Ser. 276).

We seek not just freedom but opportunity. We seek not just legal equity, but human ability. Not just equality as a right and a theory but equality as a fact and equality as a result.

> LYNDON B. JOHNSON, Address, *Howard University Commencement Exercises, June 4, 1965.* N.Y. Times, June 5, 1965 § 1, p. 14.

The principle of democracy is corrupted not only when the spirit of equality is extinct, but likewise when they fall into a spirit of extreme equality, and when each citizen would fain be upon a level with those whom he has chosen to command him. Then the people, incapable of bearing the very power they have delegated, want to manage everything themselves, to debate for the senate, to execute for the magistrates, and to decide for the judges.

> MONTESQUIEU, *Spirit of the Laws,* bk 8, ch. 2 (trans. Nugent).

All animals are equal, but some animals are more equal than others.

> GEORGE ORWELL, *Animal Farm,* ch. 10.

Equal rights to unequal possessions, equal justice to the rich and poor; this is what men come out to fight for and to defend.

> SYDNEY SMITH, *Assize Sermon, March 28, 1824, at York.*

195

Equity

A correction of law where it is defective owing to its universality.

ARISTOTLE, *Ethica Nicomachea,* bk 5, ch. 10.

Equity is that idea of justice, which contravenes the written law.

ARISTOTLE, *Rhetoric,* bk 1, ch. 13.

Equity does not demand that its suitors shall have led blameless lives.

BRANDEIS, J., *Loughran v Loughran* (1934) 292 US 216, 229, 78 L ed 1219, 1227, 54 S Ct 684.

Equity does not act for every shadowy or unsubstantial wrong.

CARDOZO, C.J., *Nann v Raimist,* 255 N. Y. 307, 319 (1931).

Equity fashions a trust with flexible adaptation to the call of the occasion.

CARDOZO, J., *Adams v Champion* (1935) 294 US 231, 237, 79 L ed 880, 884, 55 S Ct 399.

Equity acts in personam.   (*Aequitas agit in personam.*)

COWPER, L.K., *Toller v Carteret* (1705), 2 Vern. 494, 495.

He who will have equity, or comes hither for equity, must do equity.

COWPER, L.C., *Demandray v Metcalf* (1715) Prec. Ch. 419, 420.

Upon that occasion Lord Chief Justice De Grey said he never liked Equity so well as when it was like Law. The day before I had heard Lord Mansfield say he never liked Law so well as when it was like Equity.

> LORD ELDON, *Lord Dursley v Fitzhardinge Berkeley* (1801) 6 Ves. 251, 260.

A man must come into a court of equity with clean hands.

> EYRE, C.B., *Dering v Earl of Winchelsea* (1787) 1 Cox Eq. 318, 319.

Equality is equity.

> RICHARD FRANCIS, *Maxims of Equity* (1728).

And it was said by Lord Somers, that equity did delight in equality, and that the distribution according to the statute was most agreeable to natural justice.

> HOLT, C.J., *Petit v Smith* (1695) 1 P. Wms. 7, 9.

The rules of Courts of Equity are not, like the rules of the Common Law, supposed to have been established from time immemorial. It is perfectly well known that they have been established from time to time—altered, improved, and refined from time to time. In many cases we know the names of the Chancellors who invented them.

> JESSEL, M.R., *Re Hallett* (1879) 13 Ch. D. 696, 710.

To apply one general law to all particular cases, were to make all shoes by one last, or to cut one glove for all hands, which how unfit it would prove, every man can readily perceive.

> WILLIAM LAMBARDE, *Archeion 69* (1635).

Equity had come not to destroy the law, but to fulfil it.

> FREDERIC WM. MAITLAND, *Lectures on Equity* 17 (1909). See
> similar statement by Bacon, under Chancery.

We ought to think of equity as supplementary law, a
sort of appendix added on to our code, or a sort of gloss
written around our code, an appendix, a gloss, which used
to be administered by courts especially designed for that
purpose, but which is now administered by the High Court
of Justice as part of the code.

> FREDERIC WM. MAITLAND, *ibid.*

Equity without common law would have been a castle
in the air, an impossibility.

> FREDERIC WM. MAITLAND, *Lectures on Equity* 18 (1909).

Equity is a right wiseness that considereth all the particular circumstances of the Deed the which also is tempered
with the Sweetness of Mercy. And such an Equity must
always be observed in every Law of Man, and in every
general Rule thereof; And that knew he well that said thus,
Laws covet to be ruled by Equity.

> CHRISTOPHER ST. GERMAN, *Doctor and Student,* Dial. I, c. 16.

Equity is a roguish thing: for law we have a measure,
know what to trust to; equity is according to the conscience
of him that is chancellor, and as that is larger or narrower,
so is equity. 'Tis all one as if they should make the standard for the measure we call a foot, a chancellor's foot;
what an uncertain measure would this be? One chancellor
has a long foot, another a short foot, a third an indifferent
foot: 'tis the same thing in the chancellor's conscience.

> JOHN SELDEN, *Table-Talk: Equity.*

Thou robed man of justice, take thy place;
And thou, his yoke-fellow of equity,
Bench by his side.

> SHAKESPEARE, *King Lear,* Act 3, scene 6.

He who seeks equity must do equity.

> JOSEPH STORY, *Equity Jurisprudence,* section 77 (1836).   Roscoe
> Pound credits Story with the particular wording of this maxim.

Error

Some courts live by correcting the errors of others and adhering to their own. On these terms courts of final review hold their existence, or those of them which are strictly and exclusively courts of review, without any original jurisdiction, and with no direct function but to find fault or see that none can be found. With these exalted tribunals, who live only to judge the judges, the rule of *stare decisis* is not only a canon of the public good, but a law of self-preservation. At the peril of their lives they must discover error abroad and be discreetly blind to its commission at home.

> BLECKLEY, C.J., *Ellison v Georgia R.R.,* 87 Ga 691, 695 (1891).

The court erred in some of the legal propositions announced to the jury, but all the errors were harmless. Wrong directions which do not put the traveler out of his way, furnish no reasons for repeating the journey.

> BLECKLEY, J., *Cherry v Davis,* 59 Ga 454, 456 (1877).

Error (Ignorance being her inseparable twin) doth in her proceeding so infinitely multiply herself, produceth such

199

monstrous and strange chimaeras, floateth in such and so
many uncertainties and sucketh down the poison from the
contagious breath of Ignorance, as all such into whom
she infuseth any of her poisoned breath, she dangerously
infects or intoxicates.

> COKE, 5 Rep.: *Preface.*

To say that "counsel for the Authority" had a "very
heavy burden" was wrong. Whatever burden counsel for
the Authority carried was not a subject for judicial sympathy. They were counsel of ability and experience, as
the trial record shows, and it was not sagacious to intimate
that their backs might be broken by a heavy verdict and,
therefore, the jury should spare them that spinal disaster.

> MUSMANNO, J., *Taylor v Urban Redevelopment Auth. of Pitts-*
> *burgh,* 419 Pa 430, 434 (1965).

Eskgroviana

And so, gentlemen, having shown you that the pannell's
argument is utterly impossibill, I shall now proceed to show
you that it is extremely improbabill.

> LORD ESKGROVE. See Cockburn, *Memorials of His Time* 123
> (1856). Although Eskgrove was a judge of ability he was
> famous for the absurdity of his words and actions.

And not only did you murder him, whereby he was
bereav-ed of his life, but you did thrust, or push, or pierce,
or project, or propell the lethal weapon through the belly-
band of the regimental breeches which were His Majesty's.

> ibid. 121. When condemning a tailor to death for murdering a
> soldier by stabbing.

All this you did; and God preserve us! joost when they were sitten doon to their denner!

> ibid. 123. When condemning to death persons who broke into a house and assaulted and robbed the occupants.

Estimate

An estimated value is a precarious measure of justice, compared with the specific thing.

> LORD MANSFIELD, C.J., *Fisher v Prince* (1762) 3 Burr. 1363, 1365.

Ethics (Legal)

Boswell: I asked him whether, as a moralist, he did not think that the practice of the law, in some degree, hurt the nice feeling of honesty.

Johnson: Why no, Sir, if you act properly. You are not to deceive your clients with false representations of your opinion: you are not to tell lies to a judge.

> BOSWELL, *Life of Samuel Johnson:* 1768.

Boswell: But what do you think of supporting a cause which you know to be bad?

Johnson: Sir, you do not know it to be good or bad until the Judge determines it. I have said that you are to state facts fairly; so that your thinking, or what you call knowing, a cause to be bad, must be from reasoning, must be from supposing your arguments to be weak and inconclusive. But, Sir, that is not enough. An argument which does not convince yourself, may convince the Judge, to whom you urge it: and if it does convince him, why, then, Sir, you are wrong, and he is right. It is his business to judge; and you are not to be confident in your own opinion that a cause is bad, but to say all you can for your client, and then hear the Judge's opinion.

Boswell: But, Sir, does not affecting a warmth when you have no warmth, and appearing to be clearly of one opinion when you are in reality of another opinion, does not such dissimulation impair one's honesty? Is there not some danger that a lawyer may put on the same mask, in common life, in the intercourse with his friends?

Johnson: Why no, Sir. Everybody knows you are paid for affecting warmth for your client; and it is, therefore, properly no dissimulation; the moment you come from the bar you resume your usual behaviour. Sir, a man will no more carry the artifice of the bar into the common intercourse of society, than a man who is paid for tumbling upon his hands will continue to tumble upon his hands when he should walk on his feet.

  ibid.

The difference between the true lawyer and those men who consider the law merely a trade is that the latter seek to find ways to permit their clients to violate the moral standards of society without overstepping the letter of the law, while the former look for principles which will persuade their clients to keep within the limits of the spirit of the law in common moral standards.

  PIERO CALAMANDREI, *Eulogy of Judges* 62 (1942) trans. Adams and Phillips.

Ethical considerations can no more be excluded from the administration of justice, which is the end and purpose

of all civil laws, than one can exclude the vital air from his
room and live.

> JOHN F. DILLON, *Laws and Jurisprudence of England and Amer-
> ica,* Lecture I (1894).

There is a vague popular belief that lawyers are necessarily dishonest. . . . Let no young man choosing the
law for a calling for a moment yield to the popular belief—
resolve to be honest at all events; and if in your own judgment you cannot be an honest lawyer, resolve to be honest
without being a lawyer. Choose some other occupation,
rather than one in the choosing of which you do, in advance,
consent to be a knave.

> ABRAHAM LINCOLN, *Notes for a Law Lecture, July 1, 1850.*

The ultimate justification of the law is to be found, and
can only be found, in moral considerations.

> LORD MACMILLAN, *Law and Other Things* 41 (1937).

I will join with my adversary in waiving a jury trial
wherever and whenever it can possibly be done without the
sacrifice of a fundamental right.

I will join with my adversary in supporting a trial justice
in fair comment upon the evidence and reasonable direction
to a jury on the facts.

I will join with my adversary in fair concession of un-
disputed facts.

I will not put an adversary to his proof in respect to facts
whose existence my client admits.

I will refrain from merely formal or technical objections
to the admission of evidence.

I will co-operate with the trial justice and my adversary
to secure a speedy, prompt and complete presentation of
the facts of the case.

I will neither make nor oppose interlocutory motions unless they are of real and practical importance.

I will take no appeal unless I am satisfied that a substantial error has been committed and that a new trial should reasonably give a different result.

> JOSEPH M. PROSKAUER, *Credo* (1928). See 13 N.Y. Co. Lawyers Assn. Bar Bull. 146 (1956).

An eminent lawyer cannot be a dishonest man. Tell me a man is dishonest, and I will answer he is no lawyer. He cannot be, because he is careless and reckless of justice; the law is not in his heart, is not the standard and rule of his conduct.

> DANIEL WEBSTER, *Speech, Charleston, S.C. Bar, May 10, 1847.*

For your duty to particular clients you may consider that some are rich, yet with such there must be no endeavour to lengthen causes, to continue fees. Some are poor, yet their business must not be neglected, if their cause be honest, they are not the worst clients; though they fill not your purses, they will fill the ears of God with prayers for you; and he who is the defender of the poor will repay your charity. Some clients are of mean capacity, you must take the more pains to instruct yourself to understand their business. Some are of quick capacity and confidence, yet you must not trust to their information. Some are peaceable; detain them not, but send them home the sooner. Some are contentious; advise them to reconcilement with their adversary. Amongst your clients and all others endeavour to gain and preserve that estimation and respect which is due to your degree and to a just, honest, and discreet person.

> BULSTRODE WHITELOCK, *Memorials of English Affairs* 354. His speech on the call of the sergeants, 1648.

Evidence

Irrelevance can be highly enlightening. The witness who starts with what she had for breakfast and remembers it was Thursday because her husband's sister had come down with the measles when she shouldn't have if she had only gone to the other doctor, the one with glasses—should be a delight to the judge's heart and make the jury feel at home. Behind this leisurely sweep of incident they can follow her as they please, and it will give them at least her barometric pressure at the time when she signed the note at the bank without reading it. After listening to enough of it, any idiot would know that she was an accommodation endorser who had done it to help her husband and had got nothing out of it for herself.

> CURTIS BOK, *I Too, Nicodemus* 322 (1946).

To refuse evidence is to refuse to hear the cause.

> EDMUND BURKE, *Report on the Lords' Journal* [1794].

It is for ordinary minds, and not for psychoanalysts, that our rules of evidence are framed. They have their source very often in considerations of administrative convenience, of practical expediency, and not in rules of logic.

> CARDOZO, J., *Shepard v United States* (1933) 290 US 96, 104, 78 L ed 196, 202, 54 S Ct 22.

Oh, Sammy, Sammy, vy worn't there a alleybi.

> CHARLES DICKENS, *Pickwick Papers,* ch. 34.

Chops and tomata sauce.

> CHARLES DICKENS, *Pickwick Papers,* ch. 34. (From **Pickwick's** letter to Mrs. Bardell, introduced in evidence in the breach of promise action).

"You must not tell us what the soldier, or any other man, said, Sir," interposed the judge, "it's not evidence."

CHARLES DICKENS, *Pickwick Papers,* ch. 34.

They (rules of evidence) are founded in the charities of religion, in the philosophy of nature, in the truths of history, and in the experience of common life.

THOMAS ERSKINE, arguendo, *Trial of Thomas Hardy* (1794) 24 How. St. Tr. 966.

It is not required that testimony be so minute as to exclude every fantastic hypothesis that can be suggested.

JACKSON, J., *Haupt v United States* (1947) 330 US 631, 640, 91 L ed 1145, 1153, 67 S Ct 874.

It is a rule of evidence . . . that positive testimony is entitled to more weight than negative testimony, but by the latter term is meant negative testimony in its true sense and not positive evidence of a negative, because testimony in support of a negative may be as positive as that in support of an affirmative.

McALISTER, J., *Blackburn v State,* 31 Ariz 427, 442 (1927). (Trial court admitted evidence that a witness could find no hair on a blood spot.)

It is certainly a maxim that all evidence is to be weighed according to the proof which it was in the power of one side to have produced, and in the power of the other to have contradicted.

LORD MANSFIELD, C.J., *Blatch v Archer* (1774) 1 Cowp. 63, 65.

Human nature constitutes a part of the evidence in every case.

POTTER, J., *Greene v Harris,* 11 R.I. 5, 17 (1875).

Evidence (Circumstantial)

Some circumstantial evidence is very strong, as when you find a trout in the milk.

HENRY D. THOREAU, *Journal, November 11, 1850.*

Pieces of evidence, each by itself insufficient, may together constitute a signficant whole, and justify by their combined effect a conclusion.

LORD WRIGHT, *Grant v Australian Knitting Mills, Ltd.* [1936] A.C. 85, 96.

Iachimo:
                    On her left breast
A mole cinque-spotted, like the crimson drops
I' the bottom of a cowslip: here's a voucher;
Stronger than ever law could make: this
        secret
Will force him think I have pick'd the lock **and**
        ta'en
The treasure of her honour.

SHAKESPEARE, *Cymbeline,* Act 2, scene **2.**

Queen Margaret:
Then you, belike, suspect these **noble**
        noblemen
As guilty of Duke Humphrey's timeless **death.**

Earl of Warwick:

Who finds the heifer dead and bleeding fresh,
And sees fast by a butcher with an axe,
But will suspect 'twas he that made the slaughter?
Who finds the partridge in the puttock's nest,
But may imagine how the bird was dead,
Although the kite soar with unbloodied beak?
Even so suspicious is this tragedy.

    SHAKESPEARE, *Henry VI, Pt. 2,* Act 3, scene 2.

Lady Macbeth:

Why did you bring these daggers from the place?
They must lie there: go carry them, and smear
The sleepy grooms with blood.

Macbeth:

      I'll go no more. . . .

Lady Macbeth:

Give me the daggers. . . .
I'll gild the faces of the grooms withal;
For it must seem their guilt.

    SHAKESPEARE, *Macbeth,* Act 2, scene 2.

Iago:

I will in Cassio's lodging lose this napkin,
And let him find it; trifles light as air
Are to the jealous confirmations strong
As proofs of holy writ.

    SHAKESPEARE, *Othello,* Act 3, scene 3.

Othello:
That handkerchief which I so lov'd and
    gave thee
Thou gav'st to Cassio.

> SHAKESPEARE, *ibid.* Act 5, scene 2.

Exception

Th' lawyer f'r th' definse objicts to all th' questions an' whin th' coort overrules him he takes an exciption. That is as much as to say to th' judge: "I'll make a jack iv ye in th' supreem coort."

> FINLEY PETER DUNNE, *Mr. Dooley on Making a Will: On Criminal Trials.* Also in Bander, ed. *Mr. Dooley on the Choice of Law* (1963) 4.

Experiment

To stay experimentation in things social and economic is a grave responsibility. Denial of the right to experiment may be fraught with serious consequences to the Nation. It is one of the happy incidents of the federal system that a single courageous State may, if its citizens choose, serve as a laboratory; and try novel social and economic experiments without risk to the rest of the country. This Court has the power to prevent an experiment. . . . But in the exercise of this high power, we must be ever on our guard, lest we erect our prejudices into legal principles. If we would guide by the light of reason, we must let our minds be cold.

> BRANDEIS, J., dissenting, *New State Ice Co. v Liebmann* (1932) 285 US 262, 311, 76 L ed 747, 771, 52 S Ct 371.

[Legal Quotations]—14   *209*

Exposure

One thinks that an error exposed is dead, but exposure amounts to nothing when people want to believe.

OLIVER WENDELL HOLMES, 1 *Holmes-Pollock Letters* 219 (Aug. 30, 1914).

Extraordinary

We call it extraordinary, but in truth it is not an extraordinary storm which happens once in a century, or in fifty or twenty years; on the contrary it would be extraordinary if it did not happen. There is a French saying "that there is nothing so certain as that which is unexpected." In like manner, there is nothing so certain as that something extraordinary will happen now and then.

BRAMWELL, B., *Ruck v Williams* (Ex. 1858) 3 H. & N. 308, 318.

Facts

Knowledge is essential to understanding; and understanding should precede judging.

BRANDEIS, J., dissenting, *Jay Burns Baking Co. v Bryan* (1924) 264 US 504, 520, 68 L ed 813, 829, 44 S Ct 412, 32 ALR 661.

Her terrible tale
You can't assail,
With truth it quite agrees:
Her taste exact
For faultless fact
Amounts to a disease.

WILLIAM S. GILBERT, *The Mikado*, Act 2.

The main part of intellectual education is not the acquisition of facts, but learning how to make the facts live.

> OLIVER WENDELL HOLMES, *Oration before Harvard Law School Association* (1886), Speeches (1913) 29; Coll. Leg. Pap. 37.

The purpose of a hearing is that the Court may learn what it does not know and it knows least about the facts. It may sound paradoxical, but most contentions of law are won or lost on the facts. They often incline a judge to one side or the other.

> ROBERT H. JACKSON, *Advocacy Before the Supreme Court: Suggestions for Effective Case Presentations*, 37 A.B.A.J. 801, 803 (1951).

Though the the'ry's fust-rate, the facs
    wun't coincide:
Facs are contrary 'z mules, an' ez hard
    in the mouth.

> JAMES RUSSELL LOWELL, *Bigelow Papers*, Ser. 2, No. 4.

Without a known fact, it is impossible to know the law on that fact.

> VAUGHAN, C.J., *Bushel's Case* (1670) Jones (T.) 13, 16.

Fair Trade

To forbid the competition of a cocoanut grove with the American cow.

> LETTS, J., *Carolene Products Co. v Wallace*, 27 F. Supp. 110, 113 (1939). Referring to the purpose of the Filled Milk Act.

Thirsty folk want beer, not explanations.

> LORD MACNAGHTEN, *Montgomery v Thompson* [1891] A.C.
> 217, 225. Case involved the fraudulent use of the trade name,
> Stone Ale.

There is a homely proverb current in my part of the
country which says "you may not sell the cow and sup the
milk."

> LORD MACNAGHTEN, *Nordenfelt v Maxim Nordenfelt Guns
> and Ammunition Co.* [1894] A.C. 535, 572. (Case involved
> a covenant in restraint of trade.)

Faith

I die the King's servant, but God's first.

> SIR THOMAS MORE.

Is not this house as nigh heaven as mine own?

> SIR THOMAS MORE, when imprisoned in the Tower of London
> and his wife urged him to obtain his freedom by yielding to
> the king. Roper, *Life of More.*

Federation

Under a federal as under a unitarian system there exists
a sovereign power, but the sovereign is in a federal state
a despot hard to rouse. He is not, like the English Parliament, an ever-wakeful legislator, but a monarch who slumbers and sleeps. . . . But a monarch who slumbers for
years is like a monarch who does not exist. A federal

constitution is capable of change, but for all that a federal constitution is apt to be unchangeable.

> ALBERT V. DICEY, *Law of the Constitution 136 (1885) lect. 4: Parliamentary Sovereignty and Federalism.*

Federalism substitutes litigation for legislation, and none but a law-fearing people will be inclined to regard the decision of a suit as equivalent to the enactment of a law.

> ALBERT V. DICEY, *ibid.* 164.

A nation concealed under the form of a federation.

> ALBERT V. DICEY, *ibid.* App. 604 (9th ed 1939). Referring to the United States.

Feeling

Men's feelings are as different as their faces.

> BULLER, J., *Good v Elliott* (1790) 3 T.R. 693, 701.

Fees

As for lawyers' fees, I must leave it to the conscience and merit of the lawyer.

> BACON, *Speech, May 7, 1617,* on taking his seat in Chancery as Lord Keeper.

Voila! the non suit of cow beef.

> THOMAS ERSKINE, on receiving fee from Admiral Keppel for defending him in court martial proceeding. The charge was pronounced "malicious and ill-founded."

I dislike sending in professional charges to friendly people, but we have a saying here that offices like individuals have to live.

> REGINALD L. HINE, *Confessions of an Un-Common Attorney* 26
> (1945).

Ask for what Price thy Venial Tongue was sold:
A rusty Gammon of some sev'n Years old:
Tough, wither'd Treuffles; ropy Wine, a Dish
Of shotten Herring, or stale stinking Fish.
For four times talking, if one piece thou take,
That must be cantled, and the Judge go snack.

> JUVENAL, *Satires,* VII (Dryden trans.) Lawyers were paid in goods
> or produce (gammon=ham, treuffles=scallions). On the rare
> occasion that payment was a gold piece the judge took a snack
> (share).

The matter of fees is important, far beyond the mere question of bread and butter involved. Properly attended to, fuller justice is done to both lawyer and client. An exorbitant fee should never be claimed. As a general rule never take your whole fee in advance, nor any more than a small retainer. When fully paid beforehand, you are more than a common mortal if you can feel the same interest in the case, as if something was still in prospect for you, as well as for your client.

> ABRAHAM LINCOLN, *Notes for a Law Lecture, July 1, 1850.*

I have just received yours of the 16th, with check on Flagg & Savage for twenty-five dollars. You must think I am a high-priced man. You are too liberal with your money. Fifteen dollars is enough for the job. I send you a receipt for fifteen dollars, and return to you a ten dollar bill.

> ABRAHAM LINCOLN, *Letter to George P. Floyd, February 21, 1856.*

The form of their pleading is 1st, the advocates and their clients stand each on either side of the door through the bar, at the bar, and the advocates plead in Scotch before them, and in the then time of their pleading their clients will put a double piece or more, with an ordinary fee with the poorest, and will say to their advocates "thumb it thumb it," and then will the advocates plead accordingly as they feel it weigh.

> LOWTHER, *Our Journall into Scotland* (1629) 31. Reprint, 1894.

Tim'rous by nature, of the rich in awe,
I come to Counsel learned in the law,
You'll give me like a friend both sage and free,
Advice, and (as you use) without a fee.

> ALEXANDER POPE, *Imitations of Horace,* bk 2, 1st satire, line 7.

The contingent fee is the poor man's key to the court-house door.

> *Saying.*

To lying awake thinking of your case.

> *Saying.* Suggested item on lawyer's bill.

'Tis like the breath of an unfee'd lawyer; you gave me nothing for 't.

> SHAKESPEARE, *King Lear,* Act 1, scene 4.

O! then, I see, Queen Mab hath been with you. . . .
She is the fairies' midwife, and she comes . . .
O'er lawyers' fingers, who straight dream on fees.

SHAKESPEARE, *Romeo and Juliet,* Act 1, scene 4.

There was a young lady of Ci'cester,
Who went to consult her solicitor,
When he asked for his fee,
She said "Fiddle-de-dee,
I only looked in as a visitor."

Unknown.

While in bed the sick man's lying,
While in Court your client's cause you're trying,
That's the time to get your fee.
For, when the sick man has recovered,
And the lawsuit's won or smothered,
He will never think of thee.

Unknown. Inscribed on the walls of the University of Bologna,
Italy, in the Thirteenth Century.

Fiction

Fiction (in law) a wilful falsehood, uttered by a judge,
for the purpose of giving to injustice the colour of justice.

JEREMY BENTHAM, *Scotch Reform,* 5 Works 13.

There are many pleasant fictions of the law in constant
operation, but there is not one so pleasant or practically
humorous as that which supposes every man to be of equal
value in its impartial eye, and the benefits of all laws to be

216

equally attainable by all men, without the smallest reference to the furniture of their pockets.

CHARLES DICKENS, *Nicholas Nickleby,* ch. 46.

Any assumption which conceals, or affects to conceal, the fact that a rule of law has undergone alteration its letter remaining unchanged, its operation being modified.

SIR HENRY MAINE, *Ancient Law,* ch. 2.

Fictions of law hold only in respect of the ends and purposes for which they were invented.

LORD MANSFIELD, C.J., *Morris v Pugh* (1761) 3 Burr. 1241, 1243.

It is the creature of the court, and is moulded to the purposes of justice, according to the view which its inventors have taken of its capacity to effect those purposes.

MARSHALL, Cir. J., *Livingston v. Jefferson,* 15 Fed. Cas. (No. 8411) 660, 663 (1811).

Flag

We live by symbols. . . . The flag is but a bit of bunting to one who insists on prose. Yet . . . its red is our life blood, its stars our world, its blue our heaven. It owns our land. At will it throws away our lives.

HOLMES, C.J., On motion that the court adjourn on February 4, 1901, the one hundredth anniversary of the day John Marshall took his seat as Chief Justice of the United States, 178 Mass 627.

Flattery

Parliaments, palaces of princes, and pulpits should be free from adulation and flattery.

COKE, *Third Institute* 209.

Footnotes

There is no merit in plaintiff's contention made at the oral argument that the ruling of the Supreme Court was not binding since it appeared in the footnote in the opinion. A footnote is as important a part of an opinion as a matter contained in the body of the opinion and has like binding force and effect.

McCOMB, J., *Melancon v Walt Disney Productions,* 127 Cal App 2d 213, 214n (1954).

There may be narrower scope for operation of the presumption of constitutionality when legislation appears on its face to be within a specific prohibition of the Constitution, such as those of the first ten amendments, which are deemed equally specific when held to be embraced within the Fourteenth. . . .

It is unnecessary to consider now whether legislation which restricts those political processes which can ordinarily be expected to bring about repeal of undesirable legislation, is to be subjected to more exacting judicial scrutiny under the general prohibitions of the Fourteenth Amendment than are most other types of legislation. . . .

Nor need we inquire whether similar considerations enter into the review of statutes directed at particular religions, . . . or national . . . or racial minorities, . . . whether prejudice against discrete and insular minorities may be a special condition, which tends seriously to curtail the operation of those political processes ordinarily to be

218

relied upon to protect minorities, and which may call for a correspondingly more searching judicial inquiry.

> STONE, J., *United States v Carolene Products Co.* (1938) 304 US 144, 152 fn, 82 L ed 1234, 1241, 58 S Ct 778.

There was long current a remark attributed to Chief Justice Hughes to the effect that "I will not be bound by a footnote," but unfortunately it is not to be found in any opinion he wrote. Indeed, the footnote in the first *Carolene* case, to the effect that "There may be narrower scope for operation of the presumption of constitutionality when legislation appears on its face to be within a specific prohibition of the Constitution, such as those of the first ten amendments, which are deemed equally specific when held to be embraced within the Fourteenth" . . . foreshadowed, for better or worse, a good deal of constitutional doctrine of the 1940's.

> FREDERICK BERNAYS WIENER, *Briefing and Arguing Federal Appeals* (1961) 154 fn. 73.

Formula

To rest upon a formula is a slumber that, prolonged, means death.

> OLIVER WENDELL HOLMES, *Ideals and Doubts,* 10 Ill. L. Rev. 1, 3 (1915); Coll. Leg. Pap. 306.

Fraud

Fraud includes the pretense of knowledge when knowledge there is none.

> CARDOZO, C.J., *Ultramares Corp. v Touche,* 255 N.Y. 170, 179 (1931).

Fraud is infinite in variety; sometimes it is audacious and unblushing; sometimes it pays a sort of homage to virtue, and then it is modest and retiring; it would be honesty itself if it could only afford it.

> LORD MACNAGHTEN, *Reddaway v Banham* [1896] **A.C.** 199, 221.

No court has ever attempted to define fraud.

> LINDLEY, L.J., *Allcard v Skinner* (1887) 36 Ch. 145, 183.

Freedom

Many an appeal to freedom is the masquerade of privilege or inequality seeking to intrench itself behind the catchword of a principle.

> BENJAMIN N. CARDOZO, *Mr. Justice Holmes,* 44 Harv. L.R. 682, 687 (1931).

Freedom is a thing with which the nature of man has been endowed by God. For this reason if it be taken away from man it strives of its own energy always to return.

> SIR JOHN FORTESCUE, *De Laudibus Legum Angliae,* ch. 42.

Freedom of the Press

The liberty of the press is indeed essential to the nature of a free state; but this consists in laying no previous restraints upon publications, and not in freedom from censure for criminal matter when published.

> BLACKSTONE, *Commentaries,* bk. 4, 151.

To censure the licentiousness, is to maintain the liberty, of the press.

BLACKSTONE, *ibid.* 153.

This Court has not yet decided that the fair administration of criminal justice must be subordinated to another safeguard of our constitutional system—freedom of the press, properly conceived. The Court has not yet decided that, while convictions must be reversed and miscarriages of justice result because the minds of jurors or potential jurors grew poisoned, the poisoner is constitutionally protected in plying his trade.

FRANKFURTER, J., concurring, *Irvin v Dowd* (1961) 366 US 717, 730, 6 L ed 2d 751, 760, 81 S Ct 1639.

The basis of our governments being the opinion of people, the very first object should be to keep that right; and were it left to me to decide whether we should have a government without newspapers, or newspapers without a government, I should not hesitate a moment to prefer the latter. But I should mean that every man should receive those papers, and be capable of reading them.

THOMAS JEFFERSON, *Letter to Edward Carrington, Jan. 16, 1787.*

Advertisements contain the only truths to be relied on in a newspaper.

THOMAS JEFFERSON, *Letter to Nathaniel Macon, 1819.*

The liberty of the press consists in printing without any previous licence, subject to the consequences of law. The licentiousness of the press is Pandora's Box, the source of every evil. Miserable is the condition of individuals, dangerous is the condition of the State, if there is no certain

221

law, or, which is the same thing, no certain administration
of law, to protect individuals, or guard the State.

> LORD MANSFIELD, C.J., *R. v Shipley* (1784) 4 Doug. 73, 170.

If it poisons the minds of the people, it likewise admin-
isters an antidote. The same waggons, the same flys and
stages, that carry down into the county the lies and abuse
of faction, carry down also the lies and abuse of the minis-
try. If any one is bit by the tarantula of opposition, he is
cured by the music of the court.

> ALEXANDER WEDDERBURN, *Speech, House of Commons,*
> *(1770)* 16 Parl. Hist. 1290.

Freedom of Speech

Liberty of speech inviteth and provoketh liberty to be
used again, and so bringeth much to a man's knowledge.

> BACON, *Advancement of Learning,* bk 2.

Free speech is not so absolute or irrational a conception
as to imply paralysis of the means for effective protection
of all the freedoms secured by the Bill of Rights.

> FRANKFURTER, J., *Bridges v California* (1941) 314 US 252, 282,
> 86 L ed 192, 213, 62 S Ct 190, 159 ALR 1346.

This is a phrase [i.e. "the preferred position of freedom
of speech"] that has uncritically crept into some recent opinions of this Court. I deem it a mischievous phrase, if it
carries the thought, which it may subtly imply, that any
law touching communication is infected with presumptive
invalidity. . . . I say the phrase is mischievous because
it radiates a constitutional doctrine without avowing it.

> FRANKFURTER, J., concurring, *Kovacs v Cooper* (1949) 336 US
> 77, 90, 93 L ed 513, 524, 69 S Ct 448, 10 ALR2d 608.

Free-speech cases are not an exception to the principle that we are not legislators, that direct policy-making is not our province. How best to reconcile competing interests is the business of the legislatures, and the balance they strike is a judgment not to be displaced by ours, but to be respected unless outside the pale of fair judgment.

> FRANKFURTER, J., concurring, *Dennis v United States* (1951) 341 US 494, 539, 95 L ed 1137, 1168, 71 S Ct 857.

The question in every case is whether the words used are used in such circumstances and are of such a nature as to create a clear and present danger that they will bring about the substantive evils that Congress has a right to prevent.

> HOLMES, J., *Schenck v United States* (1919) 249 US 47, 52, 63 L ed 470, 473, 39 S Ct 247.

The most stringent protection of free speech would not protect a man in falsely shouting fire in a theatre and causing a panic.

> HOLMES, J., *ibid.*

The right of free speech is not absolute at all times and under all circumstances. There are certain well-defined and narrowly limited classes of speech, the prevention and punishment of which have never been thought to raise any constitutional problem. These include the lewd and obscene, the profane, the libelous, and the insulting or "fighting" words—those which by their very utterance inflict injury to tend to incite an immediate breach of the peace.

> MURPHY, J., *Chaplinsky v New Hampshire* (1942) 315 US 568, 572, 86 L ed 1031, 1035, 62 S Ct 766.

223

It is by the goodness of God that in our country we have those three unspeakably precious things: freedom of speech, freedom of conscience, and the prudence never to practice either of them.

> MARK TWAIN, *Following the Equator* (1903) v. 1, p. 198.

Speech is not an absolute, above and beyond control by the legislature when its judgment, subject to review here, is that certain kinds of speech are so undesirable as to warrant criminal sanction.   Nothing is more certain in modern society than the principle that there are no absolutes, that a name, a phrase, a standard has meaning only when associated with the considerations which gave birth to the nomenclature. . . . To those who would paralyze our Government in the face of impending threat by encasing it in a semantic straitjacket we must reply that all concepts are relative.

> VINSON, C.J., *Dennis v United States* (1951) 341 US 494, 508, 95 L ed 1137, 1152, 71 S Ct 857.

I disapprove of what you say, but I will defend to the death your right to say it.

> VOLTAIRE, attributed to in Tallentyre, *The Friends of Voltaire* (1907) 199. When not found in his works and the author was questioned she explained that it was not intended as a direct quotation but as a paraphrase. Considered characteristic, or because it serves a particular purpose, it is still quoted and ascribed to Voltaire.*

---

* cf.

In writing biography, fact and fiction shouldn't be mixed. And if they are, the fiction parts should be printed in red ink, the fact parts in black ink.

Catherine Drinker Bowen, 173 Publishers Weekly, Mar. 24, 1958, p. 15.

Freedom of Thought

It is common knowledge that the thought of man shall not be tried, for the Devil himself knoweth not the thought of man.

> BRIAN, J., Y.B. 17 Edw. 4 Pasch., f.2 (1477).

Of that freedom [freedom of thought and speech] one may say that it is the matrix, the indispensable condition, of nearly every other form of freedom.

> CARDOZO, J., *Palko v Connecticut* (1937) 302 US 319, 327, 82 L ed 288, 293, 58 S Ct 149.

No man . . . shall be examined upon secret thoughts of his heart, or of his secret opinion.

> COKE, 12 Rep. 26.

I maintain that opinion is free, and that conduct alone is amenable to the law.

> THOMAS ERSKINE, arguendo, *Trial of Thomas Paine* (1792) 22 How. St. Tr. 358, 419.

If there is any principle of the Constitution that more imperatively calls for attachment than any other it is the principle of free thought—not free thought for those who agree with us but freedom for the thought that we hate.

> HOLMES, J., *United States v Schwimmer* (1929) 279 US 644, 654, 73 L ed 889, 893, 49 S Ct 448.

Those who begin coercive elimination of dissent soon find themselves exterminating dissenters. Compulsory uni-

[Legal Quotations]—15

fication of opinion achieves only the unanimity of the graveyard.

> JACKSON, J., *West Virginia State Board of Education v Barnette*
> (1943) 319 US 624, 641, 87 L ed 1628, 1639, 63 S Ct 1178,
> 147 ALR 674.

If there is any fixed star in our constitutional constellation, it is that no official, high or petty, can prescribe what
shall be orthodox in politics, nationalism, religion, or other
matters of opinion or force citizens to confess by word or
act their faith therein.

> JACKSON, J., *West Virginia State Board of Education v Barnette*
> (1943) 319 US 624, 642, 87 L ed 1628, 1639, 63 S Ct 1178,
> 147 ALR 674.

The danger that citizens will think wrongly is serious,
but less dangerous than atrophy from not thinking at all.
. . . Thought control is a copyright of totalitarianism,
and we have no claim to it. It is not the function of our
Government to keep the citizen from falling into error; it
is the function of the citizen to keep the Government from
falling into error.

> JACKSON, J., *American Communications Asso., C.I.O. v Douds*
> (1950) 339 US 382, 442, 94 L ed 925, 967, 70 S Ct 674.

If there be any among us who would wish to dissolve this
Union or to change its republican form, let them stand
undisturbed as monuments of the safety with which error
of opinion may be tolerated where reason is left free to
combat it.

> THOMAS JEFFERSON, *First Inaugural Address, March 4, 1801.*

Human laws reach not thoughts.

> Proverb. THOMAS FULLER, *Proverbs* (1732).

Friend

I am on most friendly terms with all the judges, but I suspect that if I should be gathered to Abraham's bosom some of them would think it an advantage to the law, even if they missed a friend.

> OLIVER WENDELL HOLMES, (1930) 2 *Holmes-Pollock Letters* 268.

Gain

Every one thirsteth after gain.

> COKE, *Third Institute* 196.

Gambling

The law draws a distinction between a criminal act and yielding to a vice. It does not treat alike the spider who spins the web and the fly enmeshed in it.

> LEHMAN, C.J., *Bamman v Erickson,* 288 N.Y. 133, 136 (1942).

Generalization

To generalize is to omit.

> HOLMES, J., *Donnell v Herring-Hall-Marvin Safe Co.* (1908) 208 US 267, 273, 52 L ed 481, 487, 28 S Ct 288.

Gentleman

As for gentlemen, they be made good cheape in England. For whosoever studieth the lawes of the realme, who

studieth in the universities, who professeth liberall sciences,
and to be shorte, who can live idly and without manuall
labour, and will beare the port, charge, and countenance of
a gentleman, he shall be called master, for that is the title
which men give to esquires and other gentlemen, and shall
be taken for a gentleman.

> SIR THOMAS SMITH, *De Republica Anglorum,* bk 1, ch. 20
> (1583).

Gift

The old man has given all to his son.
O fool! to undress thy self before thou art going to bed.

> BENJAMIN FRANKLIN, *Poor Richard Almanac (Oct. 1733).*

He who gives away his goods before he
  is dead
Take a beetle and knock him on
  the head.

> Proverb. See John Ray, *English Proverbs* (1670).

Goodwill

We are not here to sell a parcel of boilers and vats, but
the potentiality of growing rich beyond the dreams of
avarice.

> SAMUEL JOHNSON, when asked what he really considered the
> value of the Thrale Brewery which, as executor, he was trying
> to sell. Boswell's *Life of Johnson:* 1781.

What is goodwill? It is a thing very easy to describe, very
difficult to define. It is the benefit and advantage of the

good name, reputation, and connection of a business. It is the attractive force which brings in custom. It is the one thing which distinguishes an old-established business from a new business at its first start. The goodwill of a business must emanate from a particular centre or source. However widely extended or *diffused* its influence may be, goodwill is worth nothing unless it has a power of attraction sufficient to bring customers home to the source from which it emanates. Goodwill is composed of a variety of elements. It differs in its composition in different trades and in different businesses in the same trade.

> LORD MACNAGHTEN, *I.R.C. v Muller & Co.'s Margarine Ltd.* [1901] A.C. 217, 223.

Government

Our Government is the potent, the omnipresent teacher. For good or for ill, it teaches the whole people by its example. . . . If the Government becomes a law-breaker, it breeds contempt for law; it invites every man to become a law unto himself; it invites anarchy. To declare that in the administration of the criminal law the end justifies the means—to declare that the Government may commit crimes in order to secure the conviction of a private criminal—would bring terrible retribution. Against that pernicious doctrine this court should resolutely set its face.

> BRANDEIS, J., dissenting, *Olmstead v United States* (1928) 277 US 438, 485, 72 L ed 944, 960, 48 S Ct 564, 66 ALR 376. (Wire-tapping case.)

The prosperity and greatness of empires ever depended, and ever must depend, upon the use their inhabitants do make of their reason in devising wise laws, and the spirit and virtue with which they watch over their just execution:

and it is impious to suppose, that men, who have made no provision for their own happiness or security in their attention to their government, are to be saved by the interposition of Heaven in turning the hearts of their tyrants to protect them.

> THOMAS ERSKINE, *arguendo, Proceedings against Dean of St. Asaph,* 21 How. St. Tr. 1015 (1783). Argument was in support of the proposition that juries had the right to decide on whether or not a publication was libelous.

Men must turn square corners when they deal with the Government.

> HOLMES, J., *Rock Island, A. & L. R. Co. v United States* (1920) 254 US 141, 143, 65 L ed 188, 189, 41 S Ct 55.

The science of government is the most abstruse of all sciences; if, indeed, that can be called a science, which has but few fixed principles, and practically consists in little more than the exercise of a sound discretion, applied to the exigencies of the state as they arise. It is the science of experiment.

> JOHNSON, J., *Anderson v Dunn* (1821, US) 6 Wheat 204, 226, 5 L ed 242, 247.

No government ought to be so defective in its organization, as not to contain within itself, the means of securing the execution of its own laws against other dangers than those which occur every day.

> MARSHALL, C.J., *Cohens v Virginia* (1821, US) 6 Wheat 264, 387, 5 L ed 257, 287.

They that govern most make least noise; you see, when they row in a barge, they that do the drudgery work slash and puff and sweat but he that governs sits quietly at the stern and scarce is seen to stir.

JOHN SELDEN, *Table-Talk: Power-State.*

Government (Laws and Men)

To the end it may be a government of laws and not of men.

JOHN ADAMS, *Draft Massachusetts Constitution: Declaration of Rights, Art. XXX (1779).* See 4 *Works* 230.

He who bids the law rule may be deemed to bid God and Reason alone rule, but he who bids man rule adds an element of the beast; for desire is a wild beast, and passion perverts the minds of rulers, even when they are the best of men.

ARISTOTLE, *Politics,* III, 16 (trans. Jowett).

A government of laws without men is as visionary as a government of men without laws; the solution will always be a compromise based on experience.

LEARNED HAND, *The Deficiencies of Trials to Reach the Heart of the Matter,* 3 Lectures on Legal Topics, Assn Bar of City of N.Y., 102 (1926).

And these I conceive to be the principles upon which Aristotle and Livy (injuriously accused by Hobbes for not writing out of nature) have grounded their assertion that a "Commonwealth is an empire of laws and not of men."

JAMES HARRINGTON, *Oceana.*

If men were angels, no government would be necessary. If angels were to govern men, neither external nor internal

231

controuls on government would be necessary. In framing a government which is to be administered by men over men, the great difficulty lies in this: You must first enable the government to controul the governed; and in the next place, oblige it to controul itself.

> JAMES MADISON, *The Federalist No. 51 (1788).*

I see that the State in which the law is above the rulers . . . has salvation.

> PLATO, *Laws* IV, 715.

There never was such a government. Constitute them how you will, governments are always governments of men, and no part of any government is better than the men to whom that part is entrusted. The gauge of excellence is not the law under which officers act, but the conscience and intelligence with which they apply it, if they apply it at all. And the courts do not escape the rule. So far as the individual is concerned, a constitutional government is as good as its courts; no better, no worse.

> WOODROW WILSON, *Constitutional Government in the United States* (1908) 17.

Government (Separation of Powers)

The doctrine of the separation of powers was adopted by the Convention of 1787, not to promote efficiency but to preclude the exercise of arbitrary power. The purpose was, not to avoid friction, but, by means of the inevitable friction incident to the distribution of the governmental powers among three departments, to save the people from autocracy.

> BRANDEIS, J., dissenting, *Myers v United States* (1926) 272 US 52, 293, 71 L ed 160, 242, 47 S Ct 21.

Last Thursday I described the American form of Government as a three-horse team provided by the Constitution to the American people so that their field might be plowed. The three horses are, of course, the three branches of government—the Congress, the Executive and the Courts. Two of the horses are pulling in unison today; the third is not. Those who have intimated that the President of the United States is trying to drive that team, overlook the simple fact that the President, as Chief Executive, is himself one of the three horses.

It is the American people themselves who are in the driver's seat.

It is the American people themselves who want the furrow plowed.

It is the American people themselves who expect the third horse to pull in unison with the other two.

> FRANKLIN D. ROOSEVELT, *Radio Address, Mar. 9, 1937.* See *Public Papers and Addresses (Rosenman ed.) 123.*

Guardian and Ward

The constitutional guardian I
Of pretty young wards in Chancery,
All very agreeable girls and none
Is over the age of twenty-one,

.   .   .

And everyone who'd marry a ward
Must come to me for my accord,
And in my court I sit all day
Giving agreeable girls away.

> WILLIAM S. GILBERT, *Iolanthe, Act 1 (Lord Chancellor's Song).*

Guilt

Now, if any fundamental assumption underlies our system, it is that guilt is personal not inheritable.

> JACKSON, J., dissenting, *Korematsu v United States* (1944) 323 US 214, 243, 89 L ed 194, 213, 65 S Ct 193.

The wicked flee when no man pursueth: but the righteous are as bold as a lion.

> Proverbs 28:1.

Habeas Corpus

A writ by which a man may be taken out of jail when confined for the wrong crime.

> AMBROSE BIERCE, *Devil's Dictionary.*

The writ of *habeas corpus,* the most celebrated writ in the English law.

> BLACKSTONE, *Commentaries,* bk 3, 129.

"Well," said the cobbler: "When I was going to take out a probate of the will, the nieces and nevys, who was desparately disappointed at not getting all the money, enters a caveat against it."

"What's that?" inquired Sam.

"A legal instrument, which is as much as to say, it's no go," replied the cobbler.

"I see," said Sam, "a sort of brother-in-law o' the have-his-carcass."

> CHARLES DICKENS, *Pickwick Papers,* ch. 44.

Hain't we saved Habus Coppers,
 improved it in fact,
By suspendin' the Unionists "stid of"
 the Act?

JAMES RUSSELL LOWELL, *Bigelow Papers,* Ser. 2, no. 4.

Headnotes

Possession in Scotland evidence of stealing in England.

> *Clement's Case* (1830) 1 Lewin C.C. 113. A popular version is:
> Possession of trousers in Scotland—evidence of larceny in
> England.

The decision depends largely, if not entirely, on facts, which are stated at great length by the court, both in the statement of the case, and in its opinion. These papers are most carefully prepared. While both deal with facts, those facts are stated with clearness, with fullness, with completeness, and with unusual care. They leave nothing untouched. Without treating them with the same fullness, the reporter feels himself unable to prepare a headnote which could convey an adequate and just account of the opinion and decision of the court. Under these circumstances he deems it best not to attempt an impossibility, but to respectfully ask the readers of this headnote to regard the opinion of the court in this case as incorporated into it.

> JOHN CHANDLER BANCROFT DAVIS, Headnote to opinion in
> *Huntting Elevator Co. v Bosworth* (1900) 179 US 415, 45
> L ed 256, 21 S Ct 183.

The reporter does not believe that the opinion in this case was intended to change the settled rule of law, as laid down in the several cases cited, and he has therefore made

235

the head-note conform to those cases, and not to the language of the opinion.

> J. W. SHEPARD (reporter), *Drake v State,* 51 Ala 30 (1874).

Hearing

"Does our Law judge a man unless it first give him a hearing, and knows what he does?" They answered and said to him, "Art thou also a Galilean? Search the Scriptures and see that out of Galilee arises no prophet."

> JOHN 7:51 (Nicodemus to the other Pharisees concerning the contemplated arrest of Christ.)

Heaven

We may not look at our pleasures to go to heaven in feather beds. It is not the way; for our Lord himself went thither with great pain and by many tribulations, which was the path wherein he walked thither, leaving us example to follow Him; for the servant may not look to be in better case than his master.

> SIR THOMAS MORE. See Harpsfield, *Life of Thomas More* 75. (Although this was a contemporary life—circa 1558—it was not pub. until 1932.)

Hindsight

The event is always a great teacher.

> BRADLEY, J., *The Nevada* (1882) 106 US 154, 157, 27 L ed 149, 150, 1 S Ct 234.

Looking back at the mishap with the wisdom born of the event, we can see that the mechanic would have done better if he had given warning of the change of pose. Extraordinary prevision might have whispered to him at the moment that the warning would be helpful. What the law exacted of him, however, was only the ordinary prevision to be looked for in a busy world.

CARDOZO, C.J., *Breene v Sibley, et al.,* 257 N.Y. 190, 192 (1931).

History

But if Maitland brought law to bear on history, he brought history to bear on law. Again and again he emphasized the danger of imposing legal concepts of a later date on facts of an earlier date—a common fault, before his time, of the majority of legal historians and of many constitutional historians. We must not read either law or history backwards. We must learn to think the thoughts of a past age—"the common thoughts of our forefathers about common things." "We must not attribute precise ideas or well defined law to the German conquerors of Britain." It is as if "we armed Hengist and Horsa with machine guns or pictured the Venerable Bede correcting proofs."

HELEN CAM, *Intoduction: Selected Historical Essays of F. W. Maitland* xix (1957).

History, in illuminating the past, illuminates the present, and in illuminating the present, illuminates the future.

BENJAMIN N. CARDOZO, *Nature of the Judicial Process* 53 (1921).

237

Undoubtedly the Court has the right to make history, as it has often done in the past, but it has no right to *remake* it.

> EDWARD S. CORWIN, *The Supreme Court as a National School Board, 14 Law & Contemp. Problems* 3, 20 (1949).

The laws of a nation form the most instructive portion of its history.

> EDWARD GIBBON, *Decline and Fall of the Roman Empire,* ch. 45.

The history of what the law has been is necessary to the knowledge of what the law is.

> OLIVER WENDELL HOLMES, *Common Law* 37 (1881).

Historic continuity with the past is not a duty, it is only a necessity.

> OLIVER WENDELL HOLMES, *Learning and Science, Speeches* 68 (1913).

A page of history is worth a volume of logic.

> HOLMES, J., *New York Trust Co. v Eisner* (1921) 256 US 345, 349, 65 L ed 963, 983, 41 S Ct 506, 16 ALR 660.

People often speak of correcting the judgment of the time by that of posterity. I think it is quite as true to say that we must correct the judgment of posterity by that of the time.

> OLIVER WENDELL HOLMES, *Answer to resolutions of the Bar, Boston (George Otis Shattuck) May 29, 1897. Speeches* (1913) 70.

The Fourteenth Amendment, itself a historical product, did not destroy history for the States and substitute mechanical compartments of law all exactly alike. If a thing has been practised for two hundred years by common consent, it will need a strong case for the Fourteenth Amendment to effect it.

> HOLMES, J., *Jackman v Rosenbaum Co.* (1922) 260 US 22, 31, 67 L ed 107, 112, 43 S Ct 9.

Law in particular becomes then only a rational study, when it is traced historically, from its first rudiments among savages, through successive changes, to its highest improvements in a civilized society.

> LORD KAMES, *Historical Law Tracts: Preface.*

Law treated historically becomes an entertaining study; entertaining not only to those whose profession it is, but to every person who hath any thirst for knowledge.

> LORD KAMES, *ibid.*

History involves comparison and the English lawyer who knew nothing and cared nothing for any system but his own hardly came in sight of the idea of legal history.

> FREDERIC WM. MAITLAND, *Why the History of English Law Is Not Written,* Inaugural Lecture in Arts School, Cambridge, 1888, in 1 *Coll. Papers* 488.

Such is the unity of all history that any one who endeavours to tell a piece of it must feel that his first sentence tears a seamless web.

> FREDERIC WM. MAITLAND, *Prologue to a History of English Law,* 14 L.Q.R. 13 (1898).

239

To-day we study the day before yesterday, in order that yesterday may not paralyse to-day, and to-day may not paralyse tomorrow.

> FREDERIC WM. MAITLAND, *Survey of the Century*, in 3 *Coll. Papers* 439.

The law is what it is today because of what the law was yesterday; it cannot escape its ancestry, and it, too, must progress against the background of its history.

> ALISON REPPY, *Common-Law Pleading*, 2 N. Y. Law Forum 1, 5 (1956).

Holmes, Oliver Wendell

It has taken a decade to elevate Mr. Justice Holmes from deity to mortality.

> WALTON H. HAMILTON, 9 Univ. Chi. L. Rev. 1 (1941).

I could carve out of a banana, a judge with more backbone than that.

> THEODORE ROOSEVELT — attributed to, after Holmes' dissent in *Northern Secur. Co. v United States* (1904) 193 US 197, 48 L ed 679, 24 S Ct 436.

Honesty

We were pressed in argument with the contention . . . that "great difficulties will arise in the administration of bankruptcy if the Court is to decide according to what it considers high-minded without regard to law or equity." I think that these difficulties are exaggerated. But while one may agree that opinions as to rules of honesty differ, the difficulty of recognizing honesty when she appears, affords no adequate reason for discarding her altogether. The advantages of maintaining a high standard of commercial morality in my judgment far outweigh the suggested inconveniences of administration.

> ATKIN, L.J., *Re Thellusson, ex parte Abdy* [1919] 2 K.B. 735, 764.

He kept his innocency when others let theirs go; . . . which raises his merit to a higher pitch. For to be honest when everybody is honest, when honesty is in fashion and is trump, as I may say, is nothing so meritorious; but to stand alone in the breach—to own honesty when others dare not to do it, cannot be sufficiently applauded, nor sufficiently rewarded.

> HOLLIS, M.P., *Speech in behalf of Sir Ranulphe Crew,* 2 pt. 2 Rushworth, *Hist. Coll.* App. 267. (Chief Justice Crew was removed from office for denying the legality of forced loans by Charles I.)

Horse Racing

For a generation or more betting at horse races was unlawful. After this prolonged burst of morality the Legislature suddenly discovered the need of "improving the breed of horses." . . . In a backhanded way this legislation restored race track betting by removing the criminal penalties. But let no one suspect that our best citizens repair to Belmont Park and other nearby tracts for the purpose of betting or gambling. Perish the thought, for their minds rest on higher things. Improving the breed of horses is their aim, and their conversation, aside from formal greetings, deals solely with sires and dams, foals and fillies, blood lines, consanguinity and inherited characteristics. These things a judge must believe, even at the risk of being chided as naive, because they are contemporary America.

> BONYNGE, J., *Reed v Littleton,* 159 Misc (N.Y.) 853, 855 (1936).

The bond . . . was given, not to pay racing debts, but to avoid the consequences of not having paid them.

> LORD ROMILLY, M.R., *Bubb v Yelverton* (1870) L.R. 9 Eq. 471, 474.

Husband and Wife

The common law does not regulate the form of agreements between spouses. Their promises are not sealed with seals and sealing wax. The consideration that really obtains for them is that natural love and affection which counts for so little in these cold Courts.

> ATKIN, L.J., *Balfour v Balfour* [1919] 2 K.B. 571, 579.

Draw up the papers, lawyer, and make 'em good and
  stout,
For things at home are crossways, and Betsy and I are
  out.

> WILL CARLETON, *Betsy and I Are Out; Farm Ballads* (1878).

The cock swan is an emblem or representation of an affectionate and true husband to his wife above all other fowls; for the cock swan holdeth himself to one female only, and for this cause nature hath conferred on him a gift beyond all others; that is, to die so joyfully, that he sings sweetly when he dies.

> COKE, *Case of Swans* (1592) 7 Rep. 17.

[You are] "the more guilty of the two in the eye of the law; for the law supposes that your wife acts under your direction." "If the law supposes that," said Mr. Bumble, squeezing his hat emphatically in both hands, "the law is a ass—a idiot. If that's the eye of the law, the law's a bachelor; and the worst I wish the law is, that his eye may be opened by experience."

CHARLES DICKENS, *Oliver Twist,* ch. 51.

While the husband is still declared by statute to be the head of the family, he, like the King of England, is largely a figurehead.

HINES, J., *Curtis v Ashworth,* 165 Ga 782, 787 (1928).

For sixty years she made life poetry for me.

OLIVER WENDELL HOLMES, 2 *Holmes-Pollock Letters* 243 (May 24, 1929).

Mrs. Barber is the kind of a wife who stands by her husband in all the troubles he would not have had if he had not married her.

JAYNE, V.C., *Bondarchuk v Barber,* 135 N.J. Eq. 334 (1944).

With regard to compensatory damages—and with due regard for the priceless gift of a good wife's affections, —we believe that when a man discovers that another man has alienated his wife's affections he has not lost something; he has merely learned something.

CHARLES A. O'NIELL, Chief Justice, Sup. Ct. Louisiana, *Address,* 57 N.Y.S.B.Rep. 585, 591 (1934).

When people understand that they must live together,
except for a very few reasons known to the law, they
learn to soften by mutual accommodation that yoke which
they know they cannot shake off; they become good husbands and good wives from the necessity of remaining husbands and wives; for necessity is a powerful master in
teaching the duties which it imposes. If it were once understood, that upon mutual disgust married persons might be
legally separated, many couples who now pass through
the world with mutual comfort, with attention to their
common offspring and to the moral order of civil society,
might have been at this moment living in a state of mutual
unkindness, in a state of estrangement from their common
offspring, and in a state of the most licentious and unre-
served immorality. In this case, as in many others, the
happiness of some individuals must be sacrificed to the
greater and more general good.

SCOTT, J., *Evans v Evans* (1790) 1 Hag. Con. 35, 36.

Petruchio:

I will be master of what is mine own.
She is my goods, my chattels; she is my house,
My household stuff, my field, my barn,
My horse, my ox, my ass, my anything.

SHAKESPEARE, *Taming of the Shrew*, Act 3, scene 2.

The husband will be accounted the common enemy; and
the mercer and the gallant will unite with the wife, and
they will combine their strength against the husband.

Wives will be their own carvers, and, like hawks, will
fly abroad and find their own prey.

It shall be left to the pleasure of a London jury to dress my wife in such apparel as they think proper.

> WYNDHAM, J., *Manby v Scott,* (K.B. 1662–3) 1 Sid. 109, 122.
> (These are the consequences which would ensue if wives could pledge their husband's credit without authority).

Ideals

It often is a merit of an ideal to be unattainable.   Its being so keeps forever before us something more to be done, and saves us from the ennui of a monotonous perfection.

> HOLMES, J., *Law in Science and Science in Law,* 12 Harv. L.R. 443, 463 (1899); Coll. Leg. Pap. 242.

Idleness

Idleness, the mother of all vice and weakness.

> COKE, 10 Rep. *Preface.*

Imitation

Customs and law, in every place
Like a disease, an heirloom dread,
Still trace their curse from race to race,
And furtively abroad they spread.
To nonsense, reason's self they turn;
Beneficence becomes a pest;
Woe unto thee, thou art a grandson born!
As for the law, born with us, unexpressed
That law, alas, none careth to discern.

> GOETHE, *Faust,* I, 4, 449.

I am immensely struck with the blind imitativeness of man when I see how a doctrine, a discrimination, even a phrase, will run in a year or two over the whole English-speaking world.

OLIVER WENDELL HOLMES, *Law in Science — Science in Law,* 12 Harv. L.R. 443, 455 (1899).

Impeachment

Behold, my desire is, . . . that mine adversary had written a book.

Job 31:35.

Imprisonment

No restraint be it never so little, but is imprisonment, and foreign employment is a kind of honorable banishment.

COKE, referring to King James' appointment of him to serve on a commission to inquire into conditions in Ireland. See 11 D.N.B. 237.

Incitement

Every idea is an incitement. It offers itself for belief, and if believed it is acted on unless some other belief outweighs it, or some failure of energy stifles the movement at its birth. The only difference between the expression of an opinion and an incitement in the narrower sense is the speaker's enthusiasm for the result.

HOLMES, J., dissenting, *Gitlow v New York* (1925) 268 US 652, 673, 69 L ed 1138, 1149, 45 S Ct 625.

Independence

American independence was then and there born. . . .
Then and there was the first scene of the first act of opposition to the arbitrary claims of Great Britain. Then and
there the child Independence was born. In fifteen years,
namely in 1776, he grew up to manhood, and declared
himself free.

> JOHN ADAMS, *Letter to William Tudor, Mar. 29, 1817.* See 10
> *Works* 247, or Tudor, *Life of Otis* 60 (1823). (Referring
> to James Otis' argument in court against the validity of the
> Writs of Assistance, Boston, 1761.)

I sat by its cradle,—I followed its hearse.

> HENRY GRATTAN, referring to the rise of Irish independence in
> 1782 and its fall twenty years later. BROUGHAM, *Statesmen
> of the Time of George III: Grattan.*

Index

A being engaged in looking through an index came to
the following entry: "Best (Mr. Justice), his great mind."
Turning to the page cited he found the following: "Mr.
Justice Best said he had a great mind to commit the man
for trial."

> Probably apocryphal. Attributed to various authors of law books.

One may recollect generally that certain thoughts or facts
are to be found in a certain book; but without a good
Index such a recollection may hardly be more available
than that of the cabin-boy, who knew where the ship's
tea-kettle was, because he saw it fall overboard. In truth,

a very large part of every man's reading falls overboard, and unless he has good Indexes he will never find it again.

> HORACE BINNEY, *Letter, February 20, 1866 to S. Austin Allibone.*

So essential did I consider an Index to be to every book, that I proposed to bring a Bill into parliament to deprive an author who publishes a book without an Index of the privilege of copyright; and moreover, to subject him, for his offence, to a pecuniary penalty.

> LORD CAMPBELL, 3 *Lives of the Chief Justices: Preface.*

Serjeant Waller was called Index; and people went for his opinion, only to bring away a list of quotations to assist other counsel that understood better.

> NORTH, 1 *Life of Lord Keeper Guilford* 24 (1826).

Sir Frederick Pollock used to say that a man who would publish a book without an index ought to be banished ten miles beyond Hell where the Devil himself could not go because of the stinging nettles.

> ROSCOE POUND, *Book Review,* 60 Yale L.J. 200 (1951).

Indictment

The indictment had never been clearly expressed,
And it seemed that the Snark had begun
And had spoken three hours before anyone guessed
What the pig was supposed to have done.

> LEWIS CARROLL, *Hunting of the Snark: The Barrister's Dream.*

The clerk then read the indictment, which was in the usual form. It charged Laura Hawkins, in effect, with the premeditated murder of George Selby, by shooting him with a pistol, with a revolver, shotgun, rifle, repeater, breech-loader, cannon, six-shooter, with a gun, or some other weapon; with killing him with a slung-shot, a bludgeon, carving knife, bowie-knife, pen-knife, rolling-pin, car-hook, dagger, hairpin, with a hammer, with a screwdriver, with a nail, and with all other weapons and utensils whatsoever, at the Southern Hotel and in all other hotels and places wheresoever, on the thirteenth day of March and all others days of the Christian era whensoever.

MARK TWAIN, *The Gilded Age,* v. 2, ch. 23.

Inference

Inference is never certainty, but it may be plain enough to justify a finding of fact.

CROUCH, J., *Tartora v State,* 269 N.Y. 167, 170 (1935).

The law has no mandamus to the logical faculty; it orders nobody to draw inferences.

JAMES BRADLEY THAYER, *Preliminary Treatise on Evidence* 314 (1898).

Injunction

I will grant no injunction merely upon priority of suit; . . . I do not mean to make it a matter of an horse racing or posting who shall be first at Westminster Hall.

BACON, *Speech, May 7, 1617,* on taking his seat in Chancery as Lord Keeper.

I care not who makes th' laws iv a nation iv I can get out an injunction.

> FINLEY PETER DUNNE, *Mr. Dooley's Philosophy: Casual Observations.*

The injunction which we sustain is "permanent" only for the temporary period for which it may last.

> FRANKFURTER, J., *Milk Wagon Drivers Union v Meadowmoor Dairies* (1941) 312 US 287, 298, 85 L ed 836, 844, 61 S Ct 552, 132 ALR 1200.

Innovation

It would be an unsound fancy and self-contradictory to expect that things which have never yet been done can be done except by means which have never yet been tried.

> BACON, *Novum Organum: Aph. 6.*

Inns of Court

To the noblest Nourceries of Humanity, and Liberty, in the Kingdome: The Innes of Court.

> BEN JONSON, *Every Man out of His Humour: Dedication.*

Cheerful Crown-office Row (place of my kindly engendure) . . . a man would give something to have been born in such places.

> CHARLES LAMB, *Old Benchers of the Inner Temple.*

Four little winged marble boys used to play their virgin fancies, spouting out ever fresh streams from their innocent-wanton lips, in the square of Lincoln's inn, when I was no bigger than they were figured. They are gone, and the spring closed up. The fashion, they tell me, is gone by, and these things are esteemed childish. Why not then gratify children by letting them stand? Lawyers, I suppose, were children once.

    CHARLES LAMB, *ibid.*

Gray's Inn for walks,
Lincoln's Inn for a wall,
The Inner Temple for a garden
And the Middle for a hall.

    Proverb. FULLER, *Worthies: London* (1662).

The Inner for a Rich Man,
The Middle for a Poor,
Lincoln's for a parchmenter,
And Gray's for the Law.

    Anon.

Those bricky towres,
The which on Themmes brode aged backe doe ryde,
Where now the studious lawyers have their bowers,
There whylome wont the Templar Knights to byde,
Till they decayd through pride.

    EDMUND SPENSER, *Prothalamion.*

I don't know whether the student of law permits himself the refreshment of enthusiam, or indulges in poetical reminiscences as he passes by historical chambers, and says, "Yonder Eldon lived—upon this site Coke mused upon Littleton—here Chitty toiled—here Barnwell and Alderson joined in their famous labors—here Byles composed his great work upon bills, and Smith compiled his immortal leading cases . . ." but the man of letters can't but love the place which has been inhabited by so many of his brethren, or peopled by their creations as real to us at this day as the authors whose children they were—and Sir Roger de Coverley walking in the Temple Garden, and discoursing with Mr. Spectator about the beauties in hoops and patches who are sauntering over the grass, is just as lively a figure to me as old Samuel Johnson rolling through the fog with the Scotch gentleman at his heels.

THACKERAY, *Pendennis*, ch. 29.

Insanity

Miserliness is not necessarily the hallmark of insanity, and is more likely to indicate the reverse.

BRUNE, C.J., *Sellers v Qualls*, 206 Md 58, 65 (1954).

In other cases, reason is not driven from her seat, but distraction sits down upon it along with her, holds her trembling upon it, and frightens her from her propriety.

THOMAS ERSKINE, arguendo, *Trial of James Hatfield* (1800). 4 Erskine's *Speeches* 176. (High, ed.)

Doth not the idiot eat? Doth not the idiot drink? Doth not the idiot know his father and his mother? He does all this because he is a man. Doth he not smile and weep? And think you he smiles and weeps for nothing? He smiles and weeps because he is moved by human joys and sorrows, and exercises his reason, however imperfectly. Hath not the idiot anger, rage, revenge? Take from him his food, and he will stamp his feet and throw his chains in your face. Think you he does this for nothing? He does it all because he is a man, and because, however imperfectly, he exercises his reason.

WILLIAM H. SEWARD, arguendo, in Freeman Case, Auburn, New York, 1846.

If then it is proved, to the satisfaction of the jury, that the mind of the accused was in a diseased and unsound state, the question will be, whether the disease existed to so high a degree, that for the time being it overwhelmed the reason, conscience, and judgment, and whether the prisoner, in committing the homicide, acted from an irresistible and uncontrollable impulse: If so, then the act was not of a voluntary agent, but the involuntary act of the body, without the concurrence of a mind directing it.

> SHAW, C.J., *Commonwealth v Rogers,* 48 Mass (7 Met.) 500, 502 (1844).

To establish a defence on the ground of insanity, it must be clearly proved that, at the time of the committing of the act, the party accused was labouring under such a defect of reason, from disease of the mind, as not to know the nature and quality of the act he was doing; or, if he did know it, that he did not know he was doing what was wrong.

> TINDAL, C.J., *M'Naghten's Case* (1943) 10 Cl. & F. 200, 210. (The House of Lords had requested the judges to define criminal insanity.)

Insurance

The attempted distinction between accidental results and accidental means will plunge this branch of the law into a Serbonian Bog.

> CARDOZO, J., *Landress v Phoenix Mut. Ins. Co.* (1934) 291 US 491, 499, 78 L ed 934, 938, 54 S Ct 461, 90 ALR 1382. See Milton, *Paradise Lost,* bk 2, 1. 592: A gulf profound, as that Serbonian bog Betwixt Damiata and Mount Casius old, Where armies whole have sunk.

253

Intent

The state of a man's mind is as much a fact as the state of his digestion.

> BOWEN, L.J., *Edgington v Fitzmaurice* (1885) 29 Ch. D. 459, 483.

Let me end with a story about Robert Browning. Toward the close of his life he received a letter from Professor Hiram Corson of Cornell, asking whether one of his early obscure poems meant what Corson supposed it did. Browning replied, "I didn't mean that when I wrote it, but I mean it now."

> CHAFEE, *Disorderly Conduct of Words,* 41 Columbia Law Rev, 381, 404.

Even a dog distinguishes between being stumbled over and being kicked.

> OLIVER WENDELL HOLMES, *Common Law* 3 (1881).

Detached reflection cannot be demanded in the presence of an uplifted knife.

> HOLMES, J., *Brown v United States* (1921) 256 US 335, 343, 65 L ed 961, 963, 41 S Ct 501, 18 ALR 1276.

Environment illuminates the meaning of acts, as context does that of words.

> JACKSON, J., *Cramer v United States* (1945) 325 US 1, 33, 89 L ed 1441, 1460, 65 S Ct 918.

In that case the voices of infallibility, by a narrow majority, held that though a misrepresentation of fact may

254

bind a man, a mere falsified statement of his future intention does not. We were told by Mr. Denning that the Law Reform Committee has had the audacity to propose the legislative abolition of this refinement, but for us it remains binding.

> MACKINNIN, L.J., *Salisbury v Gilmore* [1942] 2 K.B. 38, 51. ("the voices of infallibility" are those of the House of Lords.)

There is no surer way to find out what parties meant, than to see what they have done.

> SWAYNE, J., *Brooklyn Ins. Co. v Dutcher* (1877) 95 US 269, 273, 24 L ed 410, 412.

Interest

Interest is a great rascal; but is not an absolute reprobate. Its doom is not perdition at all events. It has a chance of salvation. It is not obliged to commit perjury.

> BLECKLEY, J., *Davis v Central R.R.,* 60 Ga 329, 333 (1878).

International Law

International law, or the law that governs between states, has at times, like the common law within states, a twilight existence during which it is hardly distinguishable from morality or justice, till at length the imprimatur of a court attest its jural quality.

> CARDOZO, J., *New Jersey v Delaware* (1934) 291 US 361, 383, 78 L ed 847, 858, 54 S Ct 407.

Interpretation

It was by no means uncommon, where the legislature had a particular object in view in making a particular statute, to extend the enactments beyond the immediate and original object, and apply it to other matter suggested by it.

ABBOTT, C.J., *Clarke v Burdett* (1819) 2 Stark 504, 505.

One half of the English language is interpreted by the context.

ALDERSON, B., *Dellevene v Percer* (1841) 9 Dowl. 244, 245.

I know of only one authority which might justify the suggested method of construction: " 'When I use a word,' Humpty Dumpty said in rather a scornful tone, 'it means just what I choose it to mean, neither more nor less.' 'The question is,' said Alice, 'whether you can make words mean so many different things.' 'The question is,' said Humpty Dumpty, 'which is to be master—that's all' ".

LORD ATKIN, *Liversidge v Anderson* [1942] A.C. 206, 245. Quoting Carroll, *Through the Looking Glass,* ch. 6.

It is never the law itself that is in the wrong; it is always some wicked interpreter of the law that has corrupted and abused it.

JEREMY BENTHAM, *Fragment on Government, Preface,* 1 Works 231.

Does not everybody see from hence, that you must first examine the law before you can apply the rule of construction? For the law must not be bent by the con-
256

struction, but that must be adapted to the spirit and sense
of the law.

> LORD CAMDEN, C.J., *Entick v Carrington* (1765) 19 How. St.
> Tr. 1029, 1060.

"If there's no meaning in it," said the King, "that saves
a world of trouble, you know, as we needn't try to find
any."

> LEWIS CARROLL, *Alice in Wonderland,* ch. 12.

And it was resolved by them, that for the sure and
true interpretation of all statutes . . . four things are to
be discerned and considered: 1st, What was the common
law before the making of the act; 2nd, What was the mischief and defect for which the common law did not provide;
3rd, What remedy the parliament hath resolved and appointed to cure the disease of the commonwealth; and 4th,
The true reason of the remedy; and then the office of all
the judges is always to make such construction as shall
suppress the mischief, and advance the remedy, and to suppress subtle inventions and evasions for continuance of the
mischief, and *pro privato commodo,* and to add force and
life to the cure and remedy according to the true intent of
the makers of the act *pro bono publico.*

> COKE, *Heydon's Case* (1584) 3 Rep. 7a, 7b (Known as the
> "mischief rule.")

The policy as well as the letter of the law is a guide to
decision.

> DOUGLAS, J., *Markham v Cabell* (1945) 326 US 404, 409, 90
> L ed 165, 168, 66 S Ct 193.

[Legal Quotations]—17

The notion that because the words of a statute are plain, its meaning is also plain, is merely pernicious oversimplification.

> FRANKFURTER, J., *United States v Monia* (1943) 317 US 424, 431, 87 L ed 376, 382, 63 S Ct 409.

In law also the emphasis makes the song.

> FRANKFURTER, J., *Bethlehem Steel Co. v New York State Labor Relations Board* (1947) 330 US 767, 780, 91 L ed 1234, 1249, 67 S Ct 1026.

But this is a case for applying the canon of construction of the wag who said, when the legislative history is doubtful, go to the statute.

> FRANKFURTER, J., *Greenwood v United States* (1956) 350 US 366, 374, 100 L ed 412, 419, 76 S Ct 410.

If Congress chooses by appropriate means for expressing its purpose to use language with an unlikely and even an odd meaning, it is not for this Court to frustrate its purpose. The Court's task is to construe not English but congressional English. Our problem is not what do ordinary English words mean, but what did Congress mean them to mean.

> FRANKFURTER, J., dissenting, *Commissioner v Acker* (1959) 361 US 87, 94, 4 L ed 2d 127, 133, 80 S Ct 144.

Rules of statutory construction are to be resorted to when there is a doubt, ambiguity, or uncertainty, and they are never to be used to create doubt, but only to remove it.

> GARDNER, J., *Helvering v Northwestern Nat. Bank*, 89 F.2d 553, 556 (1937).

The difficulties of so-called interpretation arise when the Legislature has had no meaning at all; when the question which is raised on the statute never occurred to it; when what the judges have to do is, not to determine what the Legislature did mean on a point which was present to its mind, but to guess what it would have intended on a point not present to its mind, if the point had been present.

> JOHN CHIPMAN GRAY, *Nature and Sources of the Law: Statutes.* (1921 ed. p. 173).

I have more than once had occasion to say that in construing a statute I believe the worst person to construe it is the person who is responsible for its drafting.   He is very much disposed to confuse what he intended to do with the effect of the language which in fact has been employed.

> LORD HALSBURY, L.C., *Hilder v Dexter* [1902] A.C. 474, 477. (Lord Halsbury was himself responsible for drafting the statute.)

The words he [a judge] must construe are empty vessels into which he can pour nearly anything he will.

> LEARNED HAND, *Sources of Tolerance,* 79 Univ. of Pa. L. Rev. 1, 12 (1930).   Also in Hand, *Spirit of Liberty* (Dilliard, ed.) 81.

The meaning of a sentence may be more than that of the separate words, as a melody is more than the notes, and no degree of particularity can ever obviate recourse to the setting in which all appear, and which all collectively create.

> L. HAND, J., *Helvering v Gregory,* 69 F.2d 809, 810 (1934).

There is no surer guide in the interpretation of a statute than its purpose when that is sufficiently disclosed; nor any surer mark of oversolicitude for the letter than to wince at carrying out that purpose because the words do not formally quite match with it.

> L. HAND, J., *Federal Deposit Ins. Corp. v Tremaine*, 133 F.2d 827, 830 (1943).

It is one of the surest indexes of a mature and developed jurisprudence not to make a fortress out of the dictionary; but to remember that statutes always have some purpose or object to accomplish whose sympathetic and imaginative discovery is the surest guide to their meaning.

> L. HAND, J., *Cabell v Markham*, 148 F.2d 737, 739 (1945).

Interpretation is the art of proliferating a purpose which is meant to cover many occasions so that it shall be best realized upon the occasion in question.

> L. HAND, J., *Brooklyn National Corp. v Commissioner,* 157 F.2d 450, 451 (1946).

Do not gloss the Statute; we understand it better than you do, for we made it.

> HENGHAM, C.J., Y.B. 33-35 Edw. I (Rolls Ser.) 83 (1305).

Whoever hath an absolute authority to interpret any written or spoken laws, it is he who is truly the lawgiver to all intents and purposes, and not the person who first wrote or spoke them.

> BENJAMIN HOADLY, *Sermon, March 31, 1717.*

We do not inquire what the legislature meant; we ask only what the statute means.

> OLIVER WENDELL HOLMES, *Theory of Legal Interpretation,* 12 Harv. L. Rev. 417, 419 (1899).

The Legislature has the power to decide what the policy of the law shall be, and if it has intimated its will, however indirectly, that will should be recognized and obeyed. The major premise of the conclusion expressed in a statute, the change of policy that induces the enactment, may not be set out in terms, but it is not an adequate discharge of duty for courts to say: We see what you are driving at, but you have not said it, and therefore we shall go on as before.

HOLMES. J., *Johnson v United States,* 163 Fed. 30, 32 (1908).

The meaning of a sentence is to be felt rather than proved.

HOLMES, J., *United States v Johnson* (1911) 221 US 488, 496, 55 L ed 823, 826, 31 S Ct 627.

Courts are apt to err by sticking too closely to the words of a law where those words import a policy that goes beyond them.

HOLMES, J., dissenting, *Olmstead v United States* (1928) 277 US 438, 469, 72 L ed 944, 952, 48 S Ct 564, 66 ALR 376.

We agree to all the generalities about not supplying criminal laws with what they omit, but there is no canon against using common sense in construing laws as saying what they obviously mean.

HOLMES, J., *Roschen v Ward* (1929) 279 US 337, 339, 73 L ed 722, 728, 49 S Ct 336.

If ever we are justified in reading a statute, not narrowly as through a keyhole, but in the broad light of the evils it aimed at and the good it hoped for, it is here.

JACKSON, J., *United States ex rel Marcus v Hess* (1943) 317 US 537, 557, 87 L ed 443, 456, 63 S Ct 379.

261

I should concur in this result more readily if the Court could reach it by analysis of the statute instead of by psychoanalysis of Congress.

> JACKSON, J., concurring, *United States v Public Utilities Com.* (1953) 345 US 295, 319, 97 L ed 1020, 1089, 73 S Ct 706.

Laws are made for men of ordinary understanding, and should therefore, be construed by the ordinary rules of common sense. Their meaning is not to be sought for in metaphysical subtleties, which may make anything mean everything or nothing at pleasure.

> THOMAS JEFFERSON, *Letter to William Johnson, June 12, 1823.*

I should not find any great difficulty in construing Acts of Parliament if I had no opinions to assist me.

> SIR GEORGE JESSEL. *Report of Select Committee, 1875: To Improve Manner and Language of Current Legislation, question 1202.*

Where the mind labors to discover the design of the legislature, it seizes everything from which aid can be derived.

> MARSHALL, C.J., *United States v Fisher* (1805, US) 2 Cranch 358, 386, 2 L ed 304, 313.

All laws are promulgated for this end, that every man may know his duty; and, therefore, the plainest and most obvious sense of the words is that which must be put upon them.

> SIR THOMAS MORE, *Utopia,* bk 2.

It is a very useful rule in the construction of a statute, to adhere to the ordinary meaning of the words used, and

262

to the grammatical construction, unless that is at variance with the intention of the legislature, to be collected from the statute itself, or leads to any manifest absurdity or repugnance, in which case the language may be varied or modified, so as to avoid such inconvenience, but no further.

> PARKE, B., *Becke v Smith* [1836] 2 M. & W. 191, 195. Known as the "Golden Rule."

The House of Lords is an infallible interpreter of the law. A batsman, who, as he said, had been struck on the shoulder by a ball, remonstrated against a ruling of l.b.w.; but the wicket-keeper met his protest by the remark: "It disna' maitter if the ba' hit yer neb; if the umpire says yer oot yer oot." Accordingly, if the House of Lords says "this is the proper interpretation of the statute," then it is the proper interpretation. The House of Lords has a perfect legal mind. Learned Lords may come or go, but the House of Lords never makes a mistake. That the House of Lords should make a mistake is just as unthinkable as that Colonel Bogey should be bunkered twice and take 8 to the hole. Occasionally to some of us two decisions of the House of Lords may seem inconsistent. But that is only a seeming. It is our frail vision that is at fault.

> LORD SANDS, *Assessor for Aberdeen v Collie,* 1932 S.C. 304, 311, 312.

Common Sense, as here applied, is a term of the pumpkin order. It is round, smooth, and fair to view—but hollow.

> STROUD, *Judicial Dictionary (1903, 2nd ed) Introductory Chapter.*

The sense and meaning of an Act of Parliament must be collectéd from what it says when passed into a law;

and not from the history of changes it underwent in the house where it took its rise. That history is not known to the other house, or to the Sovereign.

WILLES, J., *Millar v Taylor* (1769) 4 Burr. 2303, 2332.

Interpretation (Constitutional)

The Court's justification for consulting its own notions rather than following the original meaning of the Constitution, as I would, apparently is based on the belief of the majority of the Court that for this Court to be bound by the original meaning of the Constitution is an intolerable and debilitating evil; that our Constitution should not be "shackled to the political theory of a particular era," and that to save the country from the original Constitution the Court must have constant power to renew it and keep it abreast with this Court's more enlightened theories of what is best for our society.

BLACK, J., dissenting, *Harper v Virginia State Board of Elections* (1966) 383 US 663, 677, 16 L ed 2d 169, 178, 86 S Ct 1079.

He protested, he said, against construing this Constitution, as one would a bill of indictment.

Referring to Henry Clay, *Debate on Internal Improvements,* 31 Annals of Congress 1166 (1818).

Th' constitootion iv th' United States is applicable on'y in such cases as it is applied to on account iv its applicability.

FINLEY PETER DUNNE, *Mr. Dooley's Philosophy: President's Message.*

264

The provisions of the Constitution are not mathematical formulas having their essence in their form; they are organic living institutions transplanted from English soil. Their significance is vital not formal; it is to be gathered not simply by taking the words and a dictionary, but by considering their origin and the line of their growth.

> HOLMES, J., *Gompers v United States* (1914) 233 US 604, 610, 58 L ed 1115, 1120, 34 S Ct 693.

The interpretation of constitutional principles must not be too literal. We must remember that the machinery of government would not work if it were not allowed a little play in its joints.

> HOLMES, J., *Bain Peanut Co. v Pinson* (1931) 282 US 499, 501, 75 L ed 482, 491, 51 S Ct 228.

Far more important to the development of the country, than the decisions holding acts of Congress to be invalid, have been those in which the authority of Congress has been sustained and adequate national power to meet the necessities of a growing country has been found to exist within constitutional limitations.

> CHARLES EVANS HUGHES, *The Supreme Court of the United States* (1928) 96.

If by the statement that what the Constitution meant at the time of its adoption it means to-day, it is intended to say that the great clauses of the Constitution must be confined to the interpretation which the framers, with the conditions and outlook of their time, would have placed upon them, the statement carries its own refutation.

> HUGHES, C.J., *Home Bldg. & L. Asso. v Blaisdell* (1934) 290 US 398, 442, 78 L ed 413, 431, 54 S Ct 231, 88 ALR 1481.

265

Our peculiar security is in the possession of a written Constitution.   Let us not make it a blank paper by construction.

THOMAS JEFFERSON, *Letter to Wilson C. Nicholas, Sept. 7, 1803.*

The Constitution, on this hypothesis, is a mere thing of wax in the hands of the judiciary, which they may twist and shape into any form they please. . . .   My construction of the Constitution is very different from that you quote.   It is that each department is truly independent of the others and has an equal right to decide for itself what is the meaning of the Constitution in the cases submitted to its action.

THOMAS JEFFERSON, *Letter to Spencer Roane, Sept. 6, 1819.*

When an act of Congress is appropriately challenged in the courts as not conforming to the constitutional mandate the judicial branch of the Government has only one duty, —to lay the article of the Constitution which is invoked beside the statute which is challenged and to decide whether the latter squares with the former.

ROBERTS, J., *United States v Butler* (1936) 297 US 1, 62, 80 L ed 477, 486, 56 S Ct 312, 102 ALR 914.

Regulations, the wisdom, necessity and validity of which, as applied to existing conditions, are so apparent that they are now uniformly sustained, a century ago, or even half a century ago, probably would have been rejected as arbitrary and oppressive. . . .   And in this there is no inconsistency, for while the meaning of constitutional guaranties never varies, the scope of their application must expand or contract to meet the new and different conditions which are constantly coming within the field of their

266

operation.   In a changing world, it is impossible that it should be otherwise.

> SUTHERLAND, J., *Euclid v Ambler Realty Co.* (1926) 272 US 365, 387, 71 L ed 303, 310, 47 S Ct 114, 54 ALR 1016.

A provision of the Constitution . . . does not mean one thing at one time and an entirely different thing at another time.

> SUTHERLAND, J., dissenting *Home Bldg. & L. Asso. v Blaisdell* (1934) 290 US 398, 448, 78 L ed 413, 434, 54 S Ct 231, 88 ALR 1481.

If the provisions of the Constitution be not upheld when they pinch as well as when they comfort, they may as well be abandoned.

> SUTHERLAND, J., dissenting *Home Bldg. & L. Asso. v Blaisdell* (1934) 290 US 398, 483, 78 L ed 413, 452, 54 S Ct 231, 88 ALR 1481.

I . . . am quite willing that it be regarded hereafter as the law of this court, that its opinion upon the construction of the Constitution is always open to discussion when it is supposed to have been founded in error, and that its judicial authority should hereafter depend altogether on the force of the reasoning by which it is supported.

> TANEY, C.J., dissenting, *Passenger Cases* (1849, US) 7 How 283, 470, 12 L ed 702, 781.

Intoxication

A drunken man is as much entitled to a safe street, as a sober one, and much more in need of it.

> HEYDENFELDT, J., *Robinson v Pioche*, 5 Cal 460, 461 (1855).

There is in all men a demand for the superlative, so much so that the poor devil who has no other way of reaching it attains it by getting drunk.

> OLIVER WENDELL HOLMES, *Natural Law,* 32 Harv. L.R. 40 (1918).

Investigation

It is the proper duty of a representative body to look diligently into every affair of government and to talk much about what it sees. It is meant to be the eyes and the voice, and to embody the wisdom and will of its constituents. Unless Congress have and use every means of acquainting itself with the acts and the disposition of the administrative agents of the government, the country must be helpless to learn how it is being served; and unless Congress both scrutinize these things and sift them by every form of discussion, the country must remain in embarrassing, crippling ignorance of the very affairs which it is most important that it should understand and direct. The informing function of Congress should be preferred even to its legislative function.

> WOODROW WILSON, *Congressional Government* 303 (1885).

Invitee

A road is not an invitation to leave it elsewhere than at its end.

> HOLMES, J., *United Zinc & Chemical Co. v Britt* (1922) 258 US 268, 276, 66 L ed 615, 618, 42 S Ct 299, 36 ALR 28.

There is no ground for the argument that the plaintiff was invited upon the tracks. Temptation is not always invitation.

> HOLMES, J., *Erie R. Co. v Hilt* (1918) 247 US 97, 101, 62 L ed 1003, 1004, 38 S Ct 435.

Jest

As for jest, there be certain things which ought to be privileged from it; namely, religion, matters of state, great persons, any man's present business of importance, and any case that deserveth pity.

> BACON, *Essays: Of Discourse.*

Jew

He died in a concentration camp of an incurable blood infection—a Jewish grandmother.

> JOSEPH GROSS, 11 Shingle 79 (1948).

Judge

I thought myself as sober as a judge.

> Anon., *Terence Made English* (1694) 82.

Lewis, all the while, either by the strength of his brain or flinching his glass, kept himself sober as a judge.

> JOHN ARBUTHNOT, *Law is a Bottomless Pit (History of John Bull)* Pt 3, ch. 6 (1712).

I am as sober as a judge.

HENRY FIELDING, *Don Quixote in England,* III, 14.

Let them be lions, but yet lions under the throne.

BACON, *Essays: Of Judicature.*

The twelve Judges of the realm are as the twelve lions under Salomon's throne: they must be lions, but yet lions under the throne.

BACON, *Speech, 1617.* On the occasion of Justice Hutton being sworn in as judge of the Common Pleas.

Upon his moral faculties it [publicity] acts as a check, restraining him from active partiality and improbity in every shape: upon his intellectual faculties it acts as a spur, urging him to that habit of unremitting exertion, without which his attention can never be kept up to the pitch of his duty.

JEREMY BENTHAM, *Rationale of Judicial Evidence,* bk 2, ch. 10, sec. 2. See 6 *Works* (1843 Bowring ed.) 355.

And there was at that time Deborra, a prophetess, the wife of Lapidoth, who judged the people.

Judges 4:4.

And he (Samuel) went every year about to Bethel, and Galgal, and Masphath, and he judged Israel in the aforesaid places.

1 Kings 7:16.

They are the depositaries of the laws; the living oracles, who must decide in all cases of doubt, and who are bound by an oath to decide according to the law of the land.

> BLACKSTONE, *Commentaries*, bk 1, 69.

Conscious as we are of one another's many imperfections.

> LORD BOWEN. (On the opening of the Royal Courts in 1882 the judges were preparing an address to Queen Victoria. It began: "Conscious as we are of our manifold defects." Jessel objected and Bowen suggested the above alternative.)

Laws and customs . . . are often abusively perverted by the foolish and unlearned who ascend the judgment seat before they have learnt the laws.

> BRACTON, *De Legibus et Consuetudinibus Angliae*, f. 1 (v. 1, p. 5 Twiss ed. Rolls ser. No. 70).

The great tides and currents which engulf the rest of men, do not turn aside in their course, and pass the judges by.

> BENJAMIN N. CARDOZO, *Nature of the Judicial Process* 168 (1921).

It may truly be said that the magistrate is the speaking law, and the law a silent magistrate. *(Vere dici potest, magistratum legem esse loquentem, legem autem mutum magistratum.)*

> CICERO, *De Legibus*, III, i.

The law is the rule, but it is mute. The king judgeth by his judges, and they are the speaking law.

> COKE, *First Institute* 130. (Generally quoted: The judges are the speaking law.)

271

Anyone who will may satisfy himself, by taking down a volume of reports, old or new, that any given Judge will run in a particular direction if he fairly can.

LORD DARLING, *Scintillae Juris: Of Judges.*

"If I had me job to pick out," said Mr. Dooley, "I'd be a judge. I've looked over all th' others an that's the on'y wan that suits. I have th' judicyal timperamint. I hate wurruk."

FINLEY PETER DUNNE, *Observations by Mr. Dooley: The Law's Delays.*

I would ye should know that the Justices of England sit not in the King's courts above iij houres in a day, that is so say, from viij of the clock in the forenoone til xi, complete. In the afternoones those courts are not holden or kept. But the suters then resort to the perusing of their writings and elsewhere consulting with the Serjeants at law and other their counsaylors. Wherefore the Justices, after they have taken their refection, doe passe and bestow all the residue of the day in the study of the lawes, in reading of holy scripture and using other kind of contemplation at their pleasure. So that their life may seem more contemplative than active. And thus doe they lead a quiet life, discharged of all worldly cares and troubles.

SIR JOHN FORTESCUE, *De Laudibus Legum Angliae,* ch. 51.

And that Nisi Prius nuisance, who just now is rather rife,
The Judicial Humorist—I've got him on the list!
All funny fellows, comic men, and clowns of private life—
They'd none of 'em be missed—they'd none of 'em be missed.

WILLIAM S. GILBERT, *The Mikado,* Act 1.

All hail, great judge!

    *   *   *   *

May each decree
    As statute rank
And never be
    Reversed in banc.

    WILLIAM S. GILBERT, *Trial by Jury.*

Though homeward as you trudge,
You declare my law is fudge.
Yet of beauty I'm a judge.

    WILLIAM S. GILBERT, *ibid.*

Judges are apt to be naif, simple-minded men, and they need something of Mephistopheles.

    OLIVER WENDELL HOLMES, *Law and the Court,* in *Speeches* 102 (1913).

You seem . . . to consider the judges as the ultimate arbiters of all constitutional questions; a very dangerous doctrine indeed, and one which would place us under the despotism of an oligarchy. Our judges are as honest as other men, and not more so. They have, with others, the same passions for party, for power, and the privilege of their corps. Their maxim is "*boni judicis est amplaire jurisdictionem,*" and their power the more dangerous, as they are in office for life, and not responsible, as the other functionaries are, to the elective control. The constitution has erected so such single tribunal, knowing that to whatever hands confided, with the corruptions of time and party, its members would become despots.

    THOMAS JEFFERSON, *Letter to William Charles Jarvis, Sept. 28, 1820.*

What a wretched thing a Lord Chief Justice is, always was, and will be!

> CHARLES LAMB, *Letter to Bernard Barton, January 23, 1824.* (Referring to Leigh Hunt's conviction for libel and his sentencing by Lord Ellenborough. Hunt had written an article reflecting on the Prince Regent whom he called a fat Adonis of fifty.)

The Chief Justice was rich, quiet, and infamous.

> THOMAS MACAULAY, *Warren Hastings,* 74 Edinburgh Rev. 105 (1841).

While "an overspeaking judge is no well-tuned cymbal" neither is an amorphous dummy unspotted by human emotions, a becoming receptacle for judicial power.

> McREYNOLDS, J., dissenting, *Berger v United States* (1921) 255 US 22, 43, 65 L ed 481, 489, 41 S Ct 230.

My dear Garrick, a judge on the bench is now and then in your whimsical situation between tragedy and comedy; inclination drawing one way, and a long string of precedents the other.

> LORD MANSFIELD, Holliday, *Life of Mansfield* 211 (1797).

After all is said and done, we cannot deny the fact that a judge is almost of necessity surrounded by people who keep telling him what a wonderful fellow he is. And if he once begins to believe it, he is a lost soul.

> HAROLD R. MEDINA, *Some Reflections on the Judicial Function: A Personal Viewpoint,* 38 A.B.A.J. 107, 108 (1952).

Midnight Judges.

(Derisive term applied to the last-minute appointments of President
John Adams. Judiciary Act passed Feb. 13, 1801, created six
new federal circuit courts with sixteen judges. Many of these
commissions, including those for Justices of the Peace of the
Dist. of Col., were filled out on the last day of Adams's term
of office.)

Judges are no more than the mouth that pronounces the
words of the law, mere passive beings, incapable of moderat-
ing either its force or rigor.

MONTESQUIEU, *Spirit of the Laws,* bk 11, ch. 6 (trans. Nugent).

The judge should not be young; he should have learned
to know evil, not from his own soul, but from late and
long observance of the nature of evil in others: knowledge
should be his guide, not personal experience.

PLATO, *Republic,* bk 3 (Jowett trans.)

Judges are philologists of the highest order.

POLLOCK, C.B., *Ex parte Davis* (1857) 5 W. R. 522, 523.

Slander or poison, dread from Delia's rage,
Hard words or hanging, if your judge be Page.

ALEXANDER POPE, *Imitations of Horace,* bk 2, 1st satire.

We rate the judge who is only a lawyer higher than the
judge who is only a philosopher.

CUTHBERT W. POUND, *Address,* Fed. Bar Assn, 1 N.Y.S. Bar
Bull. 279, 285 (1929).

A good judge conceives quickly, judges slowly.

Proverb. HERBERT, *Jacula Prudentum* (1651).

Judges are lawyers who knew a governor.

Saying.

Thieves for their robbery have authority
When judges steal themselves.

SHAKESPEARE, *Measure for Measure,* Act 2, Scene 2.

And then the justice,
In fair round belly with good capon lin'd,
With eyes severe and beard of formal cut,
Full of wise saws and modern instances.

SHAKESPEARE, *As You Like It,* Act 2, Scene 7.

Shylock.

It does appear you are a worthy judge;
You know the law, your exposition
Hath been most sound: I charge you by the law,
Whereof you are a well-deserving pillar,
Proceed to judgment.

SHAKESPEARE, *Merchant of Venice,* Act 4, Scene 1.

Shylock.

A Daniel come to judgment! yea a
     Daniel!
O wise young judge, how I do honour thee!

SHAKESPEARE, *ibid.*

It is well that judges should be clothed in robes, not only, that they who witness the administration of justice should be properly advised that the function performed is one different from, and higher, than that which a man discharges as a citizen in the ordinary walks of life; but also, in order to impress the judge himself with the constant consciousness that he is a high priest in the temple of justice and is surrounded with obligations of a sacred character that he cannot escape and that require his utmost care, attention and self-suppression.

> WILLIAM HOWARD TAFT, *An Appreciation of General Grant, May 30, 1908.* See Taft, *Present Day Problems* 63 (1908).

Judge Thumb.

> (The dictum that a husband may beat his wife with a stick no thicker than his thumb was attributed to Sir Francis Buller. The story was generally believed and made the subject of caricature. Foss in his *Biographical Dictionary of the Judges of England* states that searching investigation has produced no substantial evidence that such an opinion was ever rendered by Judge Buller.)

Our judges are not monks or scientists, but participants in the living stream of our national life steering the law between the dangers of rigidity on the one hand and of formlessness on the other.

> EARL WARREN, *The Law and the Future,* 52 Fortune, Nov. 1955, p. 107.

Judge (Political Aspiration)

Every judge is politically insolvent.

> LOGAN E. BLECKLEY, 49 Alb. L. J. 409 (1894).

I notice that he says he won't be a candidate unless the President asks him to be—or something like that. *Entre nous* I have noticed a certain reserve in his speech that seems to leave possibilities open. I think a judge should extinguish such thoughts when he goes on the Bench.

> OLIVER WENDELL HOLMES, 1 *Holmes—Pollock Letters* 192 (Apr. 26, 1912).

It was not a preference but simply and solely, as I believe, a sense of duty that led Hughes to accept the nomination. I shall miss him consumedly, for he is not only a good fellow, experienced and wise, but funny, and with doubts that open vistas through the wall of a non-conformist conscience.

> *Ibid.* 237, July 12, 1916. (On June 10, 1916 Charles Evans Hughes accepted the Republican nomination for the Presidency and resigned from the Supreme Court of the United States.)

A judge has no constituents.

> GEORGE SUTHERLAND, 47 Cong. Rec. 2801 (1911). (Said when Senator).

It is dangerous to have a judge who thinks beyond the judicial in his personal ambitions.

> MORRISON R. WAITE, *Letter, Nov. 7, 1875,* to his Congressman nephew, J. T. Waite. (At the time there was talk of nominating the Chief Justice for the presidency.)

Judges (Appraisal)

He was a strong, stout man, and could endure to sit at it day and night (The picture of a common lawyer:—

278

He must have an "iron head, a brazen face, and a leaden breech."); became eminent in his calling, had good practise; called to be a Serjeant and a Judge.

> JOHN AUBREY, *Brief Lives: Sir John Popham.* Popham became Lord Chief Justice of King's Bench in 1592.

Let it go. Sit down. Life, liberty, and property are always safe in his hands.

> RUFUS CHOATE, to an associate who was rising to contest what he considered an unfair ruling by Chief Justice Lemuel Shaw of Massachusetts. See 1 Brown, *Works of Choate* 288 (1862).

I regard him as the Indian does his wooden log, curiously carved; I acknowledge he's ugly, but I bow before a superior intelligence.

> RUFUS CHOATE, referring to Chief Justice Lemuel Shaw of Massachusetts. See 1 Brown, *Works of Choate* 289 (1862).

Judge Ashhurst with his lantern jaws,
Throws light upon our English laws.

> LORD ERSKINE, attributed to.

To see him preside was like witnessing Toscanini lead an orchestra.

> FELIX FRANKFURTER, *Chief Justices I Have Known,* 39 Va. L. Rev. 883 (1953). (Referring to Chief Justice Hughes).

Left hand, right hand.

> The Bar thus frequently referred to Learned Hand and Augustus N. Hand, first cousins, both of whom served with great distinction on the bench of the U. S. District Court, Southern District, N. Y. and U. S. Circuit Court, 2nd cir., N. Y. For many years they served simultaneously in the same court.

Quote Learned, but cite Augustus.

> ROBERT H. JACKSON, attributed to. Referring to Learned Hand and Augustus Hand, Judges on the Federal Courts for New York.

Judicial Impartiality

The cold neutrality of an impartial judge.

> BURKE, *Preface to Brissot's Address.*

Contrary to the layman's belief, personal friendship between the judge and the lawyer is not an advantage to the client; for a scrupulous judge is so afraid that he will unconsciously favor his friend that in reaction he tends to be unjust to him.

> PIERO CALAMANDREI, *Eulogy of Judges* 92 (1942) trans. Adams and Phillips.

"I'll be judge, I'll be jury," said cunning old Fury;
"I'll try the whole cause, and condemn you to death."

> LEWIS CARROLL, *Alice in Wonderland,* ch. 3.

He shall know nothing about the parties, everything about the case. He shall do everything for justice; nothing for himself; nothing for his friend; nothing for his patron; nothing for his sovereign. If, on one side, is the executive power, and the legislature and the people, —the sources of his honors, the givers of his daily bread—and on the other an individual nameless and odious, his eye is to see neither, great nor small; attending only to the "trepidations of the balance".

> RUFUS CHOATE, *Massachusetts Constitutional Convention, 1853: Debates and Proceedings* 800.

The most satisfactory ideal I have ever been able to form of justice is embodied in the picture of a judge courageous enough "to give the devil his due", whether he be in the right or in the wrong.

> JOHN F. DILLON, *Laws and Jurisprudence of England and America* 152 (1894).

There is no guaranty of justice except the personality of the judge.

> EUGEN EHRLICH, *Freedom of Decision,* in *Science of Legal Method,* 9 Mod. Leg. Philos. Ser. 65 (1917 trans. by Bruncken).

His private affections are swallowed up in the common cause as rivers lose their names in the ocean.

> THOMAS FULLER, *The Holy State: The Good Judge* (1642).

Considerate men of every description ought to prize whatever will tend to beget or fortify that temper in the courts; as no man can be sure that he may not be tomorrow the victim of a spirit of injustice, by which he may be a gainer to-day.

> ALEXANDER HAMILTON, *The Federalist No. 78 (1788).*

A man may judge impartially even in his own cause.

> LORD MANSFIELD, C.J., *R. v Cowle* (1759) 2 Burr. 834, 863.

If the parties will at my hand call for justice, then were it my father stood on the one side, and the devil on the other, his cause being good, the devil should have right.

> SIR THOMAS MORE. Roper, *Life of More.*

Men cannot live apart or independent of each other . . . and yet they cannot live together without contests. These contests require some arbitrator to determine them. The necessity of a common, indifferent and impartial judge makes all men seek one.

JAMES OTIS, *Rights of the British Colonies* (1764).

He whose father is judge goes safe to his trial.

Proverb. THOMAS FULLER, *Proverbs* (1732).

It sometimes happens, also, that he who sits as judge is either our enemy or the friend of our opponent, a circumstance which ought to claim the attention of both sides, but more particularly, perhaps, of that to which the judge seems to incline. For there is sometimes, in unprincipled judges, a foolish propensity to give sentence against their friends, or in favour of parties with whom they are at enmity, and to act unjustly that they may not seem to be unjust.

QUINTILIAN, *Inst. of Oratory*, bk 4, 1, 18 (trans. Watson).

He who decides a case with the other side unheard,
Though he decide justly, is himself unjust.

SENECA, *Medea.*

No man should be a judge in his own cause.

SYRUS, *Sententiae.*

Cranmer:
I shall both find your lordship judge and juror.

SHAKESPEARE, *Henry VIII*, Act 5, Scene 3.

Judicial Independence

There is no human being whose smile or frown; there is no Government, Tory or Liberal, whose favour or disfavour can start the pulse of an English judge upon the Bench, or move by one hair's breath the even equipoise of the scales of justice.

> LORD BOWEN, at Mansion House Banquet, May 18, 1887.

That when that case should be, he would do that should be fit for a judge to do.

> CHIEF JUSTICE COKE, *Case of the Commendams*. See 1 Coll. Jur. 17. (King James directed the judges to stay the action until they should consult with him. The judges refused. They were then asked if they would obey a similar order in the future. Coke refused.)

Judges were not to give opinion by fractions, but entirely according to the vote whereupon they should settle upon conference: and that this auricular taking of opinions, single and apart, was new and dangerous.

> COKE, *Peacham's Case* (1615) 2 How. St. Tr. 873. (When James I tried to submit a case in advance to the judges.)

If you gentlemen of the red robe will not execute the law, my red coats shall.

> OLIVER CROMWELL. Newdigate, Pepys and Windham called as Judges under Cromwell in June 1654 expressed doubts as to his title and scruples as to whether they execute the law under him. See Campbell, *Lives of the Chief Justices: Richard Newdigate*.

Nothing is more striking in the history of the Court than the manner in which the hopes of those who expected a

283

Judge to follow the political views of the President appointing him have been disappointed.

> CHARLES WARREN, 1 *Supreme Court in U. S. History* 22 (1922). (Lincoln's legal tender policy was held unconstitutional by his own appointees. Judges appointed by Jefferson and Madison did not hesitate to join with Marshall in opinions obnoxious to Jefferson.)

Judicial Legislation

The childish fiction employed by our judges, that judiciary or common law is not made by them, but is a miraculous something made by nobody; existing I suppose, from eternity, and merely declared from time to time by the judges.

> JOHN AUSTIN, *Jurisprudence: Statute and Judiciary Law* (lect. 37).

Judges ought to remember that their office is *jus dicere,* and not *jus dare;* to interpret law, and not to make law, or give law.

> BACON, *Essays: Of Judicature.*

It is the judges . . . that make the common law. Do you know how they make it? Just as a man makes laws for his dog. When your dog does anything you want to break him of, you wait till he does it, and then beat him for it. This is the way you make laws for your dog: and this is the way the judges make law for you and me.

> JEREMY BENTHAM, *Truth v Ashhurst,* 5 Works 235.

[The judge is] not delegated to pronounce a new law, but to maintain and expound the old one.

> BLACKSTONE, *Commentaries,* bk 1, 69.

A *casus omissus* does not justify judicial legislation.

> BRANDEIS, J., *Ebert v Poston* (1925) 266 US 548, 554, 69 L ed 435, 438, 45 S Ct 188.

I take judge-made law as one of the existing realities of life.

> BENJAMIN N. CARDOZO, *Nature of the Judicial Process* 10 (1921).

He cannot set himself above the law which he has to administer, or make or mould it to suit the exigencies of a particular occasion.

> COCKBURN, C.J., *Martin v Mackonochie* (1878) 3 Q.B.D. 730, 775.

We must not be guilty of taking the law into our own hands, and converting it from what it really is to what we think it ought to be.

> COLERIDGE, C.J., *R. v Ramsey* (1883) 1 C. & E. 126, 136.

If a statute . . . is apt to reproduce the public opinion not so much of to-day as of yesterday, judge-made law occasionally represents the opinion of the day before yesterday.

> ALBERT V. DICEY, *Law and Opinion in England* (lecture xi).

But the ultimate touchstone of constitutionality is the Constitution itself and not what we have said about it.

> FRANKFURTER, J., concurring, *Graves v New York* (1931) 306 US 466, 491, 83 L ed 927, 939, 59 S Ct 595, 120 ALR 1466.

Justices of the Court are not architects of policy. They can nullify the policy of others; they are incapable of fashioning their own solutions for social problems.

FELIX FRANKFURTER, *Mr. Justice Holmes and the Supreme Court* 25 (1938).

The customary law of English-speaking peoples stands, a structure indubitably made by the hands of generations of judges, each professing to be a pupil, yet each in fact a builder who has contributed his few bricks and his little mortar, often indeed under the illusion that he has added nothing. A judge must manage to escape both horns of this dilemma: he must preserve his authority by cloaking himself in the majesty of an overshadowing past; but he must discover some composition with the dominant trends of his time—at all hazards he must maintain that tolerable continuity without which society dissolves, and men must begin again the weary path up from savagery.

LEARNED HAND, *Mr. Justice Cardozo,* 39 Col. L.R. 9 (1939).

Moreover, judges are seldom content merely to annul the particular solution before them; they do not, indeed they may not, say that taking all things into consideration, the legislators' solution is too strong for the judicial stomach. On the contrary they wrap up their veto in a protective veil of adjectives such as "arbitrary," "artificial," "normal," "reasonable," "inherent," "fundamental," or "essential," whose office usually, though quite innocently, is to disguise what they are doing and impute to it a derivation far more impressive than their personal preferences, which are all that in fact lie behind the decision. If we do need a third chamber it should appear for what it is, and not as the interpreter of inscrutable principles.

LEARNED HAND, *The Bill of Rights* (1964 ed.) 70.

I recognize without hesitation that judges do and must legislate, but they can do so only interstitially; they are confined from molar to molecular motions.

> HOLMES, J., *Southern P. Co. v Jensen* (1917) 244 US 205, 221, 61 L ed 1086, 1100, 37 S Ct 524.

The clearest feature of the Court's decision is that it leaves the country under an Act which is not much like any Act passed by Congress.

> JACKSON, J., *United States v Harriss* (1954) 347 US 612, 633, 98 L ed 989, 1004, 74 S Ct 808.

Courts are the mere instruments of the law, and can will nothing.

> MARSHALL, C.J., *Osborn v Bank of United States* (1824, US) 9 Wheat 738, 866, 6 L ed 204, 234.

I think we are not, as Judges, (living though we do in a more enlightened and liberal age), to be liberal above what is written, or by any method of construction, when the statutes distinctly, expressly, and imperatively require one form, to substitute another as equivalent for the object or purpose, as we may think, of the legislature.

> POLLOCK, C. B., *Miller v Salomons* (1852) 17 Ex. 475, 566.

Under the common law there is no case unprovided for, —though there may be many of which it is extremely difficult, and indeed impossible, to say before hand what the provision is. For the cases on which no decision has yet been pronounced, an unknown law exists, which must be brought to light whenever the courts are called upon for their decision. For all practical purposes, a law so unknown is the same as a law not in existence. To declare, is substantially to enact it; and the Judges, though called only expounders of law, are in reality legislators.

> SIR SAMUEL ROMILLY, *Bentham on Codification,* 29 Edinburgh Rev. 223 (1817).

The chief lawmakers in our country may be, and often are, the judges, because they are the final seat of authority. Every time they interpret contract, property, vested rights, due process of law, liberty, they necessarily enact into law parts of a system of social philosophy; and as such interpretation is fundamental they give direction to all lawmaking. The decisions of the courts on economic and social questions depend upon their economic and social philosophy; and for the peaceful progress of our people during the twentieth century we shall owe most to those judges who hold to a twentieth century economic and social philosophy and not to a long outgrown philosophy, which was itself the product of primitive economic conditions.

> THEODORE ROOSEVELT, *Message to Congress, Dec. 8, 1908.*

To vindicate the policy of the law is no necessary part of the office of a judge.

> SCOTT, J., *Evans v Evans* (1790) 1 Hag. Con. 35, 36.

The judicial function is that of interpretation; it does not include the power of amendment under the guise of interpretation.

> SUTHERLAND, J., *West Coast Hotel Co. v Parrish* (1937) 300 US 379, 404, 81 L ed 703, 715, 57 S Ct 578, 108 ALR 1330.

Thorpe (of counsel): I think you will do as others have done in the same case; or else we do not know what the law is.

Hillary, J.: It is the will of the Justices.
Stonore, C.J.: No; law is reason.

> See Y.B. 18–19 Edw. III (Rolls Ser.) 78, No. 3 Hil. (1344–45).

However the Court may interpret the provisions of the Constitution, it is still the Constitution which is the law and not the decision of the Court.

> CHARLES WARREN, 3 *Supreme Court in U.S. History* 470 (1922).

Judicial Notice

This court knows judicially there is always a chance to lose in any kind of a lawsuit.

> CLARKE, J., *Moorman v Louisville Trust Co.*, 181 Ky 30, 39 (1918).

There comes a point where the Court should not be ignorant as judges of what we know as men.

> FRANKFURTER, J., *Watts v Indiana* (1949) 338 US 49, 52, 93 L ed 1801, 1805, 69 S Ct 1347.

One need not, in the words of the plaintiff's brief, be guilty of "judicial myopia" to ascertain that the doctrine of privity is not yet moribund and that one would be guilty of impropriety if he attempted to conduct a funeral without a corpse.

> McDONALD, J., *Serrano v Riverside Dinette Products Co.*, 222 N.Y.S.2d 537, 539 (Supreme Court, Kings Co., 1961).

The King [Henry IV] demanded of Gascoign, Justice if he saw one in his presence kill J.S., and another that was innocent was indicted for it before him and found guilty of the same death, what he would do in such a case? And he answered, that he would respite judgment, because he knew the party was innocent, and make further relation to his Majesty to grant his pardon; and the King was well pleased that the law was so; but there he could not acquit him, and give judgment of his own private knowledge.

> PLOWDEN, 83.

A court must be blind not to see that the so-called tax is imposed to stop the employment of children within the age limits prescribed. Its prohibitory and regulatory effect and purpose are palpable. All others can see and understand this. How can we properly shut our minds to it?

> TAFT, C.J., *Child Labor Tax Case* (1922) 259 US 20, 37, 66 L ed 818, 819, 42 S Ct 449, 21 ALR 1432.

Judicial Precepts

A popular judge is a deformed thing: and *plaudite's* are fitter for players than magistrates.

> BACON, *Speech, Star Chamber, 1617,* to judges before the summer circuit.

That you should:
Draw your learning out of your books, not out of your brain.
Mix well the freedom of your opinion with the reverence of the opinion of your fellows.
Continue the studying of your books, and do not spend time with the old stock.
Fear no man's face, yet turn not stoutness into bravery.

*   *   *

Be a light to jurors to open their eyes, not a guide to lead them by the noses.

Affect not the opinion of pregnancy and expedition by an impatient and catching hearing of the counsellors at the bar.

Let your speech be with gravity, as one of the sages of the law, and not talkative, nor with impertinent flying out to show learning.

*   *   *

Contain the jurisdiction of your Court within the ancient mere-stones, without removing the mark.

> BACON, *Speech 1617*, on the occasion of Justice Hutton being called to be one of the judges of the Common Pleas.

Judges ought to be more learned than witty, more reverend than plausible, and more advised than confident. Above all things, integrity is their portion and proper virtue.

> BACON, *Essays: Of Judicature.*

Patience and gravity of hearing is an essential part of justice; and an overspeaking judge is no well-tuned cymbal.

> BACON, *ibid.*

Judges must be chaste as Caesar's wife, neither to be, nor so much as suspected in the least to be unjust.

> BACON, *Letter, 1616, to Villiers, Duke of Buckingham* (when he became a Favorite to King James).

The judge is under a duty, within the limits of his power of innovation, to maintain a relation between law and

291

morals, between the precepts of jurisprudence and those of reason and good conscience.

> BENJAMIN N. CARDOZO, *Nature of the Judicial Process* 133 (1921).

There are two things against which a judge ought to guard,—precipitancy, and procrastination. Sir Nicholas Bacon was made to say, which I hope never again to hear, that a speedy injustice is as good as justice which is slow.

> CLARKE, M.R., *Atherton v Worth* (1764) 1 Dick. 375, 377.

O mortal men! be wary how ye judge.

> DANTE, *Paradise,* Canto 20.

There shall be no difference of persons, you shall hear the little as well as the great: neither shall you respect any man's person, because it is the judgment of God. And if any thing seem hard to you, refer it to me, and I will hear it.

> Deuteronomy 1:17.

Thou shalt not accept person nor gifts: for gifts blind the eyes of the wise, and change the words of the just.

> Deuteronomy 16:19.

1. Be Kind.
2. Be Patient.
3. Be Dignified.
4. Don't Take Yourself Too Seriously.
5. Remember That a Lazy Judge Is a Poor One.
6. Don't Be Dismayed When Reversed.
7. Remember There Are No Unimportant Cases.

8. Don't Impose Long Sentences.
9. Don't Forget Your Common Sense.
10. Pray for Divine Guidance.

EDWARD J. DEVITT, *Ten Commandments for the New Judge,*
47 A.B.A.J. 1175 (1961). (Each of these topical headings is
followed by comment).

The greatest deterrent to taking yourself too seriously
in any respect is a wise and observing wife who period-
ically will remark, "Don't get so Judgey."

EDWARD J. DEVITT, *ibid.*

Credulity is not esteemed a paramount virtue of the
judicial mind.

HUSTON, J., *Rankin v Jauman,* 4 Idaho 394, 401 (1895).

Things necessary to be continually had in remembrance:
That in the administration of justice I am entrusted
for God, the king and country; and therefore,
That it be done, first, uprightly; secondly, deliberately,
thirdly, resolutely.
That I rest not upon my own understanding or strength,
but implore and rest upon the direction and strength of
God.
That in the execution of judgment, I carefully lay aside
my own passions and do not give way to them, however
provoked.
That I be wholly intent upon the business I am about, re-
mitting all other cares and thoughts as unseasonable and
interruptions.
That I suffer not myself to be prepossessed with any
judgment at all, till the whole business and both parties be
heard.

SIR MATTHEW HALE, History of the Common Law xv (4th ed.).

293

That I never engage myself in the beginning of any cause, but reserve myself unprejudiced 'till the whole be heard.

That in business capital, though my nature prompt me to pity; yet, to consider that there is also a pity due to the country.

That I be not too rigid in matters purely conscientious, where all the harm is diversity of judgment.

That I be not biased with compassion to the poor or favour to the rich, in point of justice.

That popular or court applause, or distaste, have no influence in any thing I do, in point of distribution of justice.

Not to be solicitous what men will say or think, so long as I keep myself exactly according to the rules of justice.

To be short, and sparing, at meals, that I may be the better for business.

SIR MATTHEW HALE, *ibid.*

For heaven's sake discard the monstrous wig which makes the English judges look like rats peeping through bunches of oakum.

THOMAS JEFFERSON, attributed to.

The judges therefore should always be men of learning and experience in the laws, of exemplary morals, great patience, calmness, coolness and attention; their minds should not be distracted with jarring interests, they should not be dependent upon any man or body of men.

THOMAS JEFFERSON, *Letter to George Wythe, June —, 1776.*

Ye shall do no unrighteousness in judgment: thou shalt not respect the person of the poor, nor honor the person of the mighty: but in righteousness shalt thou judge thy neighbour.

Leviticus 19:15.

As anger does not become a Judge, so neither doth pity; for one is the mark of a foolish woman, as the other is of a passionate man.

SCROGGS, C.J., *R. v Johnson* (1678) 2 Show. K.B. 1, 4.

These, then, are those faults which expose a man to the danger of smiting contrary to the law: a Judge must be clear from the spirit of party, independent of all favour, well inclined to the popular institutions of his country; firm in applying the rule, merciful in making the exception; patient, guarded in his speech, gentle and courteous to all. Add his learning, his labour, his experience, his probity, his practised and acute faculties, and this man is the light of the world, who adorns human life and gives security to that life which he adorns.

SYDNEY SMITH, *Assize Sermon, March 28, 1824,* at York.

Judicial Process

In cases omitted, the rule of law is to be deduced from similar cases, but with caution and judgment. And here the following rules are to be observed: Let reason be esteemed a fruitful, and custom a barren, thing, so as to breed no new cases.

BACON, *Advancement of Learning,* bk 8, Aph. 11.

The narrow compass of human wisdom cannot take in all the cases which time may discover; whence new and

295

omitted cases often present themselves. For these, the remedy or supplement is threefold; namely, by reference to similar cases, by employment of examples which have not yet grown into law, and by juries which decree according to conscience and discretion, whether in the courts of equity or common law.

> BACON, *Advancement of Learning,* bk 8, Aph. 10.

When a "political theory" embodied in our Constitution becomes outdated, it seems to me that a majority of the nine members of this Court are not only without constitutional power but are far less qualified to choose a new constitutional political theory than the people of this country proceeding in the manner provided by Article V.

> BLACK, J., dissenting, *Harper v Virginia State Board of Elections* (1966) 383 US 663, 678, 16 L ed 2d 169, 179, 86 S Ct 1079.

What judges do and what they profess to do are not always the same, and the latter is only evidence of the former,—often very misleading evidence.

> W. JETHRO BROWN, *Customary Law in Modern England,* 5 Col L.R. 561, 567 (1905).

It is when the colors do not match, when the references in the index fail, when there is no decisive precedent, that the serious business of the judge begins.

> BENJAMIN N. CARDOZO, *Nature of the Judicial Process* 21 (1921).

The restraining power of the judiciary does not manifest its chief worth in the few cases in which the legislature has gone beyond the lines that mark the limits of discre-

296

tion. Rather shall we find its chief worth in making vocal and audible the ideals that might otherwise be silenced, in giving them continuity of life and of expression, in guiding and directing choice within the limits where choice ranges.

> BENJAMIN N. CARDOZO, *Nature of the Judicial Process* 94 (1921).

We do not pick our rules of law full-blossomed from the trees.

> BENJAMIN N. CARDOZO, *Nature of the Judicial Process* 103 (1921).

The judge, even when he is free, is still not wholly free. He is not to innovate at pleasure. He is not a knight-errant, roaming at will in pursuit of his own ideal of beauty or of goodness. He is to draw his inspiration from consecrated principles. He is not to yield to spasmodic sentiment, to vague and unregulated benevolence. He is to exercise a discretion informed by tradition, methodized by analogy, disciplined by system, and subordinated to "the primordial necessity of order in the social life." Wide enough in all conscience is the field of discretion that remains.

> BENJAMIN N. CARDOZO, *Nature of the Judicial Process* 141 (1921).

Our function as judges is not to transform civilization, but to regulate and order it.

> BENJAMIN N. CARDOZO, *Paradoxes of Legal Science* 59 (1928).

A friend of mine . . . called upon the Justice [Holmes] shortly after his retirement from the Court and asked him whether he had been guided by any one principle in the decision of constitutional cases. "Young man," said he, fixing my friend's eye sternly, "Young man, I discovered about 75 years ago that I wasn't God Almighty."

> EDWARD S. CORWIN. *Standpoint in Constitutional Law,* 17 B.U.L.Rev. 513, 527 (1937).

Thwackum was for doing justice, and leaving mercy to Heaven.

> HENRY FIELDING, *Tom Jones,* bk 2, ch. 10.

No judge writes on a wholly clean slate.

> FELIX FRANKFURTER, *The Commerce Clause* 12 (1937).

We cannot escape the demands of judging or of making the difficult appraisals inherent in determining whether constitutional rights have been violated.

> GOLDBERG, J., *Haynes v Washington* (1963) 373 US 503, 515, 10 L ed 2d 513, 521, 83 S Ct 1336.

Judges are constantly sustaining the validity of legislation which as legislators they would probably condemn.

> CHARLES EVANS HUGHES, *The Supreme Court of the United States* (1928) 38.

How amazing it is that, in the midst of controversies on every conceivable subject, one should expect unanimity of opinion upon difficult legal questions! In the highest ranges of thought, in theology, philosophy and science, we find differences of view on the part of the most distinguished experts,—theologians, philosophers and scientists. The history of scholarship is a record of disagreements. And when we deal with questions relating to principles of law and their application, we do not suddenly rise into a stratosphere of icy certainty.

> CHARLES EVANS HUGHES, *Address,* 13 Proceedings Amer. Law Inst. 61, 64 (1936).

We do not write on a blank sheet. The Court has its jurisprudence, the helpful repository of the deliberate and expressed convictions of generations of sincere minds addressing themselves to exposition and decision, not with the freedom of casual critics or even of studious commentators, but under the pressure and within the limits of a definite official responsibility.

> CHARLES EVANS HUGHES, Chief Justice, speaking on the occasion of the 150th anniversary of the Court, 309 US xiv (1940).

When the case is difficult or involved, and turns upon a hairsbreadth of law or of fact, that is to say, "when there are many bags on the one side and on the other" and Judge Bridlegoose would have used his "little small dice," I, after canvassing all the available material at my command, and duly cogitating upon it, give my imagination play, and brooding over the cause, wait for the feeling, the hunch— that intuitive flash of understanding which makes the jump-spark connection between question and decision, and at the point where the path is darkest for the judicial feet, sheds its light along the way.

> JOSEPH C. HUTCHESON, *Judgment Intuitive,* 14 Corn. L.Q. 274, 278 (1929).

In feeling or "hunching" out his decisions, the judge acts not differently from, but precisely as the lawyers do in working on their cases, with only this exception; that the lawyer, having a predetermined destination in view,—to

299

win his law suit for his client—looks for and regards only those hunches which keep him in the path that he has chosen, while the judge, being merely on his way with a roving commission to find the just solution, will follow his hunch wherever it leads him, and when, following it, he meets the right solution face to face, he can cease his labors.

> JOSEPH C. HUTCHESON, *ibid.*

For we have a legal system which entrusts its case-law-making to a body who are specialists only in being unspecialized, in being the official depositaries of as much general and balanced but rather uninformed horse sense as can be mustered.

> KARL LLEWELLYN, *The Common Law Tradition: Deciding Appeals* (1960) 263.

The problem of judicial interpretation is to hold a just middle way between excess of valour and excess of caution.

> SIR FREDERICK POLLOCK, *Judicial Caution and Valour,* 45 L.Q.R. 293, 296 (1929).

For having well and exactly seen, surveyed, overlooked, reviewed, recognized, read, and read over again, turned and tossed over, seriously perused and examined the bills of complaint, accusations, impeachments, indictments, warnings, citations . . . preparatories, productions, evidences, proofs . . . contradictions, supplications, requests, petitions . . . and other such like confects, and spiceries . . . I posit on the end of a table in my closit, all the pokes and bags of the defendant, and then allow unto him the first hazard of the dice. . . . That being done, I thereafter lay down upon the other end of the same table the bags and sachels of the plaintiff. . . . Then do I

300

likeways and semblably throw the dice for him, and forth-with liver him his chance.

> RABELAIS, *Gargantua and Pantagruel,* bk 3, ch. 39. (Trial of
> Judge Bridlegoose, who decided causes and controversies in law
> by the chance and fortune of the dice.)

But, quoth Trinquamelle, my friend, how come you to know, understand, and resolve, the obscurity of these various and seeming contrary passages, in law, which are laid claim to by the suitors and pleading parties? Even just, quoth Bridlegoose, after the fashion of your other worships: to wit, when there are many bags on the one side, and on the other, I then use my little small dice. . . . I have other large great dice, fair, and goodly ones, which I employ in the fashion that your other worships use to do, when the matter is more plain, clear, and liquid, that is to say, when there are fewer bags. But when you have done all these fine things, quoth Trinquamelle, how do you, my friend, award your decrees, and pronounce judgment? Even as your other worships, answered Bridlegoose; for I give out sentence in his favour unto whom hath befallen the best chance by dice, judiciary, tribunian, pretorial, what comes first. So our laws command.

> RABELAIS, *ibid.*

When I examine a question, I go from headland to headland, from case to case; Marshall has a compass, puts out to sea, and goes directly to the result.

> JOSEPH STORY, attributed to. See Parson, *John Marshall,* 1
> Amer. L. Rev. 436 (1866).

To press forward to a great principle by breaking through every other great principle that stands in the way of its establishment . . . to procure an eminent good by means that are unlawful; is as little consonant to private morality as to public justice.

LORD STOWELL, *Re Le Louis* (1817) 2 Dods. 210, 257.

Judicial Restraint

Nor is it desirable for a lower court to embrace the exhilarating opportunity of anticipating a doctrine which may be in the womb of time, but whose birth is distant.

L. HAND, J., *Spector Motor Service Inc. v Walsh,* 139 F.2d 809, 823 (1944).

To do so is to allow zeal for our own ideas of what is good in public instruction to induce us to accept the role of a super board of education for every school district in the nation.

JACKSON, J., *Illinois ex rel. McCollum v Board of Education* (1948) 333 US 203, 237, 92 L ed 649, 672, 68 S Ct 461, 2 ALR2d 1338.

While unconstitutional exercise of power by the executive and legislative branches of the government is subject to judicial restraint, the only check upon our own exercise of power is our own sense of self-restraint.

STONE, J., *United States v Butler* (1936) 297 US 1, 78, 80 L ed 477, 495, 56 S Ct 312, 102 ALR 914.

Judicial Review

Judicial review represents an attempt by the American Democracy to cover its bet.

EDWARD S. CORWIN, *Book Review,* 56 Harv. L. Rev. 487 (1942).

Laws are a dead letter without courts to expound and define their true meaning and operation.

ALEXANDER HAMILTON, *The Federalist,* No. 22.

The interpretation of the laws is the proper and peculiar province of the courts. A constitution is in fact, and must be, regarded by the judges as a fundamental law. It therefore belongs to them to ascertain its meaning as well as the meaning of any particular act proceeding from the legislative body. . . . Nor does this conclusion by any means suppose a superiority of the judicial to the legislative power. It only supposes that the power of the people is superior to both; and that where the will of the legislature declared in its statutes, stands in opposition to that of the people declared in the constitution, the judges ought to be governed by the latter, rather than the former.

ALEXANDER HAMILTON, *The Federalist No. 78.*

It may in the last place be observed that the supposed danger of judiciary encroachments on the legislative authority, which has been upon many occasions reiterated, is in reality a phantom.

ALEXANDER HAMILTON, *The Federalist No. 81.*

I do not think the United States would come to an end if we lost our power to declare an Act of Congress void. I do think the Union would be imperiled if we could not make that declaration as to the laws of the several States.

OLIVER WENDELL HOLMES, *Law and the Court,* in *Speeches* 102 (1913).

We ought to remember the great caution shown by the Constitution in limiting the power of the States, and should

303

be slow to construe the clause in the Fourteenth Amendment as committing to the Court, with no guide but the Court's own discretion, the validity of whatever laws the States may pass.

> HOLMES, J., *Baldwin v Missouri* (1930) 281 US 586, 595, 74 L ed 1056, 1061, 50 S Ct 436, 72 ALR 1303.

In the guise of legal questions there come to the Supreme Court many of the most fundamental and divisive issues of every era, issues which judges in other lands would never dream of having to decide. The consequences are great for Court and country. For the justices power means responsibility, a responsibility the more weighty because the Supreme Court so often has the last word. Deciding cases is never easy, but a judge may sleep more soundly after sentencing a man to death—or invalidating a President's seizure of the nation's steel mills—if he knows there is an appeal to a higher court. Justices of the Supreme Court do not have that luxury.

> ANTHONY LEWIS, *Gideon's Trumpet* (1964) 80.

It is, emphatically, the province and duty of the judicial department to say what the law is.

> MARSHALL, C.J., *Marbury v Madison* (1801, US) 1 Cranch 137, 177, 2 L ed 60, 73.

Judicial power is never exercised for the purpose of giving effect to the will of the judge; always for the purpose of giving effect to the will of the legislature; or, in other words, to the will of the law.

> MARSHALL, C.J., *Osborn v Bank of United States* (1824, US) 9 Wheat 738, 866, 6 L ed 204, 234.

The power vested in the American courts of justice of pronouncing a statute to be unconstitutional, forms one of the most powerful barriers which have ever been devised against the tyranny of political assemblies.

> ALEXIS DE TOCQUEVILLE, *Democracy in America,* Pt 1, ch. 6 (trans. Reeves).

Judicial Selection

He has made judges dependent on his will alone, for the tenure of their offices, and the amount and payment of their salaries.

> Declaration of Independence, ninth specification.

Thou shalt appoint judges and magistrates in all thy gates, which the Lord thy God shall give thee, in all thy tribes: that they may judge the people with just judgment.

> Deuteronomy 16:18.

Moreover thou shalt provide out of all the people able men, such as fear God, men of truth, hating covetousness. . . . And let them judge the people at all seasons: and it shall be, that every great matter they shall bring unto thee, but every small matter they shall judge: so shall it be easier for thyself, and they shall bear the burden with thee.

> Exodus 18:21, 22. (David Delman, New York attorney suggests that this is comparable to a small claims court).

One is entitled to say without qualification that the correlation between prior judicial experience and fitness for the functions of the Supreme Court is zero.

> FELIX FRANKFURTER, *Supreme Court in the Mirror of Justices,* 105 Univ. of Pa. L. Rev. 781, 795 (1957).

[Legal Quotations]—20

There is much to be said for the view that a kindly and patient man who is not a profound lawyer will make a far better judge . . . than an ill-tempered genius.

> LORD KILMUIR, *Judicial Qualities,* 36 New Zeal. L.J. 112, 114 (1960).

We wish for a Chief Justice who will sustain what has been done in regard to emancipation and the legal tenders. We cannot ask a man what he will do, and if we should, and he should answer us, we should despise him for it. Therefore we must take a man whose opinions are known.

> ABRAHAM LINCOLN, at the time of appointing Salmon P. Chase as Chief Justice of the United States. See 2 Boutwell, *Reminiscences of Sixty Years in Public Affairs* 29 (1902).

There is no certain harm in turning a politician into a judge. He may be or become a good judge. The curse of the elective system is the converse, that it turns almost every judge into a politician.

> HENRY T. LUMMUS, *The Trial Judge,* 138 (1937).

I look out for a gentleman, and if he knows a little law so much the better.

> LORD CHANCELLOR LYNDHURST. See Ballantine, *Some Experiences of a Barrister's Life* 148 (2nd ed. 1882).

Fill the seats of justice
With good men, not so absolute in goodness,
As to forget what human frailty is.

> SIR THOMAS TALFOURD, *Ion,* V, 3.

Paradoxical though it may sound, a bipartisan judiciary is the only way in this country to achieve a nonpartisan judiciary.

> ARTHUR T. VANDERBILT, *The Challenge of Law Reform* 33 (1955).

Oh, the Old Missouri Plan,
Oh, the Old Missouri Plan,
When Wall Street lawyers all judicial
Candidates will scan,
If you're not from Fair Old Harvard,
They will toss you in the can * * *
Oh, the Old Missouri Plan,
Oh, the Old Missouri Plan.

It won't be served with sauerkraut nor
Sauce Italian.
There'll be no corned beef and cabbage,
And spaghetti they will ban;
There'll be no such dish
As gefilte fish
On the Old Missouri Plan.

> JAMES GARRETT WALLACE, *Wallace's Third Party—A Minstrel Show 8 (1948).* Privately printed.

Judiciary

Whoever attentively considers the different departments of power must perceive, that in a government in which they are separated from each other, the judiciary, from the nature of its functions, will always be the least dangerous to the political rights of the constitution; because it will be least in a capacity to annoy or injure them. The executive not only dispenses the honors, but holds the sword of the community. The legislature not only commands the purse, but prescribes the rules by which the duties and rights of every citizen are to be regulated. The judiciary on the contrary has no influence over either the sword or the purse, no direction either of the strength or of the wealth of the society, and can take no active resolution whatever. It may truly be said to have neither FORCE nor WILL, but merely judgment; and must ultimately depend upon the aid of the executive arm even for the efficacy of its judgments.

ALEXANDER HAMILTON, *The Federalist No. 78 (1788)*.

It proves incontestibly that the judiciary is beyond comparison the weakest of the three departments of power; that it can never attack with success either of the other two; and that all possible care is requisite to enable it to defend itself against their attacks. It equally proves, that though individual oppression may now and then proceed from the courts of justice, the general liberty of the people can never be endangered from that quarter: I mean, so long as the judiciary remains truly distinct from both the legislative and executive.

ALEXANDER HAMILTON, *ibid.*

If then the courts of justice are to be considered as the bulwarks of a limited constitution against legislative encroachments, this consideration will afford a strong argument for the permanent tenure of judicial offices, since nothing will contribute so much as this to that independent spirit in the judges, which must be essential to the faithful performance of so arduous a duty.

ALEXANDER HAMILTON, *ibid.*

Next to permanency in office, nothing can contribute more to the independence of the judges than a fixed provision for their support. The remark made in relation to the president, is equally applicable here. In the general course of human nature, *a power over a man's subsistence amounts to a power over his will.*

> ALEXANDER HAMILTON, *The Federalist No. 79 (1788).*

The Judicial Department comes home in its effects to every man's fireside: it passes on his property, his reputation, his life, his all. Is it not, to the last degree important, that he should be rendered perfectly and completely independent, with nothing to influence or controul him but God and his conscience?

> JOHN MARSHALL, Virginia Constitutional Convention, 1829–30, *Debates* 616.

I have always thought, from my earliest youth till now, that the greatest scourge an angry Heaven ever inflicted upon an ungrateful and a sinning people, was an ignorant, a corrupt, or a dependent Judiciary.

> JOHN MARSHALL, Virginia Constitutional Convention, 1829–30, *Debates* 619.

There is no liberty, if the judiciary power be not separated from the legislative and executive. Were it joined with the legislative, the life and liberty of the subject would be exposed to arbitrary control; for the judge would be then the legislator. Were it joined to the executive power, the judge might behave with violence and oppression.

> MONTESQUIEU, *Spirit of the Laws,* bk 11, ch. 6 (trans. Nugent).

Of the three powers above mentioned, the judiciary is in some measure next to nothing.

> MONTESQUIEU, *ibid.*

309

You can scarcely elevate a man to a seat in a Court of Justice before he catches the leprosy of the Bench.

> CAESAR RODNEY, Attorney General, *Letter to President Jefferson, Oct. 31, 1808, Jefferson Papers MSS.* See 1 Warren, *Supreme Court in United States History* 336. Referring to William Johnson, Associate Justice and an appointee of Jefferson.

Mr. Jefferson stands at the head of the enemies of the Judiciary, and I doubt not will leave behind him a numerous progeny bred in the same school. The truth is and cannot be disguised, even from vulgar observation, that the Judiciary in our country is essentially feeble, and must always be open to attack from all quarters. It will perpetually thwart the wishes and views of demagogues, and it can have no places to give and no patronage to draw around it close defenders. Its only support is the wise and the good and the elevated in society; and these, as we all know, must ever remain in a discouraging minority in all Governments. If, indeed, the Judiciary is to be destroyed, I should be glad to have the decisive blow now struck, while I am young, and can return to the profession and earn an honest livelihood.

> JOSEPH STORY, *Letter to Jeremiah Mason, Jan. 10, 1822.*

The judicial power is by its nature devoid of action; it must be put in motion in order to produce a result. When it is called upon to repress a crime, it punishes the criminal; when a wrong is to be redressed, it is ready to redress it; when an act requires interpretation, it is prepared to interpret it; but it does not pursue criminals, hunt out wrongs, or examine into evidence of its own accord.

> ALEXIS DE TOCQUEVILLE, *Democracy in America,* Pt 1, ch. 6 (trans. Reeves).

Jurisdiction

The most important thing we do is not doing.

> MR. JUSTICE BRANDEIS, *Brandeis-Frankfurter Conversations,* manuscript in Harvard Law School Library. See Bickel, *The Unpublished Opinions of Mr. Justice Brandeis* 17 (1957).

Jurisdiction exists that rights may be maintained. Rights are not maintained that jurisdiction may exist.

> CARDOZO, J., *Berkovitz v Arbib,* 230 N.Y. 261, 274 (1921).

I do not use the term "jurisdiction" because it is a verbal coat of too many colors.

> FRANKFURTER, J., dissenting, *United States v L. A. Tucker Truck Lines, Inc.* (1952) 344 US 33, 39, 97 L ed 54, 59, 73 S Ct 67.

The foundation of jurisdiction is physical power.

> HOLMES, J., *McDonald v Mabee* (1917) 243 US 90, 91, 61 L ed 608, 609, 37 S Ct 343.

Extraordinary jurisdiction succeeds only by becoming ordinary.

> SIR FREDERICK POLLOCK, *The Expansion of the Common Law* 60 (1904).

The long arm of the law.

> Proverb.

1. The King's arm is very long.

> HERODOTUS, *History of the Persian Wars; Urania,* bk 8, ch. 140.

311

2. Know you not how long are the arms of Kings.

> OVID, *Heroidas,* xvii, 166.

Jurisprudence

In certain cases jurisprudence may be defined, the art of being methodically ignorant of what every body knows.

> JEREMY BENTHAM, *Treatise on Judicial Evidence* (Dumont ed. 1825) 6.

A jurist is a person who knows a little about the laws of every country except his own.

> LORD BOWEN. Cunningham, *Biographical Sketch* 184.

The science of jurisprudence, the pride of the human intellect, which with all its defects, redundancies, and errors, is the collected reason of ages, combining the principles of original justice with the infinite variety of human concerns.

> BURKE, *Reflections on the Revolution in France.*

The gladsome light of jurisprudence.

> COKE, *First Institute: Epilogue.*

Jurisprudence is a word which stinks in the nostrils of a practising barrister.

> ALBERT V. DICEY, 5 Law Mag. and Rev. (4th Ser.) 382 (1880).

There is not, in my opinion, in the whole compass of human affairs, so noble a spectacle as that which is displayed in the progress of jurisprudence; where we may contemplate the cautious and unwearied exertions of a succession of wise men through a long course of ages; withdrawing every case as it arises from the dangerous power of discretion, and subjecting it to inflexible rules; extending the dominion of justice and reason, and gradually contracting, within the narrowest possible limits, the domain of brutal force and of arbitrary will.

SIR JAMES MACKINTOSH, *Discourse on Study of Law of Nature and Nations* 94 (Bost. ed. 1843).

Let us think of jurisprudence for a moment as a science of social engineering, having to do with that part of the whole field which may be achieved by the ordering of human relations through the action of politically organized society.

ROSCOE POUND, *Interpretations of Legal History* 152 (1923).

The knowledge of things human and divine, the science of the just and unjust.

ULPIAN, *Digest,* (Justinian) i, I, 10.

Jury

The jury injects a democratic element into the law. This element is vital to the effective administration of criminal justice, not only in safeguarding the rights of the accused, but in encouraging popular acceptance of the laws and the necessary general acquiescence in their application. It can hardly be denied that trial by jury removes a great burden from the shoulders of the judiciary. Martyrdom does not come easily to a man who has been

313

found guilty as charged by twelve of his neighbors and fellow citizens.

BLACK, J., dissenting, *Green v United States* (1958) 356 US 165, 215, 2 L ed 2d 672, 706, 78 S Ct 632.

The trial by jury ever has been, and I trust ever will be, looked upon as the glory of the English law. And if it has so great an advantage over others in regulating civil property, how much must that advantage be heightened when it is applied to criminal cases!

BLACKSTONE, *Commentaries,* bk 3, 379.

That principal criterion of truth in the law of England.

BLACKSTONE, *Commentaries,* bk 3, 348.

In my mind he was guilty of no error, he was chargeable with no exaggeration, he was betrayed by his fancy into no metaphor, who once said that all we see about us, Kings, Lords and Commons, the whole machinery of the State, all the apparatus of the system, and its varied workings, end in simply bringing twelve good men into a box.

HENRY BROUGHAM, *Present State of the Law,* Speech in House of Commons, February 7, 1828.

Then went the jury out, whose names were Mr. Blind-man, Mr. No-good, Mr. Malice, Mr. Love-lust, Mr. Live-loose, Mr. Heady, Mr. High-mind, Mr. Enmity, Mr. Lyar, Mr. Cruelty, Mr. Hate-light, and Mr. Implacable; who every one gave in his private verdict against him among themselves, and afterwards unanimously concluded to bring him in guilty before the Judge.

JOHN BUNYAN, *Pilgrim's Progress,* pt. 1. (15 Harvard Classics 101).

The name of the illustrious Charles Dickens has been called on the jury, but he has not answered. If his great Chancery suit had been still going on, I certainly would have excused him; but, as that is over, he might have done us the honor of attending here, that he might have seen how we went on at common law.

> LORD CAMPBELL. See Heard, *Curiosities of the Law Reporters* 106 (1871).

"Write that down," the king said to the jury, and the jury eagerly wrote down all three dates on their slates, and then added them up, and reduced the answer to shillings and pence.

> LEWIS CARROLL, *Alice in Wonderland,* ch. 11.

Our civilisation has decided, and very justly decided, that determining the guilt or innocence of men is a thing too important to be trusted to trained men. It wishes for light upon that awful matter, it asks men who know no more law than I know, but who can feel the things that I felt in the jury box. When it wants a library catalogued, or the solar system discovered, or any trifle of that kind, it uses up its specialists. But when it wishes anything done which is really serious, it collects twelve of the ordinary men standing round. The same thing was done, if I remember right, by the Founder of Christianity.

> GILBERT K. CHESTERTON, *Tremendous Trifles: The Twelve Men.*

As the law does think it fit
No butchers shall on juries sit.

> CHARLES CHURCHILL, *The Ghost.*

It may, perhaps, be thought singular to suppose, that the exemption from serving on juries is the foundation of the vulgar error, that a surgeon or butcher (from the barbarity of their business) may be challenged as jurors.

> DAINES BARRINGTON, *Observations on the More Ancient Statutes* (3rd ed. Lond. 1769) 422. Referring to a statute of 5 Hen. VIII by which surgeons were exempted from attendance on juries.

Justice for all was a principle they understood and believed in; but by "all" they did not perhaps really mean persons lowdown and no good. They meant that any accused person should be given a fair, open hearing, so that a man might explain, if he could, the appearances that seemed to be against him. If his reputation and presence were good, he was presumed to be innocent; if they were bad, he was presumed to be guilty. If the law presumed differently, the law presumed alone.

> JAMES G. COZZENS, *The Just and the Unjust* (1942) 57.

If it is possible that such a practice as that which has taken place in the present instance should be allowed to pass without a remedy, trial by jury itself, instead of being a security to persons who are accused, will be a delusion, a mockery, and a snare.

> LORD DENMAN, C.J., *O'Connell v R.* (1884) 11 Cl. & F. 155, 351.

"I wonder what the foreman of the jury, whoever he'll be, has got for breakfast," said Mr. Snodgrass. . . . "Ah!" said Perker, "I hope he's got a good one." "Why so?" inquired Mr. Pickwick. "Highly important—very important, my dear Sir," replied Perker. "A good, contented, well-breakfasted juryman, is a capital thing to

316

get hold of. Discontented or hungry jurymen, my dear
Sir, always find for the plaintiff."

> CHARLES DICKENS, *Pickwick Papers,* ch. 34.

The man who laugh'd but once, to see an ass
Mumbling to make the cross-grain'd thistles pass;
Might laugh again to see a jury chaw
The prickles of an unpalatable law,

> JOHN DRYDEN, *The Medal.*

Th' lawyers make th' law; th' judges make th' errors,
but th' iditors make th' juries.

> FINLEY PETER DUNNE, *The Power of the Press,* 62 American
> Mag. 608 (1906). Also in Bander, ed., *Mr. Dooley on the
> Choice of Law* (1963) 65.

In due time twelve men iv intilligence who have r-read
th' pa-papers an' can't remimber what they've r-read, or
who can't r-read, or ar-re out iv wurruk, ar-re injooced
to sarve, an' th' awful wheels iv justice begins to go round.

> FINLEY PETER DUNNE, *Mr. Dooley on Making a Will: On
> Criminal Trials.*

Whin th' case is all over, the jury'll pitch th' tistimony
out iv th' window, an' consider three questions: "Did
Lootgert look as though he'd kill his wife? Did his wife
look as though she ought to be kilt? Isn't it time we wint
to supper?"

> FINLEY PETER DUNNE, *Mr. Dooley in Peace and War: On
> Expert Testimony.*

I have heard an experienced counsellor say that he
never feared the effect upon a jury of a lawyer who does

317

not believe in his heart that his client ought to have a verdict. If he does not believe it, his unbelief will appear to the jury, despite all his protestations, and will become their unbelief.

RALPH WALDO EMERSON, *Spiritual Laws.*

Now, Jurymen, hear my advice—
All kinds of vulgar prejudice
    I pray you set aside:
With stern judicial frame of mind
From bias free of every kind,
    This trial must be tried.

WILLIAM S. GILBERT, *Trial by Jury.*

Monster, dread our damages.
We're the jury,
Dread our fury!

WILLIAM S. GILBERT, *ibid.*

That assize is a certain royal favour, given to the people by the mercy of the king, with the advice of his nobles, by means of which such healthy provision is made for the life and condition of men, that each may keep the freehold which rightfully is his, and all can avoid the doubtful issue of battle. And by this means it comes to pass that each can escape the last punishment of unexpected and untimely death, or at least the shame of perpetual infamy arising from the cry of that hateful and shocking word [Craven] which the conquered utters as the result of his disgrace by defeat. This institution is the product of the highest equity. For the establishment of the right which after many and long delays is hardly ever attained by battle, is attained by its means more easily and quickly.

The assize does not allow so many essoins as the battle, and so labour and expense are saved to the poor. Moreover by as much as the testimony of several credible witnesses outweighs in actions that of one only, by so much is this institution more equitable than the battle. For while the battle depends upon the testimony of one sworn person this institution requires the oaths of at least twelve lawful men.

> GLANVIL, *Laws and Customs of England,* bk 2, ch. 7. (The Assize of Clarendon (1166) instituted trial by jury as an alternative to trial by battle.)

The jury has the power to bring in a verdict in the teeth of both law and facts.

> HOLMES, J., *Horning v District of Columbia* (1920) 254 US 135, 138, 65 L ed 185, 186, 41 S Ct 53.

So long as accused persons who are Republicans, Dixiecrats, Socialists, or Democrats must put up with such a jury, it will have to do for Communists.

> JACKSON, J., concurring, *Dennis v United States* (1950) 339 US 162, 175, 94 L ed 734, 744, 70 S Ct 519.

I consider trial by jury as the only anchor ever yet imagined by man, by which a government can be held to the principles of its constitution.

> THOMAS JEFFERSON, *Letter to Thomas Paine* (1789).

A jury too frequently has at least one member more ready to hang the panel than to hang the traitor.

> ABRAHAM LINCOLN, *Letter to Erastus Corning,* June 12, 1863.

319

It is the duty of the judge, in all cases of general justice, to tell the jury how to do right, though they have it in their power to do wrong, which is a matter entirely between God and their own consciences.

> MANSFIELD, C.J., *Rex v Shipley* (1784) 4 Doug. 73, 170.

Gentlemen of the jury, the man stole the boots; consider your verdict.

> BARON MARTIN—attributed to—in a larceny case where the facts were beyond dispute. If not literally true it is considered in character.

You are sworn to keep the jury without meat, drink, or fire. Now, water is not fire; water is not meat; and I should certainly hold that water is not drink.

> MAULE, J.—attributed to. (Before the Juries Act, 1870 (England) the bailiff in charge of the jury was sworn to keep them without meat, drink, or fire until a verdict was reached.)

The Jury on the body sat, and gave
   their verdict in these terms,
"They found as how that certain slugs
   had sent him to the worms."

> Old ballad.

There is a constitutional right to a jury drawn from a group which represents a cross-section of the community. And a cross-section of the community includes persons with varying degrees of training and intelligence and with varying economic and social positions. Under our Constitution, the jury is not to be made the representative of the most intelligent, the most wealthy or the most successful, nor of the least intelligent, the least wealthy or the least suc-

320

cessful. It is a democratic institution, representative of all qualified classes of people.

> MURPHY, J., dissenting, *Fay v New York* (1947) 332 US 261, 299, 91 L ed 2043, 2066, 67 S Ct 1613.

The hungry judges soon the sentence sign,
And wretches hang, that jurymen may dine.

> POPE, *Rape of the Lock*, III.

A fox should not be of the jury at a goose's trial.

> Proverb. FULLER, *Proverbs* (1732).

A London jury; hang half save half.

> Proverb. FULLER, *Worthies: London* (1662). Some affirm this of an Essex, others of a Middlesex jury.

The jury, passing on the prisoner's life,
May in the sworn twelve have a thief or two
Guiltier than him they try.

> SHAKESPEARE, *Measure for Measure*, Act 2, Scene 1.

They have been grand-jurymen since before Noah was a sailor.

> SHAKESPEARE, *Twelfth Night,* Act 3, Scene 2.

Good people, you cannot agree? Go [to John Allen, marshal] and put them in a house until Monday, and let them not eat or drink. On that commandment John put them in a house without [food or drink]. At length on the same day about vesper-time they agreed.

> STANTON, J., Anon. Y.B. 4 Edw. II (Seld. Soc. IV) 188 (1310).

[Legal Quotations]—21   *321*

The institution of the jury may be aristocratic or democratic, according to the class of society from which the jurors
are selected; but it always preserves its republican character, inasmuch as it places the real direction of society
in the hands of the governed, or a portion of the governed,
instead of leaving it under the authority of the government.

> ALEXIS DE TOCQUEVILLE, *Democracy in America,* Pt 1, ch. 16
> (trans. Reeves).

The most ingenious and infallible agency for defeating
justice that human wisdom could contrive.

> MARK TWAIN, *Roughing It,* v. 2, ch. 7 (1872).

The jury system puts a ban upon intelligence and honesty, and a premium upon ignorance, stupidity and perjury.

> MARK TWAIN, *ibid.*

A man cannot see by another's eye, nor hear by another's ear, no more can a man conclude or infer the thing
to be resolved by another's understanding or reasoning.

> VAUGHAN, C.J., *Bushell's Case* (1670) Vaugh. 135, 148 (Affirm-
> ing the right of the jury to find such a verdict as they think
> right.)

When Scarlett is addressing a jury there are thirteen
jurymen.

> DUKE OF WELLINGTON. See Scarlett, *Memoir of Lord Abinger*
> 193.

I admit the jury have the power of finding a verdict
against the law, and so they have of finding a verdict

against evidence, but I deny that they have the right to do so.

> WILLES, J., *Rex v Shipley* (1784) 4 Doug. 73, 178.

Justice

You that turn judgment into wormwood, and forsake justice in the land.

> Amos 5:7.

It is true, indeed, that on account of the imperfections incident to human nature perfect truth may not always be attained, and it is well understood that exact justice cannot, because of the inability of courts to obtain truth in entire fullness, be always administered. We are often compelled to accept approximate justice as the best that courts can do in the administration of the law. But, while the law is satisfied with approximate justice where exact justice cannot be attained, the courts should recognize no rules which stop at the first when the second is in reach.

> BECK, J., *Schroeder v C., R.I. & P.R. Co.,* 47 Iowa 375, 379 (1877).

Justice is not only one of the cardinal virtues, it is the pontifical virtue.

> BLECKLEY, C.J., *Lyons v Planters' Loan & Sav. Bk.,* 86 Ga 485, 491 (1890).

For justice, tho' she's painted blind,
Is to the weaker side inclin'd.

> SAMUEL BUTLER, *Hudibras,* Pt. III, Canto III, 1. 709.

Justice, though due to the accused, is due to the accuser also. The concept of fairness must not be strained till it is narrowed to a filament. We are to keep the balance true.

> CARDOZO, J., *Snyder v Massachusetts* (1934) 291 US 97, 122, 78 L ed 674, 687, 54 S Ct 330, 90 ALR 575.

It is the worst oppression, that is done by colour of justice.

> COKE, *Second Institute* 48.

But all men, at all times, and in all places do stand in need of Justice, and of Law, which is the rule of Justice, and of the interpreters and ministers of the law, which give life and motion unto Justice.

> DAUYS REPORTS (Ireland) 1615, *Preface,* 8: Dedicated to Lord Chancellor Ellesmere.

Justice is a machine that, when some one has once given it the starting push, rolls on of itself.

> JOHN GALSWORTHY, *Justice,* Act 2.

If we are to keep our democracy, there must be one commandment: Thou shalt not ration justice.

> LEARNED HAND, *Address before the Legal Aid Society of New York, Feb. 16, 1951.* See 9 *Brief Case,* No. 4, 5.

Equal Justice under Law.
Justice the Guardian of Liberty.

> Inscriptions on the United States Supreme Court Building, Washington. Neither is a direct quotation from any identified source. See 37 A.B.A.J. 788.

The United States wins its case whenever justice is done one of its citizens in the courts.

> Inscription, U. S. Dept. of Justice Building, Washington, D. C., 5th Floor—Attorney General's rotunda.

The Solicitor General is not a neutral, he is an advocate; but an advocate for a client whose business is not merely to prevail in the instant case. My client's chief business is not to achieve victory but to establish justice. We are constantly reminded of the now classic words penned by one of my illustrious predecessors, Frederick William Lehmann, that the Government wins its point when justice is done in its courts.

> SIMON E. SOBELOFF, *Address* before Judicial Conference of the Fourth Circuit, June 29, 1954. See 373 US 87, fn 2, 10 L ed 2d 219, 83 S Ct 1194.

The most odious of all oppressions are those which mask as justice.

> JACKSON, J., concurring, *Krulewitch v United States* (1949) 336 US 440, 458, 93 L ed 790, 801, 69 S Ct 716.

Equal and exact justice to all men, of whatever state or persuasion, religious or political.

> THOMAS JEFFERSON, *First Inaugural Address, March 4, 1801.*

Justice is the end of government. It is the end of civil society. It ever has been, and ever will be pursued, until it be obtained, or until liberty be lost in the pursuit.

> JAMES MADISON, *The Federalist No. 51 (1788).*

To no one will we sell, to no one will we refuse or delay right or justice.

Magna Carta, ch. 40 (1215).

Human justice, which sees only the actions, has but one compact with men, namely, that of innocence; divine justice, which sees the thought, has two, that of innocence and repentance.

MONTESQUIEU, *Spirit of the Laws,* bk 26 (trans. Nugent).

Justice is lame as well as blind amongst us.

THOMAS OTWAY, *Venice Preserved,* Act I, scene 1 (1682).

Justice is but the interest of the stronger.

PLATO, *Republic* bk 1 (argument of Thrasymachus).

Poetic Justice, with her lifted scale;
Where in nice balance, truth with gold she weighs,
And solid pudding against empty praise.

ALEXANDER POPE, *The Dunciad,* bk 1, line 50.

Set aside justice, and what are kingdoms but enterprises of robbery.

St. AUGUSTINE, *City of God,* bk IV, c. 4.

This even-handed justice.

SHAKESPEARE, *Macbeth,* Act 1, scene 7.

Portia:

But mercy is above this sceptred sway,
It is enthroned in the hearts of kings,

326

It is an attribute to God himself
And earthly power doth then show likest God's
When mercy seasons justice.

> SHAKESPEARE, *Merchant of Venice,* Act 4, scene 1.

Justice is the constant and perpetual will to allot to every man his due.

> ULPIAN, *Digest,* (Justinian) i, I, 10.

Justice Sir, is the great interest of man on earth. It is the ligament which holds civilized beings and civilized nations together. Wherever her temple stands, and so long as it is duly honored, there is a foundation for social security, general happiness and the improvement and progress of our race. And whoever labors on this edifice with usefulness and distinction, whoever clears its foundations, strengthens its pillars, adorns its entablatures, or contributes to raise its august dome still higher in the skies, connects himself, in name and fame and character, with that which is and must be as durable as the frame of human society.

> DANIEL WEBSTER, *Funeral Oration on Mr. Justice Story,* Sept.
> 12, 1845.

Justice of the Peace

VINEGARROON
Roy Bean . . . Barrel Whiskey . . . Justice of
    the Peace . . . Law West of the Pecos

> Sign erected by Roy Bean, July 1789. He established himself without authority, save his indomitable spirit and two six-guns, as Law in that vast and lawless domain between El Paso and the Pecos River. See McDANIEL, *The Saga of Judge Roy Bean* (1936).

327

And here a very ample field is opened for a gentleman to exert his talents, by maintaining good order in his neighbourhood; by punishing the dissolute and idle; by protecting the peaceable and industrious; and, above all, by healing petty differences, and preventing vexatious prosecutions. But, in order to attain these desirable ends, it is necessary that the magistrate should understand his business; and have not only the will, but the power also, (under which must be included the knowledge) of administering legal and effective justice. Else, when he has mistaken his authority, through passion, through ignorance, or absurdity, he will be the object of contempt from his inferiors, and of censure from those to whom he is accountable for his conduct.

BLACKSTONE, *Commentaries: Introduction* 8.

The law does not require a justice of the peace to charge the jury at all. His ignorance of the law, as well as propriety, would seem to demand that he should not, but if he undertakes to instruct the jury, he must do it correctly and in accordance with law. A justice of the peace is generally a man of consequence in his neighborhood; he writes the wills, draws the deeds and pulls the teeth of the people; also he performs divers surgical operations on the animals of his neighbors. The justice has played his part on the busy stage of life from the time of Mr. Justice Shallow down to the time of Mr. Justice Riggins. Who has not seen the gaping, listening crowd assembled around his honor, the justice, on tiptoe to catch the words of wisdom as they fell from his venerated lips? Instructions given in this case exercised an undue and unwarrantable influence upon the jury.

BLANDFORD, J. *Bendheim Brothers & Co. v Baldwin,* 73 Ga 594 (1884).

A justice with grave justices shall sit;
He praise their wisdom, they admire his **wit.**

> GAY, *The Birth of the Squire,* line 77.

I'm important in the County,
I'm a Justice of the Peace,
And I disbelieve Defendants
When they contradict the P'lice.

> J.P.C., *Poetic Justice* 45 (1947).

Long ago lawyers abandoned all hope of describing
the duties of a justice in any methodic fashion, and the
alphabet has become the one possible connecting thread.

> FREDERIC WM. MAITLAND, *Justice and Police* 84 (1885). (Provisions re Justices of the Peace were so numerous and various that authors used the alphabetical approach.)

Kin

Sir Nicholas Bacon . . . by one of the malefactors
mightily importuned for to save his life . . . on account
of kindred. "Prithee," said my lord judge, "how came that
in?" "Why, if it please you my lord, your name is Bacon,
and mine is Hog, and in all ages Hog and Bacon have been
so near kindred, that they are not to be separated." "Ay,
but" replied Judge Bacon, "you and I cannot be kindred,
except you be hanged; for Hog is not bacon until it be
well hanged."

> BACON, *Apothegms.* (Considered spurious by Spedding).

Knowledge

He who would know anything well, must resolve to be ignorant of many things.

JOHN AUSTIN, *Uses of the Study of Jurisprudence.*

Knowledge is power.

BACON, *Med. Sacrae: de Haeresibus.*

I wax now somewhat ancient; one and thirty years is a great deal of sand in the hour-glass. . . . I have taken all knowledge to be my province.

BACON, *Letter, 1592, to Lord Burghley.*

People must not be wiser than the experience of mankind.

BOWEN, L. J., *Filburn v People's Palace & Aq. Co.* (1890) 25 Q.B.D. 258, 261.

When a great learned man, who is long in making, dieth, much learning dieth with him.

COKE, *First Institute: Preface.*

For there is no knowledge (seemeth it at the first of never so little moment) but it will stand the diligent observer in stead at one time or other.

COKE, *Fourth Institute: Proeme.*

No one could be so wise as Thurlow looked.

CHARLES JAMES FOX, attributed to. See Campbell, *Lives of the Lord Chancellors:* Thurlow.

He was a man of great learning, and of reputation for learning greater even than the learning itself.

> JOHN CHIPMAN GRAY, *Nature & Sources of the Law* (1921 ed.) 253. Referring to Mr. Justice Joseph Story, Associate Justice U. S. Sup. Court.

To be master of any branch of knowledge, you must master those which lie next to it.

> OLIVER WENDELL HOLMES, *Profession of the Law, Speeches* (1913) 23; Coll. Leg. Pap. 30.

This morning, Solon, Lycurgus, Demosthenes, Archimedes, Sir Isaac Newton, Lord Chesterfield, and a great many more went away in one post-chaise.

> SAMUEL ROGERS, on seeing Brougham depart one day. 1 Greville, *Journal of the Reign of George IV*, Jan. 2, 1828.

What a wonderful versatile mind has Brougham! He knows politics, Greek, history, science; if he only knew a little of law, he would know a little of everything.

> Saying. Attributed to various contemporaries of Brougham. Emerson in *Quotation and Originality*, says this sarcasm is from Lord Eldon, but you can find the original form of this gibe in Grimm who wrote that Louis XVI after hearing a sermon by the Abbé Maury said, "Si l'Abbé nous avait parlé un peu de religion, il nous aurait parlé de tout."

Knowledge (Legal)

No attorney is bound to know all the law; God forbid that it should be imagined that an attorney, or a counsel, or even a judge is bound to know all the law.

> ABBOTT, C.J., *Montriou v Jefferys* (1825) 2 C. & P. 113, 116.

331

For I think it an undeniable position, that a competent knowledge of the laws of that society in which we live, is the proper accomplishment of every gentleman and scholar; an highly useful, I had almost said essential, part of liberal and polite education.

> BLACKSTONE, *Commentaries: Introduction* 6 (Discourse on The Study of the Law, Oct. 25, 1758).

Making, therefore, due allowance for one or two shining exceptions, experience may teach us to foretell that a lawyer, thus educated to the bar, in subservience to attorneys and solicitors, will find he has begun at the wrong end.   If practice be the whole he is taught, practice must also be the whole he will ever know: if he be not instructed in the elements and first principles upon which the rule of practice is founded, the least variation from established precedents will totally distract and bewilder him: *ita lex scripta est* is the utmost his knowledge will arrive at; he must never aspire to form, and seldom expect to comprehend, any arguments drawn, *a priori,* from the spirit of the laws and the natural foundations of justice.

> BLACKSTONE, *Commentaries: Introduction* 32.   Referring to need of a broad general education for lawyers.

Whereby I set the practice of the Law
At as light count as turning of a straw,
For straight I found how John a Stiles did state it,
But I was over stile ere I came at it;
For having thought (so easy was the way)
That one might be a lawyer the first day.

> RICHARD BRATHWAITE, *Shepherd's Tales,* E. i (1621).

If again the question were, who is rightly described as learned in the law, I should say it is the man who is an

expert in the statutes, and in the customary law observed
by individuals as members of the community, and who is
qualified to advise, direct the course of a lawsuit, and safeguard a client. (*Sin autem quaereretur, quisnam iuriscon-
sultus vere nominaretur; eum dicerem, qui legum, et consue-
tudinis eius, qua privati in civitate uterentur, et ad respond-
endum, et ad agendum, et ad cavendum, peritus esset.*)

> CICERO, *De Oratore*, I, 48. (trans. Loeb Classical Lib.)

There is no jewel in the world comparable to learning;
no learning so excellent both for prince and subject as
knowledge of laws; and no knowledge of any laws (I speak
of human) so necessary for all estates and for all causes,
concerning goods, land, or life as the common laws of
England.

> COKE, 2 Rep. (1658) viii.

The knowledge of the law is like a deep well, out of
which each man draweth according to the strength of his
understanding.

> COKE, *First Institute* 71a.

True it was that God hath endowed His Majesty with
excellent science, and great endowments of nature; but
His Majesty was not learned in the laws of His realm
of England, and causes which concern the life, or inheritance, or goods, or fortunes of His subjects, are not to
be decided by natural reason but by the artificial reason
and judgment of law, which law is an act which requires
long study and experience, before that a man can attain
to the cognizance of it.

> COKE, *Prohibitions del Roy*, 12 Rep. 63, 65. (Reply to James I's
> argument that since law was founded upon reason he could
> decide as well as the judges.)

333

If it be common law, I should be ashamed if I could not give you a ready answer; but if it be statute law, I should be equally ashamed if I answered you immediately.

> COKE. Woolrych, *Life of Coke* 197.

A law, Hinnissy, that might look like a wall to you or me wud look like a triumphal arch to th' expeeryenced eye iv a lawyer.

> FINLEY PETER DUNNE, *The Power of the Press*, 62 American Mag. 608 (1906). Generally misquoted as: "What looks like a stone wall to a layman is a triumphal arch to a corporation lawyer." See Bander, *Mr. Dooley and the Law*, 36 N.Y.S.B.J. 336, 339 (1964).

No man can be a great advocate who is no lawyer.

> LORD CHANCELLOR ERSKINE, *Letter, November 13, 1819.* This was in answer to an impertinent person who had made a bet on the number of the Lord Chancellor's decrees which had been reversed and wrote to Erskine for the information. See 2 Townsend, *Lives of Twelve Eminent Judges* 70 (1846); Campbell, *Lives of the Lord Chancellors: Erskine*, ch. 185 (1847).

But how can you love justice unless you first have sufficient knowledge in the laws, whereby the knowledge of it is won and had, for the philosopher saith, that nothing can be loved except it be known.

> SIR JOHN FORTESCUE, *De Laudibus Legum Angliae*, ch. 5.

Lawyers know the law no better than other people; they only know where to find it.

> GEORGE III (according to tradition).

When I was a lad I served a term
As office boy to an Attorney's firm.

334

I cleaned the windows and I swept the floor,
And I polished the handle of the big front door.
I polished that handle so carefullee
That now I am the Ruler of the Queen's Navee!

>   WILLIAM S. GILBERT, *H.M.S. Pinafore, Act 1.*

Swift was in charge of the departments which handled
the estates, corporation matters and appeals.   He was an
able lawyer.   He read all the latest decisions of the courts
and most of the current legal periodicals.   He knew practically all the law there is.   In fact, he knew so much law
that whenever some desirable transaction for a client had
reached the point of apparent consummation, Swift could
think of at least half a dozen confusing legal obstacles which
might possibly arise in the future.   He could always fill
the minds of all concerned with the gravest apprehensions.
In short, he knew so much law that he was thoroughly
impractical.

>   FRED L. GROSS, *What is the Verdict?* 8 (1944).

In the year 1598, Sir Edward Coke, then Attorney-Gen-
eral, married the lady Hatton, according to the book of
Common Prayer, but without banns or license; and in a
private house.   Several great men were then present. . . .
They all, by their proctor, submitted to the censure of the
Archbishop, who granted them an absolution from the
excommunication they had incurred.   The act of absolution
set forth that it was granted by reason of penitence and the
act seemingly to have been done through ignorance of the
law.

>   LORD HARDWICKE, *Middleton v Croft,* Cunningham's Rep. 61.

If you want to know the law and nothing else, you must
look at it as a bad man, who cares only for the material

consequences which such knowledge enables him to predict, not as a good one, who finds his reasons for conduct, whether inside the law or outside of it, in the vaguer sanctions of conscience.

> OLIVER WENDELL HOLMES, *Path of the Law,* 10 Harv. L.R. 457, 459 (1897).

Alongside of the practitioners to whom the law is a rag-bag from which they pick out the piece and colour that they want, there have been some students who have striven to make their knowledge organic.

> OLIVER WENDELL HOLMES, Review of Holdsworth's *History of English Law,* 25 L.Q.R. 412 (1909).

The study of the law qualifies a man to be useful to himself, to his neighbors, and to the public. It is the most certain stepping stone to preferment in the political line.

> THOMAS JEFFERSON, *Letter to Thomas M. Randolph, May 30, 1790.*

Everybody is presumed to know the law except His Majesty's judges, who have a Court of Appeal set over them to put them right.

> WILLIAM HENRY MAULE (Judge, Common Pleas), attributed to. See Williams, *Criminal Law* (1953) 386.

There is no presumption in this country that every person knows the law: it would be contrary to common sense and reason if it were so.

> MAULE, J., *Martindale v Falkner* (1846) 2 C.B. 706, 719.

To say truth, although it is not necessary for counsel to know what the history of a point is, but to know how it now stands resolved, yet it is a wonderful accomplishment, and without it a lawyer cannot be accounted learned in the laws.

ROGER NORTH, *On the Study of the Laws* 40.

Everyone is conclusively presumed to know the law, although the ablest courts in the land often find great difficulty and labor in finally determining what the law is.

PATERSON, J., *Allen v Allen,* 95 Cal. 184, 199 (1892).

He is a crust of the law, he will never know a crumb of it.

Proverb. See Forby, *Vocabulary of East Anglia* (1830) 430.

The king can make a serjeant, but not a lawyer.

Proverb. THOMAS FULLER, *Proverbs* (1732).

Ignorance of the law excuses no man; not that all men know the law, but because 'tis an excuse every man will plead, and no man can tell how to confute him.

JOHN SELDEN, *Table-Talk: Law.*

Between two hawks, which flies the higher pitch;
Between two dogs, which hath the deeper mouth;
Between two blades, which bears the better temper;
Between two horses, which doth bear him best;
Between two girls, which hath the merriest eye;
I have perhaps, some shallow spirit of judgment;

But in these nice sharp quillets of the law,
Good faith, I am no wiser than a daw.

> SHAKESPEARE, *Henry VI, Pt. I,* Act 2, scene 4.

No man can be a knowing lawyer in any nation, who hath not well pondered and digested in his mind the common law of the world, from whence the interpretation, extensions and limitations of all statutes and customs must be brought.

> LORD STAIR, *Institutions of Law of Scotland* 1 (1681).

Desiring to be teachers of the Law, when they understand neither what they say nor the things about which they make assertion.

> 1 Timothy 1:7.

The worst enemy of the law is the man who knows only the technical details.

> WOODROW WILSON, *Legal Education of Undergraduates* 441.

Language

I know that; I am talking English, not law.

> ARTHUR J. BALFOUR. Retort in the House of Commons to lawyer of the opposition who interrupted to remind him that "trade unions are not corporations". See Maitland, *Coll. Pap.* 305 citing *The Standard,* April 23, 1904.

I have heard that man speak more poetry than I have ever seen written, though I saw him seldom, and but occasionally.

> LORD BYRON, referring to John P. Curran. Moore, *Life of Byron* 306 (1860).

We don't decry the vivid phrase,
    The erudite bravura,
That gives judicial mayonnaise
    A touch of Angostura.

> RICHARD H. FIELD, *Frankfurter, J., Concurring,* 71 Harv. L.
> Rev. 77 (1957). Referring to Mr. Justice Frankfurter's phrase
> "the Plimsoll line of due process" in *Fikes v. Alabama* (1957)
> 352 US 191, 199, 1 L ed 2d 246, 252, 77 S Ct 281.

"And/or," that befuddling, nameless thing, that Janus-faced verbal monstrosity, neither word nor phrase, the child of a brain of some one too lazy or too dull to express his precise meaning, or too dull to know what he did mean, now commonly used by lawyers in drafting legal documents, through carelessness or ignorance or as a cunning device to conceal rather than express meaning.

> FOWLER, J., *Employers Mut. Liability Ins. Co. v Tollefsen,* 219
> Wis. 434 (1935).

The non-lawyer, when annoyed by the way judges sometimes interpret apparently simple statutory language, is the victim of the one-word-one-meaning fallacy, based on the false assumption that each verbal symbol refers to one and only one specific subject. If the non-lawyer would reflect a bit, he would perceive that such an assumption, if employed in the non-legal world, would compel the conclusion that a clothes-horse is an animal of the equine species, and would make it impossible to speak of "drinking a toast".

> JEROME FRANK, *Courts on Trial* 299 (1949).

Language alters, and there is a fashion in judicial writings as in other things.

> FRANKFURTER, J., *Freeman v Hewit* (1946) 329 US 249, 254,
> 91 L ed 265, 273, 67 S Ct 274.

Profanity is vitriol, slang is vinegar, but reporters' English is rancid butter.   I don't know that you have the thing to which I refer in England—an intrusion into the language of sentiment, as when they call a house a home.

OLIVER WENDELL HOLMES, 2 *Holmes-Pollock Letters* 131.

Gentlemen, the chimney took fire; it poured out volumes of smoke.   Volumes did I say?   Whole encyclopedias, gentlemen!

MARRYATT — attributed to; probably apocryphal.

Gobbledygook: Talk or writing which is long, pompous, vague, involved, usually with Latinized words.   It is also talk or writing which is merely long, even though the words are fairly simple, with repetition over and over again, all of which could have been said in a few words.

MAURY MAVERICK, *New York Times, May 21, 1944, Mag. p. 11.*

"The last time I was at quarter sessions, the sheriff told us that *dies*—that *dies inceptus*—In short, you don't understand Latin, but it means that a term-day is not begun until it is ended."
"That sounds like nonsense, my dear."
"May be so, my dear: but it may be very good law for all that."

SIR WALTER SCOTT, *Guy Mannering,* ch. 9 (Mr. Bertram to his wife).

I am quite aware of the habit of some business people and some lawyers of sprinkling "and/ors" as if from a pepper pot all over their documents.

SCRUTTON, L.J., *Gurney v Grimmer* (1932) 38 Com. Cas., 7, 13.

A peculiar Cant and Jargon of their own, that no other Mortal can understand, and wherein all their laws are written.

JONATHAN SWIFT, *Gulliver's Travels: Houyhnhnms,* ch. 5.

Surely, my Lords, this lawyer here hath swallowed
Some 'pothecary's bills, or proclamations.
And now the hard and undigestable words
Come up like stones we use give hawks for physic.
Why, this is Welsh to Latin!

JOHN WEBSTER, *The White Devil,* III, 2 (c. 1608).

Law (Apothegms)

To seek to be wiser than the laws is precisely what good laws forbid.

ARISTOTLE, *Rhetoric,* bk 1, ch. 15.

Moses the lawgiver, and God's first pen.

BACON, *Advancement of Learning,* bk 1.

In this court "the unwritten law" is not worth the paper it isn't written on.

BIDDLE, J., when the theory of the unwritten law was much urged
upon the jury in a case in the common pleas of Philadelphia.

There are two, and only two, foundations of law, . . . equity and utility.

EDMUND BURKE, *Tract on Popery Laws,* Pt 1, ch. 3.

Laws, like houses, lean on one another.

BURKE, *Tracts on Popery Laws,* Pt. 1, ch. 3.

341

Law and arbitrary power are in eternal enmity.

> BURKE, *Impeachment of Warren Hastings,* February 16, 1788.

I am not determining a point of law; I am restoring tranquility.

> EDMUND BURKE, *Speech on Conciliation with America,* Mar. 22, 1775.

People crushed by law have no hopes but from power. If laws are their enemies, they will be enemies to laws; and those, who have much to hope and nothing to lose, will always be dangerous, more or less.

> EDMUND BURKE, *Letter to Charles J. Fox,* Oct. 8, 1777.

That which is law today is none tomorrow.

> ROBERT BURTON, *Anatomy of Melancholy: Democritus to the Reader* (1621).

I am ashamed that the law is such an ass.

> GEORGE CHAPMAN, *Revenge for Honour,* Act 3, scene 2.

Free from all restraint and awe
Just to the windward of the law.

> CHARLES CHURCHILL, *The Ghost,* bk 3 line 55.

Extreme law is extreme injustice. (*Summum jus, summa injuria.*)

> CICERO, *De Officiis,* I, 10, 33.

We are in bondage to the law in order that we may be free. (*Legum denique idcirco omnes servi sumus, ut liberi esse possimus.*)

CICERO, *Pro Cluentio* 53.

The laws are silent amidst the clash of arms. (*Silent enim leges inter arma.*)

CICERO, *Pro Milone,* iv.

Law is the safest helmet.

SIR EDWARD COKE. (Inscription on rings given to friends.)

Ungodly jumble.

OLIVER CROMWELL, attributed to. There is a long tradition among lawyers that Cromwell applied this phrase either to English law as a whole, or to the English law of real property in particular. R. E. Megarry, 205 Notes and Queries 76 (Feb. 1960).

Now, therefore, O king, confirm the sentence, and sign the decree: that what is decreed by the Medes and Persians may not be altered.

Daniel 6:8.

Men would be great criminals did they need as many laws as they make.

LORD DARLING, *Meditations in the Tea Room,* XIV.

And what nation is there so great, that hath statutes and judgments so righteous as all this law, which I set before you this day.

Deutronomy 4:8.

The law's made to take care o' raskills.

> GEORGE ELIOT, *The Mill on the Floss,* bk 3, ch. 4.

Every law which the state enacts indicates a fact in human nature.

> RALPH WALDO EMERSON, *Essays: History.*

I walk within the purlieus of the law.

> SIR GEORGE ETHEREGE, *Love in a Tub,* Act 1, scene 3.

The sparks of all sciences in the world are raked up in the ashes of the law.

> SIR HENRY FINCH, *Law, or Discourse,* bk 1, ch. 3.

The Law is what it is—a majestic edifice, sheltering all of us, each stone of which rests on another.

> JOHN GALSWORTHY, *Justice,* Act 2.

The Law is the true embodiment
Of everything that's excellent.
It has no kind of fault or flaw,
And I, my Lords, embody the Law.

> WILLIAM S. GILBERT, *Iolanthe,* Act I (Lord Chancellor's Song).

The law obliges us to do what is proper, not simply what is just.

> GROTIUS, *De Jure Belli ac Pacis,* bk 1, ch. 1 (1625).

I established law and justice in the land.

> HAMMURABI, *Code: Prologue.*

Law is a plant that lives long before it throws out bulbs.

> OLIVER WENDELL HOLMES, *Introduction: Rational Basis of Legal Institutions* (by various authors).

The life of the law has not been logic: it has been experience. The felt necessities of the time, the prevalent moral and political theories, intuitions of public policy, avowed or unconscious, even the prejudices which judges share with their fellow-men, have had a good deal more to do than the syllogism in determining the rules by which men should be governed.

> OLIVER WENDELL HOLMES, *Common Law* 1 (1881).

The law is the witness and external deposit of our moral life. Its history is the history of the moral development of the race.

> OLIVER WENDELL HOLMES, *Path of the Law,* 10 Harv. L.R. 457, 466 (1897); Coll. Leg. Pap. 170.

It cannot be helped, it is as it should be, that the law is behind the times.

> OLIVER WENDELL HOLMES, *Law and the Court, Speeches* 101 (1913). Coll. Leg. Pap. 294.

Of relative justice law may know something; of expediency it knows much; with absolute justice it does not concern itself.

> O. W. HOLMES, SR., *Pages from an Old Volume of Life* 324 (1883).

Laws are not made for particular cases, but for men in general.

> SAMUEL JOHNSON. Boswell, *Life of Johnson: 1776.*

Now these are the Laws of the Jungle, and many and
    mighty are they;
But the head and the hoof of the Law and the haunch and
    the hump is—Obey!

    RUDYARD KIPLING, *The Law of the Jungle.*

The law is a sort of hocuspocus science, that smiles in
yeer face, while it picks yeer pocket: and the glorious
uncertainty of it is of mair use to the professors than the
justice of it.

    CHARLES MACKLIN, *Love a la Mode,* Act 2, scene 1 (1759).

Law was the point where life and logic met.

    FREDERIC WM. MAITLAND, *Selden Society Year Book Series,*
    v.1: xxxvii.

Very happily, the more the law is looked into, the more it
appears founded in equity, reason and good sense.

    LORD MANSFIELD, C.J., *James v Price* (1773) Lofft 219, 221.

Do not think that I am come to destroy the law or the
prophets. I am not come to destroy, but to fulfil.

    Matthew 5:17.

Law can discover sin, but not remove.

    JOHN MILTON, *Paradise Lost,* XII, 1. 290.

Unlimited power is apt to corrupt the minds of those
who possess it; and this I know, my Lords, that where law
ends, there tyranny begins.

    WILLIAM PITT (Lord Chatham). In Debate in House of Lords,
    January 9, 1770, on the right of John Wilkes to take his seat
    in the House of Commons.

Law is neither a trade nor a solemn jugglery, but a science.

> SIR FREDERICK POLLOCK, *Contracts* (1885, 2nd Amer. Ed. from 4th Eng.): Dedication to Rt. Hon. Lord Justice Lindley.

Law must be stable and yet it cannot stand still.

> ROSCOE POUND, *Interpretations of Legal History* 1 (1923).

It is a bad cause that none dare speak in.

> Proverb. CLARKE, *Paroemiologia* (1639).

It is an ill cause that the lawyers think shame o'.

> Proverb. RAMSAY, *Scots Proverbs* (1737).

In a thousand pounds of law there's not an ounce of love.

> Proverb. RAY, *Proverbs* (1678).

Law, logic and Switzers may be hired to fight for anybody.

> Proverb

People subject to the law should be its author; only those who form an association may regulate the conditions of the society.

> ROUSSEAU, *Contrat Social*, bk 2, ch. 6.

For the whole law is fulfilled in one word: Thou shalt love thy neighbour as thyself.

> ST. PAUL, *Galatians*, 5:14.

347

For where there is no law, neither is there transgression.

ST. PAUL: *Romans,* 4:15.

Law's like laudanum, it's much more easy to use it as a quack does, than to learn to apply it like a physician.

SIR WALTER SCOTT, *Guy Mannering,* ch. 56.

Old father antic the law.

SHAKESPEARE, *Henry IV,* Pt. I, Act 1, scene 2.

We must not make a scarecrow of the law,
Setting it up to fear the birds of prey,
And let it keep one shape, till custom make it
Their perch and not their terror.

SHAKESPEARE, *Measure for Measure,* Act 2, scene 1.

In law, what plea so tainted and corrupt
But, being seasoned with a gracious voice,
Obscures the show of evil?

SHAKESPEARE, *Merchant of Venice,* Act 3, scene 2.

Still you keep o' the windy side of the law.

SHAKESPEARE, *Twelfth Night,* Act 3, scene 4.

No laws, however stringent, can make the idle industrious, the thriftless provident, or the drunken sober.

SAMUEL SMILES, *Self-Help,* ch. 1.

Within the dusty purlieus of the law.

> TENNYSON, *In Memorian,* xxxv.

We know that the law is good, if a man uses it rightly, knowing that the law is not made for the just, but for the unjust and rebellious.

> 1 Timothy 1:8

In crossing France, laws changed as often as one changed horses.

> VOLTAIRE, *Dictionnaire Philosophique: Lois.*

An Act of Parliament is everything to the English; they love law.

> VOLTAIRE, *Essai sur les Moeurs, ch.* 168.

The law,—it has honored us, may we honor it.

> DANIEL WEBSTER, *Speech, Dinner of Charleston, S.C., Bar, May 10, 1847.*

Law (Definition)

Law is intelligence without passion.

> ARISTOTLE, *Politics,* III, 16 (trans. Weldon).

A rule of civil conduct prescribed by the supreme power in a state, commanding what is right and prohibiting what is wrong.

> BLACKSTONE, *Commentaries,* bk 1, 44.

349

For law, remember, is not a dead corpus of blackletter wisdom. It is an elastic tissue which clothes the living body of society.

> JOHN BUCHAN, *Homilies and Recreations* 218.

Law is whatever is boldly asserted and plausibly maintained.

> AARON BURR. See 1 Parton, *Life and Times of Aaron Burr* 149 (1889).

Law is the technique of justice. (*Jus est ars boni et aequi.*)

> CELSUS, *Digest* (Justinian) i. I, 1 (trans. Radin). This inscription will be found on many courthouses.

It is the absolute justice of the State, enlightened by the perfect reason of the State.

> RUFUS CHOATE, *Address: Conservative Force of the American Bar,* July 3, 1845.

Law is the highest reason, implanted in nature, which commands what ought to be done and forbids the opposite. (*Lex est ratio summa, insita in natura, quae iubet ea quae facienda sunt, prohibetque contraria.*)

> CICERO, *De Legibus,* I, vi.

The design and object of laws is to ascertain what is just, honorable and expedient; and, when that is discovered, it is proclaimed as a general ordinance, equal and impartial to all. This is the origin of law, which, for various reasons, all are under an obligation to obey, but especially because all law is the invention and gift of heaven, the resolution of wise men, the correction of every offence, and the general compact of the state; to live in conformity with which is the duty of every individual in society.

> DEMOSTHENES, *Contra Aristogeitan*, I, 16.

The Law of the State or of any organized body of men is composed of the rules which the courts, that is, the judicial organs of that body, lay down for the determination of legal rights and duties.

> JOHN CHIPMAN GRAY, *Nature and Sources of the Law*, ch. 4 (2nd ed. 1921) 84.

The Law of a great nation means the opinions of half-a-dozen old gentlemen. . . . If those half-a-dozen old gentlemen form the highest tribunal of a country, then no rule or principle which they refuse to follow is Law in that country.

> JOHN CHIPMAN GRAY, *Nature and Sources of the Law*, ch. 4 (2nd ed. 1921) 84.

Law is a statement of the circumstances in which the public force will be brought to bear upon men through the courts.

> HOLMES, J., *American Banana Co. v United Fruit Co.* (1909) 213 US 347, 356, 53 L ed 826, 832, 29 S Ct 511.

The prophecies of what the courts will do in fact, and nothing more pretentious, are what I mean by the law.

> OLIVER WENDELL HOLMES, *Path of the Law*, 10 Harv. L. Rev. 457, 460 (1897).

The law is the last result of human wisdom acting upon human experience for the benefit of the public.

> SAMUEL JOHNSON. *Johnsoniana: Piozzi* 58.

Human law is framed for a number of human beings, the majority of whom are not perfect in virtue. Wherefore human laws do not forbid all vices, from which the virtuous abstain, but only the more grievous vices, from which it is possible for the majority to abstain.

ST. THOMAS AQUINAS, *Summa Theologica* I–II q. 96 art. 2.

It is nothing other than a certain rule of reason for the purpose of the common good, laid down by him who is entrusted with the welfare of the community and promulgated.

ST. THOMAS AQUINAS, *Summa Theologica*, I-II, q. 90, art. 4 (trans. Dr. Wu).

Law is common sense as modified by the legislature.

Saying.

Law is law, law is law, and as in such and so forth, and hereby, and aforesaid, provided always, nevertheless, notwithstanding. Law is like a country dance, people are led up and down in it till they are tired. Law is like a book of surgery, there are a great many terrible cases in it. It is also like physic, they that take least of it are best off. Law is like a homely gentlewoman, very well to follow. Law is also like a scolding wife, very bad when it follows us. Law is like a new fashion, people are bewitched to get into it; it is also like bad weather, most people are glad when they get out of it.

GEORGE ALEXANDER STEVENS, *Lecture on Heads* 85 (1799).

Law (A Jealous Mistress)

As the law is a jealous science, and will not have any partnership with the Eastern Muses, I must absolutely renounce their acquaintance for ten or twelve years to come.

> SIR WILLIAM JONES, *Letter, October 4, 1774 to Mr. Howard* (after his call to the bar).

As to the profession of the law, I must say of it in general, that it requires the whole man, and must be his north star, by which he is to direct his time, from the beginning of his undertaking it, to the end of his life. It is a business of that nature, that it will not be discontinued, nor scarce endure a cessation; but he that will reap the fruit expected from it, that is, raising of an estate by the strength of that, must pursue the subject without interruption, and he must not only read and talk, but eat, drink, and sleep law.

> ROGER NORTH, *On the Study of the Laws* 7.

When I say daily, without intermission or cessation, I do not mean every hour and minute in every day, but only, as the philosophers meant by *nulla dies sine linea,* no day is to pass without somewhat of study or practice of the law, except such as order and necessity will have exempted.

> ROGER NORTH, *On the Study of the Laws* 8.

I will not say with Lord Hale that "The law will admit of no rival, and nothing to go even with it;" but I will say, that it is a jealous mistress, and requires a long and constant courtship. It is not to be won by trifling favors, but by lavish homage.

> JOSEPH STORY, *Miscellaneous Writings* 456 (1835). Speech on his inauguration as Dane Professor of Law, Harvard Univ., August 25, 1829.

The phrase, "The law is a jealous mistress" has been variously attributed but without documentary source. In 1945, after considerable research, M. Eugene Culver (19 Conn. B. J. 90) unearthed this expression of the phrase by Story in 1829. This, however, is not final. See Roger North, *On the Study of the Laws* (pub. 1824), with Notes by a member of the Inner Temple—Note at p. 55: "Mr. North's observations are correct and sensible; the law is not so jealous a mistress as to exclude every other object from the mind of her devotee, although she will vindicate the first place in his affections."

Law (Letter and Spirit)

The case books are full of reports of cases where lay arbitrators have found contracts to be frustrated and the court has held they were wrong. Lawyers have ever been more prone than merchants to cling to the letter of the contract; see, for example *Shylock v. Antonio,* a case which might have been decided on grounds of public policy but, in fact, turned on a pure question of construction.

DIPLOCK, J., *Tsakiroglou v Noblee Thorl* [1959] 2 W.L.R. 179, 185, 186.

If courts of law will adhere to the mere letter of law, the great men who preside in Chancery will ever devise new ways to creep out of the lines of the law, and temper with equity.

LORD MANSFIELD, C.J., *Doe d. Perrin v Blake* (1769) 1 Coll. Jurid. 283, 321.

Wherefore a man ought not to rest upon the letter of an act, nor think that when he has the letter on his side, he has the law on his side in all cases.

PLOWDEN (reporter), *Eyston v Studd* (1574) 2 Plow. 464.

From this judgment and the cause of it, the reader may observe that it is not the words of the law, but the internal sense of it that makes the law, and our law (like all others) consists of two parts, viz.: a body and soul; the letter of the law is the body of the law, and the sense and reason of the law is the soul of the law, *quia ratio legis est anima legis.* And the law may be likened to a nut which has a shell and within it a kernel; the letter of the law represents the shell and the sense of it the kernel, and as you will be no better for the nut if you make use only of the shell, so you will receive no benefit by the law if you rely only upon the letter, and as the fruit and profit of the nut lies in the kernel and not in the shell, so the fruit and profit of the law consists in the sense more than in the letter.

PLOWDEN (reporter), *Eyston v Studd* (1574) 2 Plow. 465.

Not in the letter but in the spirit; for the letter killeth, but the spirit quickeneth.

ST. PAUL: 2 Corinthians 3:6.

Extreme right wiseness is extreme wrong: as who saith, if thou take all that the words of the law giveth thee, thou shalt sometime do against the law.

CHRISTOPHER ST. GERMAN, *Doctor and Student,* Dial. I, ch. 16.

All of the defendants being covered by the spirit and intent of the law, are covered by the letter of the law.

TERRELL, J., *Beard v Viser,* 86 Fla 265, 269 (1923).

Law (Obedience To)

In all well-attempered governments there is nothing which should be more jealously maintained than the spirit of obedience to law, more especially in small matters; for transgression creeps in unperceived and at last ruins the state, just as the constant recurrence of small expenses in time eat up a fortune.

ARISTOTLE, *Politics*, bk 5, ch. 8 (Jowett trans.).

Until the people have by some solemn and authoritative act annulled or changed the established form, it is binding upon themselves collectively, as well as individually; and no presumption, or even knowledge of their sentiments, can warrant their representatives in a departure from it, prior to such an act. But it is easy to see that it would require an uncommon portion of fortitude in the judges to do their duty as faithful guardians of the constitution, where legislative invasion of it had been instigated by the major voice of the community.

ALEXANDER HAMILTON, *The Federalist No. 78 (1788)*.

After all, prohibition is better than no liquor at all.

RING LARDNER, attributed to.

Judicial decisions have two uses—first, to absolutely determine the case decided; and secondly, to indicate to the public how other similar cases will be decided when they arise. . . . We think its decisions on constitutional questions, when fully settled, should control not only the particular cases decided, but the general policy of the country, subject to be disturbed only by amendments of the Constitution as provided in the instrument itself. More than this would be revolution. But we think the *Dred Scott* decision is erroneous. We know the Court that made it has often overruled its own decisions, and we shall do what

356

we can to have it overrule itself. We offer no resistance to it.

> ABRAHAM LINCOLN, *Speech, Springfield, Ill.,* June 26, 1857.
> See 2 Nicolay & Hay, *Complete Works* (1894) 320.

I do not forget the position assumed by some that constitutional questions are to be decided by the Supreme Court, nor do I deny that such decisions must be binding in any case upon the parties to a suit as to the object of that suit, while they are also entitled to very high respect and consideration in all parallel cases by all other departments of the Government. And while it is obviously possible that such decision may be erroneous in any given case, still the evil effect following it, being limited to that particular case, with the chance that it may be overruled and never become a precedent for other cases, can better be borne than could the evils of a different practice.

> ABRAHAM LINCOLN, *First Inaugural Address,* March 4, 1861.

At the same time, the candid citizen must confess that if the policy of the Government, upon vital questions affecting the whole people is to be irrevocably fixed by decisions of the Supreme Court, the instant they are made in ordinary litigation between parties in personal actions the people will have ceased to be their own rulers, having to that extent practically resigned their Government into the hands of that eminent tribunal. Nor is there in this view any assault upon the court or the judges. It is a duty from which they may not shrink to decide cases properly brought before them, and it is no fault of theirs if others seek to turn their decisions to political purposes.

> ABRAHAM LINCOLN, *ibid.*

357

Are all the laws but *one* to go unexecuted, and the government itself to go to pieces, lest that one be violated? Even in such a case, would not the official oath be broken, if the government should be overthrown, when it was believed that disregarding the single law, would tend to preserve it?

ABRAHAM LINCOLN, *Message to Congress, July 4, 1861*. Referring to the suspension of the writ of habeas corpus in the *Merryman* case.

I did understand, however, that my oath to preserve the Constitution to the best of my ability imposed upon me the duty of preserving, by every indispensable means, that government—that nation, of which the Constitution was the organic law. Was it possible to lose the nation and yet preserve the Constitution? By general law, life and limb must be protected, yet often a limb must be amputated to save a life; but a life is never wisely given to save a limb. I felt that measures otherwise unconstitutional might become lawful by becoming indispensable to the preservation of the Constitution through the preservation of the nation.

ABRAHAM LINCOLN, *Letter Apr. 4, 1864, to A. G. Hodges*. See 10 Nicolay & Hay, *Complete Works* (1894) 66.

Without prophecy the people become demoralized; but happy is he who keeps the law.

Proverbs 29:18.

If in the opinion of the people the distribution or modification of the Constitutional powers be in any particular wrong, let it be corrected by an amendment in the way which the Constitution designates. But let there be no change by usurpation; for though this, in one instance, may be the instrument of good, it is the customary weapon by which free governments are destroyed. The precedent must always greatly overbalance in permanent evil any partial or transient benefit which the use itself can at any time yield.

GEORGE WASHINGTON, *Farewell Address, Sept. 17, 1796.*

Law (Publication)

It was not thought fit nor convenient, to publish either those or any of the statutes enacted in those days in the vulgar tongue, lest the unlearned by bare reading without right understanding might suck out errors, and trusting to their conceit, might endamage themselves and some times fall into destruction.

SIR EDWARD COKE, 3 Rep.: *Preface.*

Law (Purpose)

The aim of the law is not to punish sins, but is to prevent certain external results.

HOLMES, J., *Commonwealth v Kennedy,* 170 Mass 18, 20 (1897).

The end of law is not to abolish or to restrain, but to preserve and enlarge freedom: for in all the states of created beings capable of laws, where there is no law, there is no freedom.

JOHN LOCKE, *Second Treatise of Government,* sec. 57.

The end of the law is peace. The means to that end is war. So long as the law is compelled to hold itself in readiness to resist the attacks of wrong—and this it will be

359

compelled to do until the end of time—it cannot dispense with war.   The life of the law is a struggle,—a struggle of nations, of the state power, of classes, of individuals. All the law in the world has been obtained by strife.

> RUDOLPH VON JHERING, *The Struggle for Law* (trans. Lalor).

Law (Respect For)

They presume that the law doth speak with all indifferency; that the law hath no side-respect to their persons; that the law is as it were an oracle proceeded from wisdom and understanding.

> RICHARD HOOKER, *Laws of Ecclesiastical Polity,* bk 1, ch. 10, 7 (1594).

Let reverence for the laws be breathed by every American mother to the lisping babe that prattles on her lap; let it be taught in schools, seminaries, and in colleges; let it be written in primers, spelling books, and in almanacs; let it be preached from the pulpit, proclaimed in legislative halls, and enforced in courts of justice.   And, in short, let it become the political religion of the nation, and let the old and young, the rich and the poor, the grave and the gay of all sexes and tongues and colors and conditions sacrifice unceasingly upon its altars.

> ABRAHAM LINCOLN, *Speech, Springfield, Ill.,* January 27, 1837.

Let every American, every lover of liberty, every well-wisher to his posterity, swear by the blood of the Revolution never to violate in the least particular the laws of the country, and never to tolerate their violation by others.

> ABRAHAM LINCOLN, *ibid.*

These things my heart prompteth me to teach the Athenians, and to make them understand that lawlessness worketh more harm to the state than any other cause. But a law-abiding spirit createth order and harmony, and at the same time putteth chains upon evil-doers; it maketh rough things smooth, it checketh inordinate desires, it dimmeth the glare of wanton pride and withereth the budding bloom of wild delusion; it maketh crooked judgments straight and softeneth arrogant behavior; it stoppeth acts of sedition and stoppeth the anger of bitter strife. Under the reign of law, sanity and wisdom prevail ever among men.

SOLON, *Fragments* (trans. Linforth).

Law (Source)

When the element of long time is introduced, the absurdity of the view of Law preexistent to its declaration is obvious. What was the Law in the time of Richard Coeur de Lion on the liability of a telegraph company to the persons to whom a message was sent? It may be said that though the Law can preexist its declaration, it is conceded that the Law with regard to a natural force cannot exist before the discovery of the force.

GRAY, *Nature and Sources of the Law,* (1921, 2nd ed.) ch. 4, 98.

Human beings do not ever make laws; it is the accidents and catastrophes of all kinds happening in every conceivable way, that make laws for us.

PLATO, *Laws* IV, 709.

Law (Symbolic)

Law is the scripture of Justice, the gospel of Right, and Truth is the minister at its altars. Error is a pretender to holy orders, a wolf in sheep's clothing, always striving to usurp the sacred office, or to share in the exercise of its functions.

LOGAN E. BLECKLEY, *Truth at the Bar*, 3 Ga. Bar Rep. 106 (1886).

Our Lady of the Common Law—I say it with the humility that is due from an old and faithful servant—our Lady in these days is no longer an easy one to please. She has become insatiate in her demands. Not law alone, but almost every branch of human knowledge, has been brought within her ken, and so within the range of sacrifice exacted of her votaries. Those who would earn her best rewards must make their knowledge as deep as the science and as broad and universal as the culture of their day. She will not be satisfied with less.

BENJAMIN N. CARDOZO, *Commencement Address to First Graduating Class, 1928,* 13 St. John's L. R. 231, 232 (1939).

The Law was the golden met-wand, and measure to try the causes of the subjects; and which protected his Majesty in safety and peace.

COKE, *Prohibitions del Roy,* 12 Rep 65.

The law, wherein, as in a magic mirror, we see reflected, not only our own lives, but the lives of all men that have been! When I think on this majestic theme, my eyes dazzle.

OLIVER WENDELL HOLMES, *The Law. Speeches* 17 (1913). Coll. Leg. Pap. 26.

When I think thus of the law, I see a princess mightier than she who once wrought at Bayeux, eternally weaving into her web dim figures of the ever-lengthening past— figures too dim to be noticed by the idle, too symbolic to be interpreted except by her pupils, but to the discerning eye disclosing every painful step and every world-shaking contest by which mankind has worked and fought its way from savage isolation to organic social life.

OLIVER WENDELL HOLMES, *ibid.*

When I think of the Law as we know her in the court-house and the market, she seems to me a woman sitting by the wayside, beneath whose overshadowing hood every man shall see the countenance of his deserts or needs. The timid and overborne gain heart from her protecting smile. Fair combatants, manfully standing to their rights, see her keeping the lists with the stern and discriminating eye of even justice. The wretch who has defied her most sacred commands, and has thought to creep through ways where she was not, finds that his path ends with her, and beholds beneath her hood the inexorable face of death.

OLIVER WENDELL HOLMES, *The Law. Speeches* 18 (1913). Coll. Leg. Pap. 27.

Of Law there can be no less acknowledged, than that her seat is the bosom of God, her voice the harmony of the world. All things in heaven and earth do her homage, the very least as feeling her care, and the greatest as not exempted from her power: both Angels and Men and creatures of what condition soever, though each in different sort and manner, yet all with uniform consent, admiring her as the mother of their peace and joy.

RICHARD HOOKER, *Laws of Ecclesiastical Polity,* bk 1, 16 (1594).

363

Law Enforcement

Judges must beware of hard constructions and strained inferences; for there is no worse torture than the torture of laws.

BACON, *Essays: Of Judicature.*

Let penal laws, if they have been sleepers of long, or if they be grown unfit for the present time, be by wise judges confined in the execution.

BACON, *Essays: Of Judicature.*

After an existence of nearly twenty years of almost innocuous desuetude these laws are brought forth.

PRESIDENT CLEVELAND, *Message, March 1, 1886, to the Senate.*

The laws sometimes sleep, never die.

COKE, *Second Institute* 161.

He threatens the innocent who spares the guilty.

COKE, 4 Rep. 45.

The innocent and the just you shall not put to death, nor shall you acquit the guilty.

Exodus 23:7.

The bite of law is in its enforcement.

FRANKFURTER, J., *Fisher v United States* (1946) 328 US 463, 484, 90 L ed 1382, 1394, 66 S Ct 1318, 166 ALR 1176.

Ours is the accusatorial as opposed to the inquisitorial system.

> FRANKFURTER, J., *Watts v Indiana* (1949) 338 US 49, 54, 93 L ed 1801, 1806, 69 S Ct 1347.

In applying the Bill of Rights to the states, the Supreme Court should not regard these declarations of fundamental principles as if they were a detailed code of criminal procedure, allowing no room whatever for reasonable difference of judgment or play in the joints.

> HENRY J. FRIENDLY, *The Bill of Rights as a Code of Criminal Procedure,* 53 Calif. L. Rev. 929, 953 (1965).

Laws are to govern all alike—those opposed as well as those who favor them. I know no method to secure the repeal of bad or obnoxious laws so effective as their stringent execution.

> ULYSSES S. GRANT, *Inaugural Address,* March 4, 1869.

Of what use are laws, inoperative through public immorality? (*Quid leges sine moribus vanae proficiunt.*)

> HORACE, *Odes,* bk 3, 35.

I concur in the result in this case . . . with considerable misgivings. This is because the case in its particulars seems to present the theory of fair play in a criminal investigation and prosecution as though it were a one way street, instead of presenting it as it is, a two way street. I am the more troubled because it seems to me that both state and federal courts are making it increasingly more difficult to obtain a conviction in the present climate of opinion which so over-emphasizes and slants in the defendant's favor the social and ethical requirements of criminal investi-

365

gation and prosecution as to almost completely overlook
the at least equal good of bringing a criminal to justice.

> HUTCHESON, J., in *Wiman v Powell,* 293 F. 2d 605, 608 (1961).

Perhaps the basic trouble in cases like the one here
[habeas corpus to review a state conviction] is that . . .
the courts and the prosecution are so concerned with questions of fair play from a purely technical standpoint as to
lose sight entirely of the primary question whether the
defendant in whose interest these questions of fair play are
raised, is in fact innocent. It may well be that when a
defendant seeks to invoke in his favor these ideas of fair
play, he must first lay the predicate of showing his innocence of the crime charged. As it is, his hands may be red
with blood and his guilt may shriek to high heaven, but
if he can invoke some of these overattenuated and highly
technical ideas of theoretical fair play, he may escape altogether the consequences of his crime.

> HUTCHESON, J., *ibid.*

Questioning is an indispensable instrumentality of justice.

> JACKSON, J., dissenting, *Ashcraft v Tennessee* (1944) 322 US 143,
> 160, 88 L ed 1192, 1202, 64 S Ct 921.

                              The Gods
Grow angry with your patience. 'Tis their care,
And must be yours, that guilty men escape not:
As crimes do grow, justice should rouse itself.

> BEN JONSON, *Catiline his Conspiracy,* Act 3, scene 5.

It is a public scandal when the law is forced to uphold a
dishonest act.

> LORD MACNAGHTEN, *Nordenfelt v Maxim Nordenfelt Guns*
> [1894] A.C. 535, 573.

Enormous offences call for a greater axe.

> SIR FREDERICK POLLOCK, *The Expansion of the Common Law* 82 (1904).

The law hath not been dead, though it hath slept.

> SHAKESPEARE, *Measure for Measure,* Act 2, scene 2.

We have strict statutes and most biting laws,—
The needful bits and curbs to headstrong steeds,—
Which for this fourteen years we have let sleep;
Even like an o'ergrown lion in a cave,
That goes not out to prey . . . so our decrees,
Dead to infliction, to themselves are dead;
And liberty plucks justice by the nose.

> SHAKESPEARE, *Measure for Measure,* Act 1, scene 3.

A sign of the loss of freedom is the new compassion which extends pity not to the raped but to the rapist.

> FULTON J. SHEEN, *Sermon at Red Mass.* See Hofstadter and Levittan, *Lest the Constable Blunder,* 20 Record (Assn Bar N.Y.C.) 637 (1965).

Law of the Land

This Constitution, and the Laws of the United States which shall be made in Pursuance thereof; and all Treaties made, or which shall be made under the Authority of the United States, shall be the supreme Law of the Land.

> Constitution of the United States, Art. VI, cl. 2.

No freeman shall be taken or imprisoned or disseised, or outlawed, or exiled, or in any ways destroyed; nor shall we go upon him, nor will we send upon him, but by the lawful judgment of his peers or by the law of the land.

Magna Carta, ch. 39 (1215).

Law Review

Judges have at last awakened, or at all events a number of them not wholly negligible, to the treasures buried in the law reviews.

BENJAMIN N. CARDOZO, *Growth of the Law* 14 (1924).

I have thought in certain moods that there is only one test of merit for a decision, and that is whether it was in favor of the critic or against him.   In the old fable of the Greeks, Midas, King of Phrygia, was chosen to decide between Pan and Apollo when they engaged in a musical contest on the flute and lyre.   Midas gave his vote to Pan, whereupon Apollo turned his ears into those of an ass. There are times in reading the comments in the law reviews when I wonder whether Phoebus Apollo is at his elfish tricks again.

BENJAMIN N. CARDOZO, Address, December 17, 1931, 1932 N.Y. County Lawyers Yearbook 369, 371.

Lawyer

Hocus was an old cunning Attorney. What he wanted of skill in law, was made by a Clerk which he kept, that was the prettiest fellow in the world. He loved money, was smooth-tongued, gave good words, and seldom lost his temper.

JOHN ARBUTHNOT, *Law is a Bottomless Pit (History of John Bull)* ch. 5 (1712).

368

It is as impossible for a lawyer to wish men out of litigation, as for a physician to wish them in health.

JEREMY BENTHAM, *Commonplace Book,* 10 Works 74.

Advisers of particular men, in particular difficulties, for
particular fees.

AUGUSTINE BIRRELL, *Introductory Lecture on Law of Fraud,*
University College, December, 1896. See 13 L.Q.R. 264.

But once a lawyer always a lawyer. Though it is fifteen
years since I ceased to practise I find that I still read the
law reports first in the morning paper, and that fragments
of legal jargon still tend to adorn my dubious literary style.

JOHN BUCHAN, *Homilies and Recreations* 209.

We may justly tax our wrangling lawyers, they do grow
old in lawsuits, are so litigious and busy here on earth,
that I think they will plead their clients' causes hereafter,
some of them in hell.

ROBERT BURTON, *Anatomy of Melancholy: Democritus to the
Reader* (1621).

A sergeant of the lawe, war and wys,
That often hadde been at the parvys,
Ther was also, ful riche of excellence.
Discreet he was, and of greet reverence:
He semed swich, his wordes weren so wyse.
Justyce he was ful often in assyse,
By patente, and by pleyn commissioun;
For his science, and for his heigh renoun
Of fees and robes hadde he many oon.

So greet a purchasour was no-wher noon.
Al was fee simple to him in effect,
His purchasing mighte nat been infect,
No-wher so bisy a man as he ther nas,
And yet he semed bisier than he was.
In termes hadde he caas and domes alle,
That from the tyme of king William were falle.
Therto he coude endyte, and make a thing,
Ther coude no wight pinche at his wryting;
And every statut coude he pleyn by rote.

> CHAUCER, *Canterbury Tales: Prologue.*

The lawyer's vacation is the space between the question
put to a witness and his answer.

> RUFUS CHOATE. See 1 Brown, *Works of Choate* 137 (1862).

The greatest orator among the lawyers, the greatest
lawyer among the orators. (*Iuris peritorum eloquentis-
simus, eloquentium iuris peritissimus.*)

> CICERO, *De Oratore*, I, 39 (Referring to Quintus Scaevola).

For the house of a great lawyer is assuredly the oracular
seat of the whole community. (*Est enim sine dubio domus
iurisconsulti, totius oraculum civitatis.*)

> CICERO, *De Oratore*, I, 45.

[Gaius Acquilius] so just and virtuous a man that he
seems to be a lawyer by nature rather than training. (*Qui
ita iustus est et bonus vir, ut natura, non disciplina con-
sultus esse videatur.*)

> CICERO, *Pro Caecina*, xxvii.

370   [Legal Quotations]

The lawyer has spoiled the statesman.

> BENJAMIN DISRAELI, *The Young Duke,* bk 5, ch. 6. Referring to Lord Brougham.

The legal mind chiefly consists in illustrating the obvious, explaining the self-evident and expatiating on the commonplace.

> BENJAMIN DISRAELI, attributed to.

A most learned species of profoundly ignorant men. (*Doctissimum genus indoctissimorum hominum.*)

> ERASMUS, referring to English lawyers and his impression that they knew little outside their profession. 1 North, *Life of Lord Keeper Guilford* 200 (1826).

Necessity knows no law; I know some attorneys of the same.

> BENJAMIN FRANKLIN, *Poor Richard's Almanac for 1734.*

One that will not plead that cause wherein his tongue must be confuted by his conscience.

> THOMAS FULLER, *The Holy State: The Good Advocate* (1642).

I know you lawyers can, with ease,
Twist words and meaning as you please;
That language, by your skill made pliant,
Will bend to favor every client;
That 'tis the fee directs the sense,
To make out either side's pretense,
When you peruse the clearest case,
You see it with a double face,

For scepticism is your profession;
You hold there's doubt in all expression.

> JOHN GAY. *Fables: Dog and the Fox.*

All thieves who could my fees afford
Relied on my orations,
And many a burglar I've restored
To his friends and his relations.

> WILLIAM S. GILBERT, *Trial by Jury.*

To protect his clients from being persuaded by persons whom they do not know to enter into contracts which they do not understand to purchase goods which they do not want with money which they have not got.

> LORD GREENE. Lord Evershed, *Practical and Academic Characteristics of English Law* 40 (1956), says Lord Greene was fond of quoting this old definition of a lawyer's function.

Come, you of the law, who can talk if you please,
Till the man in the moon will allow it's a cheese.

> O. W. HOLMES, Sr., *Lines Recited at Berkshire Jubilee.*

You know my division of able lawyers into kitchen knives, razors, and stings.

> OLIVER WENDELL HOLMES, 1 *Holmes-Laski Letters* 692.

A simple barefoot Wall Street lawyer.

> HAROLD L. ICKES, 3 *Secret Diary (Dec. 21, 1940)* 396. Referring to Wendell Willkie as the Republican presidential nominee. Ickes says he borrowed the phrase, using it in a speech, from columnist Jay Franklin (John Franklin Carter).

In a peaceful Cambridge college,
  Far remote from active law,
I dissect the Courts' decisions—
  I of course detect the flaw:
I correct their learned Lordships,
  (Though I do it from afar);
Though I'm good at academics,
  I'd be useless at the Bar.

J.P.C., *Poetic Justice* 15 (1947).

He did not care to speak ill of any man behind his back, but he believed the gentleman was an attorney.

SAMUEL JOHNSON.   Boswell, *Life of Johnson: 1770.*

Lawyers know life practically.   A bookish man should always have them to converse with, they have what he wants.

SAMUEL JOHNSON.   Boswell, *Life of Johnson: 1778.*

Woe to you lawyers also! because you load men with oppressive burdens and you yourselves with one of your fingers do not touch the burdens.

Luke 11:46.

Woe to you lawyers! for you have taken away the key of knowledge; you yourselves have not entered in, and those that were entering in you have hindered.

Luke 11:52.

A cock-brained solicitor, a law puddler, a mere and arrant pettifogger, a pork who never read any philosophy, an unbuttoned fellow, a boar in a vineyard, a snout in pickle

. . . the shame of all honest attorneys, an unswilled hogshead, a tradesman of the law, whose best ware is only gibberish, a serving man and solicitor compounded into one mongrel—an apostate scarecrow, a vagabond and ignoramous, a beetle, a daw, a horsefly, a nuisance and brazen ass.

> JOHN MILTON, *Colasterion,* (A composite of the epithets which Milton applied to an opponent who disagreed with him on the subject of divorce.)

Some allured to the trade of law, grounding their purposes not on the prudent and heavenly contemplation of justice and equity, which was never taught them, but on the promising and pleasing thoughts of litigious terms, fat contentions, and flowing fees.

> JOHN MILTON, *Of Education.*

Sometimes a man who deserves to be looked down upon because he is a fool is despised only because he is a lawyer.

> MONTESQUIEU, *Persian Letters,* XLIV.

They have no lawyers among them, for they consider them as a sort of people whose profession it is to disguise matters.

> SIR THOMAS MORE, *Utopia,* bk 2.

An Honest Lawyer—a trusted Pilot, a true priest of justice, one who wears the conscience as well as the gowne, weighs the cause as well as the gold, and knows, but never uses, the nice snapperadoes of Practice.

> OVERBURY, *Characters: An Honest Lawyer.*

The lawyer is always in a hurry.

>PLATO: *Theaetetus.*

Your lawyer in practice spends a considerable part of his life in doing distasteful things for disagreeable people who must be satisfied, against an impossible time limit and with hourly interruptions, from other disagreeable people who want to derail the train; and for his blood, sweat, and tears he receives in the end a few unkind words to the effect that it might have been done better, and a protest at the size of the fee.

>WILLIAM L. PROSSER, 1 Jl. Leg. Educ. 260.

The devil makes his Christmas-pies of lawyers' tongues and clerks' fingers.

>Proverb.

Of three things the Deuill makes his messe, Of Lawyers tongues, of Scriueners fingers, you the third may gesse.

>FLORIO, *Second Frutes* (1591) 179.

Sir Robert Pye, attorney of the court of wardes, was his neighbour, but there was no great goodwill between them. Sir Robert was haughty. He happened to dye on Christmas day: the newes being brought to the serjeant, said he "the devill haz a christmas pye."

>AUBREY, *Brief Lives: John Hoskyns, Serjeant-at-lawe.*

St. Ives was a Breton,
Lawyer and not a robber,
A thing that made the people wonder.

>Proverb.

A barrister of extended practise, if he has any talents at all, is the best companion in the world.

SIR WALTER SCOTT, *Journal, April 30, 1828.*

Why might not that be the skull of a lawyer? Where be his quiddities now, his quillets, his cases, his tenures, and his tricks?

SHAKESPEARE, *Hamlet,* Act 5, scene 1.

Dick (the Butcher): The first thing we do, let's kill all the lawyers.

Jack Cade: Nay, that I mean to do.

SHAKESPEARE, *Henry the Sixth,* Pt. 2, Act 4, scene 2. (Read in its full context these words show that Shakespeare knew that you cannot set up a totalitarian form of government unless you first get rid of all the lawyers. Edwin M. Otterbourg, 39 A.B.A.J. 424.)

And do as adversaries do in law,
Strive mightily, but eat and drink as friends.

SHAKESPEARE, *Taming of the Shrew,* Act 1, scene 2.

He piqued himself on understanding the practice of the courts, and in private company he took pleasure in laying down the law.

SMOLLETT, *Sir Launcelot Greaves,* ch. 1 (referring to Tom Clarke, a young lawyer).

There are three sorts of lawyers—able, unable, lamentable.

ROBERT SMITH SURTEES, *Plain or Ringlets,* ch. 40.

There was a society of men among us, bred up from their youth in the art of proving, by words multiplied for the purpose, that white is black and black is white, according as they are paid.

JONATHAN SWIFT, *Gulliver's Travels: Houyhnhnms*, ch. 5.

An *advocat* is a man who, not having money enough to buy one of those brilliant offices on which the universe has its eyes fixed, studies for three years the laws of Theodosius and Justinian so as to know the custom of Paris, and who at length having got matriculated has the right of pleading for money, if he has a loud voice.

VOLTAIRE, *Dictionnaire Philosophique*, 3 Works 378.

He is never in the company of a lawyer but he fancies himself in a witness-box.

WARD, *Illustrations of Human Life.* Quoted in 1 Grant, *Bench and Bar* 157 (1841).

I can give it as the condensed history of most, if not all good lawyers, that they lived well and died poor.

DANIEL WEBSTER, *Speech, Charleston, S.C. Bar,* May 10, 1847.

I have given my life to law and politics. Law is uncertain and politics are utterly vain.

DANIEL WEBSTER, to Professor Silliman, May 1852. Lodge, *Life of Webster 346.*

He is the very miracle of a lawyer,
One that persuades men to peace, and compounds quarrels
Among his neighbours, without going to law.

JOHN WEBSTER, *Devil's Law Case,* Act 2, scene 1 (1619).

377

Weary lawyers with endless tongue.

WHITTIER, *Maud Muller.*

[Lawyers] have been known to wrest from reluctant juries triumphant verdicts of acquittal for their clients, even when those clients, as often happens, were clearly and unmistakably innocent.

OSCAR WILDE, *The Decay of Lying.*

A modest lawyer! a silent woman! a paradox in nature.

JOHN WILSON, *The Cheats,* I, 4 (1664).

O lady, lady, all interruption and no sense between us, as if we were lawyers at the bar; but I had forgot Apollo and Littleton never lodge in a head together.

WILLIAM WYCHERLY, *The Plain Dealer,* Act 4, scene 1.

That litigious pettifogger.

WILLIAM WYCHERLEY, *The Plain Dealer,* Act 4, scene 1.

Lawyer (Fledgling)

Young men who feel drawn to the legal profession may rest assured that they will find in it an opportunity for usefulness which is probably unequalled elsewhere.

LOUIS D. BRANDEIS, Interview by Ernest Poole, 71 Amer. Mag. 493 (1911).

"Phunky, Phunky," said the Serjeant; "I never heard the name before. He must be a very young man."

"Yes, he is a very young man," replied the attorney. "He was only called the other day. Let me see—oh, he hasn't been at the Bar eight years yet."

CHARLES DICKENS, *Pickwick Papers*, ch. 31.

Mr. Bellby, the junior—not as junior as he might have been, for Soames only employed barristers of established reputation; it was, indeed, something of a mystery to him how barristers ever managed to establish that which made him employ them.

JOHN GALSWORTHY, *In Chancery*, Pt. 2, ch. 4.

When I went to the Bar as a very young man,
   (Said I to myself, said I,)
I'll work on a new and original plan,
   (Said I to myself, said I,)
I'll never assume that a rogue or a thief
Is a gentleman worthy implicit belief,
Because his attorney has sent me a brief,
   (Said I to myself, said I!)

WILLIAM S. GILBERT, *Iolanthe*, Act 1.

I'll never throw dust in a juryman's eyes,
   (Said I to myself, said I,)
Or hoodwink a judge who is not over-wise,
   (Said I to myself, said I,)
Or assume that the witnesses summoned in force
In Exchequer, Queen's Bench, Common Pleas, or Divorce,
Have perjured themselves as a matter of course,
   (Said I to myself, said I!)

WILLIAM S. GILBERT, *ibid.*

379

Ere I go into court I will read my brief through,
　(Said I to myself, said I,)
And I'll never take work I'm unable to do,
　(Said I to myself, said I,)
My learned profession I'll never disgrace
By taking a fee with a grin on my face,
When I haven't been there to attend to the case,
　(Said I to myself, said I!)

　　WILLIAM S. GILBERT, *ibid.*

When I, good friends, was called to the bar,
I'd an appetite fresh and hearty,
But I was, as many young barristers are,
An impecunious party:
I'd a swallow-tail coat of beautiful blue—
A brief which I bought of a booby—
A couple of shirts and a collar or two,
And a ring that looked like a ruby!

　　WILLIAM S. GILBERT, *Trial By Jury.*

In Westminster Hall I danced a dance,
　　Like a semi-despondent fury;
For I thought I should never hit on a chance
　　Of addressing a British Jury—
But I soon got tired of third-class journeys,
　　And dinners of bread and water;
So I fell in love with a rich attorney's
　　Elderly, ugly daughter.

　　WILLIAM S. GILBERT, *ibid.*

The rich attorney, he jumped with joy,
　　And replied to my fond professions:

"You shall reap the reward of your pluck, my boy,
    At the Bailey and Middlesex Sessions.
You'll soon get used to her looks," said he,
    "And a very nice girl you'll find her!
She may very well pass for forty-three
    In the dusk, with a light behind her!"

WILLIAM S. GILBERT, *ibid.*

I was speaking of my first brief, when he asked, "Did you not exclaim,—'Thou great first cause, least understood'?"

CRABB ROBINSON, *Diary, November 14, 1815.* Referring to conversation with Charles Lamb, who quoted from Pope's *Universal Prayer.*

O, how can a modest young man
E'er hope for the smallest progression,—
The profession's already so full
Of lawyers so full of profession!

JOHN GODFREY SAXE, *The Briefless Barrister.*

Lawyer (Gentlemen of the Long Robe)

I wish thee all the success that thy heart can desire! and that these Gentlemen of the long robe may have their bellyful of Law!

JOHN ARBUTHNOT, *Law is a Bottomless Pit (History of John Bull)* pt 4, ch. 7 (1712).

But what occasion had you to present them, and what authority had you to swear him.   You are a gentleman of the long robe, and should have known better.

JEFFREYS, C.J., *Sacheverell's Case* (1684) 10 How. St. Tr. 91.

381

Lawyer (Philadelphia)

It would (to use a Yankee phrase) puzzle a dozen Philadelphia lawyers.

The Balance, Nov. 15, 1803.
Proverb. There would seem to be little doubt but that the origin of this expression grew out of the Zenger trial. Zenger's New York lawyers were disbarred by the court. Andrew Hamilton (then eighty years of age) came from Philadelphia to defend him and succeeded in obtaining an acquittal. The expression is used both in praise and in opprobrium. Hamilton was given the Freedom of the Corporation by the Mayor of New York. See *Zenger Trial* (1735) 17 How. St. Tr. 723. Remarks on the trial by two lawyers, defending the arguments of the Crown repeatedly use the expression in a disparaging manner. See *ibid.* 740, 754, 763.

Many historians credit him (Andrew Hamilton) with being the one who, through his successful defense of John Peter Zenger, not only established in the New World the freedom of the press, but also created the appellation you here have enjoyed of being "Philadelphia lawyers".

LOYD WRIGHT, 41 A.B.A.J. 797 (1955).

Legal Advice

It is not what a lawyer tells me I *may* do; but what humanity, reason, and justice, tell me I ought to do.

EDMUND BURKE, *Speech on Conciliation with America,* March 22, 1775.

It is well known that on every question the lawyers are about equally divided, . . . and were we to act but in cases where no contrary opinion of a lawyer can be had, we should never act.

THOMAS JEFFERSON, *Letter to Secretary of Treasury,* Sept. 20, 1808.

Legal Advice (Right to Counsel)

Not only these precedents but also reason and reflection require us to recognize that in our adversary system of criminal justice, any person haled into court, who is too poor to hire a lawyer, cannot be assured a fair trial unless counsel is provided for him. . . . Governments, both state and federal, quite properly spend vast sums of money to establish machinery to try defendants accused of crime. . . . Similarly, there are few defendants charged with crime, few indeed, who fail to hire the best lawyers they can get to prepare and present their defenses.   That government hires lawyers to prosecute and defendants who have the money hire lawyers to defend are the strongest indications of the widespread belief that lawyers in criminal courts are necessities, not luxuries.

> BLACK, J., *Gideon v Wainwright* (1963) 372 US 335, 344, 9 L ed 2d 799, 805, 83 S Ct 792, 93 ALR2d 733.

It does not militate against respect for the deeply rooted systems of criminal justice in the states that such an abrupt innovation as recognition of the constitutional claim here made implies, would furnish opportunities hitherto uncontemplated for opening wide the prison doors of the land.

> FRANKFURTER, J., *Foster v Illinois* (1947) 332 US 134, 139, 91 L ed 1955, 1959, 67 S Ct 1716.

Gideon's Trumpet has been heard throughout the land by all potential defendants.

> SAMUEL H. HOFSTADTER and SHIRLEY LEVITTAN, *Lest the Constable Blunder,* 20 Record (Assn Bar N.Y.C.) 629, 643, fn. 59. Referring to *Gideon v Wainwright* (1963) 372 US 335, 9 L ed 2d 799, 83 S Ct 792, 93 ALR2d 733, and title of book "Gideon's Trumpet" by Anthony Lewis.

Bolingbroke:
What would you have me do? I am a subject,
And challenge law: attorneys are denied me,
And therefore personally I lay my claim
To my inheritance of free descent.

SHAKESPEARE, *Richard II*, Act 2, scene 3.

Legal Aid

Ye who plead for the poor, and take money at their hands,
Ye lawyers, ye advocates, be sure of this:
When ye draw near to death, and pray for pardon,
Your pardon at your parting hence will be but small.
Saint Matthew bids me tell you this, and if I lie, blame him.

LANGLAND, *Piers Plowman:* Gods's Bull of Pardon.

For the sake of God, I will help you. (*Pro Deo te adjuvabo.*)

ST. IVES (his maxim).

Legislation

As in other sciences, so in politics, it is impossible that all things should be precisely set down in writing; for enactments must be universal, but actions are concerned with particulars.

ARISTOTLE, *Politics,* bk 2, 8.

It is better that all things be regulated by law, than left to be decided by judges.

ARISTOTLE, *Rhetoric,* bk 1, 1.

384

It is far easier to conceive justly what would be useful law, than so to construct that same law that it may accomplish the design of the lawgiver.

> JOHN AUSTIN, *Jurisprudence: Codification* (Lect. 39 pt. 2).

That law may be set down as good which is certain in meaning, just in precept, convenient in execution, agreeable to the form of government, and productive of virtue in those that live under it.

> BACON, *Advancement of Learning,* bk 8, Aph. 7.

The laws of the most kingdoms and states have been like buildings of many pieces, and patched up from time to time according to occasions, without frame or model.

> BACON, *An Offer to the King of a Digest to be Made of the Laws of England.*

Solon being asked; *Whether he had given the Athenians the best laws?* answered; *Yes, the best of those that they would have received.*

> BACON, *Apothegms New and Old,* no. 93.

No law can be made that does not take something from liberty.

> JEREMY BENTHAM, *Anarchical Fallacies: Preamble.* See 2 *Works* (1843 Bowring ed.) 493.

The founders of this Nation entrusted the lawmaking power to Congress alone in both good and bad times.

> BLACK, J., *Youngstown Sheet & Tube Co. v Sawyer* (1952) 343 US 579, 589, 96 L ed 1153, 1168, 72 S Ct 863, 26 ALR2d 1378. (Referring to seizure of steel mills by executive order of President Truman.)

Legislatures are not grammar schools; and, in this country at least, it is hardly reasonable to expect legislative acts to be drawn with strict grammatical or logical accuracy.

> CHRISTIANCY, C.J., *Whipple v Judge of Saginaw Circuit*, 26 Mich 342, 344 (1873).

I knew a very wise man . . . he believed if a man were permitted to make all the ballads, he need not care who should make the laws of a nation.

> ANDREW FLETCHER *Letter to Marquis of Montrose.* See Political Works (1749 Edin. ed.) 266.

Law has always been unintelligible, and I might say that perhaps it ought to be. And I will tell you why, because I don't want to deal in paradoxes. It ought to be unintelligible because it ought to be in words—and words are utterly inadequate to deal with the fantastically multiform occasions which come up in human life.

> LEARNED HAND, *Speech at Seventy-Fifth Anniversary Dinner, Legal Aid Society of N.Y.*, Feb. 16, 1951, 9 Brief Case, No. 4, 4.

Each one of us must in the end choose for himself how far he would like to leave our collective fate to the wayward vagaries of popular assemblies. No one can fail to recognize the perils to which the last forty years have exposed such governments. We are not indeed forced to choose between absolutism and the kind of democracy that so often prevailed in Greek cities during the sixth to fourth centuries before our era. The Founding Fathers were acutely, perhaps overacutely, aware of the dangers that had followed that sort of rule, though, as you all know, they differed widely as to what curbs to impose. For myself it would be most irksome to be ruled by a bevy of

Platonic Guardians, even if I knew how to choose them, which I assuredly do not.

LEARNED HAND, *The Bill of Rights* (1964 ed.) 73.

If Congress has not, by the words used in this act, described this and like cases, it would, we apprehend, be impossible to find words that would describe them.

HARLAN, J., *Northern Secur. Co. v United States* (1904) 193 US 197, 360, 48 L ed 679, 709, 24 S Ct 436.

It might be possible, but I doubt if it would be easy, to compress in the same number of lines more fertile opportunities for doubt and error.

LORD HEWART, C.J., *London County Council v Lees* [1939] 1 All E. R. 191, 194. Referring to the Sunday Trading Restrictions Act, 1936.

It is not wisdom but authority that makes a law.

THOMAS HOBBES, *Dialogue of the Common Laws,* 6 Works 5.

I am so skeptical as to our knowledge about the goodness or badness of laws that I have no practical criterion except what the crowd wants. Personally I bet that the crowd if it knew more wouldn't want what it does—but that is immaterial.

OLIVER WENDELL HOLMES, 1 *Holmes-Pollock Letters* 163 (1910).

The Constitution does not make it a condition of preventive legislation that it should work a perfect cure. It is enough if the questioned act has a manifest tendency to cure or at least make the evil less.

HOLMES, J., dissenting, *Louis K. Liggett Co. v Baldridge* (1928) 278 US 105, 115, 73 L ed 204, 209, 49 S Ct 57.

An Act of Parliament can do no wrong, though it may do several things that look pretty odd.

HOLT, C.J., *City of London v Wood* (1701) 12 Mod. 669, 687.

Algebraic formulae are not lightly to be imputed to legislators.

HOUGH, J., *Edwards v Slocum*, 287 Fed. 651, 654 **(1923).**

I'm the Parliamentary Draftsman,
   I compose the country's laws,
And of half the litigation
   I'm undoubtedly the cause.
I employ a kind of English
   Which is hard to understand:
Though the purists do not like it,
   All the lawyers think it's **grand.**

J.P.C., *Poetic Justice* 31 (1947).

I'm the Parliamentary Draftsman,
   And they tell me it's a fact
That I often make a muddle
   Of a simple little Act.
I'm a target for the critics,
   And they take me in their stride—
Oh, how nice to be a critic
   Of a job you've never tried!

J.P.C., *Poetic Justice* 32 (1947).

Laws are formed by the manners and exigencies of particular times, and it is but accidental that they last longer than their causes.

SAMUEL JOHNSON. *Boswell, Life of Johnson: 1776.*

Three corrective words turn whole legal libraries into waste paper.

JULIUS VON KIRCHMANN, attributed to (1847).

Legislation in the United States is a digestive process by Congress with frequent regurgitations by the Supreme Court.

SIR WILMOT LEWIS, attributed to. See Pearson and Allen, *Nine Old Men* (1936) 44.

It was incongruous and impossible of operation; and its absurdities were so great that the framers themselves had no very distinct notion of its meaning.

MAULE, J., *Stratton v Pettit* (1885) 16 C.B. 420, 432.

The laws should be adapted in such a manner to the people for whom they are framed that it should be a great chance if those of one nation suit another. . . . They should be in relation to the climate of each country, to the quality of its soil, to its situation and extent, to the principal occupation of the natives.

MONTESQUIEU, *Spirit of the Laws,* bk 1.

I first thought it would be possible to reduce laws to simple geometrical demonstrations, so that whoever could read and tie two ideas together would be capable of pronouncing on them; but I almost immediately convinced myself that this was an absurd idea.

NAPOLEON.

The law does not perfectly comprehend what is noblest and most just for all and therefore cannot enforce what is best. The differences of men and actions, and the endless irregular movements of human things, do not admit of any universal and simple rule. And no art whatsoever can lay down a rule which will last for all time.

PLATO, *Statesman* (Jowett trans.)

I will drive a coach and six through the Act of Settlement.

STEPHEN RICE. Macaulay, *History of England,* ch. 12.

Every law which originated in ignorance and malice, and gratifies the passions from which it sprang, we call the wisdom of our ancestors.

SYDNEY SMITH, *Peter Plymley Letters* (Letter no. 5).

It is not enough to attain to a degree of precision which a person reading in good faith can understand; but it is necessary to attain if possible to a degree of precision which a person reading in bad faith cannot misunderstand.

STEPHEN, J., *In re Castioni* [1891] 1 Q.B. 149, 167.

No law of that country must exceed in words the number of letters in their alphabet, which consists only of two and twenty. But, indeed few of them extend even to that length. They are expressed in the most plain and simple terms, wherein those people are not mercurial enough to discover above one interpretation; and to write a comment upon any law is a capital crime. As to the decision of civil causes, or proceedings against criminals, their precedents are so few, that they have little reason to boast of any extraordinary skill in either.

JONATHAN SWIFT, *Gulliver's Travels: Brobdingnag,* ch. 7.

Do you want good laws? Burn those which you have at present, and make fresh ones.

VOLTAIRE, *Dictionnaire Philosophique: Lois.*

Legislature

Mr. Popham, when he was Speaker, and the Lower House had sat long, and done in effect nothing; coming one day to Queen Elizabeth, she said to him: *Now, Mr. Speaker, what hath passed in the Lower House?* He answered, *If it please your Majesty, seven weeks.*

BACON, *Apothegms New and Old,* no. 59.

England is the mother of Parliaments.

JOHN BRIGHT, *Speech* at Birmingham, Jan. 18, 1865.

It is a fundamental principle with the English lawyers that Parliament can do everything, except making a woman a man or a man a woman.

DE LOLME, *Constitution of England,* bk 1, ch. x (1775). Although De Lolme is invariably given as the source of this saying, it appears earlier in a satirical pamphlet published in 1648. See, *News from Pembroke and Montgomery* in *The Harleian Miscellany.* The words are there put into the mouth of Philip Herbert, 4th Earl of Pembroke.

I think a Court of Law is bound to proceed upon the assumption that the legislature is an ideal person that does not make mistakes.

LORD HALSBURY, L.C., *Comm'rs. for Special Purpose of Income Tax v Pemsel* [1891] A.C. 531, 549.

391

It must be remembered that legislatures are ultimate guardians of the liberties and welfare of the people in quite as great a degree as the courts.

> HOLMES, J., *Missouri, K. & T. R. Co. v May* (1904) 194 US 267, 270, 48 L ed 971, 973, 24 S Ct 638.

If the present Congress errs in too much talking, how can it be otherwise, in a body to which the people send one hundred and fifty lawyers, whose trade it is to question everything, yield nothing, and talk by the hour? That one hundred and fifty lawyers should do business together, ought not to be expected.

> THOMAS JEFFERSON, *Autobiography.*

These are the *Bounds* which the trust that is put in them by the Society, and the Law of God and Nature, have *set to the Legislative* Power of every Commonwealth, in all Forms of Government.

First, They are to govern by *promulgated establish'd Laws,* not to be varied in particular Cases, but to have one Rule for Rich and Poor, for the Favourite at Court, and the Country Man at Plough.

Secondly, These *Laws* also ought to be designed *for* no other end ultimately but *the good of the People.*

Thirdly, they must *not raise Taxes* on the Property of the People *without the Consent of the People,* given by themselves, or their Deputies. . . .

Fourthly, The *Legislative* neither must *nor can transfer the Power of making Laws* to any Body else, or place it any where but where the People have.

> JOHN LOCKE, *Second Treatise of Government,* sec. 142.

He [Monk] also acquainted them that he had sent a letter to the Parliament, that they would fill up the House, and put an end to their sitting by the 6th of May. By this means he gave such encouragement to the Cavalierish party, that the rabble of them, as he passed by from Guildhal, cried out for a free Parliament; and perceiving him not displeased with their insolence, they made bonfires in London and Westminster for roasting the Rump, as they presumed to call that Parliament, who in the five years' time that they governed without interruption, had raised the glory of the nation from the dust wherein it had been buried by the negligence and corruption of the preceding governments.

> EDMUND LUDLOW, *Memoirs,* entry. Feb. 11, 1660.

The bill for incorporating the Bank of the United States did not steal upon an unsuspecting legislature, and pass unobserved.

> MARSHALL, C.J., *M'Culloch v Maryland* (1819, US) 4 Wheat 316, 401, 4 L ed 579, 600.

The old argument often heard, often repeated, and in this court never assented to, that when a question of the power of Congress arises the advocate of the power must be able to place his finger on words which expressly grant it.

> MILLER, J., *Ex parte Yarbrough* (1884) 110 US 651, 658, 28 L ed 274, 276, 4 S Ct 152.

The Capitol Comedy Company of Washington.

> WILL ROGERS. See *Autobiography of Will Rogers* (selected and ed. by Day) entry Feb. 18, 1923. Referring to Congress.

No man's life, liberty, or property are safe while the Legislature is in session.

> Saying. See 1 Tucker (N.Y. Surr.) 249 (1866).

The House of Commons is called the lower house in twenty acts of Parliament, but what are twenty acts of Parliament amongst friends.

　　JOHN SELDEN, *Table-Talk: House of Commons.*

The most high and absolute power of the realme of Englande, consisteth in the Parliament. . . . That which is done by this consent is called firme, stable and sanctum, and is taken for lawe. The Parliament abrogateth olde lawes, maketh newe, giveth orders for things past, and for thinges hereafter to be followed, changeth rightes, and possessions of private men, legittimateth bastards, establisheth formes of religion, altereth weightes and measures, giveth formes of succession to the crowne, defineth of doubtfull rightes, whereof is no lawe alreadie made, appointeth subsidies, tailes, taxes, and impositions, giveth most free pardons and absolutions, restoreth in bloud and name as the highest court, condemneth or absolveth them whom the Prince will put to that triall: And to be short, all that ever the people of Rome might do either in Centuriatis comitiis or tributis, the same may be doone by the parliament of Englande, which representeth and hath the power of the whole realme both the head and the bodie. For everie Englishman is entended to bee there present, either in person or by procuration and attornies, of what preheminence, state dignitie, or qualitie soever he bee, from the Prince (be he King or Queene) to the lowest person of Englande. And the consent of the Parliament is taken to be everie mans consent.

　　SIR THOMAS SMITH, *De Republica Anglorum,* bk 2, ch. 1.

For protection against abuses by legislatures the people must resort to the polls, not to the courts.

　　WAITE, C.J., *Munn v Illinois* (1876) 94 US 113, 134, 24 L ed 77, 87.

The king being in great want of money, and fearing that if the lawyers were parliament men they would oppose his excessive demaunds and hinder his illegall purposes (according to their knowledge and learning in the lawes and publique affayres); to prevent this the King issued forth writs of summons with a clause of "nolumus" to this effect: "We will not that you or any other sherife of our kingdome or any other man of lawe by any means be chosen." This parliament was held 6 Hen. 4, and was called the lacke-learning parliament, either (saith our historian) for the unlearnedness of the persons or for their malice to learned men. It is stiled by Sir Thomas Walsingham in his *Margent* "the parliament of unlearned men," and from them, thus packed, the king (saith our author) obtained a graunt of an unusual taxe and to the people "full of trouble and very grievous." . . . They who will have a "nolumus" of learned senators must be contented with a "volumus" of uncouth lawes which I hope will never be the fate of England.

BULSTRODE WHITELOCK, *Notes upon the King's Writ.*

Liability

Wherever one of two innocent persons must suffer by the acts of a third, he who has enabled such third person to occasion the loss must sustain it.

ASHHURST, J., *Lickbarrow v Mason* (1787) 2 T.R. 63, 70.

Suppose that some intelligent member of the public—a juryman, for example . . . were to look into a series of courts to observe what is actually going on . . . he will almost certainly find a person . . . who has suffered bodily injuries in a collision between two stationary motor-cars, each on its proper side of the road, and each keeping a good look-out, endeavouring to convince a judge and a jury that the liability rests upon the defendant, and to collect suitable compensation in the way of damages.

LORD HEWART, *Not Without Prejudice* 230.

A blind man is not required to see at his peril.

OLIVER WENDELL HOLMES, *Common Law* 109 (1881).

Legal obligations that exist but cannot be enforced are ghosts that are seen in the law but that are elusive to the grasp.

HOLMES, J., *The Western Maid* (1922) 257 US 419, 433, 66 L ed 299, 303, 42 S Ct 159.

Libel and Slander

It had been adjudged, that where one says of a Lawyer, That he had as much Law as a Monkey, that the words were not actionable; because he hath as much Law, and more also. But if he had said, That he hath no more Law than a Monkey, those words were actionable.

BARCKLEY (BERKELEY) J., *Dickes v Fenne* (1639) March N.R. 60.

For supposing they were true, the law says they are not the less libellous for that; nay indeed the law says, their being true is an aggravation of the crime.

RICHARD BRADLEY (Atty. Gen. for King, Province of N.Y.) arguendo, *Trial of Peter Zenger* (1735) 17 How. St. Tr. 694.

Dost not know that old Mansfield who writes like the Bible
Says the more 'tis a truth, sir, the more 'tis a libel.

> ROBERT BURNS, *Lines written at Stirling.*

Many things that are defamatory may be said with
impunity through the medium of speech. Not so, however,
when speech is caught upon the wing and transmuted
into print. What gives the sting to the writing is its
permanence of form. The spoken word dissolves, but the
written one abides and "perpetuates the scandal".

> CARDOZO, C.J., *Ostrowe v Lee,* 256 N.Y. 36, 39 (1931).

Political parties, like public men are, as it were, public
property.

> FRANKFURTER, J., *Beauharnais v Illinois* (1952) 343 US 250,
> 263, n. 18, 96 L ed 919, 931, 72 S Ct 725.

It hath ever been agreed, that it is not the matter but the
manner which is punishable; for libelling against a common strumpet is as great an offense as against an honest
woman, and perhaps more dangerous to the breach of the
peace; for as the woman said she would never grieve to
have been told of her red nose if she had not one indeed,
neither is it a ground to examine the truth or falsehood of
a libel, because it is *sub judice* whether it be a libel or not.

> HUDSON, *Star Chamber* (2 Coll. Jurid., 102).

I adopt, in this case, as perfectly correct, the comprehensive and accurate definition of one of the counsel at
the bar (Gen. Hamilton) that the liberty of the press
consists in the right to publish with impunity, truth, with

good motives, and for justifiable ends, whether it respects government, magistracy or individuals.

> KENT, J., *People v Croswell,* 3 John. Cas. (N.Y.) 337, 393 (1804). This definition by Alexander Hamilton antedated by almost forty years Lord Campbell's Act of 1843 and is the basis of modern criminal libel statutes.

Whenever a man publishes he publishes at his peril.

> LORD MANSFIELD, C.J., *R. v Woodfall* (1774) Lofft, 776, 781.

The greater the truth the greater the libel.

> *Maxim.* This maxim was applicable to the criminal law of defamation prior to the passage of Lord Campbell's Libel Act of 1843, which permitted the truth to be given in evidence on the subject of malice. The maxim has been attributed to both Lord Mansfield and Lord Ellenborough but the particular wording has not been found in the reports.

And oh, 'twas nuts to the Father of Lies,
(As this wily fiend is named in the Bible)
To find it settled by laws so wise,
That the greater the truth, the worse the libel.

> THOMAS MOORE, *A Case of Libel. Odes on Cash, Corn, etc.*

The question is not so much who was aimed at, as who was hit.

> POUND, J., *Corrigan v Bobbs-Merrill Co.,* 228 N.Y. 58, 63, 64 (1920).

For Sir Philip well knows,
That his innuendos
Will serve him no longer
In verse or in prose;

For twelve honest men have decided the cause,
Who are judges of fact, though not judges of law.

> SIR WILLIAM PULTENEY, *Ballad,* published on the occasion of
> an acquittal of *The Craftsman,* for libel. This version of the
> ballad Lord Mansfield quoted from memory in the Trial of
> the Dean of St. Asaph, 21 How. St. Tr. 1037. Ridgeway, ed. of
> *Speeches of Lord Erskine* (see, 17 How. St. Tr. 672) and Lord
> Campbell (see, *Lives of Chancellors: Erskine,* ch. 178) assert
> that the last two lines read: For twelve honest men have deter-
> mined the cause, Who are judges alike of the facts and the laws.

"You are too easily surprised," said Mr. Towkington.
"Many words have no legal meaning. Others have a legal
meaning very unlike their ordinary meaning. For example, the word 'daffy-down-dilly.' It is a criminal libel to
call a lawyer a daffy-down-dilly. Ha! Yes, I advise you
never to do such a thing. No, I certainly advise you *never*
to do it."

> DOROTHY SAYERS, *Unnatural Death,* ch. 14. (In Peares' Case
> (1634) 1 Roll. Abr. 55, it was held actionable to call a lawyer
> a "daffa-down-dilly".)

Juliet:
That is no slander, sir, which is a truth;
And what I spake, I spake it to my face.

> SHAKESPEARE, *Romeo and Juliet,* Act 4, scene 1.

Convey a libel in a frown,
And wink a reputation down.

> JONATHAN SWIFT, *Journal of a Modern Lady.*

If wisdom's ways you would early seek,
   Five things observe with care,

To whom you speak, of whom you speak,
    And how, and when, and where.

Unknown.

A strange wild jurisdiction; where the jurors are judges
both of law and of fact, and ignorant country fellows are
to determine the nicest points of law.

WILMOT, J., *Doe v Roe* (1760) 2 Burr. 1046, 1047.

Liberty

Liberty is a term of two hundred definitions.

LORD ACTON. See *Essays on Freedom and Power* **14.**

Experience should teach us to be most on our guard
to protect liberty when the Government's purposes are
beneficent. Men born to freedom are naturally alert to
repel invasion of their liberty by evil-minded rulers. The
greatest dangers to liberty lurk in insidious encroachment
by men of zeal, well-meaning but without understanding.

BRANDEIS, J., *Olmstead v United States* (1928) 277 US 438, 479,
72 L ed 944, 957, 48 S Ct 564, 66 ALR 376.

Liberty to be enjoyed, must be limited by law, for law
ends where tyranny begins, and the tyranny is the same,
be it the tyranny of a monarch, or of a multitude—nay,
the tyranny of the multitude may be the greater, since it
is multiplied tyranny.

EDMUND BURKE, *Letter to the Sheriffs of Bristol.*

The liberty of a man's person is more precious to him than all the rest that follow.

COKE, *Second Institute* 46.

It is the common fate of the indolent to see their rights become prey to the active. The condition upon which God hath given liberty to man is eternal vigilance.

JOHN P. CURRAN, *Speech on the Right of Election, July 10, 1790.*

A country, preserved at the sacrifice of all the cardinal principles of liberty, is not worth the cost of preservation.

DAVIS, J. *Ex parte Milligan* (1866, US) 4 Wall 2, 126, 18 L ed 281, 297.

Would we hold liberty, we must have charity—charity to others, charity to ourselves, crawling up from the moist ovens of a steaming world, still carrying the passional equipment of our ferocious ancestors, emerging from black superstition amid carnage and atrocity to our perilous present. What shall it profit us, who come so by our possession, if we have not charity?

LEARNED HAND, *Sources of Tolerance,* 79 Univ. Pa. L. Rev. 1, 14 (1930). Also in Hand, *Spirit of Liberty* (Dilliard, ed.) 83.

Liberty is so much latitude as the powerful choose to accord to the weak.

LEARNED HAND, *Sources of Tolerance, ibid.*

I often wonder whether we do not rest our hopes too much upon constitutions, upon laws and upon courts. These are false hopes; believe me, these are false hopes. Liberty lies in the hearts of men and women; when it dies there, no constitution, no law, no court can save it; no constitution, no law, no court can even do much to help it. While it lies there it needs no constitution, no law, no court to save it.

> LEARNED HAND, *Spirit of Liberty* 189. Speech to newly naturalized citizens, May 21, 1944.

What then is the spirit of liberty? I cannot define it; I can only tell you my own faith. The spirit of liberty is the spirit which is not too sure that it is right; the spirit of liberty is the spirit which seeks to understand the minds of other men and women; the spirit of liberty is the spirit which weighs their interests alongside its own without bias; the spirit of liberty remembers that not even a sparrow falls to earth unheeded; the spirit of liberty is the spirit of Him who, near two thousand years ago, taught mankind that lesson it has never learned, but has never quite forgotten; that there may be a kingdom where the least shall be heard and considered side by side with the greatest.

> LEARNED HAND, *ibid.* 190.

Liberty implies the absence of arbitrary restraint, not immunity from reasonable regulations and prohibitions imposed in the interests of the community.

> HUGHES, J., *Chicago, B. & Q. R. Co. v McGuire* (1911) 219 US 549, 567, 55 L ed 328, 338, 31 S Ct 259.

There is no such thing as an achieved liberty; like electricity, there can be no substantial storage and it must be generated as it is enjoyed, or the lights go out.

> ROBERT H. JACKSON, *Task of Maintaining Our Liberties*, 39 A.B.A.J. 962 (1953).

Not every defeat of authority is a gain for individual freedom, nor every judicial rescue of a convict a victory for liberty.

ROBERT H. JACKSON, *ibid. 964.*

It is something never established for the future, but something which each age must provide for itself.

ROBERT H. JACKSON, *The Supreme Court in American System of Government* 76 (1955).

But he who has looked carefully into the perfect law of liberty and has remained in it, not becoming a forgetful hearer but a doer of the work, shall be blessed in his deed.

James 1:25.

Civil liberty consists, not in a right to every man to do just what he pleases, but it consists in an equal right to all the citizens to have, enjoy, and do, in peace, security, and without molestation, whatever the equal and constitutional laws of the country admit to be consistent with the public good.

JAY, C.J., *First Charge to Grand Jury as a Federal Judge,* 1st Cir., N.Y., 1790. See 3 Jay, *Correspondence and Public Papers* 395.

I believe that there are more instances of the abridgement of the freedom of the people, by gradual and silent encroachments of those in power, than by violent and sudden usurpations.

JAMES MADISON, *Debates in Virginia Constitutional Convention, June 6, 1788.*

403

To suppose that any form of government will secure liberty or happiness without any virtue in the people, is a chimerical idea.

> JAMES MADISON, *Debates in Virginia Constitutional Convention, June 20, 1788.*

To be free is to live under a government by law.

> LORD MANSFIELD, C.J., *R. v Shipley* (1784) 4 Doug. 73, 170.

He that would make his own liberty secure must guard even his enemy from oppression; for if he violates this duty he establishes a precedent that will reach himself.

> THOMAS PAINE, *Dissertation on First Principles of Government* (1795).

For you have been called to liberty, brethren.

> ST. PAUL, Galatians 5:13.

Freedom is not a mere intellectual abstraction; and it is not merely a word to adorn an oration upon occasions of patriotic rejoicing.

> SUTHERLAND, J., *Associated Press v N.L.R.B.* (1937) 301 US 103, 137, 81 L ed 953, 963, 57 S Ct 650.

For the saddest epitaph which can be carved in memory of a vanished liberty is that it was lost because its possessors failed to stretch forth a saving hand while yet there was time.

> SUTHERLAND, J., *Associated Press v N.L.R.B.* (1937) 301 US 103, 141, 81 L ed 953, 965, 57 S Ct 650.

There is no such thing as corporate liberty. Liberty belongs to the individual, or it does not exist.

> WOODROW WILSON, *Constitutional Government in the United States* (1908) 16.

Life

Life has relations not capable always of division into inflexible compartments. The moulds expand and shrink.

> CARDOZO, J., *Glanzer v Shepard*, 233 N.Y. 236, 241 (1922).

The life of a man is much favoured in law, but the life of the law itself which protects all in peace and safety ought to be more favoured.

> COKE, 9 Rep. 68.

A man's life, like a piece of tapestry, is made up of many strands which interwoven make a pattern; to separate a single one and look at it alone, not only destroys the whole, but gives the strand itself a false value.

> JUDGE LEARNED HAND, *Proceedings in Memory of Mr. Justice Brandeis*, 317 U.S. xi (1942).

The riders in a race do not stop short when they reach the goal. There is a little finishing canter before coming to a standstill. There is time to hear the kind voice of friends and to say to one's self: "The work is done." But just as one says that, the answer comes: "The race is over, but the work never is done while the power to work remains." The canter that brings you to a standstill need not be only coming to rest. It cannot be while you still live. For to live is to function. That is all there is in living. And so I end with a line from a Latin poet who uttered the message more than fifteen hundred years ago. "Death plucks my ears and says, Live—I am coming."

> OLIVER WENDELL HOLMES, *Radio Address*, Mar. 8, 1931, on his 90th birthday.

I was on the point of asking you for the original of the quotation with which you wind up your speech of thanks (not the least of your minor works and I hope not the last), when I found in Miss Waddell's reprint that *Mors aurem vellens, Vivite, ait, venio,* is the end line of the pseudo-Virgilian *Copa.* The author understood life in a pretty different fashion from yours, but all is fair in quotation and especially of tags. Your approximate dating leaves room for conjecture to place that curious poem anywhere in the whole range of ancient Latin verse. To my mind the rather affected use of out of the way words can hardly be earlier than the silver age, and some of the lines are too good to be much later.

> SIR FREDERICK POLLOCK, 2 *Holmes-Pollock Letters* 285.

Literature

And as to the lawyers, they are well known to have been very little acquainted with the commonwealth of literature, and to have always acted and written in defiance to its laws.

> HENRY FIELDING, *The Literary Commonwealth* (1752). See *Convent Garden Journal* (reprint, Jansen, ed. 1915) 271.

I am in one of my moods of wholesale impatience with all fiction and all verging on it, reading instead, with rapture, *Fountainhall's Decisions.* . . . Fountainhall is prime, two big folio volumes, and all dreary and all true, and all terse as an obituary; and about one interesting fact on an average in twenty pages, and ten of them unintelligible for technicalities. There's literature, if you like.

ROBERT L. STEVENSON, *Letter to Henry James, July, 1893.*

The style . . . of the legal decisions of the Supreme Court of the United States . . . in purity, in elegance, and in technical precision, is equaled only by that of the best British authors, and surpassed by that of no English compositions of a similar kind.

NOAH WEBSTER, *Dictionary: Preface* (1828 ed.).

Litigation

To him that goes to law, nine things are requisite: A good deal of money, a good deal of patience, a good cause, a good attorney, good counsel, good evidence, a good jury, a good judge—and lastly, good luck.

Anon. *Hone, Every-day Book, under February 14.*

Law is a bottomless pit! It is a cormorant, a harpy that devours everything!

JOHN ARBUTHNOT, *Law is a Bottomless Pit (History of John Bull)* ch. 6 (1712).

A machine which you go into as a pig and come out of as a sausage.

AMBROSE BIERCE, *Devil's Dictionary.*

407

Going tew law iz like skinning a new milch cow for the hide, and giving the meat tew the lawyers.

JOSH BILLINGS, *Sollum Thoughts.*

He that goes to law (as the proverb is) holds a wolf by the ear.

ROBERT BURTON, *Anatomy of Melancholy: Democritus to the Reader* (1621).

While lawyers have more sober sense,
Than t' argue at their own expense,
But make their best advantages
Of others' quarrels, like the Swiss.

SAMUEL BUTLER, *Hudibras,* Pt. III, Canto III, 1. 455.

The litigious spirit is more often found with ignorance than with knowledge of law.   (*Potius ignoratio iuris litigiosa est quam scientia.*)

CICERO, *De Legibus,* I, vi.

Litigation is the pursuit of practical ends, not a game of chess.

FRANKFURTER, J.. *Indianapolis v Chase Nat. Bank* (1941) 314 US 63, 69, 86 L ed 48, 50, 62 S Ct 15.

I must say that, as a litigant, I should dread a lawsuit beyond almost anything else short of sickness and death.

LEARNED HAND, *Deficiencies of Trials to Reach the Heart of the Matter,* 3 Lectures on Legal Topics, Assn. Bar City of N. Y. 89, 105.

It would also seem evident that each of the parties to this litigation possesses ample independent financial means. It sometimes seems that litigation is pursued only to experience a rapturous warmth from the heat of battle.

JAYNE, J., *Schulter v Schulter,* 23 N. J. Super. 409, 413 (1952).

No Cause is try'd at the litigious Bar,
But Women Plaintiffs or Defendants are.
They form the Process, all the Briefs they write;
The Topicks furnish, and the Pleas indite;
And teach the toothless Lawyer how to bite.

JUVENAL, *Satires,* VI (Dryden trans.)

Sainthood is not a prerequisite to entering the portals of the courts; and if it were few litigants (and perhaps no lawyers) would enter therein, and the judges could go fishing as often as they heard the call of the waters. Nor will it be amiss to say (as probably will be said) that if such test should be applied to the bench, many judges (including this writer) would be "recalled"; for it is here and now frankly conceded that the adoption of such a test would create more vacancies than the bar could furnish saints to fill.

KEY, J., *Heidenheimer v Beer,* 155 S.W. 352, 356 (Tex. Civ. App., 1913).

Discourage litigation. Persuade your neighbors to compromise whenever you can. Point out to them how the nominal winner is often a real loser—in fees, expenses and waste of time. As a peacemaker the lawyer has a superior opportunity of being a good man.

ABRAHAM LINCOLN, *Notes for a Law Lecture, July 1, 1850.*

409

And if anyone would go to law with thee and take thy tunic, let him take thy cloak as well.

Matthew 5:40.

One suit carried through the three courts,* Gargilianus, is wearing you out, now numbering, as you do, the colds of twenty winters since its commencement. Wretched, infatuated man! does any one continue at law for twenty years, Gargilianus, who has the option of losing his suit?

MARTIAL, *Epigrams*, bk 7, no. 65.

Lawsuits are an absolute leprosy, a social cancer. My code has singularly diminished lawsuits, by placing numerous causes within the decision of every individual. But there still remained much for the legislator to accomplish. Not that he could hope to prevent men from quarrelling: that they have done in all ages; but he might have prevented a third party in society, from living upon the quarrels of the two others, and even stirring up disputes, to promote their own interest. It was therefore my intention to establish the rule that lawyers should never receive fees, except when they gain causes.

NAPOLEON. See Parkes, *History of Court of Chancery* 457 (1828).

It is altogether a defect in you that you have lawsuits one with another.

ST. PAUL, 1 Corinthians 6:7.

The object our laws had in view was that our people should be supremely happy and devotedly attached to one

_____
* The old Roman court, that of Julius Caesar, and that of Augustus.

another, but citizens will never be thus attached where there
are many suits at law between them, and numerous wrongs
committed, but where both are rarest and of least consequence.

> PLATO, *Laws* V. 743 (A.E. Taylor trans.).

You little know what a ticklish thing it is to go to law.

> PLAUTUS, *Mostellaria*, V., 1.

The parties before the court are wholly answerable for
the conduct of their own cases. Litigation is a game in
which the court is umpire. The rules are in the knowledge
of the court and will be declared and applied by it as
required. It is for the parties to learn the rules and play
the game correctly at their peril. The court will not tell
the plaintiff what step he ought to take next, neither will
it tell the defendant whether the plaintiff has made a slip
of which he can take advantage. The umpire will speak
when his judgment is demanded; it is not his business if
the players throw away chances.

> SIR FREDERICK POLLOCK, *The Expansion of the Common Law*
> 32 (1904).

Once, says an author, where I need not say,
Two travellers found an oyster on their way.
Both fierce, both hungry, the dispute grew strong,
When scale in hand, Dame Justice passed along.
Before her each with clamor pleads the laws,
Explains the matter, and would win the cause.
Dame Justice, weighing long the doubtful right,
Takes, opens, swallows it before their sight.
The cause of strife removed so rarely well,
"There, take," says Justice, "take you each a shell,

411

We thrive in courthouses on fools like you.
'Twas a fat oyster; live in peace—adieu."

> POPE, *Miscellanies* (trans. from Boileau).

He'll go to law for the wagging of a straw.

> Proverb. RAY, *Proverbs* (1678).

Fond of lawsuits, little wealth; fond of doctors, little health.

> Proverb.

Law-suits consume time, and money, and rest, and friends.

> Proverb. HERBERT, *Jacula Prudentum* (1651).

Sue a beggar and catch a louse.

> Proverb. RAY, *Proverbs* (1678).

It is not the saints of the world who chiefly give employment to our profession.

> RYAN, C.J., *Motion to admit Miss Lavinia Goodell to the Bar,* 39 Wis 232, 245 (1875).

When fools fall out, for ev'ry flaw,
They run horn mad to go to law,
A hedge awry, a wrong plac'd gate,
Will serve to spend a whole estate,
Your case the lawyer says is good,
And justice cannot be withstood;
By tedious process from above

412

From office they to office move;
Thro' pleas, demurrers, the dev'l and all,
At length they bring it to the hall;
The dreadful hall by Rufus rais'd,
For lofty Gothick arches prais'd.

> *Unknown.* Inscription on an engraving of Westminster Hall by C. Mosley. See Hone, *Everyday Book,* under Jan. 23.

Sancho: But if this is hell, why do we see no lawyers?

Clarindo: They won't receive them, lest they bring lawsuits here.

Sancho: If there are no lawsuits here, hell's not so bad.

> LOPE de VEGA, *The Star of Seville,* Act 3, scene 2.

Logic

I told him that I thought it was law logic—an artificial system of reasoning, exclusively used in Courts of justice, but good for nothing anywhere else.

> JOHN QUINCY ADAMS, Sec'y of State, to Wm. Wirt, Atty. Gen. (1819). See 4 *Memoirs of Adams* 372.

Loss

When baggage is lost, it is not simple privation; it is bereavement.

> BLECKLEY, J., *Western R. R. v Thornton,* 60 Ga 300, 302 (1878).

Loyalty

Loyalty is a matter of mind and of heart not of race. That indeed is the history of America.

> DOUGLAS, J., *Hirabayashi v United States* (1943) 320 US 81, 107, 87 L ed 1774, 1790, 63 S Ct 1375.

Magna Charta

Magna Charta is such a fellow that he will have no sovereign.

> COKE, *Speech in the House of Commons, May 17, 1628,* 2 Parl. Hist. 357.

Majority

To give a minority a negative upon the majority (which is always the case where more than a majority is requisite to a decision) is in its tendency to subject the sense of the greater number to that of the lesser number. . . . The public business must in some way or other go forward. If a pertinacious minority can controul the opinion of a majority respecting the best mode of conducting it; the majority in order that something may be done, must conform to the views of the minority; and thus the sense of the smaller number will over-rule that of the greater, and give a tone to the national proceedings.

> ALEXANDER HAMILTON, *The Federalist No. 22 (1787).*

Man

A man's happiness depends upon the state of his digestion, and not the station he fills.

> LORD ABINGER. 1 Hardcastle, ed., *Life of Lord Campbell,* ch. 13 (Amer. ed. 1881, p. 394).

The best men are but men, and are sometimes transported with passion.

> SIR ROBERT ATKYNS, *Enquiry into the Power of Dispensing with Penal Statutes* (1686). See *Trial of Sir Edward Hales,* 11 How. St. Tr. 1206.

A great man represents a great ganglion in the nerves of society, or, to vary the figure, a strategic point in the campaign of history, and part of his greatness consists in his being *there.*

> HOLMES, C.J. On motion that the court adjourn on February 4, 1901, the one hundredth anniversary of the day John Marshall took his seat as Chief Justice of the United States, 178 Mass 625.

I only mean that when one thinks coldly I see no reason for attributing to man a significance different in kind from that which belongs to a baboon or to a grain of sand.

> OLIVER WENDELL HOLMES, 2 *Holmes-Pollock Letters* 252.

Man with all his wisdom, *toils for heirs he knows not who.*

> KIRKPATRICK, C.J., *Nevison v Taylor,* 8 N.J.L. 43, 46 (1824).

If parts allure thee, think how Bacon shin'd,
The wisest, brightest, meanest of mankind.

> POPE, *Essay on Man,* iv, 281. Referring to Sir Francis Bacon.

Manners

Manners are of more importance than laws. Upon them in a great measure the laws depend. The law touches us but here and there, and now and then. Manners are what vex or smooth, corrupt or purify, exalt or debase, barbarize or refine us by a constant, steady, uniform, insensible operation, like that of the air we breathe in. They give their whole form and color to our lives. According to their quality, they aid morals, they support them, or they totally destroy them.

> EDMUND BURKE, *Letters on a Regicide Peace.*

Mansfield, Lord

Mansfield was not a mere lawyer. When he came to town he "drank champagne with the wits"; he was the friend of Pope.

> SAMUEL JOHNSON (indirect quote). Boswell, *Life of Johnson: 1772.* (The expression "drank champagne with the wits" is from Prior's Chameleon.)

Much may be made of a Scotchman, if he be caught young.

> SAMUEL JOHNSON. Boswell, *Life of Johnson: 1772.*

Graced as thou art, with all the power of words,
So known, so honoured, at the House of Lords.

> POPE, *Imitations of Horace*, **I, vi.**

Marbury v. Madison

The Court determined at once, that being an original process, they had no cognizance of it; and therefore the question before them was ended. But the Chief Justice went on to lay down what the law would be, had they jurisdiction of the case, to wit: that they should command the delivery. The object was clearly to instruct any other court having the jurisdiction, what they should do if Marbury should apply to them. Besides the impropriety of this gratuitous interference, could anything exceed the perversion of law? . . . Yet this case of Marbury and Madison is continually cited by bench and bar, as if it were settled law, without any animadversion on its being an *obiter* dissertation of the Chief Justice.

> THOMAS JEFFERSON, *Letter to [Justice] William Johnson, June 12, 1823.*

Marriage

In me heart I think if people marry it ought to be f'r life. Th' laws ar-re altogether too lenient with thim.

> FINLEY PETER DUNNE, *Dissertations by Mr. Dooley: Short Marriage Contracts.*

I believe marriages would in general be as happy, and often more so if they were all made by the Lord Chancellor, upon a due consideration of characters and circumstances, without the parties having any choice in the matter.

> SAMUEL JOHNSON. Boswell, *Life of Johnson: 1776.*

If people are drunk or delirious,
The marriage of course would be bad;
Or if they're not sober and serious,

But acting a play or charade.
It's bad if it's only a cover
For cloaking a scandal or sin,
And talking a landlady over,
To let the folks lodge in her inn.

> LORD NEAVES, *The Tourist's Matrimonial Guide Through Scot-land.*

What was once a holy estate enduring for the joint lives of the spouses, is steadily assuming the characteristics of a contract for a tenancy at will.

> LORD RUSSELL of Killowen, *Fender v St. John-Mildmay* [1938] A.C. 1, 34.

Quoth Dick to Tom,—This Act appears
Absurd, as I'm alive;
To take the Crown at eighteen years,
The Wife at twenty-five.
The myst'ry how shall we explain?
For sure, as Dowdeswell said,
Thus early if they're fit to *reign*
They must be fit to *wed*.
Quoth Tom to Dick,—Thou art a **fool,**
And little know'st of life;
Alas! 'tis easier far to rule
A kingdom than a wife.

> Saying, 1772 in England at the time of the passage of the Royal Marriage Act. The law placed restraints on the freedom of marriage in the case of the Heir-Apparent and other members of the Royal Family. 17 Parl. Hist., 401.

Of all actions of a man's life, his marriage does least concern other people, yet of all actions of our life 'tis most meddled with by other people.

> JOHN SELDEN, *Table-Talk: Marriage.*

Marshall, John

When conversing with Marshall, I never admit anything. So sure as you admit any position to be good, no matter how remote from the conclusion he seeks to establish, you are gone. So great is his sophistry you must never give him an affirmative answer or you will be forced to grant his conclusion. Why, if he were to ask me if it were daylight or not, I'd reply, "Sir, I don't know, I can't tell."

> THOMAS JEFFERSON, attributed to by Joseph Story. See *Diary and Letters of Rutherford B. Hayes* (Williams ed.) diary entry Sept. 20, 1843.

Martyr

One . . . does not prove by his martyrdom that he has kept within the law.

> CARDOZO, J., *Hamilton v Regents of University of California* (1934) 293 US 245, 268, 79 L ed 343, 355, 55 S Ct 197.

Maxim

If this is a maxim, is it any the worse? What are maxims but the expression of that which good sense has made a rule.

> LORD BRAMWELL, J., *Smith v Charles Baker & Sons* [1891] A.C. 325, 344.

I detest the attempt to fetter the law by maxims. They are almost invariably misleading: they are for the most part so large and general in their language that they always include something which really is not intended to be included in them.

> LORD ESHER, M.R., *Yarmouth v France* (1887) 19 Q.B.D. 647, 653.

It certainly is very hard upon a Judge, if a rule which he generally lays down, is to be taken up and carried to its full extent. This is sometimes done by counsel, who have nothing else to rely on; but great caution ought to be used by the Court in extending such maxims to cases which the Judge who uttered them never had in contemplation.

> LORD MANSFIELD, C.J., *Brisbane v Dacres* (1813) 5 Taunt., 143, 162.

Measure

The breadth of an acre is still known to all Englishmen, for it is the distance between the wickets.

> FREDERIC W. MAITLAND, *Domesday Book and Beyond* (1897) 372.

Memory

For my name and memory, I leave it to men's charitable speeches, and to foreign nations, and the next ages.

> BACON, *From His Will.*

Verses at the first were invented for the helpe of memorie and it standeth well with gravitie of our lawyer to cite them.

> COKE, *First Institute* 237.

I would sooner trust the smallest slip of paper for truth, than the strongest and most retentive memory, ever bestowed on mortal man.

> LUMPKIN, J., *Miller v Cotton,* 5 Ga 341, 349 (1848).

I do not remember.   (Non mi ricordo.)

> MAJORCHI, an Italian witness, testifying against Queen Caroline (1820) when cross-examined by Lord Brougham, made this statement nine out of ten times. It became a catchword.

Metaphor

Metaphors in law are to be narrowly watched, for starting as devices to liberate thought, they end often by enslaving it.

> CARDOZO, J., *Berkey v Third Ave. Ry. Co.,* 244 N.Y. 84, 94 (1926).

When I can't talk sense, I talk metaphor.

> JOHN P. CURRAN. 2 Thomas Moore, *Memoirs* 170 (1853).

Nothing in law is so apt to mislead as a metaphor.

> LORD MANSFIELD. Attributed to him by Lord Westbury in *Knox v Gye* (1872) 42 L.J. Ch. 234, 239.

Meum and Tuum

These two great pronouns, *meum* and *tuum.*

> COKE, *Third Institute: Proeme.*

421

Minimum Wage

It is difficult to imagine any grounds, other than our own personal economic predilections, for saying that the contract of employment is any the less an appropriate subject of legislation than are scores of others, in dealing with which this Court has held that legislatures may curtail individual freedom in the public interest.

> STONE, J., dissenting, *Morehead v New York* (1936) 298 US 587, 633, 80 L ed 1347, 1367, 56 S Ct 918, 103 ALR 1445.

Mistake

Mistakes are the inevitable lot of mankind.

> JESSEL, M. R., *Re Taylor's Estate* (1882) 22 Ch.D. 495, 503.

Monster

Thou are a monster; thou hast an English face, but a Spanish heart.

> COKE, *Trial of Sir Walter Raleigh* (1603) 2 How. St. Tr. 1, 7.

Morality

Our system of morality is a body of imperfect social generalizations expressed in terms of emotion. To get at its truth, it is useful to omit the emotion and ask ourselves what these generalizations are and how far they are confirmed by fact accurately ascertained.

> OLIVER WENDELL HOLMES, *Ideals and Doubts,* 10 Ill. L. Rev. 1, 3 (1915) Coll. Leg. Pap. 306.

Men who are knaves by retail are extremely honest in the gross; they love morality.

MONTESQUIEU, *Spirit of the Laws,* bk 25.

Mortgage

A common foreclosure altho the inventive genius of Col. Burr has worked out of the case a great deal of trouble for me.

THOMAS ADDIS EMMET, *Letter, Nov. 6, 1816 to John V. Henry, Esq.* in Mss Section N. Y. State Library.

I remember what my father said when I was a law student. He gave me a mortgage to foreclose. I had foreclosed a few before, but this was a bigger one than I had tried before, and I asked the old gentleman some questions. He said, "Don't worry about that. You foreclose a big mortgage just the same as you do a little one."

HAMILTON WARD, 55 N.Y.S. Bar Assn Rept. 528 (1930).

Motions

We need not consider all the reasons advanced by defendant in support of its motion. One arrow, if fatal, is fatal enough.

HOOVER, J., *Inland Properties Co. v Union Properties, Inc.,* 60 Ohio L. Abs. 150, 151 (Com. Pleas, Cuyahoga Co., 1951).

Motive

The illustrious Lucius Cassius, whom the Roman people considered the wisest and most conscientious of judges, was in the habit of asking repeatedly in trials, "who had profited by it?" (*L. Cassius ille quem populus Romanus verissimum et sapientissimum iudicem putabat, indentidem in causis quaerere solebat, "cui bono" fuisset.*)

> CICERO, *Pro Roscio Amerino,* xxx, 84.

Murder

Lizzie Borden took an axe
And gave her Mother forty whacks;
When she saw what she had done,
She gave her Father forty-one.

> Anon. (Lizzie Borden was tried for the murder of her father and step-mother at Fall River, Mass., Aug. 4, 1892.)

Gentlemen, do not hang me high, for the sake of decency.

> MARY BLANDY (hanged April 16, 1752, for the murder by poison of her father). See MacKinnon, *Inner Temple Papers* 123.

Gentlemen of the jury, the charge against the prisoner is murder, and the punishment of murder is death; and that simple statement is sufficient to suggest to us the awful solemnity of the occasion which brings you and me face to face.

> JOHN INGLIS, *Address to the Jury, July 8, 1857,* Trial of Madeleine Smith before the High Court of Justiciary, Edinburgh. (Regarded in England as the finest opening by the counsel for the defense in a murder case ever known.)

I have just heard of your deep affliction, and the arrest of your son for murder. I can hardly believe he can be capable of the crime alleged against him. It does not seem possible. I am anxious that he should be given a fair trial at any rate; and gratitude for your long continued kindness to me in adverse circumstances prompts me to offer my humble services gratuitously in his behalf. It will afford me an opportunity to requite, in a small degree, the favors I received at your hand, and that of your lamented husband, when your roof afforded me a grateful shelter, without money and without price.

> ABRAHAM LINCOLN, *Letter to Mrs. Hannah Armstrong,* September, 1857.

Mrs. Manning insisted on being hanged in black satin, and ruined the trade in that material in consequence for several years for ladies' dresses.

> SERJEANT ROBINSON. See Manson, *Builders of Our Law* 119 (2nd ed. 1904).

Murder will out.

> Proverb.

Mordre wol out that see we day by day.
Mordre is so wlatsom* and abhominable
To God, that is so just and reasonable,
That he ne wol nat suffre it heled** be.

> CHAUCER, *The Nun's Priest's Tale,* line 232.

---

* heinous
** hidden

First Murderer:

Well, I'll go hide the body in some hole,
Till that the duke give order for his burial;
And when I have my meed I will away,
For this will out, and here I must not stay.

> SHAKESPEARE, *Richard III,* Act 1, scene 4.

Name

A self-made man may prefer a self-made name.

> L. HAND, J., on granting the application of Samuel Goldfish to
> change his name to Samuel Goldwyn.

[Filoramo] is an honorable name of parents of Italian
ancestry. . . . To the court it sounds more beautiful
than that of Michaels.

> SANTANGELO, J., *Petition of Anthony and Rosemary Filoramo
> for leave to assume the name of Michaels,* 40 M.2d 598 (Civil
> Ct. N.Y.C. 1963).

Natural Law

For there are in nature certain fountains of justice whence
all civil laws are derived but as streams; and like as waters
do take tinctures and tastes from the soils through which
they run, so do civil laws vary according to the regions
and governments where they are planted, though they proceed from the same fountain.

> BACON, *Advancement of Learning,* bk 2.

This law of nature, being coeval with mankind, and dictated by God himself, is of course superior in obligation to any other. It is binding over all the globe, in all countries, and at all times: no human laws are of any validity, if contrary to this; and such of them as are valid derive all their force, and all their authority, mediately or immediately, from this original.

BLACKSTONE, *Commentaries,* bk 1, 41.

There is but one law for all, namely that law which governs all law, the law of our Creator, the law of humanity, justice, equity,—the Law of Nature and of Nations.

BURKE, *Impeachment of Warren Hastings,* May 28, 1794.

There is in fact a true law—namely, right reason—which is in accordance with nature, applies to all men, and is unchangeable and eternal. By its commands this law summons men to the performance of their duties; by its prohibitions it restrains them from doing wrong. Its commands and prohibitions always influence good men, but are without effect on the bad. To invalidate this law by human legislation is never morally right, nor is it permissible ever to restrict its operation, and to annul it wholly is impossible. Neither the senate nor the people can absolve us from our obligation to obey this law, and it requires no Sextus Aelius to expound and interpret it. It will not lay down one rule at Rome and another at Athens, nor will it be one rule today and another tomorrow. But there will be one law, eternal and unchangeable, binding at all times upon all peoples; and there will be, as it were, one common master and ruler of men, namely God, who is the author of this law, its interpreter, and its sponsor. The man who will not obey it will abandon his better self, and in denying the true nature of a man, will thereby suffer the severest of penalties, though he has escaped all the other consequences which men call punishment.

CICERO, *De Re Publica,* III, xxii (trans. by Sabine and Smith).

The law of nature is that which God at the time of creation of the nature of man infused into his heart, for his preservation and direction; and this is *lex aeterna,* the moral law, called also the law of nature. And by this law, written with the finger of God in the heart of man, were the people of God a long time governed, before the law was written by Moses, who was the first reporter or writer of law in the world.

COKE, *Calvin's Case* (1608) 7 Rep. 12 b.

Natural law is the dictate of right reason, showing the moral turpitude, or moral necessity of any act from its agreement or disagreement with a rational nature, and consequently that such an act is either forbidden or commanded by God, the author of nature.

GROTIUS, *De Jure Belli ac Pacis* (1625) bk 1, ch. 1.

When the first principles of civil society are violated, and the rights of a whole people are invaded, the common forms of municipal law are not to be regarded. Men may then betake themselves to the law of nature; and if they but conform their actions to that standard, all cavils against them betray either ignorance or dishonesty. There are some events in society to which human laws can not extend; but when applied to them lose all their force and efficacy. In short, when human laws contradict or discountenance the means which are necessary to preserve the essential rights of any society, they defeat the proper end of all laws, and so become null and void.

> ALEXANDER HAMILTON, *The Farmer Refuted* (1775).

In the forum of conscience, duty to a moral power higher than the State has always been maintained.

> HUGHES, C.J., dissenting, *United States v Mackintosh* (1931) 283 US 605, 633, 75 L ed 1302, 1315, 51 S Ct 570.

When the Gentiles who have no law do by nature what the Law prescribes, these having no law are a law unto themselves. They show the work of the Law written in their hearts. Their conscience bears witness to them, even when conflicting thoughts accuse or defend them.

> ST. PAUL, *Romans* 2:14.

The natural law always buries its undertakers.

> HEINRICH ROMMEN, *Natural Law* (1947) 267 (paraphrasing an expression of Etienne Gilson, French philosopher).

We must say that the natural law, as to first common principles, is the same for all, both as to rectitude and as to knowledge. But as to certain matters of detail, which are conclusions, as it were of those common principles, it is the same for all in the majority of cases, both as to rectitude and as to knowledge; and yet in some few cases it may fail, both as to rectitude, by reason of certain obstacles (just as natures subject to generation and corruption fail in some few cases on account of some obstacle), and as to knowledge, since in some the reason is perverted by passion, or evil habit, or an evil disposition of nature.

> ST. THOMAS AQUINAS, *Summa Theologica*, I–II, q.94, art. 4 (trans. English Dominican Fathers).

429

Every human law has just so much of the character of
law as it is derived from the law of nature.   But if in
any point it differs from the law of nature, it is no longer
a law but a corruption of law.

> ST. THOMAS AQUINAS, *Summa Theologica*, I–II, q.95, art. 2.

I cannot fancy to myself what the law of nature means,
but the law of God.   How should I know I ought not to
steal, I ought not to commit adultery, unless some body
had told me so?   Surely 'tis because I have been told so?
'Tis not because I think I ought not to do them, nor because
you think I ought not; if so, our minds might change,
whence then comes the restraint?   From a higher Power,
nothing else can bind.

> JOHN SELDEN, *Table-Talk: Law of Nature.*

Yea! for not Zeus, I ween, proclaimed this thing;
Nor Justice, co-mate with the Nether Gods,
Not she ordained men such unnatural laws!
Nor deemed I that thine edict had such force,
That thou, who are but mortal, couldst o'erride
The unwritten and unswerving laws of Heaven,
Not of today and yesterday are they,
But from everlasting * * * .

> SOPHOCLES, *Antigone.*   Antigone's response to Creon when asked
> if she had buried her brother's body against his command.

Necessity

Necessity is always a suspicious argument and never
wanting to support the worst of measures.

> JOSHUA EVANS, *arguendo, Home v Bentinck* (1820) 2 Brod. &
> B. 130, 148.

430

Neck Verse

Have mercy on me, O God, according to thy great mercy. And according to the multitude of thy tender mercies blot out my iniquity.

> Psalm 50. This psalm was called the "neck verse" since it was the one invariably chosen by persons claiming benefit of clergy to prove that they were able to read.

Negligence

Negligence is the omission to do something which a reasonable man . . . would do, or doing something which a prudent and reasonable man would not do.

> ALDERSON, B., *Blyth v Birmingham Waterworks Co.* (1856) 11 Exch. 781, 784.

Whenever one person is by circumstances placed in such a position with regard to another that every one of ordinary sense who did think would at once recognize that if he did not use ordinary care and skill in his own conduct with regard to those circumstances he would cause danger of injury to the person or property of the other, a duty arises to use ordinary care and skill to avoid such danger.

> BRETT, M.R. *Heaven v Pender* (1883) 11 Q.B.D. 503, 509.

Negligence is not actionable unless it involves the invasion of a legally protected interest, the violation of a right. "Proof of negligence in the air, so to speak will not do."

> CARDOZO, C.J., *Palsgrave v Long Island R. R. Co.*, 248 N.Y. 339, 341 (1928). Cardozo is quoting Pollock, *Torts* (11th ed.) 455.

Standards of prudent conduct are declared at times by courts, but they are taken over from the facts of life.

> CARDOZO, J., *Pokora v Wabash R. Co.* (1934) 292 US 98, 104, 78 L ed 1149, 1154, 54 S Ct 580, 97 ALR 1049.

If a man is negligently run over or otherwise negligently injured in his body, it is no answer to the sufferer's claim for damages that he would have suffered less injury, or no injury at all, if he had not had an unusually thin skull or an unusually weak heart.

> KENNEDY, J., *Dulieu v White & Sons* [1901] 2 K.B. 669, 679. (This is the classic quotation in the "eggshell" skull cases. Tortfeasor must take his victim as he finds him.)

We are admonished that hard cases are the quicksands of the law. Neither equity nor the law relieves those who seek aid in Court merely to avoid the effects of their own negligence. . . . Negligence always has misfortune for a companion.

> LAMM, J., *Lipscomb v Talbott*, 243 Mo 1, 36 (1912).

The State cannot be expected to "child proof" its entire highway system.

> REYNOLDS, J., *Harrow v State*, 21 A.D.2d 571, 573 (1964).

I said I could see no difference between negligence and gross negligence—that it was the same thing, with the addition of a vituperative epithet.

> ROLFE, B., *Wilson v Brett* (1843) 11 M. & W. 113, 115.

Negotiable Instrument

It is a key which in the hands of a rightful owner is intended to unlock the door of the warehouse, floating or fixed, in which the goods may chance to be.

> BOWEN, L. J., *Sanders Bros. v MacLean & Co.* (1883) 11 Q.B.D. 327, 341 (referring to a bill of lading).

A negotiable bill or note is a courier without luggage.

> GIBSON, C.J., *Overton v Tyler,* 3 Pa. St. 346, 347 (1846).

No party can be charged as principal upon a negotiable instrument unless his name is thereon disclosed.—The reason of this rule is that each party who takes a negotiable instrument makes his contracts with the parties who appear on its face to be bound for its payment; it is "a courier without luggage," whose countenance is its passport.

> 1 DANIEL, *Negotiable Instruments* (2d ed. 1879) 249.

Nonsuit

A nonsuit . . . is but like blowing out of a candle, which a man at his own pleasure lights again.

> JOHN MARCH, *Slander and Arbitrements* 215 (1648).

Notary Public

The Notary Public like the domestic dog is found everywhere.

> JOHN CADMAN ROPES (attributed to). See 1 *Holmes-Pollock Letters* 267.

Nuisance

One ought not to have so delicate a nose, that he cannot bear the smell of hogs.

COKE, 9 Rep. 58.

It would have been wrong, as it seems to me, for this Court in the reign of Henry VI to have interfered with the further use of sea coal in London, because it had been ascertained to their satisfaction, or predicted to their satisfaction, that by the reign of Queen Victoria both white and red roses would have ceased to bloom in the Temple Gardens. If some picturesque haven opens its arms to invite the commerce of the world, it is not for this Court to forbid the embrace, although the fruit of it should be the sights, and sounds, and smells of a common seaport and shipbuilding town, which would drive the Dryads and their masters from their ancient solitudes.

JAMES, L.J., *Salvin v North Brancepeth Coal Co.* (1874) 9 Ch. 705, 709.

A nuisance may be merely a right thing in the wrong place—like a pig in the parlor instead of the barnyard.

SUTHERLAND, J., *Euclid v Ambler Realty Co.* (1926) 272 US 365, 388, 71 L ed 303, 311, 47 S Ct 114, 54 ALR 1016.

Numbers

And it seemeth to me, that the law in this case delighteth herselfe in the number of twelve; for there must not onely be twelve jurors for the tryall of matters of fact but twelve judges of ancient time for tryall of matters of law in the Exchequer Chamber. Also for matters of state there were in ancient time twelve counsellors of state. He that wageth his law must have eleven others with him, which thinke he says true. And that number of twelve is much respected in holy writ, as twelve apostles, twelve stones, twelve tribes etc.

COKE, *First Institute* 155.

Oath

I will not counsel or maintain any suit or proceeding which shall appear to me to be unjust, nor any defense except such as I believe to be honestly debatable under the law of the land.

American Bar Association, model oath for candidates for admission to the bar, 33 A.B.A. Rep. 585 (1908).

Oh, will you swear by yonder skies,
Whatever question may arise,
'Twixt rich and poor, 'Twixt low and high,
That you will well and truly try?

WILLIAM S. GILBERT, *Trial by Jury.*

Every pleader is bound by oath that he will not knowingly maintain or defend wrong or falsehood, but will abandon his client immediately that he perceives his wrongdoing. That he will never have recourse to false delays or false witnesses, and never allege, proffer, or consent to any corruption, deceit, lie, or falsified law, but loyally will maintain the right of his client, so that he may not fail through his folly, or negligence, nor by default of him, not by default of any argument that he could urge; and that he will not by blow, contumely, brawl, threat, noise, or villain

435

conduct disturb any judge, party, serjeant, or other in court, nor impede the hearing or the course of justice.

> ANDREW HORN, *Mirror of Justice* (c. 1307), 7 Seld. Soc. Pub. 48.

Obscenity

All ideas having even the slightest redeeming social importance—unorthodox ideas, controversial ideas, even ideas hateful to the prevailing climate of opinion—have the full protection of the guaranties, unless excludable because they encroach upon the limited area of more important interests. But implicit in the history of the First Amendment is the rejection of obscenity as utterly without redeeming social importance. . . . We hold that obscenity is not within the area of constitutionally protected speech or press.

> BRENNAN, J., *Roth v United States* (1957) 354 US 476, 484, 1 L ed 2d 1498, 1507, 77 S Ct 1304.

Some American courts adopted this standard [Regina v Hicklin] but later decisions have rejected it and substituted this test: whether to the average person, applying contemporary community standards, the dominate theme of the material taken as a whole appeals to prurient interest.

> BRENNAN, J., *Roth v United States* (1957) 354 US 476, 489, 1 L ed 2d 1498, 1509, 77 S Ct 1304.

I think the test of obscenity is this, whether the tendency of the matter charged as obscenity is to deprave and corrupt those whose minds are open to such immoral influences, and into whose hands a publication of this sort may fall. Now, with regard to this work it is quite certain that it

436

would suggest to the minds of the young of either sex, or even to persons of more advanced years, thoughts of a most impure and libidinous character.

> LORD COCKBURN, C.J., *Regina v Hicklin* (1868) 3 Q.B. 360, 371.

From first to last page it is a filthy, cynical, disgusting narrative of sordid amours. Not only is there in it no word or suggestion of the romantic, sentimental, poetic or spiritual aspects of the sex relation, but it is not even bawdy sex or comic sex or sex described with vulgar good humor. No glory, no beauty, no stars—just mud.

> DESMOND, C.J., concurring, *People v Fritch,* 13 N.Y.2d 119, 126 (1963).

The exquisite vagueness of the word "obscenity" is apparent from the way the judicial definition of that word has kept shifting.

> FRANK, J., concurring, *United States v Roth,* 237 F.2d 796, 826 (1956).

What is pornography to one man is the laughter of genius to another.

> D. H. LAWRENCE, *Pornography and Obscenity* 5 (1929).

If the trend continues unabated, by the time some author writes of "Lady Chatterley's Granddaughter," "Lady Chatterley" herself will seem like a prim and puritanical housewife. However the case must be decided in accordance with contemporary judicial standards and: I reluctantly concur.

> MOORE, J., *Grove Press v Christenberry,* 276 F.2d 433, 443 (1960).

437

Occupation

Are you a member of the Society of Jobbists, or do you know the guild? If not, let me tell you of it. All may join, though few can qualify. Its president is a certain white-haired gentleman, with a keen blue eye, and a dangerous turn for dialectic. . . . It is an honest craft, which gives good measure for its wages, and undertakes only those jobs which the members can do in proper workmanlike fashion, which of course means no more than that they must like them. . . . It demands right quality, better than the market will pass, and perhaps it is not quite as insistent as it should be upon standards of living, measured by radios and motor-cars and steam heat. But the working hours are rigorously controlled, because for five days alone will it labor, and the other two are all the members' own. These belong to them to do with what they will, be it respectable or not; they are nobody's business, not even that of the most prying moralists.

> LEARNED HAND, *Mr. Justice Holmes,* 43 Harv. L. Rev. 857, 860 (1930). Also in Hand, *Spirit of Liberty* (Dilliard, ed.) 62.

Office

Officialdom, however it displays itself, is the husk and that what is precious is the man within.

> BENJAMIN N. CARDOZO, *Law and Literature* 189 (1931).

The officers of our government, from the highest to the lowest, are equally subjected to legal restraint.

> JOHNSON, J., *Gilchrist v Collector of Charleston,* 10 Fed. Cas. 355, 356 (1808).

438

The only road to the highest stations in this country is that of the law.

SIR WILLIAM JONES, *Letter March 17, 1771, to C. Reviczki.*

Although an office is "an employment," it does not follow that every employment is an office.

MARSHALL, Cir. J., *United States v Maurice,* 26 Fed. Cas. (No. 15,747) 1211, 1214 (1823). This is an opinion of the Chief Justice, on circuit.

No man in this country is so high that he is above the law. No officer of the law may set that law at defiance with impunity. All the officers of the government, from highest to the lowest, are creatures of the law, and are bound to obey it.

MILLER, J., *United States v Lee* (1882) 106 US 196, 220, 27 L ed 171, 182, 1 S Ct 240.

In our country, the highest man is not above the people; the humblest is not below the people.

JOSEPH STORY, Speech, Massachusetts Constitutional Convention, 1820. 1 Story, *Life of Joseph Story* 392.

Opinion

Opinion has a significance proportioned to the sources that sustain it.

CARDOZO, C.J., *Petrogradsky M.K. Bank v National City Bank,* 253 N.Y. 23, 35 (1930).

Order

I should like to stipulate for some kind of order. . . .
There is the chronological, the botanical, the metaphysical,
the geographical—even the alphabetical order would be
better than no order at all.

> MAULE, J. See Robinson, *Bench and Bar* 109 (1894).

Paradox

In the Blue Grass region,
A "Paradox" was born,
The corn was full of kernels
And the "colonels" full of corn.

> JOHN MARSHALL. 4 Beveridge, *Life of Marshall*, ch. 2. At a
> social gathering a game was being played which required each
> one present to make a rhyme upon a word suddenly given.
> This doggerel was Marshall's contribution.

Parchment

There is no magic in parchment or in wax.

> ASHHURST, J., *Master v Miller* (1791) 4 T.R. 320, 331.

The mysterious virtue of wax and parchment.

> EDMUND BURKE, *Speech on Conciliation with America*, Mar. 22,
> 1775.

Is not this a lamentable thing, that of the skin of an
innocent lamb should be made parchment? that parchment,
being scribbled o'er, should undo a man?

> SHAKESPEARE, *Henry VI, pt. II,* Act 4, scene 2.

440

Partnership

Of legal knowledge I acquired such a grip
That they took me into the partnership.
And that junior partnership, I ween,
Was the only ship that I ever had seen.
　　But that kind of ship so suited me,
　　That now I am the Ruler of the Queen's Navee!

> WILLIAM S. GILBERT, *H.M.S. Pinafore, Act 1.*

Past

The past cannot be recalled by the most absolute power.

> MARSHALL, C.J., *Fletcher v Peck* (1810, US) 6 Cranch 87, 135, 3 L ed 162, 177.

Though the Court may order an election *nunc pro tunc* it is beyond the power of the Courts, or of an Act of Parliament, to recall a day that has passed, or make a thing which happened not have happened.

> MAULE, J., *Berwick (Mayor of) v Osward* (1854) 3 El. & Bl. 653, 670.

Perjury

Once forsworn, and ever forlorn.

> COKE, *Second Institute* 238.

Perpetuities

Perpetuities were born under some unfortunate constellation.

> COKE, 10 Rep. 42 b.

The *fertile octogenarian.*

> W. BARTON LEACH (felicitous descriptive phrase used in his writings). See *Perpetuities in a Nutshell,* 51 Harv. L. Rev. 638 (1938). The outstanding example of the traditional rigour of the Rule against Perpetuities is the rule, derived from ancient cases, that it is conclusively presumed that any person is capable of having children, no matter what his or her age and regardless of such physiological facts as change of life, impotence or surgical removal of productive organs. See Morris and Leach, *The Rule Against Perpetuities* (2d ed. 1962) 76.

The *precocious toddler.*

> W. BARTON LEACH (felicitous descriptive phrase used in his writings in relation to cases concerning the minimum age at which a person can have a child). See Morris and Leach, *The Rule Against Perpetuities* (2d ed. 1962) 84.

The *unborn widow.*

> W. BARTON LEACH (felicitous descriptive phrase used in his writings).
>
> This type of case repeatedly occurs. Gifts to children are held too remote because of the possibility that their father, now married, can lose his wife by death or divorce, and then marry a woman who is now unborn. See Morris and Leach, *The Rule Against Perpetuities* (2d ed. 1962) 72.

"Lives" means human lives. It was suggested that the last of the dogs could in fact not outlive the testator by more than twenty-one years. I know nothing of that. The Court does not enter into the question of a dog's expectation of life. In point of fact neighbour's dogs and cats are unpleasantly longlived; but I know nothing of their precise expectation of life.

> MEREDITH, J., *Matter of Kelly, Cleary v Dillon* [1932] Ir. R. 255, 260.

There can be no doubt that "lives" means lives of human beings, not of animals or trees in California.

MEREDITH, J., *ibid.*, 260.

For let the lives be never so many, there must be a survivor, and so it is but the length of that life; for Twisden used to say, the candles were all lighted at once.

POWELL, J., *Scatterwood v Edge* (1699) 1 Salk, 229.

If all the candles be light at once it is good.

TWISDEN, J., *Love v Wyndham & Wyndham* (1669) 1 Mod. 50, 54.

Persecution

Persecution is a very easy form of virtue.

COLERIDGE, C.J., *R. v Ramsey* (1883) 1 C. & E. 126, 145.

Philosophy

As for the philosophers, they make imaginary laws for imaginary commonwealths; and their discourses are as the stars, which give little light because they are so high. For the lawyers, they write according to the states where they live, what is received law, and not what ought to be law: for the wisdom of a lawmaker is one, and of a lawyer is another.

BACON, *Advancement of Learning*, bk 2.

You think perhaps of philosophy as dwelling in the clouds. I hope you may see that she is able to descend to earth. You think that in stopping to pay court to her, when you should be hastening forward on your journey, you are loitering in bypaths and wasting precious hours. . . . Here you will find the key for the unlocking of bolts and combinations that shall never be pried open by clumsier or grosser tools. You think that there is nothing practical in a theory that is concerned with ultimate conceptions. That is true perhaps while you are doing the journeyman's work of your profession. You may find in the end, when you pass to higher problems, that instead of its being true that the study of the ultimate is profitless, there is little that is profitable in the study of anything else.

> BENJAMIN N. CARDOZO, *Growth of the Law* 23 (1924).

As a bettabilitarian I bet the cosmos has in it a somewhat that would strike us as pretty queer if we were capable of being struck by it with our present faculties. But I am swamped in the law.

> OLIVER WENDELL HOLMES, *Holmes-Cohen Correspondence,* Journal of the History of Ideas (1948).

As to the universe my formula as a bettabilitarian (one who thinks you can bet about it but not know) is a spontaneity taking an irrational pleasure in a moment of rational sequence.

> OLIVER WENDELL HOLMES, 2 *Holmes-Pollock Letters* 22 (Aug. 21, 1919).

At times the work purports clearly to travel on the level of considered and buttressed scholarly discussion; at times on the level of bed-time stories for the tired bar;

> KARL N. LLEWELLYN, *A Realistic Jurisprudence,* 30 Col. L. Rev. 431, 435 (1930). Referring to the writings of Roscoe Pound.

444

Plaintiff and Defendant

John Doe and Richard Roe his crony,
Good men, and true, who never fail
The needy and distress'd to bail
Direct unseen the dire dispute,
And pledge their names in ev'ry suit.

JOHN ANSTEY, *Pleader's Guide,* bk 1 **(1796).**

Oh, listen to the plaintiff's case:
Observe the features of her face—
The broken-hearted bride.
Condole with her distress of mind:
From bias free of every kind,
This trial must be tried!

WILLIAM S. GILBERT, *Trial by Jury.*

And when amid the plaintiff's shrieks,
The ruffianly defendant speaks—
Upon the other side;
What *he* may say you needn't mind—
From bias free of every kind,
This trial must be tried.

WILLIAM S. GILBERT, *ibid.*

Planning

Nor can you without the influence of the law enable a mere group of sheds to become a great city throbbing with life.

LORD BUCKMASTER, *Address before Canadian Bar Association,* 3 Can. B. Rev. 361, 363 (1925).

445

Aviation is today an established method of transportation. The future, even the near future, will make it still more general. The city that is without the foresight to build the ports for the new traffic may soon be left behind in the race of competition. Chalcedon was called the city of the blind, because its founders rejected the nobler site of Byzantium lying at their feet. The need for vision of the future in the governance of cities has not lessened with the years. The dweller within the gates, even more than the stranger from afar, will pay the price of blindness.

CARDOZO, C.J., *Hesse v Rath,* 249 N.Y. 436, 438 (1928).

Pleading

Whoe'er has drawn a special plea,
Has heard of old Tom Tewkesbury,
Deaf as a post, and thick as mustard,
He aim'd at wit, and bawl'd and bluster'd,
And died a *nisi prius* leader—
That genius was my special pleader.

JOHN ANSTEY, *Pleader's Guide,* bk 1 (1796).

Good pleading—the heart-string of the common law.

COKE, *First Institute: Preface.*

Hear me, hear me, if you please,
These are very strange proceedings—
For permit me to remark
On the merits of my pleadings,
You're at present in the dark.

WILLIAM S. GILBERT, *Trial by Jury.*

The wisdom of Solomon, accentuated by the legal lore of Coke and Mansfield, could not devise a judgment which this complaint would support.

HUSTON, J., *Wilson v Thompson,* 4 Idaho 678, 680 (1896).

In law it is good policy to never plead what you need not, lest you oblige yourself to prove what you can not.

ABRAHAM LINCOLN, *Letter to Usher F. Linder, Feb. 20, 1848.*

And know ye this, my son, that this is one of the most honorable, laudable and profitable things in our law; to have the science of well pleading in actions real and personal; and therefore I counsel thee especially to set all thy courage and care to learn this.

LITTLETON, *Tenures,* bk 3, ch. 9, sec. 534 (1481).

The prayer for general relief—that India-rubber prayer.

LUMPKIN, J., *Rutherford v Jones,* 14 Ga 521, 525 (1854).

So great is the ascendancy of the Law of Actions in the infancy of Courts of Justice, that substantive law has at first the look of being gradually secreted in the interstices of procedure.

SIR HENRY MAINE, *Early Law and Custom* 389 (1907).

Procedure . . . is the prime bread-and-butter subject of the practitioner.

ARTHUR T. VANDERBILT, *Cases and Materials on Modern Procedure* 4 (1952).

447

Police Power

All rights tend to declare themselves absolute to their logical extreme. Yet all in fact are limited by the neighborhood of principles of policy which are other than those on which the particular right is founded, and which become strong enough to hold their own when a certain point is reached. The limits set to property by other public interests present themselves as a branch of what is called the police power of the State.

> HOLMES, J., *Hudson County Water Co. v McCarter* (1908) 209 US 349, 355, 52 L ed 828, 832, 28 S Ct 529.

The power to direct the removal of gunpowder is a branch of the police power, which unquestionably remains, and ought to remain, with the states.

> MARSHALL, C.J., *Brown v Maryland* (1827, US) 12 Wheat 419, 443, 6 L ed 678, 687.

Politics

Questions of political expediency belong to the legislative halls, not to the judicial forum.

> BRADLEY, J., concurring, *Legal Tender Cases* (1870, US) 12 Wall 457, 562, 20 L ed 287, 316.

It is hostile to a democratic system to involve the judiciary in the politics of the people. And it is not less pernicious if such judicial intervention in an essentially political contest be dressed up in the abstract phrases of the law.

> FRANKFURTER, J., *Colegrove v Green* (1946) 328 US 549, 553, 90 L ed 1432, 1434, 66 S Ct 1198.

The constitution does not allow reasons of State to influence our judgment: God forbid it should! We must not regard political consequences, how formidable soever they might be: if rebellion was the certain consequence, we are bound to say, *"Fiat justitia ruat coelum."*

> LORD MANSFIELD, C.J., *R. v Wilkes* (1770) 4 Burr. 2527, 2561. The maxim: "Let justice be done though the heavens fall" became widely popular after its use by Lord Mansfield.

Some odd old Whig
Who never changed his principle, or wig.

> POPE, *Imitations of Horace, Epilogue to Satires,* I (Referring to Sir Joseph Jekyl, Master of the Rolls).

Scarcely any political question arises in the United States which is not resolved sooner or later into a judicial question.

> ALEXIS DE TOCQUEVILLE, *Democracy in America,* Pt. 1, ch. 16.

The American judge is brought into the political arena independently of his own will. He only judges the law because he is obliged to judge a case. The political question which he is called upon to resolve is connected with the interest of the parties, and he cannot refuse to decide it without abdicating the duties of his post.

> ALEXIS DE TOCQUEVILLE, *Democracy in America,* Pt. 1, ch. 6 (trans. Reeves).

Popularity

Experience might inform them that many who have been saluted with the huzzas of a crowd one day, have received their execrations the next; and many who by the

popularity of their times have been held up as spotless
patriots, have, nevertheless, appeared upon the historian's
page, when truth has triumphed over delusion, the assassins
of liberty. Why then, can the noble lord think I am ambitious of present popularity, that echo of folly and shadow
of renown.

> LORD MANSFIELD, reply to Chatham in House of Lords, May 9,
> 1770, 16 Parl. Hist. 977.

I wish popularity: but, it is that popularity which follows; not that which is run after. It is that popularity
which, sooner or later, never fails to do justice to the
pursuit of noble ends, by noble means. I will not do that
which my conscience tells me is wrong upon this occasion;
to gain the huzzas of thousands, or the daily praise of all
the papers which come from the press: I will not avoid
doing what I think is right; though it should draw on me
the whole artillery of libels; all that falsehood and malice
can invent, or the credulity of a deluded populace can
swallow.

> LORD MANSFIELD, C.J., *R. v Wilkes* (1770) 4 Burr. 2527, 2562.

Possession

The plaintiff being a chimney sweeper's boy found a
jewel and carried it to the defendant's shop (who was a
goldsmith) to know what it was, and delivered it into
the hands of the apprentice, who under pretence of weighing it, took out the stones, and calling to the master to let
him know it came to three halfpence, the master offered
the boy the money, who refused to take it, and insisted
to have the thing again; whereupon the apprentice delivered
him back the socket without the stones. And now in
trover against the master these points were ruled: That

the finder of a jewel, though he does not by such finding acquire an absolute property or ownership, yet he has such a property as will enable him to keep it against all but the rightful owner. . . . That the action well lay against the master, who gives a credit to his apprentice. . . . As to the value of the jewel several of the trade were examined to prove what a jewel of the finest water that would fit the socket would be worth; and the Chief Justice directed the jury, that unless the defendant did produce the jewel, and shew it not to be of the finest water, they should presume the strongest against him, and make the value of the best jewels the measure of their damages: which they accordingly did.

PRATT, C.J., *Armory v Delamirie* [1721] 1 Stra. 504.

Possession is eleven points of the law and they say there are but twelve.

Proverb, RAY, *Proverbs* (1678).

Poverty

Poverty is the parent of revolution and crime.

ARISTOTLE, *Politics*, bk 2, ch. 6 (Jowett trans.).

Poverty and immorality are not syonymous.

BYRNES, J., *Edwards v California* (1941) 314 US 160, 177, 86 L ed 119, 127, 62 S Ct 164.

Power

Arbitrary power has seldom or never been introduced into any country at once. It must be introduced by slow

451

degrees, and as it were step by step lest the people should see its approach.   The barriers and fences of the people's liberty must be plucked up one by one, and some plausible pretences must be found for removing or hoodwinking, one after another, those sentries who are posted by the constitution of a free country, for warning the people of their danger.

> THOMAS ERSKINE, arguendo, *Trial of Thomas Paine* (1792) 22 How. St. Tr. 443.

The prize of the general is not a bigger tent, but command.

> OLIVER WENDELL HOLMES, *Law and the Court, Speeches* 100 (1913).

Evil men are rarely given power; they take it over from better men to whom it had been entrusted.

> Justices ROBERTS, FRANKFURTER, and JACKSON, dissenting in *Screws v United States* (1945) 325 US 91, 160, 89 L ed 1495, 1534, 65 S Ct 1031, 162 ALR 1330.

There is no stretching of power: 'tis a good rule, eat within your stomach, act within your commission.

> JOHN SELDEN, *Table-Talk: Power-State.*

Arbitrary power and the rule of the Constitution cannot both exist.   They are antagonistic and incompatible forces; and one or the other must of necessity perish whenever they are brought into conflict.

> SUTHERLAND, J., *Jones v Securities & Exch. Com.* (1936) 298 US 1, 24, 80 L ed 1015, 1025, 56 S Ct 654.

Prayers

Almighty God, the giver of wisdom, without whose help resolutions are vain, without whose blessing study is ineffectual, enable me, if it be Thy will, to attain such knowledge as may qualify me to direct the doubtful, and instruct the ignorant, to prevent wrongs and terminate contentions; and grant that I may use that knowledge which I shall attain, to Thy glory and my own salvation, for Jesus Christ's sake, Amen.

> SAMUEL JOHNSON, *Prayer Before the Study of Law.* Boswell, *Life of Johnson: 1765.*

Give therefore to thy servant an understanding heart, to judge thy people, and discern between good and evil. For who shall be able to judge this people, thy people which is so numerous?

> 1 Kings 3:9 (Solomon's prayer for wisdom).

St. Thomas More, be our advocate and counsel before the Divine tribunal that alone is without error.

Bespeak for us the wisdom to apply the precepts of God's eternal law to the problems of our daily practice.

Intercede for us that we may emulate the sense of humor which made your heart echo with the mirth of heaven.

Pray that we may spurn false oaths and live as you did, faithful to our trust as members of the Bar, even though by doing so we may be called upon to sacrifice our lives as you sacrificed yours.

These things seek for us through the merits of Jesus Christ, Our Lord. Amen.

> MILES F. McDONALD, *Prayer for Lawyers.*

453

O God of all truth, knowledge and judgment, without whom nothing is true or wise, or just, look down with mercy upon Thy servants whom Thou sufferest to sit in earthly seats of judgment, to administer Thy justice to Thy people. Enlighten their ignorance and inspire them with Thy judgments. Grant them grace, truly and impartially to administer Thy justice and to maintain Thy truth in the glory of Thy name. And of Thy infinite mercy so direct and dispose of my heart that I may this day fulfill all my duty in Thy fear, and fall into no error of judgment. Give me grace to hear patiently, to consider diligently, to understand rightly, and to decide justly. Grant me due sense of humility, that I be not mislead by my wilfulness, vanity or egotism. Of myself I humbly acknowledge my own unfitness and unworthiness in Thy sight, and without Thy gracious guidance I can do nothing right. Have mercy upon me, a poor, weak, frail sinner, groping in the dark; and give me grace so to judge others now, that I may not myself be judged when Thou comest to judge the world with Thy truth. Grant my prayer, I beseech Thee, for the love of Thy son, our Saviour, Jesus Christ. Amen.

> EDWARD G. RYAN, Chief Justice of Wisconsin Supreme Court. Prayer was found among his papers after his death.

Preamble

Of all instruments of longwindedness, the most unmerciful is that which is called a Preamble. It is a sort of excrescence growing out of the head of a section.

> JEREMY BENTHAM, *Nomography*, ch. 5, in 3 *Works* 249 n.

A specious frontispiece.

> COKE, *Darcy v Allein* (1603) 11 Rep. 84b, 88b.

A key to open the minds of the makers of the Act and the mischiefs which they intended to redress.

DYER, C.J., See 1 Plowd. 369.

Precedent

Shall not we give judgment because it is not adjudged in the books before? We will give judgment according to reason; and if there be no reason in the books I will not regard them.

ANDERSON, C.J., *Case of the Resceit,* Gouldes. 96. (c. 1600).

Consequence does not draw consequence, but the extension should stop within the next cases; otherwise there will be a gradual lapse into dissimilar cases, and sharpness of wit will have greater power than authority of law.

BACON, *De Augmentis Scientiarum,* bk 8, ch. 3, aph. 16.

Precedents and rules must be followed, unless flatly absurd or unjust.

BLACKSTONE, *Commentaries,* bk 1, 70.

It is of dangerous consequence for judges, in their judgments, to rely too much on precedents, that perhaps went forth through the necessity of the present times.

BRAMSTON, L.C.J., *Hampden's Case* (1637) 3 How. St. Tr. 1245.

Precedents drawn from the days of travel by stage coach do not fit the conditions of travel to-day. The principle that the danger must be imminent does not change, but

455

the things subject to the principle do change.   They are
whatever the needs of life in a developing civilization require
them to be.

> CARDOZO, J., *MacPherson v Buick Motor Co.*, 217 N.Y. 382, 391
> (1916).

Precedents will be misleading if separated from the statutes they interpret.   Opinions get their color and significance from the subject of the controversy.

> CARDOZO, J., *Cott v Erie R.R. Co.*, 231 N.Y. 67, 73 (1921).

I will look, your Honor, and endeavor to find a precedent,
if you require it; though it would seem to be a pity that
the Court should lose the honor of being the first to establish so just a rule.

> RUFUS CHOATE.   See 1 Brown, *Works of Choate* 292 (1862).

We must peruse our ancient authors for out of the old
fields must come the new corn.*

> COKE, 4 *Inst.* 109.

The slaves of custom and established mode,
With packhorse constancy we keep the road,
Crooked or straight, through quags and thorny dells,
True to the jingling of our leader's bells.
To follow foolish precedents, and wink
With both our eyes, is easier than to think.

> WILLIAM COWPER, *Tirocinium*, *"A Review of Schools"*, 1. 251.

---

* For out of olde feldys, as men seith,
  Cometh al this newe corn fro yeer to yere.
    CHAUCER, *The Parlement of Foules*, 1, 22.

To make precedents the fount and origin of the law is to compel their study; to compel their study is to put a premium upon the knowledge so acquired; and to put a premium upon this knowledge is to encourage its over-exhibition by the overzealous. We should think of the case lawyer at least with the charity due to one who has been led into temptation.

> JOHN W. DAVIS, *The Case for the Case Lawyer,* 3 Mass. L.Q. 102 (1917).

A precedent embalms a principle.

> BENJAMIN DISRAELI, *Speech,* House of Commons, Feb. 22, 1848. (Also attributed to William Scott (Lord Stowell) in an opinion when Advocate-General, 1788).

Every precedent had first a commencement.

> ELLESMERE, L.C., *Case of Proclamations* (1611) 2 How. St. Tr. 723, 725.

One day through the primeval wood
A calf walked home, as good calves should;
But left a trail all bent askew,
A crooked trail, as all calves do.

*   *   *

And men two centuries and a half
Trod in the footsteps of that calf.

*   *   *

A hundred thousand men were led
By one calf near three centuries dead.
They followed still his crooked way,
And lost one hundred years a day;
For thus such reverence is lent
To well-established precedent.

> SAM WALTER FOSS, *The Calf-Path.*

I should be sorry that any opinion of mine should shake the authority of an established precedent; since it is better for the subject that even faulty precedents should not be shaken than that the law should be uncertain.

> GROSE, J., *King v Thompson* (1787) 2 T.R. 18, 24.

All the sentences of precedent judges that have ever been, cannot altogether make a law contrary to natural equity.

> THOMAS HOBBES, *Leviathan*, Pt. 2, ch. 26.

It is revolting to have no better reason for a rule of law than that so it was laid down in the time of Henry IV. It is still more revolting if the grounds upon which it was laid down have vanished long since, and the rule simply persists from blind imitation of the past.

> OLIVER WENDELL HOLMES, *Path of the Law,* 10 Harv. L.R. 457, 469 (1897).

But I know of no way that we can have equal justice under law except we have some law.

> JACKSON, J., dissenting, *Brown v Allen* (1953) 344 US 443, 546, 97 L ed 469, 536, 73 S Ct 397.

Constitutional precedents are accepted only at their current valuation and have a mortality rate almost as high as their authors.

> ROBERT H. JACKSON, *Task of Maintaining Our Liberties,* 39 A.B.A.J. 962 (1953).

Every doubtful point is regularly answered both ways by authority. . . . There is the Janus face of Precedent.

> KARL LLEWELLYN, *The Bramble Bush* (1930) 149.

The reason and spirit of cases make law; not the letter of particular precedents.

> LORD MANSFIELD, C.J., *Fisher v Prince* (1762) 3 Burr. 1363, 1364.

The law of England would be a strange science indeed if it were decided upon precedents only. Precedents serve to illustrate principles, and to give them a fixed certainty. But the law of England, which is exclusive of positive law, enacted by statute, depends upon principles; and these principles run through all the cases according as the particular circumstances of each have been found to fall within the one or other of them.

> LORD MANSFIELD, C.J., *Jones v. Randall* (1774) Cowp. 37, 39.

Precedent, though it be evidence of law, is not law in itself.

> LORD MANSFIELD, C.J., *Jones v Randall* (1774) Lofft 383, 385.

I have heard that lawyers in one of the Western states, when they cite a decided case as a precedent in support of an argument, never say, as the Louisiana lawyers say, that the precedent "fits like a glove," or is "on all fours," or is a "ringer" for the case being argued. They say that the precedent is a "goose case." The expression arose from the perplexity of a so-called "case lawyer," who was unprepared to advise his client whether he was liable in damages because his geese had trespassed on his neighbor's lawn. The lawyer said he had found several cases where the owners were held liable because their horses, cows, sheep, goats, or dogs had committed acts of trespass; but he could not find a "goose case." The distinction which he observed was that his "goose case" was not "on all fours."

> O'NIELL, J., dissenting, *Taylor v Allen*, 151 La. 82, 118 (1921).

Our common-law system consists in the applying to new combinations of circumstances those rules of law which we derive from legal principles and judicial precedents; and for the sake of attaining uniformity, consistency and certainty, we must apply those rules, where they are not plainly unreasonable and inconvenient, to all cases which arise; and we are not at liberty to reject them, and to abandon all analogy to them, in those to which they have not yet been judicially applied, because we think that the rules are not as convenient and reasonable as we ourselves could have devised.

> PARKE, J., *Mirehouse v Rennell* (1833) 1 Cl. & F. 527, 546.

It must not be; there is no power in Venice
Can alter a decree established.
'Twill be recorded for a precedent,
And many an error by the same example
Will rush into the state.

> SHAKESPEARE, *Merchant of Venice,* Act 4, scene 1.

The most that can be said is that the point was in the cases if anyone had seen fit to raise it. Questions which merely lurk in the record, neither brought to the attention of the court nor ruled upon, are not to be considered as having been so decided as to constitute precedents.

> SUTHERLAND, J., *Webster v Fall* (1925) 266 US 507, 511, 69 L ed 411, 413, 45 S Ct 148.

It is a maxim among these lawyers, that whatever has been done before may legally be done again; and therefore they take especial care to record all the decisions formerly made against common justice and the general reason of mankind. These, under the name of precedents, they produce as authorities to justify the most iniquitous opinions; and the judges never fail of directing accordingly.

JONATHAN SWIFT, *Gulliver's Travels: Houyhnhnms,* ch. 5.

A land of settled government,
A land of just and old renown,
Where Freedom slowly broadens down
From precedent to precedent.

TENNYSON, *You Ask me, Why,* iii.

Justice, moral fitness and public convenience . . . when applied to a new subject, make common law without a precedent.

WILLES, J., *Millar v Taylor* (1769) 4 Burr. 2303, 2312.

Prefaces

Beseeching you that where you shall finde any faultes, which either by my insufficiency, the intricatenes of the worke, or the Printer's recklesnes, are committed, either friendly to pardon, or by some means to admonish me thereof.

RICHARD BELLEW (E), *Cases, Temp. Rich. II: Preface* (1585).

Wherefore accept in good part the Author's pains, and bestowe your own in the perusal of them, before you proceed to censure, and then no doubt you will find very good advantage thereby.

WILLIAM BENDLOES, *Reports: Preface* (1661).

This seems a very little book to introduce to so large a continent. No such enterprise would ever have suggested itself to the homekeeping mind of the Author, who, none the less, when this edition was proposed to him by Messrs. Scribner on terms honorable to them and grateful to him, found the notion of being read in America most fragrant and delightful.

> AUGUSTINE BIRRELL, *Obiter Dicta: Preface* to American Edition.

I . . . have, for the instruction, at least of the younger generation, undertaken the task of diligently examining the ancient judgments of righteous men, not without much loss of sleep and labour, and by reducing their acts, counsels, and answers, and whatever thereof I have found noteworthy, into one summary, I have brought it into order under titles and paragraphs (without prejudice against any better system), to be commended to perpetual memory by the aid of writing; requesting the reader, if he should find anything superfluous or erroneously stated in this work, to correct and amend it, or to pass it over with eyes half closed, since to retain everything in memory, and to make no mistakes, is an attribute of God rather than of man.

> BRACTON, *De Legibus et Consuetudinibus Angliae*, f.1 (v.l, p. 5 Twiss ed. Rolls ser. No. 70).

I found myself reduced to the necessity of either destroying or publishing these papers; (which were originally intended for my own private use, and not for public inspection). For as it was become generally known "that I had taken some account (good or bad) of all the cases which had occured in the Court of King's Bench for upwards of forty years", I was subject to continual interruption and even persecution, by incessant applications for searches into my notes; for transcripts of them; sometimes for the note-books themselves (not always returned without trouble and solicitation), not to mention frequent conversations upon very dry and unentertaining subjects, which my consulters were paid for considering, but I had no sort of concern in. This inconvenience grew from bad to worse, till it became quite insupportable; and from thence arised the present publication.

SIR JAMES BURROW, 1 *Reports: Preface* (1765).

I anticipate slippered readers rather than academicians.

GEORGE W. DALZELL, *Benefit of Clergy: Preface* (1955).

The function of the preface is to ingratiate the author with the reader in a naive effort to forestall criticism by a show of modesty.

GEORGE W. DALZELL, *ibid.*

I still consider the fundamental idea of the work so undoubtedly true and irrefutable that I look upon every word said in opposition to it as lost.

RUDOLPH VON JHERING, *Struggle for Law*, xlvi (Amer. ed. 1915). Preface from the 5th German edition in which Jhering stated that he was making no change in the subject matter.

It is anticipated that in such a work as the present, embracing periods of history by no means satisfactorily explored, numerous omissions and errors may be pointed out by those who make it more their business to detect them than to appreciate the contribution to the common stock of knowledge. He will no further notice or answer any

463

disingenuous criticism than by perfecting and extending a future edition of his work.

> JOSEPH PARKES, *History of the Court of Chancery: Preface* (1828).

Prejudice

There are only two ways to be quite unprejudiced and impartial. One is to be completely ignorant. The other is to be completely indifferent. Bias and prejudice are attitudes to be kept in hand, not attitudes to be avoided.

> CHARLES P. CURTIS, *Commonplace Book* (1957) 7.

It is doubtful if the sinister influence of the remarks . . . made to the jury . . . could be erased by withdrawal or any admonition the Court could give. In fact, this thing of softening prejudices and erasing sinister influences once created is extremely tenuous and of doubtful consummation and if it is in the nature of a prejudice, it is more difficult to get rid of. . . . It clings to the mind like a tattoo on the epidermis.

> TERRELL, J., *Carlile v State*, 129 Fla 860, 865 (1937).

Prescription

Prescription and custom are brothers and ought to have the same age, and reason ought to be the father and congruence the mother, and use the nurse, and time out of memory to fortify them both.

> COKE, C.J., *Rowles v Mason* (1612) 2 Brownl. & Golds. 192, 198.

For whereas prescription and antiquity of time fortifies all other titles, and supposeth the beginning that law can give them: in this case it works clean contrary.

>   HOBART, C.J., *Slade v Drake* (1617) Hobart 295, 297.

President

The duty of the President to see that the laws be executed is a duty that does not go beyond the laws or require him to achieve more than Congress sees fit to leave within his power.

>   HOLMES, J., dissenting, *Myers v United States* (1926) 272 US 52, 177, 71 L ed 160, 191, 47 S Ct 21.

Presumptions

Weigh a bushel of horsefeathers against next Thursday.

>   Attributed to an unidentified English judge, referring to the weight to be given a presumption.

The presumption does not consecrate as truth the extravagantly improbable.

>   CARDOZO, C.J., *Matter of Findlay,* 253 N.Y. 1, 8 (1930).

There are breaths of human nature at which presumptions shrink and wither.

>   CARDOZO, C.J., *Matter of Findlay,* 253 N.Y. 1, 11 (1930).

Experience is not sufficiently uniform to raise a presumption that one who has the means of paying a debt will actually pay it.

>   CHAPMAN, C.J., *Atwood v Scott,* 99 Mass 177, 178 (1868).

[Legal Quotations]—30   *465*

If a man stay away from his wife for seven years, the law presumes the separation to have killed him; yet, according to our daily experience, it might well prolong his life.

LORD DARLING, *Scintillae Juris: Of Evidence.*

"That is no excuse," replied Mr. Brownlow. "You were present on the occasion of the destruction of these trinkets, and, indeed, are the more guilty of the two, in the eye of the law; for the law supposes that your wife acts under your direction."

"If the law supposes that," said Mr. Bumble, . . . "the law is a ass—a idiot. If that's the eye of the law, the law's a bachelor; and the worst I wish the law is, that his eye may be opened by experience—by experience."

CHARLES DICKENS, *Oliver Twist*, ch. 51.

In England a man is presoomed to be innocent till he's proved guilty an' they take it f'r granted he's guilty. In this counthry a man is presoomed to be guilty ontil he's proved guilty an' after that he's presoomed to be innocent.

FINLEY PETER DUNNE, *Mr. Dooley on Making a Will: On Criminal Trials.*

"Presumptions", as happily stated by a scholarly counselor, ore tenus, in another case, "may be looked on as the bats of the law, flitting in the twilight but disappearing in the sunshine of actual facts."

LAMM, J., *Mockowith v Kansas City, St. J. & C.B. R.R.,* 196 Mo 550, 571 (1906).

Principle

The tendency of a principle to expand itself to the limit of its logic. . . .

> BENJAMIN N. CARDOZO, *Nature of the Judicial Process* 51 (1921).

Privilege

The moment confidence ceases, privilege ceases.

> LORD ELDON, L.C., *Parkhurst v Lowten* (1819) 2 Swanst. 194, 216.

Probability

It is always probable that something improbable will happen.

> BLECKLEY, J., *Warren v Purtell*, 63 Ga. 428, 430 (1879).

The improbable—by definition being not impossible— sometimes does occur.

> FRANK, J., dissenting, *Old Colony Bondholders v N. Y., N. H. & H. R. Co.* 161 F. 2d 413, 443 (1947).

Profession

I hold every man a debtor to his profession; from the which as men of course do seek to receive countenance and profit, so ought they of duty to endeavour themselves by way of amends, to be a help and ornament thereunto.

> BACON, *Maxims of the Law: Preface.*

He did not like his children to come and see him act, and was always regretting—heaven help him!—that he wasn't a barrister-at-law. Look upon this picture and on that. Here we have Macbeth, that mighty thane; Hamlet, the intellectual symbol of the whole world of modern thought; Strafford, in Robert Browning's fine play; splendid dresses, crowded theatres, beautiful women, royal audiences; and on the other side, a rusty gown, a musty wig, a fusty court, a deaf judge, an indifferent jury, a dispute about a bill of lading, and ten guineas on your brief—which you have not been paid, and which you can't recover—why, " 'tis Hyperion to a satyr!"

> AUGUSTINE BIRRELL, *Obiter Dicta* (First Ser.): *Actors*. Referring to the noted actor William Charles Macready.

There are abuses incident to every branch of industry, to every profession. It would not be thought very just or wise to arraign the honorable professions of law and physic, because the one produces the pettifogger, and the other the quack.

> HENRY CLAY, *Debate on Revision of the Tariff*, 36 Annals of Cong. 2037 (1820).

Commonly, physicians, like beer, are best when they are old; and lawyers, like bread, when they are young and new.

> THOMAS FULLER, *The Holy State: The Good Advocate* (1642).

Every calling is great when greatly pursued.

> OLIVER WENDELL HOLMES, *The Law. Speeches* 17 (1913).

The lawyers are the cleverest men, the ministers are the most learned, and the doctors are the most sensible.

> O. W. HOLMES, Sr., *Poet at the Breakfast Table*, ch. 5.

Historically, there are three ideas involved in a profession, organization, learning, and a spirit of public service. These are essential. The remaining idea, that of gaining a livelihood, is incidental.

> ROSCOE POUND, *What is a Profession?* 19 Notre Dame Law. 203, 204 (1944).

An old physician and a young lawyer.

> Proverb. HERBERT, *Jacula Prudentum* (1651).

All professions are conspiracies against the laity.

> GEORGE BERNARD SHAW, *The Doctor's Dilemma,* Act 1.

Profession (Legal)

It [the Bar] is an order as ancient as the magistracy, as noble as virtue, as necessary as justice; it is distinguished by a character which is peculiar to itself, and it alone always maintains the happy and peaceful possession of independence.

> HENRI D'AGUESSEAU, Speech on opening of French Parliament, 1693. See Young, *French Bar* (1869) 61.

We must never forget that the profession of law exists in order that the administration of justice shall be carried on.

> SIR NORMAN BIRKETT, informal remarks at dinner by New Jersey Bar to American Bar Association officers. See 32 A.B.A.J. 861 (1946).

Then welcome business, welcome strife,
Welcome the cares and thorns of life,

The visage wan, the pore-blind sight
The toil by day, the lamp by night,
The tedious forms, the solemn prate,
The pert dispute, the dull debate,
The drowsy bench, the babbling hall,
For thee fair justice, welcome all.

BLACKSTONE, *Farewell to His Muse.*

Law,—in its nature the noblest and most beneficial to mankind, in its abuse and debasement the most sordid and most pernicious.

LORD BOLINGBROKE, *On the Study and Use of History: Letter* 5 (1739).

There have been lawyers that were orators, philosophers, historians; there have been Bacons and Clarendons, my lord.   There will be none such any more, till, in some better age true ambition, or the love of fame, prevails over avarice; and till men find leisure and encouragement to prepare themselves for the exercise of this profession, by climbing up to the "vantage ground" (so my Lord Bacon calls it) of science, instead of grovelling all their lives below, in a mean but gainful application of all the little arts of chicane.   Till this happens, the profession of the law will scarce deserve to be ranked among the learned professions.   And whenever it happens, one of the vantage grounds to which men must climb, is metaphysical, and the other, historical knowledge.

LORD BOLINGBROKE, *ibid.*

The law is a profession which abounds with honourable men, and in which I believe there are fewer scamps, than in any other.   The most honourable men I have known

470

have been lawyers; they were men whose word was their bond, and who would have preferred ruin to breaking it.

GEORGE BORROW, *Wild Wales,* ch. 55.

Instead of holding a position of independence, between the wealthy and the people, prepared to curb the excesses of either, able lawyers have, to a large extent, allowed themselves to become adjuncts of great corporations and have neglected their obligation to use their powers for the protection of the people. We hear much of the "corporation lawyer", and far too little of the "people's lawyer". The great opportunity of the American bar is and will be to stand again as it did in the past, ready to protect also the interests of the people.

LOUIS D. BRANDEIS, *The Opportunity in the Law,* 39 Am. L. Rev. 559.

Membership in the bar is a privilege burdened with conditions.

CARDOZO, J., *Matter of Rouss,* 221 N.Y. 81, 84 (1917).

The quest is greater than what is sought, the effort finer than the prize, or, rather, that the effort *is* the prize—the victory cheap and hollow were it not for the rigor of the game.

BENJAMIN N. CARDOZO, *Law and Literature* 164 (1931).

I grieved because there was taken away from me, not, as many thought, a rival, who stood in the way of my reputation, but a partner and companion, in a glorious calling.

CICERO, *Brutus,* I, 2 (on the death of Hortensius).

471

Though holding larger trusts than all other vocations combined, and without security, the record of the profession in its fiduciary relations is of unexampled purity.

CHAUNCEY M. DEPEW, *Speech to Graduates of Columbia Law School,* May 17, 1882.

"How do you like the law, Mr. Micawber?" "My dear Copperfield," he replied, "to a man possessed of the higher imaginative powers the objection to legal studies is the amount of detail they involve. Even in our professional correspondence," said Mr. Micawber, glancing at some letters he was writing, "the mind is not at liberty to soar to any exalted form of expression. Still, it is a great pursuit, a great pursuit."

CHARLES DICKENS, *David Copperfield,* ch. 39.

To be a great lawyer, I must give up my chance of being a great man.

BENJAMIN DISRAELI, *Vivian Grey,* bk 1, ch. 9 (1826).

And then there is the blessed assurance that, as a lawyer, his "works do follow him", not into the grave, but into the workaday lives of his clients. Long after he is dead and gone, men and women will be acting upon his advice, will be carrying out his directions, will be ordering their affairs in strict observance of his written word. Estates will go on devolving under the settlements he drew. Husbands, wives, children will go on being protected by the trusts he created. Beneficiaries will rise up and bless him for the wills he made. Year after year, tenants will occupy or trade or farm, relying on the agreements and the leases he approved.

REGINALD L. HINE, *Confessions of an Un-Common Attorney* 112.

Law is the business to which my life is devoted, and I should show less than devotion if I did not do what in me lies to improve it, and, when I perceive what seems to me the ideal of its future, if I hesitated to point it out and to press toward it with all my heart.

> OLIVER WENDELL HOLMES, *Path of the Law*, 10 Harv. L. Rev. 457, 473 (1897).

Of course, the law is not the place for the artist or the poet. The law is the calling of thinkers.

> OLIVER WENDELL HOLMES, *Profession of the Law*, Speeches 22 (1913), Coll. Leg. Pap. 29.

A man may live greatly in the law as well as elsewhere; that there as well as elsewhere his thought may find its unity in an infinite perspective; that there as well as elsewhere he may wreak himself upon life, may drink the bitter cup of heroism, may wear his heart out after the unattainable.

> OLIVER WENDELL HOLMES, *Profession of the Law, Speeches* 23 (1913). Coll. Leg. Pap. 30.

The glory of lawyers, like that of men of science, is more corporate than individual.

> OLIVER WENDELL HOLMES, Answer to Resolution of the Bar on Daniel S. Richardson, April 15, 1890, Speeches 47 (1913).

Lawyers and magistrates wore a long scarlet robe trimmed with ermine (which was generally of feline origin, whence Rabelais's qualification "furred cats," which is synonymous with "pettifoggers").

> R. T. HOUSE, *A Celebrated Legal Corporation*, 24 Green Bag, 294 (1912). (From article on the one hundredth anniversary of the Paris Bar Assn).

473

The highest reward that can come to a lawyer is the esteem of his professional brethren. That esteem is won in unique conditions and proceeds from an impartial judgment of professional rivals. It cannot be purchased. It cannot be artificially created. It cannot be gained by artifice or contrivance to attract public attention. It is not measured by pecuniary gains. It is an esteem which is born in sharp contests and thrives despite conflicting interests. It is an esteem commanded solely by integrity of character and by brains and skill in the honorable performance of professional duty. . . . In a world of imperfect humans, the faults of human clay are always manifest. The special temptations and tests of lawyers are obvious enough. But, considering trial and error, success and defeat, the bar slowly makes its estimate and the memory of the careers which it approves are at once its most precious heritage and an important safeguard of the interests of society so largely in the keeping of the profession of the law in its manifold services.

> Chief Justice CHARLES EVANS HUGHES, *Remarks in Reference to the late George Wickersham,* 13 Proceedings Amer. Law Inst. 61 (1936).

A barrister's profession is such an uncertain thing, especially if he won't take unsavory cases.

> IBSEN, *A Doll's House,* Act 1.

The bar is not a bed of roses,—it is either all bed and no roses, or all roses and no bed.

> RUFUS ISAACS. See Hewart, *Not Without Prejudice* 35: I remember Rufus Isaacs when he was working at the highest pressure saying that before he came to the Bar "he was told it was a bed of roses; but that was quite wrong—it is all bed and no roses or all roses and no bed."

The office of the lawyer . . . is too delicate, personal and confidential to be occupied by a corporation.

> ROBERT H. JACKSON, *Functions of the Trust Co.,* 52 N.Y.S. Bar Rept. 144 (1929).

This vanishing country lawyer left his mark on his times, and he was worth knowing. He "read law" in the *Commentaries* of Blackstone and Kent and not by the case system. He resolved problems by which he called "first principles". He did not specialize, nor did he pick and choose clients. He rarely declined service to worthy ones because of inability to pay. Once enlisted for a client, he took his obligation seriously. He insisted on complete control of the litigation—he was no mere hired hand. But he gave every power and resource to the cause. He identified himself with the client's cause fully, sometimes too fully. He would fight the adverse party and fight his counsel, fight every hostile witness, and fight the court, fight public sentiment, fight any obstacle to his client's success. He never quit. . . . He moved for new trials, he appealed; and if he lost out in the end, he joined the client at the tavern in damning the judge—which is the last rite in closing an unsuccessful case, and I have officiated at many.

> ROBERT H. JACKSON, *Tribute to Country Lawyers,* 30 A.B.A.J. 139 (1944).

He loved his profession, he had a real sense of dedication to the administration of justice, he held his head high as a lawyer, he rendered and exacted courtesy, honor and straightforwardness at the Bar. He respected the judicial office deeply, demanded the highest standards of competence and disinterestedness and dignity, despised all political use of or trifling with judicial power, and had an affectionate regard for every man who filled his exacting prescription

475

of the just judge. The law to him was like a religion, and its practice was more than a means of support; it was a mission. He was not always popular in his community, but he was respected. Unpopular minorities and individuals often found in him their only mediator and advocate. He was too independent to court the populace—he thought of himself as a leader and lawgiver, not as a mouthpiece. . . . Often his name was in a generation or two, forgotten. It was from this brotherhood that America has drawn its statesmen and its judges. A free and self-governing Republic stands as a monument for the little known and unremembered as well as for the famous men of our profession.

ROBERT H. JACKSON, *ibid.*

It too often is overlooked that the lawyer and the law office are indispensable parts of our administration of justice. Law-abiding people can go nowhere else to learn the ever changing and constantly multiplying rules by which they must behave and to obtain redress for their wrongs.

JACKSON, J., *Hickman v Taylor* (1947) 329 US 495, 514, 91 L ed 451, 464, 67 S Ct 385.

Boswell: I mentioned that a gay friend had advised me against being a lawyer, because I should be excelled by plodding block-heads.

Johnson: Why Sir, in the formulary and statutory part of law, a plodding block-head may excel; but in the ingenious and rational part of it a plodding block-head can never excel.

SAMUEL JOHNSON. Boswell, *Life of Johnson: 1766.*

Judges and lawyers took to wigs when other men in a frivolous moment took to them; unfortunately they retained the silliest adornment that human head has yet invented for itself when even physicians and bishops had recovered their wonted sobriety.

> FREDERIC WM. MAITLAND, *From the Old Law Courts to the New,* 1 Eng. Illus. Mag. 6 (1883).

There you shall see in very truth how the spark, fostered in our own land by Glanvill and Bracton, waxed into a clear flame under the care of Brian and Choke, Littleton and Fortescue, was tended by Coke and Hale, and was made a light to shine round the world by Holt and Mansfield, and the Scotts, and others whom living men remember. You shall understand how great a heritage is the law of England, whereof we and our brethren across the ocean are partakers, and you shall deem treaties and covenants a feeble bond in comparison of it; and you shall know with certain assurance that, however arduous has been your pilgrimage, the achievement is a full answer. So venerable, so majestic, is this living temple of justice, that immemorial yet freshly growing fabric of the Common Law, that the least of us is happy who hereafter may point to so much as one stone thereof, and say, The work of my hands is there.

> SIR FREDERICK POLLOCK, *Oxford Lectures and Discourses* (1890) 111.

There is no law without lawyers.

> ROSCOE POUND, *A Hundred Years of American Law,* in 1 *Law a Century of Progress* (1937) 8.

Craft is the vice, not the spirit of the profession. Trick is professional prostitution. Falsehood is professional apostasy. The strength of a lawyer is in thorough knowl-

edge of legal truth, in thorough devotion to legal right.
Truth and integrity can do more in the profession than
the subtlest and wiliest devices. The power of integrity is
the rule; the power of fraud is the exception. Emulation
and zeal lead lawyers astray; but the general law of the
profession is duty, not success. In it, as elsewhere in
human life, the judgment of success is but the verdict of
little minds. Professional duty, faithfully and well performed, is the lawyer's glory. This is equally true of the
bench and of the bar.

> JUDGE EDWARD G. RYAN, *Address, Univ. of Wisconsin Law
> School,* June, 1880.

The three proverbial roads to success at the bar—influence, a book, or a miracle.

> Saying.

In a profession, where unbounded trust is necessarily
reposed, there is nothing surprising that fools should neglect
it in their idleness, and tricksters abuse it in their knavery,
but it is the more to the honour of those, and I will vouch
for many, who unite integrity with skill and attention, and
walk honourably upright where there are so many pitfalls
and stumbling blocks for those of a different character.
To such men their fellow citizens may safely entrust the
care of protecting their patrimonial rights, and their country
the more sacred charge of her laws and privileges.

> SIR WALTER SCOTT, *The Antiquary,* ch. 43.

It is the pest of our profession that we seldom see the
best side of human nature. People come to us with every
selfish feeling newly pointed and grinded. . . . In
civilized society, law is the chimney through which all that

smoke discharges itself, that used to circulate through the whole house and put every one's eyes out; no wonder, therefore, that the vent itself should sometimes get a little sooty.

SIR WALTER SCOTT, *Guy Mannering,* ch. 39.

The law is the only profession which records its mistakes carefully, exactly as they occurred, and yet does not identify them as mistakes.

ELLIOTT DUNLAP SMITH, Conference on Teaching of Law in Liberal Arts Curriculum, November, 1954. See 39 J. Am. Jud. Soc. 47.

To be wholly devoted to some intellectual exercise is to have succeeded in life; and perhaps only in law and the higher mathematics may this devotion be maintained, suffice to itself without reaction, and find continual rewards without excitement.

ROBERT L. STEVENSON, *Weir of Hermiston,* ch. 2.

Yes, my lords, I am amazed at his grace's speech. The noble duke cannot look before him, behind him, or on either side of him, without seeing some noble peer, who owes his seat in this house to his successful exertions in the profession to which I belong. Does he not feel that it is as honourable to owe it to these, as to being the accident of an accident?

LORD THURLOW, reply to Duke of Grafton during the inquiry into Lord Sandwich's administration of Greenwich Hospital. The Duke belittled the legal profession and Thurlow's recent admission into the peerage. See Butler, *Reminiscences* 165 (1824).

Every person who enters into a learned profession undertakes to bring to the exercise of it a reasonable degree of care and skill. He does not undertake, if he is an attorney, that at all events you shall gain your case, nor does a surgeon undertake that he will perform a cure; nor does he undertake to use the highest possible degree of skill. There may be persons who have a higher education and greater advantages than he has, but he undertakes to bring a fair, reasonable, and competent degree of skill.

TINDAL, C.J., *Lanphier v Phipos* (1838) 8 C. & P. 475, 479.

I cannot believe that a republic could subsist at the present time if the influence of lawyers in public business did not increase in proportion to the power of the people.

ALEXIS DE TOCQUEVILLE, *Democracy in America,* Pt. 1, ch. 16.

The more that we reflect upon all that occurs in the United States the more we shall be persuaded that the lawyers as a body form the most powerful, if not the only, counterpoise to the democratic element.

ALEXIS DE TOCQUEVILLE, *ibid.*

The profession of the law is the only aristocratic element which can be amalgamated without violence with the natural elements of democracy, and which can be advantageously and permanently combined with them.

ALEXIS DE TOCQUEVILLE, *ibid.*

As the lawyers constitute the only enlightened class which the people do not mistrust, they are naturally called upon to occupy most of the public stations. They fill the legislative assemblies, and they conduct the administration;

they consequently exercise a powerful influence upon the formation of the law, and upon its execution.

> ALEXIS DE TOCQUEVILLE, *ibid.*

When every iniquity of the lawyers of the past has been admitted, we still find that there were abundant gentlemen of the long robe, haunted, even if they were not inspired and pervaded, by the spirit of righteousness. The illumination they shed may not always have been a beacon, but at any rate the wick never ceased altogether to glow, and down the centuries we see a succession of these unloved men boring away in their tedious frowsty courts, really struggling in that dim mediaeval light to import some semblance of justice, some thought for the common weal, into the limitless greed of robber barons, the unqualified imperatives of feudal chiefs and the grasping cunning of the baser sort.

> H. G. WELLS, *The Work, Wealth and Happiness of Mankind* 353 (1931).

You are not a mere body of expert business advisers in the field of civil law or a mere body of expert advocates for those who get entangled in the meshes of the criminal law. You are servants of the public, of the state itself. You are under bonds to serve the general interest, the integrity and enlightenment of law itself, in the advice you give individuals. It is your duty also to advise those who make the laws,—to advise them in the general interest, with a view to the amelioration of every undesirable condition that the law can reach, the removal of every obstacle to progress and fair dealing that the law can remove, the lightening of every burden the law can lift and the righting of every wrong the law can rectify.

> WOODROW WILSON, *The Lawyer and the Community,* 35 A.B.A.R. 419, 435 (1910).

Profession (Overcrowded)

Never fear the want of business. A man who qualifies himself well for his calling never fails of employment in it.

THOMAS JEFFERSON, *Letter to Peter Carr, June 22, 1792.*

You must not indulge too sanguine hopes, should you be called to our bar. I was told, by a very sensible lawyer, that there are a great many chances against any man's success in the profession of the law; the candidates are so numerous, and those who get large practice so few. He said, it was by no means true that a man of good parts and application is sure of having business, though he, indeed, allowed that if such a man could but appear in a few causes, his merit would be known, and he would get forward; but that, the great risk was, that a man might pass half a lifetime in the courts, and never have an opportunity of shewing his abilities.

SAMUEL JOHNSON. Boswell, *Life of Johnson: 1777.*

Whereas the Number of Attorneys at Law that practice at the Barr in this Province are but few and that many persons Retain most of them on one side to the great prejudice and discouragement of others that have or may have suits at Law to the end therefore that Justice may be Equally administered and no Room left for Complaint be it Enacted by the Governour and Councill and Representatives Convened in Generall Assembly and by the Authority of the same that from and after the publication hereof that no person or persons That shall have any suit at Law in any of the Courts of Record Within this Province shall Retain more than two Attorneys at Law for the prosecution or management of any such Suit or process at Law that they shall have and if they Retain any more it shall be Lawful for the Justices of the bench where the Suit is Depending to order all such Attorneys as shall be Retained more than two as aforesaid to plead for the other side Without Returning the fee Received.

> Laws of N.Y. 1695, c. 49.

When one said that the numbers of Lawyers would marr the occupation, he answered, "No, for always the more Spaniels in the field, the more game."

> Proverb. Camden, *Remains Concerning Britain: Wise Speeches* (quoting John Heywood) (1674).

Two attorneys can live in a town where one cannot.

> Proverb. 4 Lean, *Collect.* 169 (1902).

There is always room at the top.

> DANIEL WEBSTER—ascribed to. See 190 N.&Q. 262, Latham, *Famous Sayings and Their Authors* 65.

Profits

Their argument was that "past and future profits" is merely "profits" writ large—for this reason, that time is exhaustively divided into past and future, and the present is merely a dividing line between the two. This is, of course, a profound and impressive truth, but there are times and places for everything, and I should hardly have thought a Tramway Act exactly the occasion which Parliament would choose for teaching business men metaphysics unawares— more especially as this statute applies to England as well as Scotland.

> ROBERTSON, Lord Pres., *Edinburgh Street Tramways Co. v Lord Provost*, 1894, 21 S.C. (4th ser.) 688, 704.

483

Progress

The center of gravity of legal development lies not in legislation, nor in juristic science, nor in judicial decision, but in society itself.

> EUGEN EHRLICH, *Fundamental Principles of the Sociology of Law: Foreword* (1936, trans. by Moll).

Public opinion's always in advance of the **Law.**

> JOHN GALSWORTHY, *Windows,* Act I.

[Law] like all human systems, will ever advance nearer to perfection, and ever fall short of it.

> SIR WILLIAM JONES, *Isaeus: Preface.*

Social necessities and social opinions are always more or less in advance of Law. We may come indefinitely near to the closing of the gap between them, but it has a perpetual tendency to reopen. Law is stable; the societies we are speaking of are progressive. The greater or less happiness of a people depends on the degree of promptitude with which the gulf is narrowed.

> SIR HENRY MAINE, *Ancient Law,* ch. 2.

Promotion

Who should succeed the captain but the lieutenant?

> SIR HENEAGE FINCH. When appointed Lord Keeper in 1673, Charles II asked him who should succeed him as Attorney General he thus replied, referring to Francis North. See Roger North, *Examen* 515.

Proof

That which is obvious need not be proved. (*Ea que manifesta sunt, non indigent probacione.*)

BRACTON, Note Book case 194 (1222) marginal notation.

If . . . enough can be squeezed from these poor and puny anonymities to turn the color of legal litmus paper.

HOLMES, J., dissenting, *Abrams v United States* (1919) 250 US 616, 629, 63 L ed 1173, 1180, 40 S Ct 17.

Property

Property and law are born and must die together.

JEREMY BENTHAM, *Principles of the Civil Code*, 1 Works 309.

There are topics in Real Property
    both awkward and abstruse,
Like the shifting and the springing
    of that awful thing, the Use.

J.P.C., *Poetic Justice* 6 (1947).

Personal property has no locality.

LORD LOUGHBOROUGH, C.J., *Sill v Worswick* (1791) 1 H. Bl. 665, 690.

Public Interest

It is to the interest of the public that the suppression of a prosecution should not be made matter of private bargain.

ERLE, C.J., *Clubb v Hutson* (1865) 18 C.B. (N.S.) 414, 417.

485

For now the wharf and crane and other conveniences are affected with a publick interest, and they cease to be *juris privati* only; as if a man set out a street in new building on his own land, it is now no longer bare private interest, but it is affected with a publick interest.

> SIR MATTHEW HALE, *De Portibus Maris* (in Hargrave, *Law Tracts* 77).

The notion that a business is clothed with a public interest and has been devoted to the public use is little more than a fiction intended to beautify what is disagreeable to the sufferers.

> HOLMES, J., *Tyson & Bro.-United Theatre Ticket Officers v Banton* (1927) 273 US 418, 446, 71 L ed 718, 729, 47 S Ct 426, 58 ALR2d 1236.

Property does become clothed with a public interest when used in a manner to make it of public consequence, and affect the community at large.

> WAITE, C.J., *Munn v Illinois* (1876) 94 US 113, 126, 24 L ed 77, 84.

Public Policy

It is a very unruly horse, and when once you get astride it you never know where it will carry you. It may lead you from the sound law. It is never argued at all but when other points fail.

> BURROUGH, J., *Richardson v Mellish* (1824) 2 Bing. 229, 252.

Judges are more to be trusted as interpreters of the law than as expounders of what is called public policy.

> CAVE, J., *Re Mirams* [1891] 1 Q.B. 594, 595.

That principle of the law which holds that no subject can lawfully do that which has a tendency to be injurious to the public, or against the public good.

LORD TRURO, *Egerton v Brownlow* (1853) 4 H.L. Cas 1, 196.

Public Welfare

The public good is in nothing more essentially interested than the protection of every individual's private rights.

BLACKSTONE, *Commentaries,* bk 1, 139.

Public wrongs are but popular rights in embryo.

LORD DARLING, *Meditations in the Tea Room,* VII.

Sometime when the public good is pretended, a private benefit is intended.

COKE, 10 Rep. 142b.

Publicity

Publicity is justly commended as a remedy for social and industrial diseases. Sunlight is said to be the best of disinfectants; electric light the most efficient policeman.

LOUIS D. BRANDEIS, *Other People's Money,* ch. 5 (1914 ed. p. 92).

Two classes of people have poor public relations— mothers-in-law and attorneys-at-law.

ERLE STANLEY GARDNER (under pseud. A. A. Fair) *Some Women Won't Wait: Foreword* (paperback reissue).

Publicity is an evil substitute [for personal acquaintance] and the art of publicity is a black art; but it has come to stay, every year adds to its potency and to the finality of its judgments. The hand that rules the press, the radio, the screen and the far-spread magazine, rules the country; whether we like it or not, we must learn to accept it.

JUDGE LEARNED HAND, *Proceedings in Memory of Justice Brandeis,* 317 U.S. xv (1942).

Question (Law and Fact)

Every question of law arises out of a fact situation, and if there be no state of facts there can be no question of law.

DICKINSON, J., *United States v Rodenbough,* 14 F. 2d 989, 990 (1926).

Question (Leading)

All interrogatories must, to some extent, make a suggestion to the witness. It would be perfectly nugatory to ask a witness, if he knew anything about something.

LORD LANGDALE, M.R., *Lincoln v Wright* (1841) 4 Beav. 166, 171.

Quotations

I was told recently by a learned judge that I had in two or three instances attributed certain sayings or incidents to wrong personages. I think this by no means improbable, although I believe such instances to be very few. There is always a number of smart things straying about the world, like orphans, devoid of ostensible parentage, till some admirer takes pity upon them, and from ignorance or from mere whim affiliates them upon some well-known wit, who is not unlikely to have been their progenitor. On the Home Circuit, whenever we stumbled over one of these waifs, if it was of a respectable character, we in general ascribed it to Thesiger; if it was not sufficiently clothed to be presentable in decent society, we fathered it upon Serjeant Murphy; and if it savoured of conceit or self-complacency, Warren was sure to become the recipient.

ROBINSON, *Bench and Bar* 281 (4th ed. 1894).

Reading

A cursory and tumultuary reading doth ever make a confused memory, a troubled utterance, and an uncertain judgment.

COKE, 6 Rep.: *Preface.*

I had many an exciting day . . . reading the statutes and the dictionary and wondering how the characters would turn out.

MARK TWAIN, *Roughing It,* ch. 3 (Twain, while on the way to Nevada to become secretary to his brother, the Governor of the Territory, relieved the tedium of the journey by reading the U.S. Rev. Statutes.)

Reason

No man (out of his own private reason) ought to be wiser than the law, which is the perfection of reason.

COKE, *First Institute 97b.*

Reason is the life of the law; nay, the common law itself is nothing else but reason.

COKE, *First Institute 97*b.

The reason of the law is the life of the law; for though a man can tell the law, yet, if he know not the reason thereof, he shall soon forget his superficial knowledge. But when he findeth the right reason of the law, and so bringeth it to his natural reason, that he comprehendeth it as his own, this will not only serve him for the understanding of that particular case, but of many others.

COKE, *First Institute* 183.

The reason of a resolution is more to be considered than the resolution itself.

HOLT, C.J., *Cage v Acton* (1699) 12 Mod. 288, 294.

It's my will, my command, let that for reason stand. (*Hoc volo, sic ubeo, sit pro ratione voluntas.*)

JUVENAL, *Satires,* VI, 219.

Let us consider the reason of the case; for nothing is law that is not reason.

POWELL, J., *Coggs v Bernard* (1703) 2 Ld. Raym. 909, 911.

Neither rhyme nor reason.

Proverb. This brings to mind the story that Sir Thomas More, when asked by an author his opinion of an impertinent book, desired him by all means to put it into verse and bring it to him again. This being done, Sir Thomas looking upon it said, Yea, now it is somewhat like; now it is rhyme; before, it was neither rhyme nor reason. Ray, *Proverbs* (1670).

The reason of a thing is not to be inquired after, till you are sure the thing itself be so. We commonly are at "What's the reason of it?" before we are sure of the thing. It was an excellent question of my Lady Cotton, when Sir Robert Cotton was magnifying of a shoe which was Moses' or Noah's, and wondering at the strange shape and fashion of it; "but Mr. Cotton," says she, "are you sure it is a shoe?"

> JOHN SELDEN, *Table Talk: Reason.*

Reasonable Man

The man on the Clapham omnibus.

> LORD BOWEN—attributed to. See Collins, M.R., *McQuire v Western Morning News Co.* [1903] 2 K.B. 100, 109.

"Errors of judgment," however, would not count against him, if they resulted "from the excitement and confusion of the moment". The reason that was exacted of him was not the reason of the morrow. It was reason fitted and proportioned to the time and the event.

> CARDOZO, J., *Wagner v International R. R.,* 232 N.Y. 176, 177 (1921).

No court has ever given, nor do we think ever can give, a definition of what constitutes a reasonable or an average man.

> LORD GODDARD, C.J., *R. v McCarthy* [1954] 2 Q.B. 105, 112.

The person concerned is sometimes described as "the man in the street" or "the man in the Clapham omnibus," or, as I recently read in an American author, "the man

491

who takes the magazines at home, and in the evening
pushes the lawn mower in his shirt sleeves."

> GREER, L. J., *Hall v Brooklands Auto Racing Club* [1933] 1 K.B.,
> 205, 224.

He is one who invariably looks where he is going, and
is careful to examine the immediate foreground before he
executes a leap or bound; who neither star-gazes nor is lost
in meditation when approaching trap-doors or the margin
of a dock; who records in every case upon the counterfoils
of cheques such ample details as are desirable, scrupulously
substitutes the word 'Order' for the word 'Bearer', crosses
the instrument 'a/c Payee only', and registers the package
in which it is despatched; who never mounts a moving
omnibus, and does not alight from any car while the train
is in motion; who investigates exhaustively the *bona fides*
of every mendicant before distributing alms, and will inform himself of the history and habits of a dog before
administering a caress.

> A. P. HERBERT, *Uncommon Law: Fardell v Potts.*

Devoid, in short, of any human weakness, with not one
single saving vice, *sans* prejudice, procrastination, ill-nature,
avarice, and absence of mind, as careful for his own safety
as he is for that of others, this excellent but odious character
stands like a monument in our Courts of Justice, vainly
appealing to his fellow-citizens to order their lives after
his own example.

> A. P. HERBERT, *ibid.*

A "reasonable man" does not mean a paragon of circum-
spection.

> LORD REID, *A. C. Billings & Sons Ltd. v Riden* [1958] A.C. 240,
> 255.

Recreations

Recreations should not be used as professions, and trades, but to be used as medicines, to make men more able and fit for higher and greater affairs.

COKE, *Fourth Institute* 319.

Red Tape

Whatever was required to be done, the Circumlocution Office was beforehand with all the public departments in the art of perceiving HOW NOT TO DO IT.

DICKENS, *Little Dorritt,* bk 1, ch. 10.

A little bundle of Papers, tied with a red Tape, were lost on Friday last was a seven night, between Worcester-house and Lincoln's-Inn Also a Paper-Book bound in Leather and blue colored Leafs.   If any one who hath found them, will bring or send them to *Mr. Graves* his Chamber in Lincoln's Inn, they shall receive satisfaction for their pains.

The *Public Intelligencer,* December 6, 1658 (No. 158).   See S.H.H. Notes & Queries, v. 11, 2d ser. 376 (1861).

Referendum

No plebiscite can legalize an unjust discrimination.

Per curiam, *Hall v St. Helena Parish School Bd.,* 197 F.Supp. 648, 659 (1961).

A citizen's constitutional rights can hardly be infringed simply because a majority of the people choose that it be.

WARREN, C.J., *Lucas v Forty-Fourth General Assembly* (1964) 377 US 713, 736, 12 L ed 2d 632, 647, 84 S Ct 1459.

493

Reform

He that will not apply new remedies must expect new evils; for time is the greatest innovator; and if time of course alter things to the worse, and wisdom and counsel shall not alter them to the better, what shall be the end?

> BACON, *Essays: Of Innovations.*

It was the boast of Augustus . . . that he found Rome of brick, and left it of marble; a praise not unworthy a great prince, and to which the present reign also has its claims. But how much nobler will be the Sovereign's boast, when he shall have it to say, that he found law dear, and left it cheap; found it a sealed book—left it a living letter; found it the patrimony of the rich—left it the inheritance of the poor; found it the two-edged sword of craft and oppression—left it the staff of honesty and the shield of innocence.

> HENRY BROUGHAM, *Present State of the Law,* Speech in House of Commons, February 7, 1828.

To innovate is not to reform.

> EDMUND BURKE, *Letter to a Noble Lord* (1796).

"The sons of Zeruiah are yet too strong for us;" and we cannot mention the reformation of the law, but they presently cry out, we design to destroy propriety: whereas the law, as it is now constituted, serves only to maintain the lawyers, and to encourage the rich to oppress the poor.

> OLIVER CROMWELL. See Ludlow, *Memoirs,* entry, June 26, 1650.

Ignorance is the best of law reformers.

> OLIVER WENDELL HOLMES, *The Common Law* (1881) 78.

Lord Eldon, like the Spartan lawgiver, would have fain sworn his countrymen not to alter their laws after his death till they heard from him on the subject, and, in imitation of the Locrian penal law, would have soon ordained that every proposer of a new statute should come publicly with a halter around his neck, and adventure a hanging if he failed in his undertaking.

JOSEPH PARKES, *History of the Court of Chancery: Preface* (1828).

As for the possibility of the House of Lords preventing, ere long, a reform of Parliament, I hold it to be the most absurd notion that ever entered into human imagination. I do not mean to be disrespectful, but the attempt of the lords to stop the progress of reform, reminds me very forcibly of the great storm of Sidmouth, and of the conduct of the excellent Mrs. Partington on that occasion. In the winter of 1824, there set in a great flood upon that town— the tide rose to an incredible height—the waves rushed in upon the houses, and everything was threatened with destruction. In the midst of this sublime and terrible storm, Dame Partington, who lived upon the beach, was seen at the door of her house, with mop and pattens, trundling her mop, squeezing out the sea-water, and vigorously pushing away the Atlantic Ocean. The Atlantic was roused. Mrs. Partington's spirit was up; but I need not tell you that the contest was unequal. The Atlantic Ocean beat Mrs. Partington. She was excellent at a slop, or a puddle, but she should not have meddled with a tempest. Gentlemen, be at your ease—be quiet and steady. You will beat Mrs. Partington.

SYDNEY SMITH, *Speech on the Reform Bill,* reported in the Taunton Courier, Oct. 12, 1831.

Judicial reform is no sport for the short-winded.

> ARTHUR T. VANDERBILT (a frequent expression of his). See, e.g., N.Y. Times Mag. May 5, 1957.

Remedy

Want of right and want of remedy are in one equipage.

> COKE, 6 Rep. 58b.

It is a vain thing to imagine a right without a remedy; for want of right and want of remedy are reciprocal.

> Holt, C.J., *Ashby v White* (1703) 2 Ld. Raym. 938, 953.

The categories of negligence are never closed.

> LORD MACMILLAN, *Donoghue v Stevenson* [1932] A.C. 562, 619.

Torts are infinitely various, not limited or confined, for there is nothing in nature but may be an instrument of mischief.

> PRATT, C.J., *Chapman v Pickersgill* (1762) 2 Wils. K.B., 145, 146.

Unkindness has no remedy at law.

> Proverb. Ray, *Proverbs* (1678).

Reports and Reporting

Let this be the method of taking down judgments, and committing them to writing. Record the cases precisely, the judgments themselves word for word; add the reasons which the judges allege for their judgments; do not mix up the authority of cases brought forward as examples with the principal case; and omit the perorations of counsel, unless they contain something very remarkable.

BACON, *Advancement of Learning,* bk 8, Aph. 74.

Cases reported with too great prolixity would be drawn into a more compendious report, not in the nature of an abridgement, but tautologies and impertinences to be cut off; as for misprinting and insensible reporting, which many times confound the students, that will be *obiter* amended; but more principally if there be anything in the report, which is not well warranted by the record, that is also to be rectified.

BACON, *Proposition Touching the Compilation and Amendment of Laws* (1616).

Had it not been for Sir Edward Coke's Reports . . . the law by this time had been almost like a ship without ballast, for that the cases of modern experience are fled from those that are adjudged and ruled in former time.

BACON, *ibid.*

All the cases which are at this day clearly no law, but constantly ruled to the contrary, are to be left out; they do but fill the volumes and season the wits of students in a contrary sense of law.

BACON, *ibid.*

To give judgment privately, is to put an end to Reports. And to put an end to Reports is to put an end to the law of England.

BURKE, *Impeachment of Warren Hastings: Report on the Lords' Journals,* 1794.

When I was a nisi prius reporter, I had a drawer marked
"Bad Law," into which I threw all the cases which seemed
to me improperly ruled.   I was flattered to hear Sir James
Mansfield, C.J., say: "Whoever reads Campbell's Reports
must be astonished to find how uniformly Lord Ellenborough's decisions were right."   My rejected cases, which
I kept as a curiosity—not maliciously—were all burnt in
the great fire in the Temple when I was Attorney General.

> LORD CAMPBELL, *Lives of the Lord Chancellors: Harcourt,* ch.
> 119.

And for that it is hard for a man to report any part
or branch of any art or science justly and truly, which
he professeth not, and impossible to make a just and true
relation of anything that he understands not; I pray thee
beware of chronicle law.

> COKE, 3 Rep.: *Preface.*

The fellow taks doon ma' very words.

> LORD ESKGROVE, objecting to a law reporter.   Cockburn, *Me-*
> *morials of His Time* 161 (1856).

Poetical reports of law cases are not very common, yet
it appears to me desirable that they should be so.   Many
advantages would accrue from such a measure.   They
would, in the first place, be more commonly deposited in
the memory. . . .   In the next place, being divested of
that infinite circumlocution and the endless embarrassment
in which they are involved by it, they would become sur-
prisingly intelligible in comparison with their present obscurity.   And lastly they would by that means be rendered
susceptible of musical embellishment; and instead of being
quoted in the country with that dull monotony which is so

wearisome to bystanders, and frequently lulls even the judges themselves to sleep, might be rehearsed in recitation, which would have an admirable effect in keeping the attention fixed and lively, and could not fail to disperse that heavy atmosphere of sadness and gravity which hangs over the jurisprudence of our country.

> WILLIAM COWPER, *Report of an Adjudged Case.*

When a man has a working knowledge of his business, he can spend his leisure better than in reading all the reported cases he has time for. They are apt to be only the small change of legal thought.

> OLIVER WENDELL HOLMES, *Introduction* to *Continental Legal History Series,* v.1. Coll. Leg. Pap. 300.

As to the multiplication of reports I don't bother much— I always say the last twenty years takes up most of the law into itself.

> OLIVER WENDELL HOLMES, 2 *Holmes-Pollock Letters* 20.

This is an appeal from Bow County Court. In my view it is a disastrous example of the results of the misapplied industry of the compilers of law reports. A decided case is only worthy of report if it decides some principle of law and it is only deserving of citation in a later case if the same principle of law is involved. Unhappily very many cases are reported unnecessarily, and the practice has arisen, in a case involving no principle of law but purely a question of fact, of saying: "Here is a report of another case rather like this, so please decide it in the same way".

> MACKINNON, L.J., *O'Grady v. M. Saper, Ltd.* [1940] 2 K.B. 469, 472.

Hamlet:
Report me and my cause aright.

> SHAKESPEARE, *Hamlet,* Act 5, scene 2.

Reputation

He that hath an ill name is half hang'd ye know.

> Proverb. Heywood, *Proverbs* (1546) bk 2, ch. 6.

Resemblance

With a pencil dipped in the most vivid colors, and guided by the hand of a master, a splendid portrait has been drawn exhibiting this vessel and her freighter as forming a single figure, composed of the most discordant materials, of peace and war. So exquisite was the skill of the artist, so dazzling the garb in which the figure was presented, that it required the exercise of that cold investigating faculty which ought always to belong to those who sit on this bench, to discover its only imperfection; its want of resemblance.

> MARSHALL, C.J., *The Nereide* (1815, US) (9 Cranch) 388, 430, 3 L ed 769, 783.

Residence

A woman having a settlement
Married a man with none,
The question was, he being dead,
If that she had was gone?
Quoth Sir John Pratt, the settlement
Suspended did remain,

Living the husband; but him dead,
It doth revive again.
> Chorus of Puisne Judges:
Living the husband; but him dead,
It doth revive again.

> See *Shadwell v St. John's Wapping* (1723) Burr. Sett. Cases 124.

A woman having a settlement,
Married a man with none;
He flies and leaves her destitute;
What then is to be done?
Quoth Ryder, the Chief Justice,
"In spite of Sir John Pratt,
You'll send her to the parish
In which she was a brat
Suspension of a settlement
Is not to be maintained;
That which she had by birth subsists
Until another's gained."
> Chorus of Puisne Judges:
That which she had by birth subsists
Until another's gained.

> See *R. v Inhabitants of St. Botolph's* (1755) Burr. Sett. Cases 367.

Res Ipsa Loquitor

Judges, the case speaks for itself, than which there is no more powerful advocacy. *Res loquitur ipsa, judices, quae semper valet plurimum.*

CICERO, *Pro Milone*, xx.

As to the law, I see little or no real difference between us . . . beyond some variety of expression as to the

501

meaning of what is known as *res ipsa loquitor*. If that phrase had not been in Latin, nobody would have called it a principle. . . . In my opinion, the day for canonizing Latin phrases has gone past.

> LORD SHAW of Dunfermline, *Ballard v North British Railway Co.* 1923 S. C. (H. L.) 43, 56.

Restitution

King Claudius:
My fault is past. But, O! what form of prayer
Can serve my turn? "Forgive me my foul murder?"
That cannot be; since I am still possess'd
Of those effects for which I did the murder,
My crown, mine own ambition, and my queen.
May one be pardon'd and retain the offence?
In the corrupted currents of this world
Offence's gilded hand may shove by justice,
And oft 'tis seen the wicked prize itself
Buys out the law; but 'tis not so above.

> SHAKESPEARE, *Hamlet,* Act 3, scene 3.

Retaliation

Life for life, eye for eye, tooth for tooth, hand for hand, foot for foot.

> Exodus 21:24.

An Eye for an Eye and a Tooth for a Tooth: that does not mean that if I put out another man's eye, therefore I must loose one of my own (for what is he the better for

502

that? tho' this be commonly received) but it means that I shall give him what satisfaction an eye shall be judged to be worth.

> JOHN SELDEN, *Table-Talk: Retaliation.*

The penalty for depriving a one-eyed man of his single eye should be the loss of the offender's two eyes.

> SOLON. See Diogenes Laertius, *Solon* I, 57.

Retirement

I am not to be paragraphed out of my place.

> Chief Justice MELVILLE W. FULLER, to Holmes when newspapers were reporting his imminent retirement. Theodore Roosevelt was sending up trial balloons. See 2 *Holmes-Pollock Letters* 161.

I come here in the closing busy hours of my judicial life, before I relapse into constitutional second childishness and mere oblivion.

> CUTHBERT W. POUND, 7 N.Y. S. B. Bull. 43 (1935) (referring to compulsory retirement at age 70).

Revenge

Revenge is a kind of wild justice; which the more man's nature runs to, the more ought law to weed it out.

> BACON, *Essays: Of Revenge.*

Reversal

The matter does not appear to me now as it appears
to have appeared to me then.

> BRAMWELL, B., *Andrews v Styrap* (1872) 26 L.T. 704, 706.

In entering the order here appealed from vacating the
probate court order allowing the mentioned fees, the circuit
judge made it plain that he did so reluctantly, feeling that
he was impelled by precedent to effect what he considered
an unjust result. In his written opinion he said:

"The court fervently hopes the petitioners in this case
will appeal his decision and that it will be promptly and
definitely reversed by the Supreme Court in which event
the court will join a host of others in dancing in the streets."

Let him prepare to dance. The order of the circuit court
is reversed, with costs to defendants.

> DETHMERS, C.J., *Detroit Edison Co. v Janosz,* 350 Mich 606,
> 614 (1957).

My Lords, this is a case of great importance not only
to the parties themselves, but for the effect which your
Lordships' judgment may have on future cases. Indeed,
Russell J. and Bankes and Scrutton, L.JJ., embodied in
their judgments an appeal for guidance so touching as to
recall the prayer of Ajax . . . "Reverse our judgment
an it please you, but at least say something clear to help
in the future." In the state of the authorities this is, I
think, a reasonable request. It may not be easy to comply
with, but for my own part I shall do my best. The case
was admirably argued on both sides, which makes the task
an easier one.

> LORD DUNEDIN, *Sorrell v Smith* [1925] A.C. 700, 716.

I feel myself bound to state that I must, when I decided
that case, have seen it in a point of view, in which, after
most laborious consideration, I cannot see it now.

> LORD ELDON, L.C., *Ex parte Nolte* (1826) 2 Glynn & Jam. 295,
> 307.

Wisdom too often never comes, and so one ought not
to reject it merely because it comes late.   Since I now
realize that I should have joined the dissenters in the
Merchants Nat. Bank Case (1943) 320 US 256, 88 L ed
35, 64 S Ct 108, I shall not compound error by pushing
that decision still farther.   I would affirm the judgment,
substantially for the reasons given below.

> FRANKFURTER, J., dissenting, *Henslee v Union Planters Nat.
> Bank* (1949) 335 US 595, 600, 93 L ed 259, 264, 69 S Ct 290.

If a judge pass judgment, render a decision, deliver a
verdict, signed and sealed, and afterwards alter his judgment which he has rendered, he shall be called to account
for the alteration of the judgment, and he shall pay twelve-
fold the penalty which was in the said judgment; and in
the assembly, they shall expel him from his judgment
seat, and he shall not return, and he shall no more take his
seat with the judges in a case.

> HAMMURABI, *Code,* sec. 5.

We now think that we were then wrong and that the
decision must be overruled for reasons we shall state.

> L. HAND, J., *Metallizing Eng. Co. v Kenyon,* 153 F.2d 516, 518
> (1946).

Upon this case being re-argued and re-considered, I am
thoroughly convinced that my former decree was wrong.

> LORD HARDWICKE, L.C., *Walmesley v Booth* (1741) 2 Atk. 25,
> 27.

I see no reason why I should be consciously wrong today because I was unconsciously wrong yesterday.

> JACKSON, J., *Massachusetts v United States* (1948) 333 US 611, 639, 92 L ed 968, 986, 68 S Ct 747.

I am entitled to say of that opinion what any discriminating reader must think of it—that it was as foggy as the statute the Attorney General was asked to interpret. It left the difficult borderline questions posed by the Secretary of War unanswered, covering its lack of precision with generalities which, however, gave off overtones of assurance. . . . It would be charitable to assume that neither the nominal addressee nor the nominal author of the opinion read it. That, I do not doubt, explains Mr. Stimson's acceptance of an answer so inadequate to his questions. But no such confession and avoidance can excuse the then Attorney General.

> JACKSON, J., *McGrath v Kristensen* (1950) 340 US 162, 176, 95 L ed 173, 184, 71 S Ct 224. On the decision in this case, Jackson voted with the majority of the court contrary to an opinion he had rendered when Attorney General.

Since I have endured in the present case the refined but well-merited torture of listening to almost the whole of my somewhat prolix judgment in the previous case read to me viva voce, I will say at once that I have found very little therein which has been of any assistance to me in this case.

> LANGTON, J., *The Torni* [1932] P. 27, 33.

Revolution

The advocacy of violence may, or may not, fail; but in neither case can there be any "right" to use it. Revolutions are often "right," but a "right of revolution" is a contradiction in terms, for a society which acknowledged it, could not stop at tolerating conspiracies to overthrow it, but must include their execution.

> L. HAND, J., *United States v Dennis,* 183 F.2d 201, 213 (1950).

Rich and Poor

The law doth punish man or woman
That steals the goose from off the common,
But lets the greater felon loose
That steals the common from the goose.

> *Anon.* There were several versions prompted by the Enclosure Acts. This one was written when Sir Charles Pratt (Lord Camden) enclosed a strip of land in front of Camden House in 1764.

One of the Seven was wont to say; *That laws were like cobwebs; where the small flies were caught and the great brake through.*

> BACON, *Apothegms New and Old,* no. 181. (Also in *Diogenes Laertius, Solon* I).

Should I sigh, because I see
Laws like spider-webs to be?
Lesser flies are quickly ta'en
While the great break out again.

> RICHARD BRAITHWAITE, *Care's Cure.*

The law in its majestic equality, forbids the rich as well as the poor to sleep under bridges, to beg in the streets, and to steal bread.

> ANATOLE FRANCE, *Le Lys Rouge (The Red Lily),* ch. 7.

Laws grind the poor, and rich men rule the law.

> OLIVER GOLDSMITH, *The Traveller*, line 386.

I am for lifting everyone off the social bottom.   In fact, I am for doing away with the social bottom altogether.

> CLARE BOOTH LUCE, 83 Time, Feb. 14, 1964, p. 15 Col. 3.

River

A river is more than an amenity, it is a treasure.   It offers a necessity of life that must be rationed among those who have power over it.

> HOLMES, J., *New Jersey v New York* (1931) 283 US 336, 342, 75 L ed 1104, 1106, 51 S Ct 478.

Roman Law

The grand destinies of Rome are not yet accomplished; she reigns throughout the world by her reason, after having ceased to reign by her authority.

> HENRI D'AGUESSEAU—attributed to.

Arms, eloquence, and the study of the civil law, promoted a citizen to the honours of the Roman state; and the three professions were sometimes more conspicuous by their union in the same character.

> GIBBON, *Decline and Fall of the Roman Empire*, ch. 44.

Only in a sense was it true that our Common Law was not based on the Roman law, for we had used the Roman law as the Turks used the remains of the splendid temples of antiquity. We had pulled out the stones and used them in constructing buildings which we called our own.

> SIR GEORGE JESSEL, *Speech in House of Commons on the Bankruptcy Bill,* 1869, Hansard, 3rd ser. cxcv, 143.

English lawyers seem from the outset to treat the Roman law much as our church treats the Apocrypha; it is instructive but not authoritative.

> FREDERIC WM. MAITLAND, *Bracton's Notebook: Introduction* 6 (1887).

This, in my opinion, is the universal significance of the classical Roman jurists; this, their permanent worth. They had the courage to raise their glance from the ordinary questions of the day to the whole. And in reflecting on the narrow status of the particular case, they directed their thoughts to the guiding star of all law, namely the realization of justice in life.

> RUDOLPH STAMMLER, *The Theory of Justice* (trans. Isaac Husik, 1925) 127.

The Roman law forms no rule, binding in itself, upon the subject of these realms; but, in deciding a case upon principle, where no direct authority can be cited from our books, it affords no small evidence of the soundness of the conclusion at which we have arrived, if it proves to be supported by that law, the fruits of the researches of the most learned men, the collective wisdom of ages and the groundwork of the municipal law of most of the countries in Europe.

> TINDAL, C.J., *Acton v Blundell* (1843) 12 M. & W. 324, 353.

Rule of Law

When we say that . . . the rule of law is a characteristic of the English constitution . . . we mean, in the first place, that no man is punishable or can be lawfully made to suffer in body or goods except for a distinct breach of law established in the ordinary legal manner before the ordinary Courts of the land.

> ALBERT V. DICEY, *Law of the Constitution 172 (1885) lect. 5: Rule of Law.*

We mean in the second place . . . not only that with us no man is above the law, but (what is a different thing) that here every man, whatever be his rank or condition, is subject to the ordinary law of the realm and amenable to the jurisdiction of the ordinary tribunals.

> *Ibid.,* 177.

There remains yet a third and a different sense. . . . We may say that the constitution is pervaded by the rule of law on the ground that the general principles of the constitution (as for example the right to personal liberty or the right of public meeting) are with us the result of judicial decisions determining the rights of private persons in particular cases brought before the Courts.

> *Ibid.,* 208.

If a beachhead of cooperation may push back the jungles of suspicion, let both sides join in creating a new endeavor —not a new balance of power, but a new world of law, where the strong are just and the weak secure and the peace preserved.

> JOHN F. KENNEDY, *Inaugural Address, January 20, 1961.*

May we not conceive of us living beings to be a puppet of the Gods, either their plaything only, or created with a purpose—which of the two we cannot certainly know? But we do know, that these affections in us are like cords and strings, which pull us different and opposite ways, and to opposite actions; and herein lies the difference between virtue and vice. According to the argument there is one among these cords which every man ought to grasp and never let go, but to pull with it against all the rest; and this is the sacred and golden cord of reason, called by us the common law of the State; there are others which are hard and of iron, but this one is soft because golden; and there are several other kinds. Now we ought always to cooperate with the lead of the best, which is law. For inasmuch as reason is beautiful and gentle, and not violent, her rule must needs have ministers in order to help the golden principle in vanquishing the other principles. And thus the moral of the tale about our being puppets will not have been lost, and the meaning of the expression "superior or inferior to a man's self" will become clearer; and the individual, attaining to right reason in this matter of pulling the strings of the puppet, should live according to its rule; while the city, receiving the same from some god or from one who has knowledge of these things, should embody it in a law, to be her guide in her dealings with herself and with other states.

PLATO, *Laws* I, 644 (Jowett trans.).

Salvage

As the boat appears to have saved him quite as much as he the boat that account is in equilibrio.

LOWELL, J., *Price v Sears,* 19 Fed. Cas. (No. 11,416) 1321, 1322 (1877).

Search and Seizure

One would naturally expect that the law to warrant it should be clear in proportion as the power is exorbitant. If it is law, it will be found in our books; if it is not to be found there, it is not law.

> LORD CAMDEN, C.J., *Entick v Carrington* (1765) 19 How. St. Tr. 1029, 1030.

It is very certain, that the law obligeth no man to accuse himself; because the necessary means of compelling self-accusation, falling upon the innocent as well as the guilty, would be both cruel and unjust; and it should seem, that search for evidence is disallowed upon the same principle. There too the innocent would be confounded with the guilty.

> *Ibid.*, 1073.

The criminal is to go free because the constable has blundered.

> CARDOZO, J., *People v Defore*, 242 N.Y. 13, 21 (1926).

The criminal goes free, if he must, but it is the law that sets him free.

> CLARK, J., *Mapp v Ohio* (1961) 367 US 643, 659, 6 L ed 2d 1081, 1092, 81 S Ct 1684, 84 ALR2d 933.

For a man's house is his castle.

> COKE, *Third Institute* 162.

The house of every one is to him as his castle and fortress, as well for his defence against injury and violence, as for his repose.

> COKE, *Semayne's Case*, 5 Rep. 91 (b).

512

No room is private to his Majesty when the street door's once passed. That's law. Some people maintain that an Englishman's house is his castle. That's gammon.

> DICKENS, *Pickwick Papers,* ch. 24. (Mr. Grummer, constable, to Mr. Snodgrass).

The knock at the door, whether by day or by night, as prelude to a search, without authority of law but solely on the authority of the police, did not need the commentary of recent history to be condemned as inconsistent with the conception of human rights enshrined in the history and the basic constitutional doctrines of English speaking peoples.

> FRANKFURTER, J., *Wolf v Colorado* (1949) 338 US 25, 28, 93 L ed 1782, 1785, 69 S Ct 1359.

The crux of that doctrine is that a search is a search by a federal official if he had a hand in it; it is not a search by a federal official if evidence secured by state authorities is turned over to the federal authorities on a silver platter.

> FRANKFURTER, J., *Lustig v United States* (1949) 338 US 74, 78, 93 L ed 1819, 1823, 69 S Ct 1372.

This is conduct that shocks the conscience. Illegally breaking into the privacy of the petitioner, the struggle to open his mouth and remove what was there, the forcible extraction of his stomach's contents—this course of proceeding by agents of government to obtain evidence is bound to offend even hardened sensibilities. They are methods too close to the rack and screw to permit of constitutional differentiation.

> FRANKFURTER, J., *Rochin v California* (1952) 342 US 165, 172, 96 L ed 183, 190, 72 S Ct 205, 25 ALR2d 1396.

I regret that I find so unwise in principle and so in-expedient in policy a decision motivated by the high purpose of increasing respect for Constitutional rights. But in the last analysis I think this Court can increase respect for the Constitution only if it rigidly respects the limitations which the Constitution places upon it, and respects as well the principles inherent in its own processes. In the present case I think we exceed both, and that our voice becomes only a voice of power, not of reason.

> HARLAN, J., dissenting, *Mapp v Ohio* (1961) 367 US 643, 686, 6 L ed 2d 1081, 1107, 81 S Ct 1684, 84 ALR2d 933.

A search is not to be made legal by what it turns up. In law it is good or bad when it starts and does not change character from its success.

> JACKSON, J., *United States v Di Re* (1948) 332 US 581, 595, 92 L ed 210, 220, 68 S Ct 222.

Our law calleth a man's house, his castle, meaning that he may defend himself therein.

> LAMBARD(E), *Eirenarcha,* bk 2, cap. 7 (1588 ed.) 257.

Your Honours will find in the old books concerning the office of a Justice of the Peace, precedents of general war-rants to search suspected houses. But in more modern books, you will find only special warrants to search such and such houses, specially named, in which the complainant has before sworn that he suspects his goods are concealed; and will find it adjudged, that special warrants only, are legal. In the same manner I rely on it, that the writ prayed for in this petition, being general is illegal. It is a power, that places the liberty of every man in the hands of every petty officer.

> JAMES OTIS, arguing against the Writs of Assistance, Boston, 1761. See Tudor, *Life of James Otis (1823) 66.*

The poorest man may in his cottage bid defiance to all the forces of the crown. It may be frail—its roof may shake—the wind may blow through it—the storm may enter—the rain may enter—but the King of England cannot enter!—all his force dares not cross the threshold of the ruined tenement!

> WILLIAM PITT. See Brougham, *Statesmen in the Time of George III: Lord Chatham.*

Mr. *Pitt* spoke against this measure, particularly against the dangerous precedent of admitting the officers of excise into private houses. Every man's house was his castle, he said. If this tax is endured, it will necessarily lead to introducing the laws of excise into the domestic concerns of every private family, and to every species of the produce of land. The laws of excise are odious and grievous to the dealer, but intolerable to the private person. The precedent, he contended, was particularly dangerous, when men by their birth, education, and profession, very distinct from the trader, become subjected to those laws.

> Proceedings in the House of Commons on the Cyder Tax, Mar. 1763. See 15 *(Hansard) Parliamentary History*, 1756–65, p. 1307.

Self Confidence

I have never swum, but I have no doubt I could if I tried.

> HENRY BROUGHAM. Lord Grey and Brougham were crossing a ford when the tide rendered it not too safe. Grey turned and asked Brougham if he could swim. See Trevelyan, *Lord Grey of the Reform Bill* (1920) 191.

Self Incrimination

A man may plead. not guilty, and yet tell no lie, for by
the Law, no man is bound to accuse himself.   So when I
say, Not guilty, the meaning is as if I should say by way of
paraphrase, I am not so guilty as to tell you, if you will
bring me to trial and have me punished for this you lay
to my charge; prove it against me.

JOHN SELDEN, *Table-Talk: Law.*

Shakespeare

The bard play-writing in his room,
The bard a humble lawyer's clerk,
The bard a lawyer—parson—groom—
The bard deer-stealing after dark.
The bard a tradesman—and a Jew—
The bard a botanist—a beak—
The bard a skilled musician too—
A sheriff and a surgeon eke!

WILLIAM S. GILBERT, *The Bab Ballads: An Unfortunate Like-
ness.*

He who would Bacon place where Shakespeare sits
Must have unbaken brains or shaken wits.

SIR FREDERICK POLLOCK.

What about Bacon?   He meant to prove some day that, so
far from Bacon having written Shakespeare, it was Shakespeare who wrote Bacon's literary works.   Bacon being
the wisest and also the meanest of mankind paid Shakespeare to write these works.   It was of a piece with his
meanness to make Shakespeare take legal tips for the

516

plays in part payment.   Still, Bacon incurred heavy debts to Shakespeare, and thus was driven to take bribes.   The detailed proof not being yet fit for the public eye, they must avoid the whole topic.

> SIR FREDERICK POLLOCK, *Talk* at Authors' Club in London, as reported in 32 Can. L. T. 450, 452 (1912).

Mr. Fox [attorney for next of kin] described it as a wild goose chase; but wild geese can, with good fortune, be apprehended.

> WILBERFORCE, J., *In re Hopkins' Will Trusts* [1965] 1 Ch. 669, 674.   Testatrix left fund to be used in finding Bacon-Shakespeare manuscripts.

Shelley's Case

The rule in Shelley's Case, the Don Quixote of the law, which, like the last Knight errant of chivalry, has long survived every cause that gave it birth and now wanders aimlessly through the reports, still vigorous, but equally useless and dangerous.

> DOUGLAS, J., *Stamper v Stamper*, 121 N.C. 251, 254 (1897).

That was putting the case in a nutshell.   But it is one thing to put a case like Shelley's in a nutshell and another thing to keep it there.

> LORD MACNAGHTEN, *Van Grutten v Foxwell* [1897] A.C. 658, 671.

It was always being disparaged, and, what was perhaps worse, it was always being explained.

> LORD MACNAGHTEN, *Van Grutten v Foxwell* [1897] A.C. 658, 670.

517

Sheriff

The whole history of English justice and police might be brought under this rubric. "The Decline and Fall of the Sheriff."

> FREDERIC WM. MAITLAND, *Justice and Police* 69 (1885).

Ship

A ship is the most living of inanimate things.

> OLIVER WENDELL HOLMES, *Common Law* 26 (1881).

Silence

He has occasional flashes of silence, that make his conversation perfectly delightful.

> SYDNEY SMITH, referring to Thomas Macaulay. See 1 Holland, *Memoir of Smith* 320.

With regard to one of the terms, "state", this authority is declared: with regard to the other, "sovereign," the authority is implied only; but it is equally strong: for, in an instrument well drawn, as in a poem well composed, silence is sometimes most expressive.

> WILSON, J., *Chisholm v Georgia* (1793, US) 2 Dall. 419, 455, 1 L ed 440, 453.

Slavery

As soon as a negro comes into England he becomes free: one may be a villein in England, but not a slave.

> HOLT, C.J., *Smith v Brown* (1706) 2 Salk. 666.

518

You do not go back to the original proprietor. You need a bill of sale from God Almighty.

> JUDGE THEOPHILUS HARRINGTON, in a Vermont case, refusing to turn over a slave to a plaintiff who claimed ownership under the Fugitive Slave Act. See Russell, *Supreme Court of Vermont*, 6 Green Bag 77 (1894).

A slave is not a mere chattel. He bears the impress of his Maker, and is amenable to the laws of God and man; and he is destined to an endless existence.

> McLEAN, J., *Dred Scott v Sandford* (1857, US) 19 How. 393, 550, 15 L ed 691, 761.

The state of slavery is of such a nature, that it is incapable of being introduced on any reasons, moral or political, but only by positive law, which preserves its force long after the reasons, occasion, and time itself from whence it was created, is erased from memory. It is so odious, that nothing can be suffered to support it, but positive law. Whatever inconveniences, therefore, may follow from the decision, I cannot say this case is allowed or approved by the law of England; and therefore the black must be discharged.

> LORD MANSFIELD, C.J., *Sommersett Case* (1772) 20 How. St. Tr. 1, 82.

The air of England has long been too pure for a slave, and every man is free who breathes it. Every man who comes into England is entitled to the protection of English law, whatever oppression he may heretofore have suffered, and whatever may be the colour of his skin: *"Quamvis*

519

ille niger quamvis tu candidus esses."   Let the negro be discharged.

> Ascribed to Lord Mansfield by Campbell in his *Lives of the Chief Justices,* ch. 34 but not found in the reports. Hargrave, *arguendo,* used the expression that England was "too pure an air for a slave to breathe in" and gave as his source, 2 Rushworth, *Hist. Coll.* 468. See *Sommersett Case,* 20 How. St. Tr. 1, 51.

Socialism

The notion that with socialized property we should have women free and a piano for everybody seems to me an empty humbug.

> OLIVER WENDELL HOLMES, *Ideals and Doubts,* 10 Ill. L.R. 1, 3 (1915). Coll. Leg. Pap. 306.

Sovereignty

The popular theory of the English Constitution involves two errors as to the sovereign. First, in its oldest form at least, it considers him as an "Estate of the Realm," a separate co-ordinate authority with the House of Lords and the House of Commons. This and much else the sovereign once was, but this he is no longer. That authority could only be exercised by a monarch with a legislative veto. He should be able to reject bills, if not as the House of Commons rejects them, at least as the House of Peers rejects them. But the Queen has no such veto. She must sign her own death-warrant if the two Houses unanimously send it up to her.

> BAGEHOT, *The English Constitution* (5th ed. 1888) 57.

The King, moreover, is not only incapable of doing wrong, but even of thinking wrong; he can never mean to do an improper thing; in him is no folly or weakness.

BLACKSTONE, *Commentaries,* bk 1, 246.

The King himself ought not to be subject to any man, but he ought to be subject to God and the law, since law makes the King. Therefore let the King render to the law what the law has rendered to the King, viz. dominion and power for there is no King where will rules and not the law.

BRACTON, *De Legibus et Consuetudinibus Angliae,* f. 5b.

The Constitution of the United States established a government, and not a league, compact, or partnership. It was constituted by the people. It is called a government. In the eighth section of Article I it is declared that Congress shall have power to make all laws which shall be necessary and proper for carrying into execution the foregoing powers, and all other powers vested by this Constitution in *the government of the United States,* or in any department or office thereof. As a government it was invested with all the attributes of sovereignty. It is expressly declared in Article VI that the Constitution, and the laws of the United States made in pursuance thereof, and all treaties made under the authority of the United States, shall be the supreme law of the land.

BRADLEY, J., concurring, *Legal Tender Cases* (1870, US) 12 Wall 457, 554, 20 L ed 287, 313.

The doctrine so long contended for, that the Federal Union was a mere compact of States, and that the States, if they chose, might annul or disregard the acts of the

National legislature, or might secede from the Union at
their pleasure, and that the General government had no
power to coerce them into submission to the Constitution,
should be definitely and forever overthrown. This has been
finally effected by the National power, as it had often been
before, by overwhelming argument.

> BRADLEY, J., *Legal Tender Cases* (1870, US) 12 Wall 457, 554,
> 20 L ed 287, 313.

The King hath no prerogative but that which the law
of the land allows him.

> COKE, *Case of Proclamations* (1611) 12 Rep. 74, 76.

The King can never be poor when his subjects are rich.

> COKE, *Third Institute* 194.

It is a favorite maxim of the Civil Law that whatsoever
pleases the Prince has the effect of law. The laws of
England do not sanction any such maxim, since the King
of that land rules his people not only regally but also politically, and so he is bound by oath at his coronation to the
observance of his law.

> SIR JOHN FORTESCUE, *De Laudibus Legum Angliae,* ch. 34.

I wish the state of society was so far improved, and
the science of government advanced to such a degree of
perfection, as that the whole nation could in the peaceable
course of law, be compelled to do justice, and be sued
by individual citizens.

> JAY, C.J., *Chisholm v Georgia* (1793, US) 2 Dall 419, 478, 1 L ed
> 440, 465.

Judge Douglas has sung peans to his "popular sovereignty" doctrine until his Supreme Court, cooperating with
him, has squatted his squatter sovereignty out.   But he
will keep up this species of hum-buggery about squatter
sovereignty.   He has at last invented this sort of do-nothing
sovereignty—that the people may exclude slavery by a
sort of "sovereignty" that is exercised by doing nothing
at all.   Is not that running his popular sovereignty down
awfully?   Has it not got down as thin as the homeopathic
soup that was made by boiling the shadow of a pigeon
that had starved to death?   . . .   The Dred Scott decision
covers the whole ground, and while it occupies it, there is
not room even for the shadow of a starved pigeon to occupy
the same ground.

ABRAHAM LINCOLN, *Debate, Quincy, Oct. 13, 1858.*

The government proceeds directly from the people; is
"ordained and established" in the name of the people; and
is declared to be ordained, "in order to form a more perfect
union, establish justice, ensure domestic tranquility, and
secure the blessings of liberty to themselves and to their
posterity."   The assent of the States, in their sovereign
capacity, is implied in calling a Convention, and thus submitting that instrument to the people.   But the people
were at perfect liberty to accept or reject it, and their act
was final.   It required not the affirmance, and could not
be negatived, by the State governments.   The constitution,
when thus adopted, was of complete obligation, and bound
the State sovereignties.

MARSHALL, C.J., *M'Culloch v Maryland* (1819, US) 4 Wheat 316,
403, 4 L ed 579, 601.

The sovereignty of a State extends to everything which
exists by its own authority, or is introduced by its permis-

sion; but does it extend to those means which are employed by Congress to carry into execution powers conferred on that body by the people of the United States? We think it demonstrable that it does not. Those powers are not given by the people of a single State. They are given by the people of the United States, to a government whose laws, made in pursuance of the constitution, are declared to be supreme. Consequently, the people of a single State cannot confer a sovereignty which will extend over them.

> MARSHALL, C.J., *M'Culloch v Maryland* (1819, US) 4 Wheat 316, 429, 4 L ed 579, 607.

It has been said, that they [the states] were sovereign, were completely independent, and were connected with each other only by a league. This is true. But, when these allied sovereigns converted their league into a government, when they converted their Congress of Ambassadors, deputed to deliberate on their common concerns, and to recommend measures of general utility, into a Legislature, empowered to enact laws on the most interesting subjects, the whole character in which the States appear, underwent a change, the extent of which must be determined by a fair consideration of the instrument by which that change was effected.

> MARSHALL, C.J., *Gibbons v Ogden* (1824, US) 9 Wheat 1, 187, 6 L ed 23, 68.

The prince is not above the laws, but the laws above the prince. (*Non est princeps super leges, sed leges super principem.*)

> PLINY, *Panegyricus 65.*

Willy, Willy, Harry, Ste,
Harry, Dick, John, Harry 3;

524

One, two, three Neds, Richard 2,
Henry 4, 5, 6.   Then who?
Edward 4, 5, Dick the Bad,
Harrys twain and Ned the Lad;
Mary, Bessie, James the Vain,
Charlie, Charlie, James again;
Will and Mary, Anna Gloria,
Georges four, Will, Victoria.

> Popular catch, for memorizing the order of English sovereigns.

When I forget my King, may my God forget me.

> LORD THURLOW, Speech, House of Lords, December 15, 1788,
> at the time of the incapacity of George III.   2 Stanhope, *Life
> of Pitt* 10.

The will of the Emperor has the force of law, because
by the passage of the *lex regia* the people transfers to him
and vests in him all its own power and authority.

> ULPIAN, *Digest,* (Justinian) i, IV, 1.

Speed (Deliberate)

The cases are remanded to the District Courts to take
such proceedings and enter such orders and decrees consistent with this opinion as are necessary and proper to
admit to public schools on a racially nondiscriminatory
basis with all deliberate speed the parties to these cases.

> WARREN, C.J., *Brown v Board of Education* (1955) 349 US 294,
> 301, 99 L ed 1083, 1106, 75 S Ct 753.

"But with unhurrying chase,
And unperturbed pace,
Deliberate speed, majestic instancy."

525

There is no good reason to think that the United States Supreme Court was quoting from Francis Thompson's *The Hound of Heaven,* when in May 1955 Chief Justice Warren used the words "deliberate speed" in its opinion on the enforcement of its decrees in desegregation cases. But Thompson clearly anticipated, and very precisely described how the Court expects us to go about it.

> CHARLES CURTIS, *Commonplace Book* 111 (1957).

A question like the present should be disposed of without undue delay. But a State cannot be expected to move with the celerity of a private business man; it is enough if it proceeds, in the language of the English Chancery, with all deliberate speed.

> HOLMES, J., *Virginia v West Virginia* (1911) 222 US 17, 19, 56 L ed 71, 72, 32 S Ct 4.

For that portion which he had controverted into cash and expended in his own or on political intrigues, there was no mode of recovering it but by a suit at law, which was forthwith commenced, and proceeded, as our law-agents assured us, with all deliberate speed.

> WALTER SCOTT, *Rob Roy,* ch. 36 (or v. 2, ch. 19).

There has been entirely too much deliberation and not enough speed in enforcing the constitutional rights which we held in *Brown v. Board of Education* had been denied Prince Edward County Negro children.

> BLACK, J., *Griffin v County School Board* (1964) 377 US 218, 229 12 L ed 2d 256, 264, 84 S Ct 1226.

Stare Decisis

If it be that previous decisions must be rescinded, at least let them be interred with honour.

BACON, *Advancement of Learning,* bk 8, Aph. 95.

Stare decisis is ordinarily a wise rule of action.   But it is not a universal, inexorable command.

BRANDEIS, J., *Washington v W. C. Dawson & Co.* (1924) 264 US 219, 238, 68 L ed 646, 657, 44 S Ct 302.

The doctrine of *stare decisis* does not command that we err again when we have occasion to pass upon a different statute.

BRANDEIS, J., *Di Santo v Pennsylvania* (1927) 273 US 34, 42, 71 L ed 524, 529, 47 S Ct 267.

Stare decisis is usually the wise policy, because in most matters it is more important that the applicable rule of law be settled than that it be settled right. . . . But in cases involving the Federal Constitution, where correction through legislative action is practically impossible, this Court has often overruled its earlier decisions.   The Court bows to the lessons of experience and the force of better reasoning.

BRANDEIS, J., dissenting, *Burnett v Coronado Oil & Gas Co.* (1932) 285 US 393, 406, 76 L ed 815, 823, 52 S Ct 443.

They said that those things which have been so often adjudged ought to rest in peace.

CROKE, *Spicer v Spicer* (1620) Cro. Jac. 527.

We are not here compelled by Erie R. Co. v. Tompkins, 304 U.S. 64 . . . to play the role of ventriloquist's dummy to the courts of some particular state.

> FRANK, J., *Richardson v Comm'r Int. Rev.*, 126 F.2d 562, 567 (1942).

This Court, unlike the House of Lords, has from the beginning rejected a doctrine of disability at self-correction.

> FRANKFURTER, J., *Helvering v Hallock* (1940) 309 US 106, 121, 84 L ed 604, 614, 60 S Ct 444, 125 ALR 1368.

What is that occasional interference with what is perhaps abstract justice as compared with the inconvenience—the disastrous inconvenience—of having each question subject to being reargued and the dealings of mankind rendered doubtful by reason of different decisions, so that in truth and in fact there would be no real final Court of Appeal?

> LORD HALSBURY, L.C., *London St. Tramways v London Co. Council* [1898] A.C. 375, 380. This case finally established the rule that the House of Lords was bound by its own decisions.

A decision of this House upon a question of law is conclusive, and that nothing but an Act of Parliament can set right that which is alleged to be wrong in a judgment of this House.

> LORD HALSBURY, L.C., *London St. Tramways Co. v London Co. Council* [1898] A.C. 375, 381.*

Their Lordships regard the use of precedent as an indispensable foundation upon which to decide what is the law and its application to individual cases. It provides at least some degree of certainty upon which individuals

---

* See following entry—under Lord Chancellor Gardiner.

can rely in the conduct of their affairs, as well as a basis for orderly development of legal rules.

Their Lordships nevertheless recognize that too rigid adherence to precedent may lead to injustice in a particular case and also unduly restrict the proper development of the law. They propose, therefore, to modify their present practice and, while treating former decisions of this House as normally binding, to depart from a previous decision when it appears right to do so.

In this connection they will bear in mind the danger of disturbing retrospectively the basis on which contracts, settlements of property and fiscal arrangements have been entered into and also the especial need for certainty as the criminal law.

This announcement is not intended to affect the use of precedent elsewhere than in this House.

GARDINER, L.C., [1966] 1 Weekly L.R. 1234.

I had supposed that our judicial responsibility is for the regularity of the law, not for the regularity of pedigrees.

JACKSON, J., *Williams v North Carolina* (1942) 317 US 287, 324, 87 L ed 279, 300, 63 S Ct 207, 143 ALR 1273. Case involved status of divorced parties.

To bring adjudications of this tribunal into the same class as a restricted railroad ticket, good for this day and train only. I have no assurance, in view of current decisions, that the opinion announced today may not shortly be repudiated and overruled by justices who deem they have new light on the subject.

ROBERTS, J., *Smith v Allwright* (1944) 321 US 649, 669, 88 L ed 987, 1000, 64 S Ct 757, 151 ALR 1110.

[Legal Quotations]—34   *529*

The law becomes not a chart to govern conduct, but a game of chance; instead of settling rights and liabilities it unsettles them. . . . Respect for tribunals must fall when the bar and the public come to understand that nothing that has been said in prior adjudication has force in a current controversy.

> ROBERTS, J., *Mahnich v Southern S.S. Co.* (1944) 321 US 96, 112, 88 L ed 561, 572, 64 S Ct 455.

State

What constitutes a State?
Not high-rais'd battlements, or labour'd mound,
Thick wall, or moated gate;
Not cities proud, with spires and turrets crown'd;
Not bays and broad-arm'd ports,
Where, laughing at the storm, rich navies ride;
. . .

No: —Men, high-minded Men,
. . .

Men who their duties know,
But know their rights, and knowing, dare maintain;
Prevent the long-aim'd blow,
And crush the tyrant while they rend the chain.
These constitute a state,
And sov'reign Law, that state's collected will,
O'er thrones and globes elate
Sits empress, crowning good, repressing ill.

> SIR WILLIAM JONES, *Ode in Imitation of Alcaeus.*

Statute of Frauds

That unfortunate statute, the misguided application of which has been the cause of so many frauds.

BACON, V.C., *Morgan v Worthington* (1878) 38 L.T. 443, 445.

Statute of Uses

A law whereupon the inheritances of this realm are tossed at this day, as upon a sea, in such sort that it is hard to say which bark will sink and which will get to the haven.

BACON, *Reading Upon the Statute of Uses.*

A statute made upon great consideration, introduced in a solemn and pompous manner, by this strict construction, has had no other effect than to add at most, three words to a conveyance.

LORD HARDWICKE, L.C., *Hopkins v Hopkins* (1738) 1 Atk. 581, 591.

Then there is that marvellous monument of legislative futility, the Statute of Uses, the statute through which not mere coaches and four, but whole judicial processions with javelin-men and trumpeters have passed and re-passed in triumph.   It has been said of this ambitious statute that its sole effect has been to "add three words to a conveyance." It is not a mere Statute of Uselessness but a Statute of Abuses.

FREDERIC WM. MAITLAND, *Law of Real Property*, 112 Westminster Rev. 351 (1879); also in 1 Coll. Pap. 191.

531

Strike

The right of the police at Boston to affiliate which has always been questioned, never granted, is now prohibited. . . . There is no right to strike against the public safety by anybody, anywhere, any time.

> CALVIN COOLIDGE, *Telegram to Samuel Gompers,* President of AFL, Sept. 14, 1919. See Coolidge, *Have Faith in Massachusetts (Speeches and Messages)* 1919.

Suicide

For, he said, Sir James Hales was dead, and how came he to his death? It may be answered by drowning; and who drowned him? Sir James Hales; and when did he drown him? In his life-time. So that Sir James Hales being alive caused Sir James Hales to die; and the act of the living man was the death of the dead man.

> BROWN (ANTHONY), J., *Hales v Petit* (1562) 1 Plowd. 253, 262. (The Court held that the goods of Sir James Hales were forfeit to the Crown "as punishment upon the living man for the act done in his life time, which was the cause of his death afterwards".)

First Clown: Here lies the water; good.   Here stands the man; good.   If the man go to this water and drown himself, it is, will he, nill he, he goes,—mark you that? But if the water comes to him, and drown him, he drowns not himself; argal, he that is not guilty of his own death shortens not his own life.

Second Clown: But is this law?

First Clown: Ay, marry, is't; crowner's quest law.

> SHAKESPEARE, *Hamlet,* Act 5, scene 1.

532

Summation

But the Judge said he never had summed up before;
So the Snark undertook it instead,
And summed it so well that it came to far more
Than the Witnesses ever had said!

> LEWIS CARROLL, *The Hunting of the Snark: The Barrister's Dream.*

Mr. Justice Starleigh summed up in the old-established and most approved form. He read as much of his notes to the jury as he could decipher on so short a notice, and made running comments on the evidence as he went along. If Mrs. Bardell were right, it was perfectly clear Mr. Pickwick was wrong, and if they thought the evidence of Mrs. Cluppins worthy of credence they would believe it, and, if they didn't, why they wouldn't. If they were satisfied that a breach of promise of marriage had been committed, they would find for the plaintiff with such damages as they thought proper; and if, on the other hand, it appeared to them that no promise of marriage had ever been given, they would find for the defendant with no damages at all.

> CHARLES DICKENS, *Pickwick Papers*, ch. 34.

Surety

Almost all who sign as surety have occasion to remember the proverb of Solomon: "He that is surety for a stranger shall smart for it, and he that hateth suretyship is sure." But they are nevertheless held liable upon their contracts, otherwise there would be no smarting, and the proverb would fail.

> APPLETON, C.J., *Mayo v Hutchinson*, 57 Me 546, 547 (1870).

It would be as difficult for me to conceive of a surety's liability continuing after the principal obligation was discharged, as of a shadow's remaining after the substance was removed.

> RANSOM, C.J., *Farmers & Mech. Bk. v Kingsley,* 2 Doug. (Mich) 379, 403 (1846).

Talk

That barbers talk cannot be disputed. Some talk more, some less, some humorously, some not, but talk they do. It is traditional and hereditary with them.

> PETTE, J., *Vann v Ionta,* 157 Misc. (N.Y.) 461, 465 (1935).

Taxation

J. P. Morgan ridicules Congress for being too dumb to make an airtight revenue law. Most of us pay what we are told, but one man's tax is another man's loophole.

> HOWARD BRUBAKER, *Of All Things,* 13 New Yorker, June 19, 1937, p. 30.

To tax and to please, no more than to love and to be wise, is not given to men.

> EDMUND BURKE, *Speech on American Taxation,* April 19, 1774.

The De'il's Awa' Wi' the Exciseman.

> ROBERT BURNS, *Title of Song.*

The art of so plucking the goose as to procure the most feathers with the least possible amount of hissing.

> 18th century French Maxim.   Attributed to Jean Baptiste Colbert, also to Talleyrand.

"It was as true," said Mr. Barkis, "as turnips is.   It was as true," said Mr. Barkis, nodding his nightcap, which was his only means of emphasis, "as taxes is.   And nothing's truer than them."

> CHARLES DICKENS, *David Copperfield*, ch. 21.

They combed his mane, they pared his nails, cut off his tail, set him on end, sent him to school, and made him pay taxes.

> RALPH WALDO EMERSON, *Inspiration.*

Robin: On Tuesday I made a false income-tax return.
All: Ha! Ha!
1st Ghost: That's nothing.
2nd Ghost: Nothing at all.
3rd Ghost: Everybody does that.
4th Ghost: It's expected of you.

> WILLIAM S. GILBERT, *Ruddigore*, Act 2.

Any one may so arrange his affairs that his taxes shall be as low as possible; he is not bound to choose that pattern which will best pay the Treasury; there is not even a patriotic duty to increase one's taxes.

> L. HAND, J., *Helvering v Gregory,* 69 F.2d 809, 810 (1934).

The words of such an act as the Income Tax . . . merely dance before my eyes in a meaningless procession:

cross-reference to cross-reference, exception upon exception
—couched in abstract terms that offer no handle to seize
hold of—leave in my mind only a confused sense of some
vitally important, but successfully concealed, purport, which
it is my duty to extract, but which is within my power, if
at all, only after the most inordinate expenditure of time.
I know that these monsters are the result of fabulous industry and ingenuity, plugging up this hole and casting
out that net, against all possible evasion; yet at times I
cannot help recalling a saying of William James about
certain passages of Hegel: that they were no doubt, written
with a passion of rationality; but that one cannot help
wondering whether to the reader they have any significance
save that the words are strung together with syntactical
correctness.

> LEARNED HAND, *Thomas Walter Swan,* 57 Yale L.J. 167, 169
> (1947).

Taxes are what we pay for civilized society.

> HOLMES, J., *Compania General De Tabacos v Collector of Internal
> Revenue* (1927) 275 US 87, 100, 72 L ed 177, 183, 48 S Ct 100.

The power to tax is not the power to destroy while this
Court sits.

> HOLMES, J., *Panhandle Oil Co. v Mississippi ex rel. Knox* (1928)
> 277 US 218, 223, 72 L ed 857, 859, 48 S Ct 451, 56 ALR 583.

That seems to us the import of the statute before us
and we think that no distinction can be taken according
to the motives leading to the arrangement by which the
fruits are attributed to a different tree from that on which
they grew.

> HOLMES, J., *Lucas v Earl* (1930) 281 US 111, 115, 74 L ed 731,
> 733, 50 S Ct 241.

This petition brings up for solution one of those difficult jigsaw tax law puzzles all too common in the present deplorable crazy quilt patchwork state of the Internal Revenue laws.   Of this one we think it may be truly said, "This kind cometh not out save by fasting and by prayer."

> HUTCHESON, J., *Houston Textile Co. v Comm'r.,* 173 F.2d 464 (1949).

Chaos serves no social end.

> JACKSON, J., dissenting, *State Tax Com. v Aldrich* (1942) 316 US 174, 196, 86 L ed 1358, 1378, 62 S Ct 1008, 139 ALR 1436.

Excise: A hateful tax levied upon commodities and adjudged not by the common judges of property, but wretches hired by those to whom excise is paid.

> SAMUEL JOHNSON, *Dictionary.*

Income tax, if I may be pardoned for saying so, is a tax on income.

> LORD MACNAGHTEN, *London Co. Council v Atty. Gen.* [1901] A.C. 26, 35.

The apportionment of taxes on the various descriptions of property, is an act which seems to require the most exact impartiality; yet, there is perhaps no legislative act in which greater opportunity and temptation are given to a predominant party, to trample on the rules of justice.

> JAMES MADISON, *The Federalist, No. 10 (1787).*

No country ever takes notice of the revenue laws of another.

> LORD MANSFIELD, C.J., *Holman v Johnson* (1775) 1 Cowp. 341, 343.

537

If taxation and representation were to go hand in hand, then, this country had an undoubted right to tax America, because she was represented in the British parliament: she was represented by the members for the county of Kent, of which the thirteen provinces were a part or parcel; for in their charters they were to hold of the manor of Greenwich in Kent, of which manor they were by charter to be parcel.

> SIR JAMES MARRIOTT, *Speech in House of Commons (1782)* 22 Parl. Hist. 1184. Reporter stated that this opinion raised a very loud laugh.

The power to tax involves the power to destroy.

> MARSHALL, C.J., *M'Culloch v Maryland* (1819, US) 4 Wheat 316, 431, 4 L ed 579, 607.

It is true that taxes are the lifeblood of any government, but it cannot be overlooked that that blood is taken from the arteries of the taxpayers and, therefore, the transfusion is not to be accomplished except in accordance with the scientific methods specifically prescribed by the sovereign power of the State, the Legislature.

> MUSMANNO, J., *Urban Redevelopment Condemnation Case,* 406 Pa. 6, 11 (1962).

When there is an income tax, the just man will pay more and the unjust less on the same amount of income.

> PLATO, *Republic,* bk 1, 343-d.

Names were made to matter more than mathematics or economics.

> THOMAS REED POWELL, *More Ado About Gross Receipts Taxes,* 60 Harv. L.R. 501, 503 (1947).

538

Taxes are the life-blood of government.

> ROBERTS, J., *Bull v United States* (1935) 295 US 247, 259, 79 L ed 1421, 1427, 55 S Ct 695.

My Lords, of recent years much ingenuity has been expended in certain quarters in attempting to devise methods of disposition of income by which those who were prepared to adopt them might enjoy the benefits of residence within this country while receiving the equivalent of such income without sharing in the appropriate burden of British taxation. Judicial dicta may be cited which point out that, however elaborate and artificial such methods may be, those who adopt them are "entitled" to do so. There is, of course, no doubt that they are within their legal rights, but that is no reason why their efforts, or those of the professional gentlemen who assist them in the matter, should be regarded as a commendable exercise of ingenuity or as a discharge of the duties of good citizenship.

> LORD SIMON, L.C., *Latilla v Inland Revenue Commissioners* [1943] A.C. 377, 381.

They incur no legal penalties and strictly speaking, no moral censure if, having considered the lines drawn by the Legislature for the imposition of taxes, they make it their business to walk outside them.

> LORD SUMNER, *Levene v Inland Rev. Commrs.* [1928] A.C. 217, 227.

He was a bird of passage of almost mechanical regularity.

> LORD SUMNER, *ibid.*, 226.

539

Television

The function of trial is not to provide an educational experience; and there is a serious danger that any attempt to use a trial as an educational tool will both divert it from its proper purpose and lead to suspicions concerning the integrity of the trial process.

> WARREN, C.J., concurring in *Estes v Texas* (1965) 381 US 532, 575, 14 L ed 2d 543, 568, 85 S Ct 1628.

Theory

Theory is the most important part of the dogma of the law, as the architect is the most important man who takes part in the building of a house.

> OLIVER WENDELL HOLMES, *Path of the Law,* 10 Harv. L.R. 457 (1896); Coll. Leg. Pap. 200.

Third Degree

There is a torture of mind as well as body; the will is as much affected by fear as by force.

> FRANKFURTER, J., *Watts v Indiana* (1949) 338 US 49, 52, 93 L ed 1801, 1805, 69 S Ct 1347.

Not only is the pen mightier than the sword, the test-tube is more effective than the rubber hose.

> J. EDGAR HOOVER, *Fifty Years of Crime in America,* Address, May 20, 1939, before the National Fifty Years in Business Club, Nashville, Tennessee. See 2 Amer. Jl. Med. Jur. 263, 266.

There is a great deal of laziness in it. It is far pleasanter to sit comfortably in the shade rubbing pepper into a poor

devil's eyes than to go about in the sun hunting up
evidence.

> SIR JAMES STEPHEN, quoting an experienced native Indian police
> officer. See Stephen, 1 *History of the Criminal Law* (1883)
> 442, n.1.

This Court has recognized that coercion can be mental
as well as physical, and that the blood of the accused is
not the only hallmark of an unconstitutional inquisition.

> WARREN, C.J., *Blackburn v Alabama* (1960) 361 US 199, 206,
> 4 L ed 2d 242, 247, 80 S Ct 274.

Thought

Most men think dramatically, not quantitatively.

> OLIVER WENDELL HOLMES, *Law and the Court, Speeches* 99
> (1913).

The secret isolated joy of the thinker, who knows that, a
hundred years after he is dead and forgotten, men who
never heard of him will be moving to the measure of his
thought.

> OLIVER WENDELL HOLMES, *Profession of the Law, Speeches* 24
> (1913).

Time

Whence it is, that in our law, the goodness of a custom
depends upon its having been used time out of mind; or,
in the solemnity of our legal phrase, time whereof the
memory of man runneth not to the contrary.

> BLACKSTONE, *Commentaries: Introduction* 67.

Time hath his revolution, there must be a period and an end of all temporal things, *finis rerum,* an end of names and dignities, and whatsoever is terrene, and why not of De Vere?   For where is Bohun? where's Mowbray? where's Mortimer? etc.   Nay, which is more and most of all, where is Plantagenet? they are entombed in the urns and sepulchres of mortality.   And yet let the name and dignity of De Vere stand so long as it pleaseth God.

> CREW, C.J., *Oxford Peerage Case* (1625) W. Jones 101, 102.

Time has been on Marshall's side, and that theory for which Hamilton argued, and he decided, and Webster spoke, and Grant fought, and Lincoln died, is now our corner-stone.

> HOLMES, C.J., on motion that the court adjourn on February 4, 1901, the one hundredth anniversary of the day Marshall took his seat as Chief Justice, 178 Mass 627.

Orlando: Who stays it still withal?
Rosalind: With lawyers in the vacation, for they sleep between term and term and they perceive not how Time moves.

> SHAKESPEARE, *As You Like It,* Act 3, scene 2.

Title

And the English poet saith,
"For true it is, that neither fraud nor might
Can make a title where there wanteth right."

> COKE, 8 Rep. 153.

Cursed be he that removeth his neighbor's landmarks.

> Deuteronomy 27:17.

If Time destroys the evidence of title, the laws have wisely and humanely made length of possession a substitute for that which has been destroyed. He comes with his scythe in one hand to mow down the muniments of our rights; but, in his other hand the law-giver has placed an hour-glass, by which he metes out incessantly those portions of duration, which render needless the evidence that he has swept away.

> WM. C. PLUNKET, *arguendo,* in Irish Court of Chancery on behalf of Trinity College. See Brougham, *Statesmen of Time of George III: Lord Chief Justice Bushe.*

Tort

Thoughts much too deep for tears subdue the Court
When I assumpsit bring, and godlike waive a tort.

> J. L. ADOLPHUS, *The Circuiteers.* See 1 L.Q.R. 233 (1885).

Treason

'Tis not seasonable to call a man Traitor that has an Army at his heels; one with an Army is a gallant man.

> JOHN SELDEN, *Table-Talk: Traitor.*

To compass or imagine the death of the king.

> See statute, 21 Rich. 2, c. 3 (1397).

After this kind of reasoning they will not be guilty, till they have success; and if they have success enough, it will be too late to question them.

> TREBY, C.J., *Trial of Captain Vaughan* (1696) 13 How. St. Tr. 485, 533. The indictment was for adhering to and giving aid and comfort to the enemy.

543

Treaty

Great nations, like great men, should keep their word.

> BLACK, J., dissenting, *Federal Power Com. v Tuscarora Indian Nation* (1960) 362 US 99, 142, 4 L ed 2d 584, 611, 80 S Ct 543.

They never enter into any alliance with any other state. They think leagues are useless things, and reckon that, if the common ties of human nature do not knit men together, the faith of promises will have no great effect upon them: and they are the more confirmed in this by that which they see among nations round about them, who are no strict observers of leagues and treaties.

> SIR THOMAS MORE, *Utopia*, bk 2.

Trespass

By the laws of England, every invasion of private property, be it ever so minute, is a trespass. No man can set his foot upon my ground without my licence, but he is liable to an action, though the damage be nothing.

> LORD CAMDEN, C.J., *Entick v Carrington* (1765) 19 How. St. Tr. 1029, 1066.

Trial

Nothing is more incumbent upon courts of justice, than to preserve their proceedings from being misrepresented; nor is there any thing of more pernicious consequence, than to prejudice the minds of the public against persons concerned as parties in causes, before the cause is finally heard.

> LORD HARDWICKE, L.C., *Roach v Garvan* (1742) 2 Atk. 469.

There cannot be anything of greater consequence, than to keep the streams of justice clear and pure, that parties may proceed with safety both to themselves and their characters.

LORD HARDWICKE, L.C., *ibid.* 471.

Gracious lady, we implore,
Go away and sin no more,
And if that effort be too great,
Go away at any rate.

> Popular ballad at the time of the trial of Queen Caroline for adultery, 1821. George IV's harsh treatment of his consort aroused much sympathy for the Queen. In her defense, however, Lord Denman made use of an unfortunate quotation: "If no one come forward to condemn thee, neither will I condemn thee. Go, and sin no more."

A jury trial is a fight and not an afternoon tea.

RIDDELL, J., *Dale v Toronto R. W. Co.* (1915) 34 Ont. L.R. 104, 108.

The law itself is on trial, quite as much as the cause which is to be decided.

HARLAN F. STONE, *The Common Law in the United States,* 50 Harv. L. Rev. 4 (1936).

Tears have always been considered legitimate arguments before a jury, and while the question has never arisen out of any such behavior in this Court, we know of no rule or jurisdiction in the Court below to check them. It would appear to be one of the natural rights of counsel, which no Court or constitution could take away. It is certainly, if no more, a matter of the highest personal privilege. Indeed, if counsel has them at command, it may be seriously questioned whether it is not his professional duty to shed them whenever proper occasion arises, and the trial Judge would not feel constrained to interfere unless they were indulged in to such excess as to impede or delay the business of the Court.

WILKES, J., *Ferguson v Moore*, 98 Tenn 342, 351 (1897).

Trusts

A trust is altogether the same that a use was before 27 Hen. 8, and they have the same parents, fraud and fear; and the same nurse, a court of conscience.

ROBERT ATKYNS, arguendo, *Attorney General v Sands* (1669) Hard. 488, 491.

Trusts are children of equity; and in a court of equity they are at home—under the family roof-tree, and around the hearth of their ancestor.

BLECKLEY, J., *Kupferman v McGhee*, 63 Ga 250, 256 (1879).

A constructive trust is the formula through which the conscience of equity finds expression.

CARDOZO, J., *Beatty v Guggenheim Exploration Co.*, 225 N.Y. 380, 386 (1919).

A trustee is held to something stricter than the morals of the market place. Not honesty alone, but the punctilio of an honor the most sensitive, is then the standard of behavior.

CARDOZO, C.J., *Meinhard v Salmon*, 249 N.Y. 458, 464 (1928).

My old master, the late Lord Justice Selwyn, used to say, "The main duty of a trustee is to commit *judicious* breaches of trust."

> LINDLEY, M.R., *Perrins v Bellamy* [1899] 1 Ch. 797, 798. In a later case Lord Lindley remarked that the words "main duty" are a mistake. They ought to be "great use". See *National Trustees Co. of Australasia v General Finance Co.* [1905] A.C. 373, 376.

Truth

What is truth? said jesting Pilate; and would not stay for an answer.

> BACON, *Essays: Of Truth.*

The half truths of one generation tend at times to perpetuate themselves in the law as the whole truths of another, when constant repetition brings it about that qualifications, taken once for granted, are disregarded or forgotten.

> CARDOZO, C.J., *Allegheny College v National Chautauqua Co. Bank,* 246 N.Y. 369, 373 (1927).

Truth, the mother of justice.

> COKE, *Second Institute 524.*

If the respondent is, as we must take him to be, sincere, there are many ways open to him of telling the public that he is not a surgeon other than the way of telling the public that he is a surgeon.

> LORD HEWART, C.J., *Jutson v Barrow* [1936] 1 K.B. 236, 245. The respondent's argument was that the placing of the word "manipulative" before the word surgeon was intended to show that he was not registered as a surgeon under the Medical Act.

547

I used to say, when I was young, that truth was the majority vote of that nation that could lick all others.

> OLIVER WENDELL HOLMES, *Natural Law,* 32 Harv. L.R. 40 (1918). Coll. Leg. Pap. 310.

When men have realized that time has upset many fighting faiths, they may come to believe even more than they believe the very foundations of their own conduct that the ultimate good desired is better reached by free trade in ideas—that the best test of truth is the power of the thought to get itself accepted in the competition of the market, and that truth is the only ground upon which their wishes safely can be carried out.

> HOLMES, J., *Abrams v United States* (1919) 250 US 616, 630, 63 L ed 1173, 1180, 40 S Ct 17.

Truth, like all other good things, may be loved unwisely —may be pursued too keenly—may cost too much.

> KNIGHT-BRUCE, V.C., *Pearse v Pearse* (1846) 1 De Gex & Sm. 12, 28.

Truth does not always stalk boldly forth naked, but modest withal, in a printed abstract in a court of last resort. She oft hides in nooks and crannies visible only to the mind's eye of the judge who tries the case. To him appears the furtive glance, the blush of conscious shame, the hesitation, the sincere or the flippant or sneering tone, the heat, the calmness, the yawn, the sigh, the candor or lack of it, the scant or full realization of the solemnity of an oath, the carriage and mien. The brazen face of the liar, the glibness of the schooled witness in reciting a lesson, or the itching overeagerness of the swift witness, as well as the honest face of the truthful one, are alone seen by him.

> LAMM, J., *Creamer v Bivert,* 214 Mo 473, 474 (1908).

Ingenuity is one thing, and simple testimony another and "plain truth", I take it, "needs no flowers of speech."

> LORD MANSFIELD, C.J., *Wilkes v Wood* (1763) 19 How. St. Tr. 1153, 1176 n. (referring to Pope, *Imitations of Horace,* I, 6: "Plain truth, dear Murray, needs no flow'rs of speech.").

There is an idiom in truth, which falsehood never can imitate.

> NAPIER, L.C., *Low v Holmes* (1858) Drury Cases, Temp. Napier, 290, 323.

Truth will out even in an affidavit.

> Saying.

U. S. Supreme Court

Things go happily in the conference room with Taft. . . . When we differ we agree to differ, without any ill feeling. It's all very friendly.

> MR. JUSTICE BRANDEIS. See Bickel, *The Unpublished Opinions of Mr. Justice Brandeis* 203 (1957).

It is a mistake to suppose that the Supreme Court is either honored or helped by being spoken of as beyond criticism. On the contrary, the life and character of its justices should be the object of constant watchfulness by all, and its judgments subject to the freest criticism. The time is past in the history of the world when any living man or body of men can be set on a pedestal and decorated with a halo. True, many criticisms may be, like their authors, devoid of good taste, but better all sorts of criticism than no criticism at all. The moving waters are full of

549

life and health; only in the still waters is stagnation and death.

DAVID JOSIAH BREWER, *Lincoln's Day Address*, 1898.

The Supreme Court is the living voice of the Constitution.

JAMES BRYCE, *American Commonwealth*, ch. 24 (1888).

The Supreme Court feels the touch of public opinion.

JAMES BRYCE, *ibid.*

It is not necessary to prove that the Supreme Court never made a mistake; but, if the power is to be taken away from them, it is necessary to prove that those who are to exercise it, would be likely to make fewer mistakes.

CALVIN COOLIDGE, *Speech before U.S. Chamber of Commerce, Wash., D.C., Oct. 23, 1924.*

No matther whether th' constitution follows th' flag or not, th' supreme coort follows th' iliction returns.

FINLEY PETER DUNNE, *Mr. Dooley's Opinions: The Supreme Court's Decisions.*

The United States Supreme Court has wittily been called the "court of ultimate conjecture."

JEROME FRANK, *Law and the Modern Mind* 46n. (1930).

The Constitution is not a panacea for every blot upon the public welfare, nor should this Court, ordained as a judicial body, be thought of as a general haven for reform movements.

HARLAN, J., dissenting, *Reynolds v Sims* (1964) 377 US 533, 624, 12 L ed 2d 506, 563, 84 S Ct 1362.

We are very quiet there, but it is the quiet of a storm centre, as we all know.

OLIVER WENDELL HOLMES, *Law and the Court, Speeches* (1913) 98; Coll. Leg. Pap. 292.

Putting aside the long course of criticism of the Court . . . with respect to which the Court has either been vindicated in public opinion or the criticism has had but slight effect upon the general reputation of the Court, it remains true that in three notable instances the Court has suffered severely from self-inflicted wounds.

CHARLES EVANS HUGHES, *The Supreme Court of the United States* 50 (1928). Referring to the Dred Scott case, the Legal Tender cases and the Income Tax cases.

It sat almost as a continuous constitutional convention which, without submitting its proposals to any ratification or rejection, could amend the basic law.

ROBERT H. JACKSON, *Struggle for Judicial Supremacy* x (1941).

The Court functions less as one deliberative body than as nine, each Justice working largely in isolation except as he chooses to seek consultation with others. These working methods tend to cultivate a highly individualistic rather than a group viewpoint.

ROBERT H. JACKSON, *The Supreme Court in American System of Government* 16 (1955).

551

The real strength of the position of the Court is probably in its indispensability to government under a written Constitution. It is difficult to see how the provisions of a 150-year-old written document can have much vitality if there is not some permanent institution to translate them into current commands and to see to their contemporary application.

> ROBERT H. JACKSON, *The Supreme Court in the American System of Government* 26 (1955).

We are not final because we are infallible, but we are infallible only because we are final.

> JACKSON, J., *Brown v Allen* (1953) 344 US 443, 540, 97 L ed 469, 533, 73 S Ct 397.

The judiciary of the United States is the subtle corps of sappers and miners constantly working under ground to undermine the foundations of our confederated fabric. They are construing our constitutions from a coordination of a general and special government to a general and supreme one alone.

> THOMAS JEFFERSON, *Letter to Thomas Ritchie, Dec. 25, 1820.*

There is no danger I apprehend so much as the consolidation of our government by the noiseless, and therefore unalarming, instrumentality of the supreme court.

> THOMAS JEFFERSON, *Letter to Judge William Johnson, March 4, 1823.*

The judges of the Supreme Court of the land must be not only great jurists, they must be great constructive statesmen. And the truth of what I say is illustrated by every study of American statesmanship. For in not one serious study of American political life will it be possible to omit the immense part played by the Supreme Court in the creation, not merely the modification, of the great policies, through and by means of which the country has moved on to its present condition.

> THEODORE ROOSEVELT, *Dinner of the Bar in Honor of Mr. Justice Harlan, Washington, D.C., Dec. 9, 1902.* See 1 *Presidential Addresses and State Papers* (Collier & Sons, pub.) 221.

When there are grave doubts about the "constitutionality" of a statute, the Supreme Court has always been ready to remove them, but unfortunately it has only too often removed these doubts by holding the statute unconstitutional. It is in the advantageous position of being able not only to declare constitutional acts unconstitutional, but unconstitutional acts constitutional.

> WILLIAM SEAGLE, *The Quest for Law* 314 (1941).

It was to prevent an appeal to the sword and a dissolution of the compact that this Court, by the organic law, was made equal in origin and equal in title to the legislative and executive branches of the government: its powers defined, and limited, and made strictly judicial, and placed therefore beyond the reach of the powers delegated to the Legislative and Executive Departments.

> TANEY, C.J., *Gordon v United States* (1865) 117 US 697, 701, Appx, 76 L ed 1347, 1350.

The Supreme Court is placed at the head of all known tribunals, both by the nature of its rights and the class of justiciable parties which it controls.

> ALEXIS DE TOCQUEVILLE, *Democracy in America,* Pt. 1, ch. 8.

Their power is enormous, but it is the power of public opinion.

ALEXIS DE TOCQUEVILLE, *ibid.*

It is with singular pleasure that I address you as Chief Justice of the Supreme Court of the United States, for which office your commission is enclosed. In nominating you for the important station which you now fill, I not only acted in conformity to my best judgment, but I trust I did a grateful thing to the good citizens of these United States; and I have a full confidence that the love which you bear to our country, and a desire to promote the general happiness, will not suffer you to hesitate a moment to bring into action the talents, knowledge and integrity which are so necessary to be exercised at the head of that department which must be considered as the keystone of our political fabric.

GEORGE WASHINGTON, *Letter, Oct. 5, 1789 to John Jay.* See *Writings,* v. 10, Sparks ed.; v. 11, Ford ed.

In the largest proportion of causes submitted to its judgment, every decision becomes a page of history.

GEORGE W. WICKERSHAM, *Address before the Bar of the Court, on the death of Chief Justice Fuller,* 219 U.S. xv (1911).

Validity

A statute valid as to one set of facts may be invalid as to another. A statute valid when enacted may become invalid by change in the conditions to which it is applied.

BRANDEIS, J., *Nashville, C. & St. L. R. Co. v Walters* (1935) 294 US 405, 415, 79 L ed 949, 955, 55 S Ct 486.

Not what has been done under a statute, but what may reasonably be done under it, is the test of its validity.

CARDOZO, C.J., *Matter of Richardson,* 247 N.Y. 401, 420 (1928).

Verbosity

O judge not a book by its cover
Or else you'll for sure come to grief,
For the lengthiest things you'll discover
Are contained in what's known as a Brief.

J.P.C., 116 Just. P. 640 (1952).

He can compress the most words into the smallest ideas of any man I ever met.

ABRAHAM LINCOLN. Hill, *Lincoln, the Lawyer* 218.

Windy attorneys to their client woes.

SHAKESPEARE, *Richard III,* Act 4, scene 4.

Verdict (Not Proven)

In Scottish criminal procedure the jury is not restricted to a verdict of "Guilty" or "Not Guilty". There is a third possibility—"Not Proven" where there is a suspicion of guilt but not sufficient to remove all reasonable doubt.

Not guilty but don't do it again.

Proverb. See 4 Lean, *Collectanea* 64 (1904).

Waited to see the poisoning woman. She is clearly guilty, but as one or two witnesses said the poor wench

555

hinted an intention to poison herself, the jury gave that bastard verdict, *Not proven.* I hate that Caledonian *medium quid.* One who is not *proven guilty* is not innocent in the eye of law.

SIR WALTER SCOTT, *Journal, February 20, 1827.*

Voting

This is not a test but a trap, sufficient to stop even the most brilliant man on his way to the voting booth.

BLACK, J., *Louisiana v United States* (1965) 380 US 145, 153, 13 L ed 2d 709, 714, 85 S Ct 817. Referring to a state law requirement that voters be able to interpret state or federal constitution.

Wealth, like race, creed, or color, is not germane to one's ability to participate intelligently in the electoral process. Lines drawn on the basis of wealth or property, like those of race are traditionally disfavored. To introduce wealth or payment of a fee as a measure of a voter's qualifications is to introduce a capricious or irrelevant factor. The degree of the discrimination is irrelevant.

DOUGLAS, J., *Harper v Virginia State Board of Elections* (1966) 383 US 663, 668, 16 L ed 2d 169, 173, 86 S Ct 1079.

The political franchise of voting . . . is regarded as a fundamental political right, because preservative of all rights.

MATTHEWS, J., *Yick Wo v Hopkins* (1886) 118 US 356, 370, 30 L ed 220, 226, 6 S Ct 1064.

War

But hardships are part of war, and war is an aggregation of hardships. All citizens alike, both in and out of uniform, feel the impact of war in greater or lesser measure. Citizenship has its responsibilities as well as its privileges, and in time of war the burden is always heavier. Compulsory exclusion of large groups of citizens from their homes, except under circumstances of direst emergency and peril, is inconsistent with our basic governmental institutions. But when under conditions of modern warfare our shores are threatened by hostile forces, the power to protect must be commensurate with the threatened danger.

> BLACK, J., *Korematsu v United States* (1944) 323 US 214, 219, 89 L ed 194, 200, 65 S Ct 193.

I think the finest sight I ever beheld was the great review in Hyde Park before George III. The King in passing addressed Tom Erskine, who was Colonel, asking him the name of his corps. He answered, "The Devil's Own."

> LORD ELDON. See Campbell, *Lives of the Chancellors: Erskine,* ch. 182. At the time of the threatened Napoleonic invasion the various Inns of Court maintained volunteer regiments.

This greatest of civil wars was not gradually developed by popular commotion, tumultuous assemblies, or local unorganized insurrections. However long may have been its previous conception, it nevertheless sprung forth suddenly from the parent brain, a Minerva in the full panoply of *war*. The President was bound to meet it in the shape it presented itself, without waiting for Congress to baptize it with a name; and no name given to it by him or them could change the fact.

> GRIER, J., *Prize Cases* (1862, US) 2 Black 635, 668, 17 L ed 459, 477.

557

It may not be doubted that the very conception of a just government and its duty to the citizen includes the reciprocal obligation of the citizen to render military service in the case of need and the right to compel it.

> WHITE, C.J., *Selective Draft Law Cases* (1918) 245 US 366, 378, 62 L ed 340, 353, 38 S Ct 158.

War Crimes

Civilization asks whether law is so laggard as to be utterly helpless to deal with crimes of this magnitude by criminals of this order of importance. It does not expect that you can make war impossible. It does expect that your juridical action will put the forces of International Law, its precepts, its prohibitions and most of all, its sanctions, on the side of peace, so that men and women of good will in all countries, may have "leave to live by no man's leave underneath the law." *

> ROBERT H. JACKSON, *Opening for the Prosecution, Trial of German Major War Criminals,* Proceedings of the International Military Tribunal at Nuremberg, Nov. 21, 1945.

We must never forget that the record on which we judge these defendants today is the record on which history will judge us tomorrow. To pass these defendants a poisoned chalice is to put it to our own lips as well. We must summon such detachment and intellectual integrity to our task that this trial will commend itself to posterity as fulfilling humanity's aspirations to do justice.

> ROBERT H. JACKSON, *ibid.*

---

* Kipling. *The Old Issue.*

"The warrant of no man excuseth the doing of an illegal act." Political loyalty, military obedience are excellent things, but they neither require nor do they justify the commission of patently wicked acts. There comes a point where a man must refuse to answer to his leader if he is also to answer to his conscience.

> SIR HARTLEY SHAWCROSS, Chief Prosecutor for Gt. Britain, *Opening Speech at the trial of the Major War Criminals, Nuremberg, Dec. 4, 1945.* Proceedings of International Military Tribunal (Lond. 1946, pub. by auth. of Atty. Gen.) Pt. 2, 85.

Warranties

Warranties are favoured in law, being part of a man's assurance; but estoppels are odious.

> COKE, *First Institute* 365b.

Webster, Daniel

Daniel Webster struck me much like a steam-engine in trowsers.

> SYDNEY SMITH—1 Holland, *Memoir of Smith* 238.

Will (Testamentary)

I anticipate with satisfaction that henceforth the group of ghosts of dissatisfied testators who, according to a late Chancery judge, wait on the other bank of the Styx, to receive the judicial personages who have misconstrued their wills, may be considerably diminished.

> LORD ATKIN, *Perrin v Morgan* [1943] I All E.R. 187, 194.

The nonsense of one man cannot be a guide for that of another.

BULLER, J., *Smith v Coffin* (1795) 2 H. Bl. 444, 450.

Few men pinched with the messengers of death have a disposing memory.

COKE, 10 Rep.: *Preface.*

The only authentic evidence, in spite of Sir Oliver Lodge, which we have of the survival of life after death is the ability of the judges to read the intention of the testator long after he has been buried.

FREDERICK E. CRANE, *Address,* 3 N.Y.S. Bar Bull. 168 (1931).

This is what the lawyer who drew the will has caused Miss Watson to say is her intention.

CRANE, J., *Matter of Watson,* 262 N.Y. 284, 299 (1933).

When a testator has executed a will in solemn form you must assume that he did not intend to make it a solemn farce,—that he did not intend to die intestate when he has gone through the form of making a will.

LORD ESHER, M.R., *Re Harrison* (1885) 30 Ch.D. 390, 393.

Fear, fraud, and flattery: three unfit accidents to be at the making of a will.

Maxim. See Noy, *Maxims 97.*

Knowing how quickly many are removed by death, it is weightily recommended that care be taken in each

monthly meeting that friends who have estates to dispose
of, by will or otherwise, be advised to make their wills
in time of health, and strength of judgment, and to dispose of their substance as in justice and wisdom may be
to their satisfaction; to prevent the inconveniences, loss,
and trouble that may fall upon their relations and friends,
through their dying intestate.   Making such wills in due
time can shorten no man's days, but the omission or delay
thereof has proved very injurious to many.

> *Minutes and Advices of the Yearly Meeting of Friends Held in
> London* (1802).

Friends are earnestly recommended to employ persons
skilful in law, and of good repute, to make their wills; as
great inconvenience and loss, and sometimes the ruin of
families, have happened through the unskilfulness of some
who have taken upon them to make wills.

> *ibid.*

Ye lawyers who live upon litigants' fees,
And who need a good many to live at your ease,
Grave or gay, wise or witty, whate'er your degree,
Plain stuff or Queen's Counsel, take counsel of me.
When a festive occasion your spirit unbends,
You should never forget the Profession's best friends;
So we'll send round the wine and bright bumper fill,
To the jolly testator who makes his own will.

> **LORD NEAVES,** *Jolly Testator Who Makes His Own Will.*

Testators are good; but a feeling more tender
Springs up when I think of the feminine gender;
The testatrix for me, who, like Telemarque's mother
Unweaves at one time what she wove at another.

[Legal Quotations]—36   *561*

She bequeaths, she repeats, she recalls a donation,
And she ends by revoking her own revocation,
Still scribbling or scratching some new codicil,
Oh! success to the woman who makes her own will.

   Ibid.

'Tisn't easy to say 'mid her varying vapours
What scraps should be deemed testamentary papers;
'Tisn't easy from these her intentions to find,
When perhaps she herself never knew her own mind.
Every step that we take there arises fresh trouble—
Is the legacy lapsed? is it single or double?
No customer brings so much grist to the mill
As the wealthy old woman who makes her own will.

   Ibid.

You had better pay toll when you take to the road
Than attempt by a bye-way to reach your abode;
You had better employ a conveyancer's hand
Than encounter the risk that your will shouldn't stand.
From the broad beaten track where the traveller strays
He may land in a bog or be lost in a maze:
And the Law, when defied, will revenge itself still
On the man and the woman who make their own will.

   Ibid.

In some instances homemade pies are superior. Wills
never.

   PAGE, SURR., *Matter of Douglas*, 195 Misc. (N.Y.) 661, 662
   (1949).

No will has a twin brother.

   Saying.

But thousands die, without or this or that,
Die, and endow a college, or a cat.

> ALEXANDER POPE, *Epistle 3, to Lord Bathurst* (1732), **line 95.**

The will is to be read in the light of what has happened, not so much for the purpose of determining its validity, as for the purpose of seeing clearly by such light what is possible in the way of separating the good from the bad. In thus construing the will the court does not perform a radical operation to remove a malignant growth, where either the disease or the operation will take the life out of the testamentary document. The irritation of invalidity has produced, not a cancer, but, at worst, an epidermal callosity which may be harmlessly removed.

> POUND, J., *Matter of Trevor*, 239 N.Y. 6, 18 (1924).

He may make a will upon his nail for any thing he has to give.

> Proverb. Fuller, *Proverbs* (1732).

Has the testator been what is called, and very properly called, his own conveyancer? Has he left it to the Court to make out from general expressions what his intention is, or has he so defined that intention that you have nothing to do but to take the limitations he has given you, and to convert them into legal estates?

> LORD ST. LEONARDS, *Egerton v Earl of Brownlow* (1853) 4 H.L. Cas. 1, 210.

Men should not sin in their graves.

> STRANGE, M.R., *Thomas v Britnell* (1751) 2 Ves. Sr. 313, 314.

563

Wills

Whatsoever I have given, granted, confirmed, or appointed to my wife, I do now, for just and great causes, utterly revoke and make void, and leave her to her right only.

> FRANCIS BACON, *Codicil to Will,* added shortly before death.

I, CHARLES LOUNSBURY, being of sound and disposing mind and memory . . . do now make and publish this my last will and testament. . . . ITEM: And first, I give to good fathers and mothers, but in trust for their children, nevertheless, all good little words of praise and all quaint pet names, and I charge said parents to use them justly but generously as the needs of their children shall require.

> WILLISTON FISH, *A Last Will,* 42 Harper's Weekly 867 (Sept. 3, 1898). This will, a fictional creation, has been frequently quoted and reprinted, often with considerable variation from the original. It has sometimes been called, for no reason, the "insane man's" will. See Josephine Fish Peabody, *Williston Fish and "A Last Will",* 52 C. & C. No. 3 (1947).

ITEM: I leave to children exclusively, but only for the life of their childhood, all and every, the dandelions of the fields and the daisies thereof, with the right to play among them freely, according to the custom of children, warning them at the same time against the thistles. And I devise to children the yellow shores of creeks and the golden sands beneath the waters thereof, with the dragonflies that skim the surface of said waters, and the odors of the willows that dip into said waters, and the white clouds that float high over the giant trees.

And I leave to children the long, long days to be merry in, in a thousand ways, and the Night and the Moon and the train of the Milky Way to wonder at, but subject, never-

theless, to the rights hereinafter given to lovers; and I
give to each child the right to choose a star that shall be
his, and I direct that the child's father shall tell him the
name of it, in order that the child shall always remember
the name of that star after he has learned and forgotten
astronomy.

Ibid.

ITEM: I devise to boys jointly all the useful idle fields
and commons where ball may be played, and all snow-clad
hills where one may coast, and all streams and ponds
where one may skate, to have and to hold the same for
the period of their boyhood.   And all meadows, with the
clover blooms and butterflies thereof; and all woods, with
their appurtenances of squirrels and whirring birds and
echoes and strange noises; and all distant places which may
be visited, together with the adventures there found, I do
give to said boys to be theirs.   And I give to said boys
each his own place at the fireside at night, with all pictures
that may be seen in the burning wood or coal, to enjoy
without let or hindrance and without any incumbrance
of cares.

Ibid.

ITEM: To lovers I devise their imaginary world, with
whatever they may need, as the stars of the sky, the red,
red roses by the wall, the snow of the hawthorn, the sweet
strains of music, or aught else they may desire to figure
to each other the lastingness and beauty of their love.

Ibid.

ITEM: To young men jointly, being joined in a brave,
mad crowd, I devise and bequeath all boisterous, inspiring

565

sports of rivalry. I give to them the disdain of weakness
and undaunted confidence in their own strength. Though
they are rude and rough, I leave to them alone the power
of making lasting friendships and of possessing companions;
and to them exclusively I give all merry songs and brave
choruses to sing, with smooth voices to troll them forth.

Ibid.

ITEM: And to those who are no longer children or
youths or lovers I leave Memory, and I leave to them the
volumes of the poems of Burns and Shakespeare, and of
other poets, if there are others, to the end that they may
live the old days over again freely and fully, without tithe
or diminution; and to those who are no longer children
or youths or lovers I leave, too, the knowledge of what a
rare, rare world it is.

Ibid.

Wasn't that a remarkable will that Oliver Wendell Holmes
left? Imagine a man giving his money to the government
at a time when 120 million people are trying to get it
away from the government, or trying to keep from paying
'em even what we owe 'em. At least 80 years of service
to his country and he accumulates some money, and is so
appreciative of what his country has done for him, that
he wants to return it.

WILL ROGERS. See *Autobiography of Will Rogers* (selected and
ed. by Day) entry March 10, 1935.

To my loving, kind sister I give and bequeath,
For her tender regard, when this world I shall leave,

If she choose to accept it, my rump-bone may take,
And tip it with silver, a whistle to make.

> WILLIAM RUFFELL, *Will.* Ruffell, a resident of Suffolk, England
> gave copies to friends but original was not found after his
> death. See 12 N. & Q. (1st ser.) 81.

Item, I gyve unto my wiefe, my second best bed with its
furniture.

> SHAKESPEARE, *Will,* March 25, 1616.

Wire-Tapping

The makers of our Constitution undertook to secure conditions favorable to the pursuit of happiness. They recognized the significance of man's spiritual nature, of his feelings and of his intellect. They knew that only a part of
the pain, pleasure and satisfactions of life are to be found
in material things. They sought to protect Americans in
their beliefs, their thoughts, their emotions and their sensa-
tions. They conferred, as against the Government, the
right to be let alone—the most comprehensive of rights
and the right most valued by civilized men.

> BRANDEIS, J., *Olmstead v United States* (1928) 277 US 438, 478,
> 72 L ed 944, 956, 48 S Ct 564, 66 ALR 376.

We have to choose, and for my part I think it less evil
that some criminals should escape than that the Government should play an ignoble part.

> HOLMES, J., *ibid.*

No distinction can be taken between the Government as
prosecutor and the Government as judge. If the existing

567

code does not permit district attorneys to have a hand in
such dirty business it does not permit the judge to allow
such iniquities to succeed.

> HOLMES, J., *ibid.*

Witch

Hark ye, if you can fly, then fly away.   There is no law
against flying.

> POWELL, J., *Case of Jane Wenham.* Dismissing the defendant, a
> woman on trial for witchcraft, who said she could fly.   See
> 46 D.N.B. under Powell.

Witnesses

I have always told a jury that if a fact is fully proved
by two witnesses, it is as good as if proved by a hundred.

> BULLER, J., *Calliland v Vaughan* (1798) 1 Bos. & Pul. 210, 212.

For witnesses, like watches, go
Just as they're set, too fast or slow.

> SAMUEL BUTLER, *Hudibras,* Pt. II, Canto II, 1.361.

By the mouth of two or three witnesses shall he die that
is to be slain.   Let no man be put to death, when only one
beareth witness against him.

> Deuteronomy 17:6 (There is a Roman maxim: *Testis unus testis*
> *nullus*—one witness is no witness).

Name, Jo.   Nothing else that he knows on.   .   .   .
Knows a broom's a broom and knows it's wicked to tell a

lie. Don't recollect who told him about the broom, or about the lie, but knows both. Can't exactly say what'll be done to him arter he's dead if he tells a lie to the gentlemen here, but believes it'll be something wery bad to punish him, and serve him right—and so, he'll tell the truth.

"This won't do, gentlemen!" says the coroner, with a a melancholy shake of the head. . . . "You have heard the boy; 'can't exactly say' won't do, you know. We can't take that in a Court of Justice, gentlemen. It's terrible depravity. Put the boy aside."

CHARLES DICKENS, *Bleak House,* ch. 11.

They cudden't get me into coort as a witness; no, sir, not if 't was to hang me best friend. 'T is hard enough with newspapers an' cinsus officers an' th' mim'ry iv cab dhrivers to live down ye'er past without bein' foorced to dhrill it in a r-red coat an' with a brass band ahead befure th' eyes iv th' multitood. I did it wanst; I'll do it no more.

FINLEY PETER DUNNE. See Bander, ed., *Mr. Dooley on the Choice of Law* 7 (1963).

Nor shall you, when testifying in a lawsuit, side with the many in perverting justice. You shall not favor a poor man in his lawsuit.

Exodus 23:2, 3.

The public has a right to every man's evidence—a maxim which in its proper sense cannot be denied. For it is undoubtedly true that the public has a right to all the assistance of every individual.

LORD CHANCELLOR HARDWICKE, *Bill for Indemnifying Evidence,* 12 Cobbett, *Parliamentary History,* 675, 693 [1742].

A cloud of witnesses.

Hebrews 12:1.

A faithful witness will not lie but a deceitful witness uttereth a lie.

Proverbs 14:5.

Witnesses are liars, damned liars, and experts.

Saying.

Witnesses (Expert)

Expert opinion, which is only an ordinary guess in evening clothes. . . .

BOK, J., *Earl M. Kerstetter, Inc. v Commonwealth*, 404 Pa 168, 173 (1961).

The testimony relating to this footing of the case has been profuse and illuminating. The experts, as too often happens, disagree leaving the problem, as Tennyson might say, dark with excessive brightness.

JAYNE, J., *International Pulverizing Corp. v Kidwell*, 7 N.J. Super., 345, 354 (1950).

Experience has disclosed that both optimism and pessimism may be found to exist in the minds of expert witnesses.

JAYNE, J., *In re Port of New York Authority*, 28 N.J. Super., 575 580 (1953).

Woman

Woman's Rights? What does a woman want iv rights whin she has priv'leges?

> FINLEY PETER DUNNE, *Women Suffrage.* See Bander, ed., *Mr. Dooley on The Choice of Law* 57 (1963).

It will need more than the Nineteenth Amendment to convince me that there are no differences between men and women.

> HOLMES, J., dissenting, *Adkins v Children's Hospital* (1923) 261 US 525, 569, 67 L ed 785, 801, 43 S Ct 394, 24 ALR 1238. Referring to minimum wage for women.

Nature has given women so much power that the law has very wisely given them little.

> SAMUEL JOHNSON, *Letter August 18, 1763, to Dr. Taylor.* See 5 Notes & Queries (6th ser.) 342.

The Nineteenth Amendment—I think that's the one that made Women humans by Act of Congress.

> WILL ROGERS. See *Autobiography of Will Rogers* (selected and ed. by Day) entry March 30, 1929.

Discussions are habitually necessary in courts of justice, which are unfit for female ears. The habitual presence of women at these would tend to relax the public sense of decency and propriety. If, as counsel threatened, these things are to come, we will take no voluntary part in bringing them about.

> RYAN, C.J., *Matter of the motion to admit Miss Lavinia Goodell to the Bar,* 39 Wis 232, 246 (1875).

When women go to Law, the Devil is full of Business.

> JOHN WEBSTER, *The Devil's Law-Case: sub title* (1619).

571

Words

The meaning of words varies according to the circumstances of and concerning which they are used.

BLACKBURN, J., *Allgood v Blake* (1873) L.R. 8 Ex. 160, 162.

The logic of words should yield to the logic of realities.

BRANDEIS, J., *Di Santo v Pennsylvania* (1927) 273 US 34, 43, 71 L ed 524, 529, 47 S Ct 267.

The search is for the just word, the happy phrase, that will give expression to the thought, but somehow the thought itself is transfigured by the phrase when found.

BENJAMIN N. CARDOZO, *Growth of the Law* 89 (1924).

Words, like men, grow an individuality; their character changes with years and with use.

CRANE, J., *Adler v Deegan,* 251 N.Y. 467, 472 (1929).

Words in themselves may be harmless, while accent and manner may make them deadly.

DENT, Pres., *State v Kerns,* 47 W. Va. 266, 269 (1899).

Words are not only the keys of persuasion, but the triggers of action.

L. HAND, J., *Masses Pub. Co. v Patten,* 244 Fed. 535, 540 (1917).

Words are not pebbles in alien juxtaposition.

L. HAND, J., *NLRB v Federbush Co. Inc.,* 121 F. 2d 954, 957 (1941).

Words are chameleons, which reflect the color of their environment.

L. HAND, J., *Commissioner v National Carbide Co.,* 167 F.2d 304, 306 (1948).

A word generally has several meanings, even in the dictionary. You have to consider the sentence in which it stands to decide which of those meanings it bears in the particular case, and very likely will see that it there has a shade of significance more refined than any given in the word-book.

> OLIVER WENDELL HOLMES, *Theory of Legal Interpretation,* 12 Harv. L.R. 417 (1899).

It is not the first use but the tiresome repetition of inadequate catch words which I am observing—phrases which originally were contributions, but which, by their very felicity, delay further analysis for fifty years.

> OLIVER WENDELL HOLMES, *Law in Science—Science in Law,* 12 Harv. L.R. 443, 455 (1899).

It is one of the misfortunes of the law that ideas become encysted in phrases and thereafter for a long time cease to provoke further analysis.

> HOLMES, J., *Hyde v United States* (1912) 225 US 347, 391, 56 L ed 1114, 1135, 32 S Ct 793.

Words express whatever meaning convention has attached to them.

> HOLMES, J., *Trimble v Seattle* (1914) 231 US 683, 688, 58 L ed 435, 438, 34 S Ct 218.

A word is not a crystal, transparent and unchanged, it is the skin of a living thought and may vary greatly in color and content according to the circumstances and the time in which it is used.

> HOLMES, J., *Towne v Eisner* (1917) 245 US 418, 425, 62 L ed 372, 376, 38 S Ct 158.

I have seldom found much good result from hypercritical severity, in examining the distinct force of words. Language is essentially defective in precision; more so, than those are aware of, who are not in the habit of subjecting it to philological analysis.

> JOHNSON, J., *Martin v Hunter* (1816, US) 1 Wheat 304, 374, 4 L ed 97, 114.

Most of the disputes in the world arise from words.

> LORD MANSFIELD, C.J., *Morgan v Jones* (1773) Lofft 160, 176.

Almost all compositions contain words, which, taken in their rigorous sense, would convey a meaning different from that which is obviously intended. It is essential to just construction, that many words which import something excessive, should be understood in a more mitigated sense—in that sense which common usage justifies. The word "necessary" is of this description. It has not a fixed character peculiar to itself. . . . A thing may be necessary, very necessary, absolutely or indispensably necessary.

> MARSHALL, C.J., *M'Culloch v Maryland* (1819, US) 4 Wheat 316, 414, 4 L ed 579, 603.

Such is the character of human language, that no word conveys to the mind, in all situations, one single definite idea; and nothing is more common than to use words in a figurative sense.

> MARSHALL, C.J., *M'Culloch v Maryland* (1819, US) 4 Wheat 316, 414, 4 L ed 579, 603.

As men, whose intentions require no concealment, generally employ the words which most directly and aptly express the ideas they intend to convey, the enlightened patriots who framed our constitution, and the people who

adopted it, must be understood to have employed words in
their natural sense, and to have intended what they have
said.

> MARSHALL, C.J., *Gibbons v Ogden* (1824, US) 9 Wheat 1, 188,
> 6 L ed 23, 68.

There is no presumption that each word used should
change the meaning of the sentence. A word may be inserted for the sake of emphasis or for greater clearness,
or descriptively, or because it occurs to the writer as suitable to the idea he is expressing, and this without any
thought whether it is or is not absolutely necessary to the
expression of his meaning. The objection to an interpretation on the ground that it would make a word or phrase
surplusage has weight only when the presence of such word
or phrase would be unusual or unaccountable if it were not
specially inserted for the purpose of altering the meaning of
the sentence. The mere fact that you could omit it without
change of meaning has in itself no weight. There is no
presumption that human beings use the irreducible minimum of words to effect their purpose.

> MOULTON, L.J., *Boden v Boden* [1907] 1 Ch. 132, 143.

For words, which are no other than the verberation of the
air, do not constitute the statute, but are only the image of
it, and the life of the statute rests in the minds of the ex-
positors of the words, that is, the makers of the statutes.

> SERJ. SAUNDERS, arguendo, *Partridge v Strange* (1552) 1 Plowd.
> 77, 82.

Syllables govern the world.

> JOHN SELDEN, *Table-Talk: Power, State.*

Words are more plastic than wax.

> SOCRATES. See Plato, *Republic* IX (588d).

That lawyer's Paradise where all words have a fixed, precisely ascertained meaning.

> JAMES BRADLEY THAYER, *Preliminary Treatise on Evidence* 428 (1898).

Writings

Little fragments of my fleece that I have left upon the hedges of life.

> OLIVER WENDELL HOLMES, *Collected Legal Papers: Preface* (1920).

Youth

Young men are fitter to invent than to judge; fitter for execution than for counsel; and fitter for new projects than for settled business.

> BACON, *Essays: Of Youth and Age.*

A man has but one youth, and considering the consequence of employing that well, he has reason to think himself very rich; for that gone, all the wealth in the world will not purchase another.

> ROGER NORTH, *On the Study of the Laws 5.*

Zoning

As someone remarked at the hearing, everyone wants churches, schools (and clubs) but not in his own neighborhood.

> DESMOND, C.J., *Von Kohorn v Morrell,* 9 N.Y.2d 27, 34 (1961).

Index of Authors

Abbott, Charles, Baron Tenterden, English judge (1762–1832) 256, 331

à Beckett, Gilbert Abbott, English journalist, humorist (1811–1856) 87

Abinger, Baron. See Sir James Scarlett

Acton, Baron (John Emerich Edward Dalberg), English historian (1834–1902) 400

Adams, John, Massachusetts lawyer, President of the United States (1735–1826) 187, 231, 247

Adams, John Quincy, Massachusetts lawyer, President of United States (1767–1848) 105, 413

Adolphus, John L., English lawyer (1795–1862) 543

Aesop, Greek fabulist (fl. 560 B. C.) 130

Aguesseau, Henri Francois d', lawyer, Chancellor of France (1668–1751) 469, 508

Alderson, Sir Edward Hall, English judge (1787–1857) 43, 139, 256, 431

Aldrich, Bailey, Massachusetts, Judge U. S. Dist. Ct., Ch. Judge U. S. Ct. App. (1907–   ) 38

Alliluyeva, Svetlana, Russian, daughter of Joseph Stalin (1926–   ) 86

Ames, Fisher, Massachusetts lawyer, statesman, orator (1758–1808) 31

Anderson, Sir Edmund, Chief Justice of Common Pleas, England (1530–1605) 455

Anstey, John, English lawyer, poet (d. 1819) 61, 84, 445, 446

Appleton, John, Assoc. Justice, Chief Justice, Supreme Court, Maine (1804–1891) 533

Aquinas. See St. Thomas Aquinas

Arabin, William St. Julien, judge, Sheriff's Court, Commissioner, Central Criminal Court, London (d. 1841) 30, 31

597

[Legal Quotations]—39   *609*

General Index

A

Abandonment of client, 435

ABC of the law, 43

Ability, I'll never take work I'm unable to do, 380

Able, three sorts of lawyers, 376

Abolish, end of law is not to abolish or to restrain, 359

About face by Supreme Court as due to outside clamor, 127

Abridgement—
of the freedom of the people, 403
reports, 497
work, printing abridgement of, 123

Abrogation of law by itself, 76

Absence, presumption arising from, 466

Absolutes—
authority to interpret any written or spoken law, 260
bill of rights, 111
law does not concern itself with absolute justice, 345
law is absolute justice of the state, 350
past cannot be recalled by absolute power, 441
speech as not absolute, 222–224

Absolutism, 386

Absorption, rights brought within Fourteenth Amendment by process of, 111

Abstract principle, old law good as, 76

Abstraction, freedom as not a mere intellectual abstraction, 404

Absurdities—
legislation, 389
nothing too absurd but what authority can be found, 44

Absurdities—Cont'd
precedents and rules must be followed, 455
reducing laws to simple geometric demonstrations as absurd idea, 389

Abuse, 1
legislature, protection against abuses by, 394
no case, abuse the plaintiff's attorney, 35
Statute of Uses as statute of abuses, 531

Academicians, slippered readers anticipated rather than, 463

Academics, though I am good at academics, I'd be useless at the bar, 373

Accent as making words deadly, 572

Acceptance, legal proposition established by, 43

Accident of an accident, 479

Accidental—
it is accidental that the laws last longer than their causes, 388
results and means, distinction between, 253

Accidents make laws for us, 361

Accommodation indorser, witness as, 205

Accord and satisfaction, 1, 2

Accounting, backward in, 54

Accuracy, 1

Accusatory as opposed to the inquisitorial system, 365

Accuser and accused, justice due to, 324

Achieved liberty, no such thing as, 402

Achievement, 2, 3
ambition, infra

Acme of judicial distinction, 51

611

Acquittal, 364, 378

Acre, the breath of an acre is still known to all Englishmen, 420

Act, 3

Action, judiciary power is by its nature devoid of action, 310

Actions or cases—
generally, 3, 4
adequate presentation of case before judge, 49
appeal, infra
authority, 43–46
cases, 61–67
circumstances alter cases, 83
citations, 83–85
complex cases, infra
costs, 126
criminal matters, infra
damages, infra
decisions or judgments, infra
defense, infra
delay, 155–158
discourage litigation, 409
distinctions, 173–175
evidence, infra
headnote conforming to case and not to language of opinion, 236
it is as impossible for a lawyer to wish men out of litigation, as for a physician to wish them in health, 369
itself, case speaks for, 501
judge as having nothing to do with getting up of case, 51
jurisdiction, infra
jury, infra
legislation as cause of, 388
litigation, generally, 407–413
negligence which is actionable, 431
no two cases are exactly alike, 174
pleadings, infra
popular names, 66, 67
precedents, infra
reports and reporting, 496–500
similar cases, infra
suppressed speech may occasion more mental torture than lost case, 49
the case is altered, says Plowden, 83

Act of God, 3

Act of Settlement, I will drive a coach and six through, 390

Actors, 468
lawyer and actor, 17

Act within your commission, 452

Adam, God passing sentence upon, 152

Add three words to a conveyance, 531

Adjective, constitutional law as not susceptible of comprehensive statement in an adjective, 114

Administration of justice. Justice, infra

Administrative matters, 7, 8
advisory opinions, 11
investigation, 268
rules of evidence, 205

Admiralty, 8

Admissions, 7, 8
law of the realm to admit nothing against the law of God, 80
when conversing with Marshall, I never admit anything, 419

Adulation, 218

Advance—
payment of fee, 214
progress in advance of law, 484
this case is a failure in advance, 189

Advancement, 484

Adversary, argument by leaving off cause and falling upon adversary, 36

Adversary proceeding, common-law trial as, 162

Adverse party is thy advocate, 8

Adverse possession, 9

Advertisements contain the only truths to be relied on in a newspaper, 221

Advertising, 9

Advice, 9–11, 382
duty of lawyers to give, 481
free advice, 215
judges ought to be more advised than confident, 291
legal knowledge, 333

Advisory opinions, 11

Advocacy, 12–17

Advocate—
adverse party as, 8
lawyers, infra

Aequitas agit in personam, 196

Affections. Love and affection, infra

Affidavits, truth will out even in an affidavit, 549

After-life, apple pie causes in, 62

Afternoon, study all the morning and talk all the afternoon, 189

Afternoon tea, jury trial is not, 545

Agate, British constitution as like layer after layer of wrapping around agate, 114

Age, 17
law books, 55
young or old, infra

Agent, attorney as client's advocate, not agent, 17

Ages—
change in laws, 76, 77
constitution as enduring for, 109
each age must provide freedom for itself, 403
jurisprudence, 312, 313
name and memory left for the next ages, 420

Agglutinative or tonsorial type, 146

Agreement of jury, 321

Agreements. Contracts or agreements, infra

Aim, the question is not so much who was aimed at, as who was hit, 398

Air—
negligence in, 431
words which are no other than the verberation of, 575

Ajax, prayer of, 504

Algebraic formulae are not likely to be imputed to legislators, 388

Alibi, 205

Alienation of affections, 243

Alien juxtaposition, words are not pebbles in, 572

Aliens, 18, 19

All—
justice, all men at all times stand in need of, 324
justice for all by all, 316
laws are to govern all alike, 365
lawyer as all in all, 40

All—Cont'd
no attorney is bound to know all the law, 331

All hail, great judge! 273

Alliance with any other state, 544

Almanacs, reverence for the law as written in, 360

Alphabet—
no law of that country must exceed in words the number of letters in their alphabet, 390
one possible connecting thread, 329

Alphabetical order would be better than no order at all, 440

Altar, people subject to the law should be its altar, 348

Alteration. Change or alteration, infra

Amazon at common law—Miss Brass, 89

Ambiguity, 19
majority opinion, ambiguities and silences of, 170
rules of statutory construction, when resorted to, 258

Ambition, 19, 20
achievement, 2, 3
judge, personal ambitions, 278
legal profession, 470
men bribed by, 59

Ambulance chasing, 20

Amendments, 20, 21
constitution, 20, 111–113
constitutional powers, 358
judicial legislation under guise of interpretation, 288
laws, generally, 74
reports and reporting, 497
Supreme Court, 551

Amenity, river as more than, 508

A mensa et thoro divorce, 176

American Bar, schoolmaster of, 189

American independence, 247

Amorphous dummy is not unspotted by human emotions, 274

Analogy, 21

Analysis, 21
judicial opinions, 150
statutes, 262

613

Bad faith. Good faith, infra
Bad law—
hard cases as making, 63, 65
I know no method to secure the repeal of bad or obnoxious laws so effective as their stringent execution, 365
no practical criterion except what the crowd wants, 387
reports of law, 498
Bad man, looking at law as, 335
Bad people as making good lawyers, 40
Bad times, lawmaking power entrusted to Congress in, 385
Bad weather, law is like, 352
Baggage, loss of, 413
Bags and sachels of the plaintiff, 300
Ballads, 386
Banana, I would carve out of a banana, a judge with more backbone than that, 240
Banc, reversed in, 273
Banishment, foreign employment as a kind of honorable banishment, 246
Banking, 47
Bank of the United States, bill for incorporating, 393
Bankruptcy or insolvency, 47
corporations, 125
debtors' court, 193
honesty, recognizing of, 240
light-hearted nature of client after seeing attorney, 39
Barbers—
a barber's talk cannot be disputed, 534
killing with kindness, 142
Bard, 516
Barefoot Wall Street lawyer, 372
Bar examination, preparation for, 186
Bargain—
chancerymen no man's bargain, 72
for contract, 121
suppression of prosecution should not be made matter of private bargain, 485
Barrel whisky, 327

Barnyard, pig in the parlor instead of, 434
Basket justice, 59
Bastards—
no illegitimate children, only illegitimate parents, 78
Parliament as legitimatizing, 394
they are his own babies, albeit often branded as illegitimates, 172
Bats of the law, presumptions as, 466
Battle—
depends upon the testimony of one sworn person, 319
litigation pursued to experience a warmth from the heat of battle, 409
Battledore and shuttlecock's a very good name, 139
Beachhead of cooperation may push back the jungles of suspicion, 510
Beard—
growing of, 25, 26
stay friend, until I put aside my beard, for that never committed treason, 142
Beavers, English constitution as compared with work of, 114
Bed—
I give unto my wife my second best bed with its furniture, 567
the bar is either all bed and no roses, or roses and no bed, 474
Bedtime stories for the tired bar, 444
Beer—
best when it is old, 468
thirsty folk want beer, not explanations, 212
Beetle—
he who gives away his goods before he is dead take a beetle and knock him on the head, 228
lawyer as, 374
Beggar, sue a beggar and catch a louse, 412
Begging in the streets, law as forbidding the rich as well as the poor, 507

Begging of question in argument, 37

Behind the times, law as, 345

Belief—
every idea offers itself for belief, 246
exposure amounts to nothing when people want to believe, 210
I'll never assume that a rogue or a thief is a gentleman worthy implicit belief, 379
unbelief of lawyer as becoming unbelief of jury, 317, 318

Belly full of law, 381

Bench and bar, 48–51
judges, infra
lawyers, infra

Bending of law by the construction, 256

Bending or breaking of constitution, 110

Beneficence becomes a pest, 245

Beneficiaries will rise up and bless him for the wills he made, 472

Benevolence, judge as not to yield to, 297

Bequeath. Wills, infra

Bereavement, when baggage is lost, it is not simple privation; it is bereavement, 413

Best, Mr. Justice, his great mind, 247

Betsy and I or else, 242

Bettabilitarian, 444

Betting. Gambling, infra

Bias. Prejudice or bias, infra

Big mortgage foreclosed just the same as a little one, 423

Bill of rights, 88, 111–113
footnotes, 218, 219
freedom of speech, 222
states, applying bill of rights to, 365

Bill of sale from God Almighty, 519

Bills and notes. Negotiable instruments, infra

Binding effect—
obedience to law, 355–359
of footnote, 218

Biography, 52

618

Bipartisan judiciary is the only way in this country to achieve a non-partisan judiciary, 307

Bird of passage of almost mechanical regularity, 539

Birds—
a swallow had built her nest under the eaves of a court of justice, 129
cage, ideas as like birds in, 124
we must not make a scarecrow of the law, 348

Bird's nest, looking at English constitution as like looking at, 114

Birth—
independence, 247
lower court anticipating a doctrine which may be in the womb of time, 302
property and law are born and must die together, 485

Biscuits, cats born in oven as, 85

Bite—
dog entitled to one bite, 23
enforcement, bite of law is in, 364

Black art, the art of publicity is, 488

Black is white, 377

Black letter man as man of the present, 188

Black letter wisdom, law as not dead corpus of, 350

Black Monday, 53

Black satin, Mrs. Manning insisted on being hanged in, 425

Blackstone's Commentaries, 53, 54

Blameless lives, equity does not demand that its suitors shall have led, 196

Blank paper, constitution made such by construction, 266

Blank sheet, we do not write on, 299

Blessed be the amending hands, 20

Blind—
Chalcedon was called the city of, 446
imitation of the past, 458
imitativeness of man, 247
jury, names of, 314

621

Color of their environment, words reflect, 572

Colors, jurisdiction as verbal coat of too many colors, 311

Comedy and tragedy, judge as between, 274

Command—
it's my will, my command, let that for reason stand, 490
prize of the General is not a bigger tent but command, 452
stare decisis, 527

Commandments—
law as depending on, 45
thou shall not ration justice, 324

Commencement, every precedent had first, 457

Commendation of judge to advocate, 48

Commendation of self, 93, 94

Comment upon any law is a capital crime, 390

Commerce—
generally, 94, 95
change in law, 75
civil rights, 86
domicil, 176
horse and buggy definition, 77
Siamese twins, commerce clause and due process clause used like, 179

Commercial morality, advantages of maintaining high standard of, 241

Commercial paper. Negotiable instruments, infra

Commission, act within, 452

Common employment, 95

Common enemy, husband will be accounted, 244

Common good, law as a certain rule of reason for the purpose of, 352

Common knowledge—
judicial notice, 289, 290
that the thought of man shall not be tried, 225

Common law—
generally, 95–99
adversary proceeding, common-law trial as, 162

[Legal Quotations]—40

Common law—Cont'd
equity without common law would have been a castle in the air, 198
good pleading—the heart-string of the common law, 446
immemorial yet freshly growing fabric of, 477
interpretation of statutes, 257
judges made, 284
legal knowledge, 333, 334, 338
main triangles of laws of England, 140
Miss Brass—a kind of amazon at common law, 89
our lady of the common law, 362
precedents, 460, 461
prose epic of, 54
reason, common law as nothing else but, 490
Roman law, common law not based on, 508
spouses, agreements between, 242
under the common law there is no case unprovided for, 287

Common means, 155

Commonplace, legal minds chiefly consist in expatiating on, 371

Common sense—
binding authority as against, 45
construing laws, 261–263
don't forget your common sense, 293
law is common sense as modified by the legislature, 352
no war between constitution and, 116
presumption that every person knows the law as contrary to, 336

Commonwealth is an empire of laws and not of men, 231

Commonwealth of literature, lawyer as very little acquainted with, 406

Communism, 99, 100
jury for communists, 319

Community, house of a great lawyer is the oracular seat of the whole community, 370

Compact—
constitution as compact between sovereigns, 106
law is compact of the state, 351

Companion—
barrister of expended practice is the best companion in the world, 376
negligence has misfortune for, 432

Company, not to keep much company, 187

Comparison, history as involving, 239

Compassion, sign of the loss of freedom, 367

Compensation—
fees, infra
profession, ideas involved in, 469
wages, infra

Competency of country lawyer, 475

Competition, fair trade, 211, 212

Competitive examinations, 88, 183

Complaint, 447

Complex cases, 65, 66
judicial process, 299

Compounding of quarrels among his neighbors, without going to law, 377

Compromise—
government of laws without men is as visionary as a government of men without laws, 231
law as ending in, 6
whenever you can, 409

Compulsion—
exclusion of large groups of citizens from their homes during war, 557
unification of opinion achieves only the unanimity of the graveyard, 226

Concealment—
nation concealed under the form of a federation, 213
warrant to search, 514

Conceit of judge in cutting off evidence or counsel, 48

Concepts as relative, 224

Concert, persons acting in, 30

Conclave, an opinion as huddled up in, 149

Conclusion—
circumstantial evidence, 207
concurrence, 100, 101
truism that conclusion is just as sound and no more so than the premises upon which it is based, 172

Conclusiveness—
presumption to know the law, 337
stare decisis, 527–530

Concrete cases, general propositions do not decide, 63

Concurrence, 100, 101
with misgivings, 365

Condemned first and inquired upon after, 138

Conditions—
liberty, eternal vigilance as condition of, 401
membership in the bar is a privilege burdened with conditions, 471

Conduct alone is amenable to the law, 225

Confederated fabric, working underground to undermine the foundations of, 552

Confessions, 101
change in law, 73
he compelled the party accused by torture to confess, 138

Confessor, deceive not, 42, 144

Confidence—
check conscience, things held in, 73
clients with, 204
constitution, adherence to, 108
dissent as endangering conclusions of courts of last resort, 168
judges ought to be more advised than confident, 291
lordships and those who assist in debates in capacity of counsel, 49
own strength, bequest of confidence in, 566
the moment confidence ceases, privilege ceases, 467

Confidential matters—
office of the lawyer is too delicate, personal and confidential to be occupied by a corporation, 475
trust of giving counsel, 9

[Legal Quotations]

Corporations—Cont'd
  glory of lawyers is more corporate than individual, 473
  office of the lawyer is too delicate, personal and confidential to be occupied by a corporation, 475
Corpse, funeral conducted without, 289
Corrections—
  law as correction of every offense, 351
  posterity, correcting judgment of the time by that of, 238
  three corrective words turn whole legal libraries into wastepaper, 389
  universality, correction of law where it is defective owing to, 196
Corruption—
  confession to guilt of, 101
  hand never given to, 93
  obscenity, 436, 437
  of law, 430
  place of justice ought to be preserved without, 130
  unlimited power is apt to corrupt the minds of those who possess it, 347
Cosmos, 444
Cost or expense—
  generally, 126
  appeal, 26
  fortune, constant recurrence of small expenses in time eat up a fortune, 356
  lawyers have more sober sense than to argue at their own expense, 408
  nominal damages are a mere peg on which to hang cost, 141
  nominal winner is often a real loser, 409
  to know what law is, 70
  truth, cost of, as too much, 548
Counselors. Lawyers, infra
Country—
  duty, 181, 182
  flag, 217
  in the administration of justice I am entrusted for God, the King and country, 293
Country dance, law as like, 352
Country man at plough, 392

Country lawyers, 475, 476
Courage, 126, 127
  adventurous youth, 127
Courier without luggage, 433
Court of Appeal—
  animals, 23
  everybody is presumed to know the law except His Majesty's judges, 336
Courthouse door, contingent fee as the poor man's key to, 215
Courts. Judiciary, infra
Courteous, judge as, 295
Cover, judge not a book by, 555
Cover of law books, 55
Covering of bet, judicial review, 302
Cow—
  copyright and patent, 123
  going to law is like skinning a new milk cow for the hide and giving the meat to the lawyers, 408
  to forbid the competition of a coconut grove with the American cow, 211
  voila! the nonsuit of cow beef, 213
  you may not sell the cow and sup the milk, 212
Cradle, independence, 247
Craft is the vice, not the spirit, of the profession, 477
Crazy quilt—
  apportionment as, 27
  patchwork state of the internal revenue laws, 537
Cream, skim milk masquerading as, 117
Creativity of advocate, 17
Creditors. Debtors and creditors, infra
Credulity is not esteemed a paramount virtue of the judicial mind, 293
Criminal matters—
  generally, 132, 133
  actions, generally, 3, 4
  attorney, right to, 383, 384
  book without index, 248
  hanging, infra
  common law, 97, 98
  communism, 99
  confessions, supra

Death—Cont'd
only in the still waters is stagnation death, 550
plucks my ears and says, live—I am coming, 406
presumption from absence, 466
property and law are born and must die together, 485
punishment, 133, 134, 137, 424
residence of woman, 500, 501
suicide, 532
the innocent and the just you shall not put to death, nor shall you acquit the guilty, 364
the laws sometimes sleep, never die, 364
to compass or imagine the death of a king, 543
to rest upon a formula is a slumber that, prolonged, means death, 219
when a great learned man, who is long in making, dieth, much learning dieth with him, 330
wills, infra
works to follow him, 472

Debate, authority resulting from, 44

Deborra to judge the people, 270

Debtors and creditors—
generally, 143
accord and satisfaction, 1, 2
arrest for debt, 143
bankruptcy, 47, 48
conflict of interest, 102
experience as not sufficiently uniform to raise a presumption of payment, 465
insolvent debtors' court, 193
racing debts, 242

Deceit, 144
fraud, infra
physician, confessor, nor lawyer, deceive not, 42, 144
witness, 570

Decency—
discussions are habitually necessary in courts of justice, which are unfit for female ears, 571
gentlemen, do not hang me high, 424

Deciding cases is never easy, 304

Decisions or judgments—
generally, 144–152
confirm the sentence and sign the decree, 343
definitions, 155
dictum, infra
doubt, 177
equal intrinsic authority, 44
every decision becomes a page of history, 554
footnote, 218
headnotes, 235
none but a law-fearing people will be inclined to regard the decision of a suit as equivalent to the enactment of a law, 213
obedience to law, 356
overruling, 151
policy as well as the letter of the law is a guide to decision, 257
precedents, infra
reports and reporting, 496–500
seriatim, 151
Solomon's judgment, 148
stare decisis, infra
technical precision of decisions of Supreme Court, 407
verdict, infra
wisdom of Solomon could not devise a judgment which this complaint would support, 447

Declarations, dying declaration, 183

Decline and fall of the sheriff, 518

Dedication of country lawyer, 475

Deeds, justice of peace as drawing, 328

Deep well, knowledge of the law as like, 333

Defamation. Libel and slander, infra

Defendant, 445
plaintiff making out case for, 33

Defense—
generally, 152–155
by advocate, 14, 17
diligence as valuable, 161
entrapment, 191
I disapprove of what you say, but I will defend to the death your right to say it, 224

633

Dogs—Cont'd
reasonable man will inform himself of the history and habits of a dog before administering caress, 492

Domestic institution, brotherhood of man as not, 60

Domicil, 176

Donkey of a question of law, 64

Donor, secret charities as genuine index of real character of, 77

Don't get too judgey, 293

Don't take yourself too seriously, 292

Do-nothing sovereignty, 523

Don Quixote of the law, Shelley's case as, 517

Doris amara suam non intermiscuit undam, 176

Double face, lawyer's seeing case with, 371

Double jeopardy, 177

Doubt—
generally, 177, 178
authority, doubtful point as regularly answered both ways by, 458
in all expression, 372
it might be possible to compress in the same number of lines more fertile opportunities for doubt and error, 387
man beginning with certainties as ending in, 68
Parliament as defining doubtful rights, 394
rules of statutory construction, when resorted to, 258

Dower, gentlemen vouching on writ of, 83

Dowry, knowledge wooed for, 183

Drachma, small claims court, 132

Drafting documents, 339

Drafter of statute, construction by, 259

Dragon flies, devise of, 564

Dramatic, most men think dramatically, not quantitatively, 541

Dreariness of literature, 407

Dred Scott decision, 356, 523

Dress. Clothes, supra

Drill sergeant, judge appearing in character of, 50

Drink—
eat, drink and sleep law, 353
strive mightily, but eat and drink as friends, 376
toast, 339

Drowning, suicide, 532

Drugs of apothecaries, new laws are like, 73

Drum and trumpet, heroic hours as not announcing their presence by, 126

Drunkenness. Intoxication, infra

Dry and unpleasant, I do not see why the study of law is called, 188

Ducere in seria mala, 91, 92

Due, justice to allot to every man his due, 327

Duel, 180, 181

Due process, 88, 178–180
amendments to constitution, 112
judges are the final seat of authority, 288

Dummy, ventriloquist's dummy, stare decisis, 528

Duplex aim of lawyer, 42

Dust—
had raised the glory of the nation from the dust, 393
judge as having vision clouded by dust of conflict, 50
purlieus of the law, 349

Duty—
generally, 181, 182
advocate to client, 12
all laws are promulgated from the end that every man may know his duty, 262
historic continuity with the past is not a duty, it is only a necessity, 238
law, definition of, 351
unconstitutional act as imposing no duties, 116

Dying declaration, 183

E

Eagle's nest, 182

Ear—
a man cannot hear by another's ear, 322

637

Essays, decisions of judge as exquisite essays, 145

Estate—
of the realm, 520
system of Britain, 114
wills, infra

Esteem, lawyers, 474

Esthetic criteria used for evaluating decisions, 145

Estimate, 201
mortuary estimates, 52

Estoppel or waiver—
jury trial, 203
odious, estoppels are, 559
tort waived to bring assumpsit, 543

Ethics—
legal ethics, 201–204
requirements of criminal investigation, overemphasis of, 365, 366
soliciting law suits, 9

Even-handed justice, 326

Evening clothes, 570

Event—
interest is not perdition at all events, 255
is always a great teacher, 236

Everlasting natural laws, 430

Evidence—
generally, 205–209
admissions, supra
battle depends upon the testimony of one sworn person, 319
circumstantial, 207–209
conceit of judge in cutting off evidence, 48
confessions, supra
insanity, 253
it is far pleasanter to sit comfortably in the shade rubbing pepper into a poor devil's eyes than to go about in the sun hunting up evidence, 541
judge's fair comment upon, 203
jury finding a verdict against the evidence, 323
legal ethics, 203
negligence in the air, 431
own case, trying of, 38
plead what you need not, 447

[Legal Quotations]—41

Evidence—Cont'd
possession in Scotland as evidence of stealing in England, 235
precedent as evidence of law, 459
presumptions, infra
res ipsa loquitur, 501, 502
search and seizure, 512–515
survival of life after death, 560
title, 543
to him that goes to law, requisites, 407
what judges do and what they profess to do are not always the same, 296
when the case is all over, the jury will pitch the testimony out the window, 317
witnesses, infra

Evil—
all punishment in itself is, 133
he that will not apply new remedies must expect new evils, 494
judge should have learned to know evil, 275
law administered with evil eye, 6
legislation as having tendency to cure or at least make the evil less, 387
natural law, 429
obscures the shadow of evil, 348
power, evil men are rarely given, 452
prayers, 453
preservation of liberty, 400
statute read in broad light of the evils it aimed at, 261

Exactness—
as policy, 2
equal protection of the laws, exact equality is no prerequisite of, 193

Examinations—
competitive examination, 88, 183
witnesses, infra
you must first examine the law before you can apply the rules of construction, 256

Excellent, law is the true embodiment of everything that's excellent, 344

Exception, 209
  judge merciful in making the exception, 295

Exception upon exception, 536

Exchequer chamber, 434

Excise laws are odious and grievous to the dealer, but intolerable to the private person, 515

Excise tax, 534, 537

Excitement—
  defense of unpopular causes, 154, 155
  errors of judgment resulting from, 491

Excommunication—
  absolution from, 335
  corporation cannot be excommunicated, 124

Excrescence growing out of the head of a section, preamble as, 454

Excursion ticket, judicial opinions no better than, 150

Excuse, ignorance of the law excuses no man, 337

Execution—
  incitement and execution as touched with equal guilt, 104
  law convenient in, 385
  penal law as confined, 364
  president, duties of, 465
  young men fitter for execution than for counsel, 576

Executive branch—
  equal in origin and equal in title to, 553
  sword of the community, executive department holds, 307
  there is no liberty if the judiciary power cannot be separated from the legislative and executive, 309
  three horse team form of government provided by the Constitution, 233
  unconstitutional exercise of power as subject to judicial restraint, 302

Exhausting vocation, advocacy as, 16

Exigencies of particular times, laws formed by, 388

Exile, law of the land, 367, 368

Existence, a law so unknown is the same as a law not in existence, 287

Expansion—
  moulds of life, 405
  tendency of a principle to expand itself to the limit of its logic, 467

Expedience—
  design and object of laws, 350
  of relative justice law may know something; of expedience it knows much, 345
  rules of evidence, purpose of, 205
  tipping scales when arguments are nicely balanced, 32

Expense. Cost or expense, supra

Experience—
  correlation between prior judicial experience and fitness for the functions of the Supreme Court is zero, 305
  government of laws without men is as visionary as a government of men without laws, 231
  judge, 275, 294
  legal knowledge, 333
  on our guard to protect liberty when the government's purposes are beneficent, 400
  optimism and pessimism may be found to exist in the minds of expert witnesses, 570
  people must not be wiser than the experience of mankind, 330
  presumption, experience as not sufficiently uniform to raise, 465
  rules of evidence as founded in experience of common life, 206
  science of the law must join hands with experience, 186
  that his eye may be opened by experience, 466
  the law is the last result of human wisdom acting upon human experience for the benefit of the public, 351
  the life of the law has been experience, 345

Experiment—
  generally, 209
  constitution as, 107
  Fourteenth Amendment used for, 112
  government is the science of experiment, 230

Experts—
  business advisers, lawyers as not a mere body of, 481
  legal knowledge, 333
  witnesses are liars, damned liars, and experts, 570

Expiration of law in constitution at end of nineteen years, 75

Explanation—
  the more you explain it, the more I don't understand it, 170
  thirsty folk want beer, not explanations, 212

Exposition, judicial opinions, 147, 150

Exposure, 210

Expounders of law, judges as, 288

Expression to the thought, 572

Extemporaneous speaking to be practiced and cultivated, 188

Extermination of dissenters, 225

Extraordinary, 210
  constitution as meeting extraordinary needs, 110
  ordinary, extraordinary jurisdiction succeeds only by becoming, 311

Extreme law is extreme injustice, 342

Extreme right with wiseness is extreme wrong, 355

Eye for eye, 502

Eye of the law, 466

Eyes. Sight, infra

F

Face—
  brazen face, supra
  I spake it to my face, 399
  men's feelings are as different as faces, 213

Fact, equality as, 195

Fact questions, 488

Facts, 210, 211
  inferences never certainty, but it may be plain enough to justify finding of fact, 249
  jury has the power to bring in a verdict in the teeth of both law and facts, 319
  statute valid as to one set of facts may be invalid as to another, 554
  the case is altered, says Plowden, 83

Fairness, generally. Justice, infra

Fair play, 6
  criminal case, 366

Fair round belly of justice, 276

Fair trade, 211, 212

Fair trial—
  murder, 425
  right to counsel, 383, 384

Faith, 212
  time has upset many fighting faiths, 548

Faithful—
  epitaph, 155
  witness who is faithful will not lie but a deceitful witness uttereth a lie, 570

False assumption that each verbal symbol refers to one and only one specific subject, 339

Falsehood—
  can never imitate truth, 549
  is professional apostasy, 477

False hopes, 401

False income tax return, 535

False opinion of attorney, paying for, 39

False witnesses, criminal justice, 136

Fame, mastering of common law as being half way out to, 99

Families, wills as ruin of, 561

Family roof-tree, 546

Fantastic hypothesis, evidence as excluding, 206

Farce, wills, 560

Fare, right to go wherever you please as long as you have money to pay fare, 86

643

Fees—Cont'd
  no advocate without very good
    cause shall refuse to act
    for any person tendering a
    reasonable fee, 154
  nominal winner is often a real
    loser, 409
  number of lawyers retained, 483
  protest of the size of the fee,
    lawyer as receiving, 375
  sense, fees of lawyers directs,
    371
  white is black and black is white,
    according as they are paid,
    377

Fee simple, 370

Felicity of catch words, 573

Felon, 132
  criminal matters, supra

Females. Women, infra

Fences, good fences make good
  neighbors, 56

Fencing, law schools belong in the
  modern university no more
  than a school of, 190

Ferocious nature of dogs, 24

Fertile octogenarian, 442

Fetter the law by maxim, 419

Fiat justitia ruat coelum, 449

Fiction, 216, 217
  childish fiction employed by
    judges as judicial legisla-
    tion, 284
  life breathed into corporation by
    state, 125

Fidelity of lawyer, 15

Fiduciary relations of legal profession, 472

Fields and playgrounds, devise of,
  565

Fight, jury trial is, 545

Fighting words, freedom of speech,
  223

Figurative sense, words used in,
  574

Figurehead, husband as, 243

Figure of speech, rule of law not
  drawn from, 82

Filament, concept of fairness must
  not be strained until it is narrowed to, 324

Filoramo, is an honorable name
  of parents of Italian ancestry,
  426

Final, Supreme Court not final because it is infallible, 552

Final seat of authority, judges as
  in, 288

Financial matters—
  bankruptcy or insolvency, supra
  country lawyer taking clients
    regardless of, 475
  criminal trial depending upon
    the amount of money one
    has, 134
  economics, supra
  equal rights, 195
  indigents, infra
  legal ethics, 204
  litigation, 409
  rich or poor, infra
  wealth, infra

Finch, Sir Henry, 189

Finding of law, knowing where to
  find law, 334

Fineux, Sir John, 163

Finger—
  clerk as finger of a court, 89,
    90
  devil makes his Christmas pies
    of lawyers' tongues and
    clerks' fingers, 375
  God writing natural law in the
    heart of man, 428

Finis rerum, 542

Fire, jury kept without, 320

Fire bell at midnight disturbs your
  sleep, 1

Fire of genius, patent system as
  adding fuel of interest to, 124

Fire shouted in theater and causing panic, 223

Fireside, judicial department comes
  home in its effects to every
  man's fireside, 309

Firm in applying the rule, 295

First Amendment, 113

First day, one might be a lawyer
  the first day, 332

Fish—
  disposed to have gift of speech,
    25
  persuasive argument, 32

645

Fortune, constant recurrence of small expenses in time eat up a fortune, 356

Foundations—
confederated fabric, undermining foundations of, 552
equity and utility as foundations of law, 341
physical power, foundation of jurisdiction is, 311
social security, justice as foundation for, 327

Founding fathers as aware of the dangers, 386

Fountainhall's decisions, 406, 407

Fountains of justice in nature, 426

Fours, on all fours, 459

Fourteenth Amendment, 111–113
equal protection, 193, 194
footnotes, 218, 219
historical product, 239
slow to construe the clause in, 304

Fox should not be of the jury at a goose's trial, 321

Fractions—
judges were not to give opinions by, 283
scruple divided to smallest fraction, 177

France, in crossing France, law changed as often as one changed horses, 349

Fraud—
generally, 219, 220
antic of the law, 348
conscience, things held in, 73
consumer fraud, 117
impeachment of foreign judgments for, 160
misrepresentation of fact may bind a man, 254, 255
oath against falsehood, 435
parents of trust, 546
professional integrity, 478
title where there wanteth right, 542
unfit accident to be at the making of a will, 560

Frauds, statute of, 531

Free—
advice, 215
gift, infra

Free—Cont'd
ideas are free, 124, 548
the criminal goes free, 512
the judge, even when he is free, is still not wholly free, 297

Freedom—
generally, 220
absolute discretion as destructive of, 163
assembly, supra
democracy, 158
due process, 179
employment contract as subject of legislation, 422
end of law is to preserve and enlarge freedom, 359
independence, 247
law of the land, 367, 368
opinion, freedom of, 290
religion, infra
sign of the loss of freedom is the new compassion which extends pity not to the raped but to the rapist, 367
sister of common law, 98
speech and press, infra
thought, freedom of, 225, 226
we are in bondage to the law in order that we may be free, 343
we seek not just freedom but opportunity, 195
where freedom slowly broadens down from President to President, 461

Free government, voluminous code of laws as one of inconveniences necessarily connected with advantages of, 90

Free men, necessitous men as not, 121

Free Parliament, 393

Fresh justice is the sweetest, 155

Fresh laws, 391

Fresh terror, death is now attended with, 52

Friction incident to the distribution of the governmental powers, 232

Friend—
generally, 227
but what are the 20 acts of Parliament amongst friends, 394
eat and drink as friends, 376

647

Government—Cont'd
no distinction can be made between the government as
prosecutor and the government as judge, 567
overthrowing government, infra
separation of powers, 232, 233
sovereignty, infra
state, infra
taxation, infra
to be free is to live under a
government by law, 404
treason, 543
wins its point when justice is
done in its courts, 325

Governor, judges are lawyers who
knew a governor, 276

Gowns of lawyers as lined with the
wilfulness of their clients, 42

Grace of God, cross-examination
of witnesses, 139

Gracious lady, we implore, go
away and sin no more, 545

Gradual encroachments upon freedom, 403

Grammar schools, legislatures are
not, 386

Grammatical accuracy, legislative
acts drawn with, 386

Grammatical construction, 263

Grand jurymen since before Noah
was a sailor, 321

Grant fought for time, 542

Grants, 122

Gratis dictum, 161

Gratuitous opinion, obiter dictum
as, 159

Gratuity, generally. Gift, supra

Graves, men should not sin in
their graves, 563

Graveyard, compulsory unification
of opinion as achieving unanimity of, 226

Gravity—
judicial precepts, 291
let your speech be with gravity,
291

Gray's Inn for walks, 251

Greatness—
authority, great men in judicial
places will never want, 45
bad law, great cases as making,
63

Greatness—Cont'd
case decided on great consideration, 64
every calling is great when
greatly pursued, 468
greatest orator among the lawyers, greatest lawyer among
the orators, 370
jest, matters privileged from,
269
justice as great interest of man
on earth, 327
nations, like great men, should
keep their word, 544
society, great man represents a
great ganglion in the nerve
of, 415
speaking of own greatness, 166
study of law as great pursuit,
472
there shall be no difference of
persons, you shall hear the
little as well as the great,
292
to be a great lawyer, I must give
up my chance of being a
great man, 472

Greek, knowledge, 331

Grief, lawyer overcome by, 41

Grievances, petitioning government for redress of, 82

Grinding stone narrow whilst they
sharpen, 186

Grin on face, taking a fee with,
380

Gross negligence, 432

Growth—
modification implies, 73
of law, 73–77
law will become entirely consistent only when it
ceases to grow, 104

Guaranty of justice, 281

Guardian and ward, 233

Guardian of liberty, justice as, 324

Guardians, legislatures are ultimate guardians, 392

Guess—
evening clothes, expert opinion
as guess in, 570
interpretation of intent of legislature, 259

Guidance, pray for divine guidance, 293

651

Guide—
    judicial opinions as, 150
    nonsense of one man cannot be
        a guide for that of another,
        560
Guilt—
    generally, 30, 31, 234
    death penalty escaped by guilty
        rather than one innocent
        person be executed, 134
    Gideon's trumpet, 383
    hands may be red with blood
        and his guilt may shriek to
        high heaven, 366
    he threatens the innocent who
        spares the guilty, 364
    presumptions, 316, 466
    the innocent and the just you
        shall not put to death, nor
        shall you acquit the guilty,
        364
    thing too important to be trust-
        ed to trained men, 315
    treason, 543
Guise—
    judicial process, 300
    legal questions and issues, Su-
        preme Court, 304
Gunpowder, power to direct re-
    moval of, 448

H

Habeas corpus, 234, 235
    enforcement of law, 366
Habitation of man, earth as, 183
Haggle, 636
Hair, splitting of, 174
Hales, Sir James, suicide, 532
Half a dozen old gentlemen, law
    of a great nation means the
    opinions of, 351
Half truths of one generation as
    perpetuating themselves as
    the whole truths of another,
    547
Half way meeting of cause by
    judge, 48
Halifax Law, 137, 138
Hallowed place, place of justice
    as, 130
Halo, Supreme Court decorated
    with, 549

Hamilton—
    establishing freedom of the
        press, 382
    theory for time as the theory for
        which Hamilton argued,
        542
Hamlet is mine, 123
Hand—
    bias and prejudice are attitudes
        to be kept in hand, 464
    brain as like the hand, 57
    hour glass, 330
    I will go down to posterity with
        the code in my hand, 91
    press, radio, screen and maga-
        zine, hand that rules the
        country, 488
    red with blood and his guilt may
        shriek to high heaven, 366
Hand for hand, 502
Hanging—
    generally, 134–138
    black satin, Mrs. Manning in-
        sisted on being hanged in,
        425
    endeth all, 157
    gentlemen, do not hang me high,
        424
    hang half save half, 321
    he that hath an ill name is half
        hanged, 500
    hog as not bacon until it be well
        hanged, 329
    jury too frequently has at least
        one member more ready to
        hang the panel than to hang
        the traitor, 319
    they couldn't get me into court
        as a witness, not if it was
        to hang my best friend, 569
    wretches hang, that jurymen
        may dine, 321
Happiness—
    happy is he who keeps the law,
        358
    laws having such view in mind,
        410, 411
    man's happiness depends upon
        the state of his digestion,
        415
Hard cases—
    are the quicksands of the law,
        432
    as making bad law, 63, 65
    no such thing as, 64
Hardship of particular case, 61

Hardships are part of war, 557

Harmless, words in themselves may be, 572

Harmless errors, 199

Harmony of the world, voice of the law is, 363

Harpy that devours everything, law is, 407

Harvard—
a whale-ship was, 184
judicial selection, 307

Hate—
freedom for the thought that we hate, 225
jury, names of, 314
storms of, 152, 153

Haunch in the hump of the law is —obey, 346

Haven for reform movements, Supreme Court not thought as, 551

Hawks—
between two hawks, which flies the higher pitch, 337
wives will be their own carvers and, like hawks, will fly abroad and find their own prey, 244

Hayes-Tilden election contest, 153

Hazardous, definitions as, 155

Head and the hoof of the law and the haunch and the hump is— obey, 346

Headland to headland, going from, 301

Headnotes, 235

Head of corporation, 125

Head of family, husband as, 243

Heady, jury, names of, 314

Health—
advising one to make his will in time of health, 561
moving waters are full of life and health, 550
physicians and surgeons, infra
sickness, infra

Hearing, 236
accused person as given a fair, open hearing, 316
he who decides a case with the other side unheard, though he decide justly, is himself unjust, 282

Hearing—Cont'd
punishment before, 138
purpose of hearing is that the court may learn what it does not know, and it knows least about the facts, 211

Hearse, I sat by its cradle—I followed its hearse, 247

Heart—
corporation as having, 126
liberty as lying and dying in hearts of men and women, 401
loyalty is a matter of mind and of heart, not of race, 414
natural law, 429

Heart attack caused by tiger on top of bed, 22

Heart condition, tortfeasor must take his victims as he finds them, 432

Heaven—
generally, 236
blue of flag as our heaven, 217
certainty, quest for, 68
criminal justice, 137
earth hath he appointed as the suburbs of, 183
greatest scourge an angry heaven ever inflicted upon a sinning people was a dependent judiciary, 309
hands may be red with blood and his guilt may shriek to high heaven, 366
interposition of heaven in turning the hearts of their tyrants to protect them, 230
is not this house as nigh heaven as my own, 212
law doing homage to, 363
law is the invention and gift of, 350
seven hours to law, and all heaven, 188
Thwackum was for doing justice, and leaving mercy to heaven, 298
time is the wisest thing under heaven, 75
unwritten laws of, 430

Hedges of life, little fragments of my fleece that I have left upon, 576

Heinous, murder as, 425

653

Heirs, man with all his wisdom, toils for heirs he knows not who, 415

Hell—
but if this is hell, why do we see no lawyers, 413
chancery and hell as always open, 73
criminal justice, 137, 138
devil citing scripture for his purpose, 85
he dismissed hell with cost, 193
I think they will plead their clients' causes hereafter, some of them in hell, 369
person publishing book without index ought to be banished ten miles beyond hell, 248
the inferno belongs to me, 123

Helmet, the law is the safest helmet, 343

Helpless and weak, courts as standing against any winds that blow as havens of refuge, 130

Hengist and Horsa armed with machine guns, 237

Hen persisting in setting after her eggs are taken away, 31

Heritage—
constitutional privileges and immunities, 86
law of England as, 477

Hermit, live like a hermit and work like a horse, 187

Heroic hours of life not announcing their presence by drum and trumpet, 126

Heroism—
a man may live greatly in law as well as elsewhere, 473
drinking a bitter cup of, 473

He who seeks equity must do equity, 199

He who will have equity, or comes hither for equity, must do equity, 196

Hide, going to law is like skinning a milk cow for the hide, 408

Hierophant, dissenter as laying aside the role of, 167

High court of chancery, 71

Higher law than constitution, 110

Highest man is not above the people, 439

Highest reason, law as, 350

Highest tribunal of a country, half a dozen old gentlemen as forming, 351

Highlows pass as patent leathers, 117

High-mind, jury, names of, 314

High priest in temple judge of justice, judge as, 277

Highways and streets—
childproof its entire highway system, 432
drunken man is as much entitled to a safe street, 367

Hindsight, 236, 237

Hippodamus, 3

Historians, legal profession, 470

History—
generally, 237–240
a great man represents a strategic point in the campaign of history, 415
ancient, supra
books, supra
consistency of law, 104
every decision becomes a page of history, 554
interpretation of acts of parliament, 263
knowledge, 331, 337
lawyer without history or literature is a mechanic, 189
liberty, history of, 87
moral development of the race, history of the law is the history of, 345
other branches of science, and especially history, are necessary to form a lawyer, 188
precedents, infra
rules of evidence as founded in truths of, 206
scholarship history is a record of disagreements, 298
when the legislative history is doubtful, go to the statute, 258

Hit, question is not so much who was aimed at, as who was hit, 398

Hocus-pocus science, law as sort of, 69, 346

Hocus was an old cunning attorney, 368

Hogs—
hog and bacon have been so near kindred, that they are not to be separated, 329
lawyer, hogshead, 374
one ought not to have so delicate a nose, that he cannot bear the smell of hogs, 434

Holes, case full of, 64

Hollow, common sense as round, smooth, fair to view but hollow, 263

Holmes, Oliver Wendell, 240
decisions, 146, 147
will of, 566

Homage, law as won by lavish homage, 353

Home. House, infra

Homely gentlewoman, law is like, 352

Homely or conversational type, 146

Homemade pies are superior in some instances, wills never, 562

Homeopathic soup, 523

Homicidal, more cross-examinations are suicidal than, 139

Homicide. Murder, infra

Honesty—
generally, 240, 241
fraud would be honesty itself if it could only afford it, 220
judges are as honest as other men, and not more so, 273
jury system puts a ban upon, 322
lawyer, 203, 204, 374
legal ethics, 201
men who are knaves by retail are extremely honest in the gross, 423
public scandal when the law is forced to uphold a dishonest act, 366
reform of law, 494

Honor—
being the first to establish so just a rule, 456
design and object of laws, 350
foreign employment as a kind of honorable banishment, 246
law as profession which abounds with honorable men, 470

Honor—Cont'd
office of counsel, 15
the law—it has honored us, may we honor it, 349

Hoof of the law is—obey, 346

Hope—
people pressed by law have no hopes but from power, 342
rested too much upon constitutions, law and courts, 401

Horns of dilemma, judgments manage to escape, 286

Horse and buggy definition of interstate commerce, 77

Horsefeathers weighed against next Thursday, 465

Horsefly, lawyer as, 374

Horseplay of crowd, 37

Horse racing, 241, 242
I will grant no injunction merely upon priority of suit, 249

Horses—
American form of government described as three horse team provided by the Constitution, 233
between two horses, which doth bear him best, 338
clothes-horse as an animal of the equine species, 339
in crossing France, law changed as often as one changed horses, 349
it is a very unruly horse, 486
I will be master of what is my own, 244
live like a hermit and work like a horse, 187

Horse sense, 300

Hostile possession, 9

Hound of heaven, 526

House—
a home, 340
is not this house as nigh heaven as my own, 212
I will be a master of what is my own, 244
laws, like houses, lean on one another, 341
man's house is his castle, 512–515
oracular seat of the whole community, house of a great lawyer is, 370
search and seizure, 515

655

House of Commons—
   common sovereignty, 520
   is called the lower house, 394
House of Lords—
   an infallible interpreter of the
      law, 263
   appeals in, 26
How not to do it, 493
Hughes, Chief Justice, 219
Human ability, we seek not just
   legal equity, but human ability, 195
Human beings—
   do not ever make laws, 361
   lives of, 442, 443
   Nineteenth Amendment made
      women humans, 571
Humanity—
   duty of society to enforce rights
      of, 47
   Inns of Court as the nourceries
      of humanity and liberty, 250
   it is not what a lawyer tells me
      I may do, 382
   natural law, 427
   second virtue of courts, 132
Human justice, 326
Human law—
   is framed for a number of hu-
      man beings, 352
   reach not thoughts, 226
Human nature—
   as constituting part of evidence
      in every case, 207
   every law which the state enacts
      indicates a fact in, 344
   presumption shrinking and with-
      ering at breaths of, 465
Human wisdom, the law is the last
   result of, 351
Humblest man is not above the
   people, 439
Humbug, empty humbug, 520
Hum-buggery about squatter sovereignty, 523
Humor—
   dining system as putting people
      in good humor, 162
   judicial humorist, 272
Humpty Dumpty, 256
Hunching out his decisions, 299
Hungry judges soon the sentence
   sign, 321

Hungry jurymen always find for the
   plaintiff, 317
Hurry, a lawyer is always in a
   hurry, 375
Husband and wife—
   generally, 242–245
   arguments, 32
   bequest to wife, 567
   divorce, supra
   judges must be as chaste as wife
      of Caesar, 291
   law is like a scolding wife, 352
   marriage, infra
   presumption that wife acts under
      your direction, 466
   residence, 500, 501
   wills, 564
Husk, officialdom as, 438
Hyperion to a satyr, 468
Hypocritical severity, 574

I

Iago, circumstantial evidence, 208
Icy certainty, controversies on
   every conceivable subject, 299
Ideal person, court of law is bound
   to proceed upon the assumption that the legislature is an
   ideal person, 391
Ideals, 245
Ideas—
   free trade in ideas, 124, 548
   he can compress the most words
      into the smallest ideas of
      any man I ever met, 555
   historically there are three ideas
      involved in a profession, 469
   incitement, every idea is, 246
   it is one of the misfortunes of the
      law that ideas become en-
      cased in phrases, 573
   no word conveys to the mind, in
      all situations, one single
      definite idea, 574
   obscenity, 436
Identification. Description or identification, supra
Idiom in truth, 549
Idiot—
   does not the idiot eat? Does
      not the idiot drink, 252
   the law is an ass—an idiot, 243
      466

656

Idleness, 245
    no laws, however stringent, can make the idle industrious, 348

I do not remember, 421

I established law and justice in the land, 344

If, avoidance by use of, 46

Ignoble part, some criminals should escape and the government should play an ignoble part, 567

Ignoramus, 91
    lawyer as, 374

Ignorance—
    a most learned species of ignorant men, 371
    excuses no man, 337
    give your judgment, but give no reasons, 149
    he who would know anything well, must resolve to be ignorant of anything, 330
    inseparable twins, ignorance and error as, 199
    jurisprudence is the art of being methodically ignorant of what everybody knows, 312
    jury system putting premium upon, 322
    justice of the peace, 328
    law originating in ignorance and malice as called the wisdom of our ancestors, 390
    litigious spirit is more often found with ignorance than with knowledge of law, 408
    marriage without license, 335
    nicest points of law, ignorant country fellows are to determine, 400
    reformers of law, 494
    there comes a point when the court should not be ignorant as judges of what we know as men, 289
    unprejudiced by being completely ignorant, 464

Ill cause that lawyers think shame of, 347

Illegal matters, admissions, 8

Illegitimates. Bastards, supra

Illness. Sickness, infra

[Legal Quotations]—42

Illusions—
    Blackstone's contribution to jurisprudence, 53
    certainty as, 69

Imaginary laws for imaginary commonwealth, 443

Imaginary world, devise of, 565

Imaginative construction, 260

Imbecility of soul, punishment, 133

Imitation, 245, 246
    of the past, 458
    of truth, 549

Immediate answer as to law, 334

Immediate overwhelming interest as distorting judgment, 63

Immorality. Morality, infra

Immunity—
    criticism of judges, 119
    liberty implies the absence of arbitrary restraint, not immunity from reasonable regulations, 402

Impartiality—
    administration of justice, 5
    disclosure as antidote to partiality and favor, 162
    equality, supra
    judicial impartiality, 280–282
    law, 350
    prejudice or bias, infra
    publicity acting as a check, 270

Impeachment, 246
    foreign judgment impeached for fraud, 160
    reasons for decision, knowing of, 152

Imperative or magisterial type, 146

Imperfections—
    conscious as we are of one another's many imperfections, 271
    incident to human nature, 323
    its want of resemblance, 500

Impertinent flying out to show learning, 291

Impetuous party, young attorney as, 380

Implacable, jury, names of, 314

Implication—
    contracts, 121
    silence is sometimes most expressive, 518

Importance, remember there are no unimportant cases, 292

[Legal Quotations]

Insects, English constitution as compared with work of, 114

Insolvency. Bankruptcy or insolvency, supra

Insolvent, every judge is politically insolvent, 277

Instinct with an obligation, 121

Instructions to jury, 30
it is the duty of the judge to tell the jury how to do right, 320
judicial opinions are written to guide the judge as to the law, not to standardize the language to be used in, 150
justice of the peace, 328
prejudice, cure of, 464

Instructive but not authoritative, Roman law as, 509

Instruments of the law, courts as, 287

Insult—
action for, 3
freedom of speech, 223

Insurance, 253

Integrity—
defense of unpopular causes, 153
esteem of professional brethren, attainment of, 474
legal profession, 478, 481
proper virtue, 291

Intellectual abstraction, freedom as not, 404

Intellectual ambition, 20

Intellectual faculties, publicity acting as a spur, 270

Intelligence—
I bow before his superior intelligence, 279
ignorance, supra
jury system puts a ban upon, 322
law is intelligence without passion, 349
selection of jury, 320

Intensity in deciding case, 64

Intent, 253–255
legislature, 260
motive, 424
wills, 560, 563
words, meaning of, 574

Intercourse, commerce as, 95

Interest, 255
conflict of interests, supra
public, 485, 486

Interference with administration of justice, 118

Interlocutory motions, making or opposing, 204

Internal sense is what makes the law, 355

International law, 255
war crimes, 558, 559

Interpretation. Construction or interpretation, supra

Interpreters of the law, judges as, 486

Interrogatories, leading questions, 488

Interstate commerce. Commerce, supra

Interstate Commerce Commission, woosh-woosh methods of, 8

Interstitially, judges can legislate only, 287

Intestate distribution of property, 561

Intoxication, 267, 268
appeal from Philip drunk to Philip sober, 26
marriage between drunk or delirious people would be bad, 417
no laws can make the drunken sober, 348
prohibition is better than no liquor at all, 356
right to be locked up in station house if found drunk, 86

Intricate nature of argument to confound court, 37

Intuitions of public policy, 345

Intuitive flash of understanding which makes the jump-spark connection between question and decision, 299

Invasion of interest, actionable negligence, 431

Invention of story by lawyer for client, 40

Inventions, young men are fitter to invent than to judge, 576

Investigation, 268
criminal investigation as becoming one way street, 365
reasonable man, 492

Invitation, temptation is not always, 269

Invitee, 268, 269

Iron head, judge must have, 279

Irregular movements of human beings do not admit of any universal and simple rule, 390

Irrelevance can be highly enlightening, 205

Irresponsible, dissenter as, 166

Isolation, justices of Supreme Court working in, 551

Israel judged by Samuel, 270

Issues, opinions, writing of, 146, 147

Ita lex scripta est, 332

Italian ancestry, names, 426

J

Jackdaws strut in peacock's feathers, 117

Jail, habeas corpus, 234

Janus—
precedent, 458
verbal monstrosity, 339

Jargon of their own, 341

Jealous mistress, law as, 353

Jedwood justice, 138

Jefferson stands at the head of the enemies of the judiciary, 310

Jest, 269

Jew, 269
confrontation for King, 102, 103

Jewel in the world comparable to learning, 333

Jewels, finding of, 450, 451

Jigsaw tax law, 537

Jill justice, 59

Joan of Arc, trial of, 140

Jobbists, society of, 438

John Doe and Richard Roe, 445

John Shaw, give us your paw, 192

Joints, constitutional principles allow a little play in its joints, 265

Jokes, contempt of court by laughing at, 118

Jolly testator who makes his own will, 561, 562

Journey, wrong directions which do not put the traveler out of his way, furnish no reasons for repeating the journey, 199

Judges—
generally, 269–277
acme of judicial distinction as looking lawyer straight in eyes and not hearing a word he says, 51
adequate presentation of case before, 49
advocate as judge, 14, 15
all hail, great judge! 273
all the law, no judge is bound to know, 331
anomaly arising from blindly following hasty decision of distinguished judge, 24
appraisal, 278–280
authority, 43–46
bench and bar, 48–51
biased attention, 50
breach of promise, 57
certainty, search for, 68
chambers, supra
chief justice, supra
clerk as finger of court, 89
complex cases, 66
concurrence, 100
constitution as what the judges say it is, 107
contempt of court, 118, 119
contentions of law as won or lcst on the facts, 211
country lawyer joining a client at the tavern in damning the judge, 475
court packing, 127–129
cutting off evidence or counsel too short, 48
decisions or judgments, supra
discretion, 162–164
dissent, 166–173
doubt, 177, 178
enforcement of law, 364–367
epitaph, 193
equity, supra
errors, judges make the errors, 317
everybody is presumed to know the law except His Majesty's judges, 336
examination of witnesses, 50
fair comment upon the evidence, 203

661

L

[Legal Quotations]—43

Matrix of every other freedom, freedom of thought as, 225

Maxim, 419, 420

Maximum wage, 422

May do, it is not what a lawyer tells me I may do, 382

Mayonnaise, that gives judicial mayonnaise a touch of angostura, 339

Meadows, devise of, 565

Meaning—
construction or interpretation, supra
definitions, supra
felt rather than proved, 261
lawyers as twisting, 371
legislation, framers themselves have no very distinct notion of its meaning, 389
many words have no legal meaning, 399
words, 572–576

Means, to procure an eminent good by means that are unlawful, 302

Measure, 420

Measure of damages. Damages, supra

Mechanic, lawyer without history or literature is a mechanic, 189

Mechanical regularity, he was a bird of passage of almost mechanical regularity, 539

Medes and Persians, 343

Medicines, recreations to be used as, 493

Mediocrity of success by men of age, 17

Melody is more than the notes, 259

Memory—
generally, 420, 421
bequest of, 566
cursory reading as making a confused memory, 489
few men pinched with the messengers of death have a disposing memory, 560
poetical reports of law cases, 498
prefaces, 462
runneth not to the contrary, 541

Men—
feelings of men are as different as their faces, 213
government of laws and men, 231, 232
laws as made for men in general, 345

Mental third degree, 540, 541

Mental torture, suppressed speech as occasion of, 49

Mental vision embraces distant scenes, 148

Mephistopheles, judges something of, 273

Mercy—
confessions, 101
equity, 198
exceptions, merciful in making, 295
have mercy on me, oh God, according to Thy great mercy, 431
justice, 326, 327
seasons justice, 327
shown to broken reed, 101
Thwackum was for doing justice, and leaving mercy to heaven, 298

Merit, lawyers' fees, 213

Metaphor, 421
Blackstone as enlivening jurisprudence with, 53

Metaphysical grounds, legal profession, 470

Metaphysical order, 440

Metaphysical subtleties, meaning of statute not to be sought for in, 262

Meum and tuum, 421

Microscope and telescope, Mr. Justice Brandeis as master of both, 148

Midas chosen to decide between Pan and Apollo, 368

Middle way, 300

Midnight judges, 275

Mighty, thou shall not honor the person of the mighty, 294, 295

Military service, 557–559

Milky Way, bequest of, 564

Mind—
if we would guide by the light of reason, we must let our minds be bold, 144

Monster, 422
    threat of damages we're the jury, threat of fury, 318

Moon, till the man in the moon will allow it's a cheese, 372

Morals and morality—
    generally, 422, 423
    betting at horse races, 241
    civilization, test of moral quality of, 87
    common law without a precedent, 461
    high standard of commercial morality, advantages of maintaining, 241
    husband and wife, 244
    judges maintaining relation between law and morals, 291
    judges should be of exemplary morals, 294
    law as moral theories, 345
    law as the witness in the external deposit of moral life, 345
    legal education, 185
    legal ethics, 202
    manners as aiding, 416
    natural law, 426–430
    of what use are laws, inoperative through public immorality, 365
    poverty and immorality are not synonymous, 451
    publicity acting as a check, 270
    they incur no legal penalties and no moral censure, 539
    to procure an eminent good by means that are unlawful, 302
    trustee as held to something stricter than morals of the marketplace, 546
    ultimate justification of the law as found in moral considerations, 203

Morning, study all the morning and talk all the afternoon, 189

Mortality—
    constitutional precedents, 458
    it has taken a decade to elevate Mr. Justice Holmes from deity to, 240

Mortal men! Be wary how ye judge, 292

Mortgage, 423

Mortuary estimates, 52

Moses—
    first reporter or writer of law in the world, 428
    law giver, and God's first pen, 341
    to be at least as old as lawyer Moses, 122

Mother—
    certainty as mother of quietness and repose, 69
    England as mother of Parliament, 391
    idleness as mother of all vice and weakness, 245
    Lizzie Borden, 424
    truth, mother of justice, 547

Mothers-in-law, two classes of people have poor public relations, 487

Motions, 423

Motive, 424
    which leaves old women to make bequest to society, 78

Motor vehicles, bodily injuries in a collision between two stationary motor cars, liability, 396

Moulds of life expand and shrink, 405

Mountain ranges of my profession, 152

Mouth—
    judges are no more than mouths that pronounce the words of law, 275
    out of thine own mouth will I judge thee, 152

Muddle made of a simple little act, 388

Mules, facts are contrary mules, 211

Multiplication of reports, 499

Multiplicity of interests and sects, civil rights as, 88

Multiplied tyranny, 400

Multiplying of words by attorneys when they argue, 34

Multitude, tyranny of, 400

Municipality. City, supra

Munificent bequest in pauper's will, 86

Negligence—Cont'd
  tort, 543
  tortfeasor must take his victims as he finds them, 432
Negotiable instruments, 433
  reasonable man, 492
Negroes—
  defense of unpopular causes, 154, 555
  deliberation too much and speed not enough in enforcing constitutional rights, 526
  discrimination, supra
  slavery, 518–520
Neighborhood—
  justice of the peace, 328
  zoning, 576
Neighbors—
  boundaries, 56
  cursed be he that removeth his neighbor's landmarks, 542
  in righteousness shalt thou judge thy neighbor, 295
  lawyer compounds quarrels among his neighbors, without going to law, 377
  love your neighbor, 181
  persuade your neighbors to compromise whenever you can, 409
  study of law qualifies a man to be useful to, 336
  the law is fulfilled in one word: thou shalt love thy neighbor as thyself, 346
Nerves of society, a great man represents a great ganglion in, 415
Nest by swallow built under the eaves of a court of justice, 129
Neutral, solicitor general is not, 325
Neutrality of an impartial judge, 280
New and omitted cases often present themselves, 295, 296
New argument never becoming old, 35
New fashion, law is like, 352
New laws—
  are like apothecaries' drugs, 73
  judges as not delegated to denounce, 284
New projects, young men fitter for, 576

Newspaper—
  contempt of court by newspaper read in presence of judge, 118
  freedom of press, 221
Newton, Sir Isaac, 331
New trial—
  country lawyer, 475
  legal ethics, 204
New world of law, 510
New York City, ambulance chasing in, 20
New York Court of Appeals as thinking what the Supreme Court of Ohio would think, 102
New York minimum wage law as unconstitutional, 128
Night and moon, bequest of, 564
Nile, common law origin as undiscoverable as the head of the Nile, 96
Nightstick, there's a lot of law at the end of, 137
Nine old men, court packing, 129
Nineteenth Amendment, men and women, differences between, 571
Nisi prius—
  cases, 84
  leader, 446
  nuisance, 272
  reporter, 498
Noah, grand-jurymen since before Noah was a sailor, 321
Noble—
  aspirations, 60
  law—in its nature the noblest and most beneficial to mankind, 470
  legal profession, 469, 479
  popularity, seeking of, 450
  the law does not perfectly comprehend what is noblest and most just for all, 389
No good, jury, names of, 314
Noise—
  argument, 36
  they that govern most make least noise, 230
  worse cause as making most noise, 35

O

Parliament—Cont'd
most high and absolute power of the realme consisteth in the Parliament, 394
reform of, 495
what are the 20 acts of Parliament amongst friends, 394

Parliamentary draftsman, 388

Parlor instead of barnyard, pig in, 434

Parricide, easier to commit than to justify, 154

Partiality. Impartiality, supra

Particular cases—
law as not consisting in, 65
laws are not made for, 345

Particulars, actions are concerned with, 384

Particular times, laws are formed by the manners and exigencies of, 388

Parties—
defendant, supra
judge shall know nothing about the parties, 280
plaintiff, infra

Partisan debate and scholarly speculations, authority resulting from, 44

Partnership, 441
glorious calling, partner and companion in, 471
law will not have any partnership with the Eastern muses, 353
state as partnership in justice, 194

Passion—
anger does not become a judge, so neither doth pity, 295
argument, passionate nature of, 37
best men are but men transported with, 415
defense of unpopular causes, 154, 155
discretion of judge as depending upon, 163
justice of the peace, 328
law is intelligence without, 349
law originating in ignorance and malice as called the wisdom of our ancestors, 390
natural law, 429
perverts the minds of rulers, 231

Passion—Cont'd
that in the execution of judgment, I carefully lay aside my own passions, 293

Passive instrument, court as, 131

Passport, negotiable instrument as, 433

Past, 441
profits, 483

Patching up of law from time to time, 385

Patchwork minds of lawyers, 186

Patent letters, highlows passing as, 117

Patents, 59, 123, 124

Paternoster Case, 66, 67

Patience—
delay, 156
he must have patience who to law will go, 156
judges, 294, 295
judicial precepts, 291
kindly and patient man who is not a profound lawyer will make a far better judge than an ill-tempered genius, 306
ten commandments for the new judge, 292
the gods grow angry with your patience, 366
to him that goes to law, requisites, 407

Patriotism—
duties of patriot from those of advocate, separating, 13
duty to increase one's taxes, lack of, 535
freedom is not a word to adorn an oration upon occasions of patriotic rejoicing, 404
popularity, 450

Patronage, judiciary, 310

Pauper's will, munificent bequest in, 86

Payment—
arrest for debt, 143
experience as not sufficiently uniform to raise a presumption, 465

Peace—
breach of, 223
decisions of judges, functions of, 145

683

[Legal Quotations]—44

Reporter—Cont'd
  headnotes, 235
  rancid butter, 340

Report me and my cause aright, 500

Reports or reporting, 496–500
  anyone who may satisfy himself, 272
  fame found in legal reports, 64

Repose is not the destiny of man, 69

Representation and taxation, 538

Representative, advocate as, 14

Reprobate, interest is a great rascal, but is not an absolute reprobate, 255

Republic—
  constitution of, 106
  influence of lawyers in public business increasing in proportion to the power of the people, 480

Republican character, jury as preserving, 322

Republican in Paris and royalist in London, 85

Reputation, 500
  convey a libel in a frown and wink a reputation down, 399
  good will, 229
  judicial department passing on, 309
  presumption of innocence or guilt, 316

Rescue, danger as inviting, 142

Resemblance, 500

Residents, 500, 501
  taxation, 539

Res ipsa loquitor, 501, 502

Resolution, the reason of, 490

Respect for law, 360, 361

Respect given dictum, 160

Responsibility—
  corporations as ingenious device for obtaining individual profit without individual responsibility, 124
  power for the justices, 304
  security against the abuse of discretion as resting on, 164
  time of war, 557

Rest, lawsuits consume, 412

Rest in peace, those things which have been so often adjudged ought to rest in peace, 527

Restitution, 502

Restraint—
  end of law is not to abolish or to restrain, 359
  imprisonment, 246
  judicial restraint, 302
  liberty implies the absence of arbitrary restraint, not immunity from reasonable regulations, 402
  officers of government as subjected to legal restraint, 438
  windward of the law, 342

Restricted railroad ticket, good for this day and train only, 529

Result—
  chance, 70
  equality as, 195
  judiciary must be put in motion in order to produce a result, 310
  Marshall has a compass, puts out to sea, and goes directly to the result, 301

Retaliation, 502, 503

Retirement, 503

Retouching of strokes on canvass, constitution, 107

Retrogression, 74

Return of part of fee, 215

Revenge, 42, 503
  have not the idiot revenge, 252

Revenue. Taxation, infra

Reverence—
  constitution looked at with, 108
  for the law, 360
  judges ought to be more reverent than plausible, 291
  precedent, reverence given, 457

Reversal, 504–506
  don't be dismayed when reversed, 292
  in banc, 273

Review. Appeals, supra

Reviews, law reviews, 368

Revocation—
  contract, 122
  will, 564

Revoking her own revocation, 562

697

699

Statutes—Cont'd
  reading of, 489
  substituted for decision, 73, 74
  the statute enjoins truth; this
    label exhales deceit, 144
  tyrant, statute as like, 97
  unconstitutional statute pre-
    sumed to have been known
    to be nullity, 115
  validity, 554, 555
  words, 575

Stealing, generally. Theft, infra

Stealing teeth out of your very
  mouth, 30

Steam engine in trousers, Daniel
  Webster struck me much like,
  559

Stepping stone to preferment in the
  political line, study of law as,
  336

Sterilized board of directors, stockholders not permitted to
  create, 125

Stings, division of able lawyers
  into kitchen knives, razors,
  and stings, 372

Stipulate, I should like to stipulate
  for some kind of order, 440

Stockholders as creating a sterilized
  board of directors, 125

Stock in trade, lawyer's advice as,
  10

Stomach—
  corporation as having, 126
  eat within, 452
  forcible extraction of contents
    of, 513
  legislators' solution as too strong
    for the judicial stomach,
    286

Storm—
  extraordinary matters, 210
  justice not to be taken by, 73
  Sidmouth, 495

Storm centre, Supreme Court as,
  551

Storms of human hate and passion,
  152, 153

Strange and wondrous thing, the
  sea as, 8

Strangers, 18, 19
  he that is a surety for, 533

[Legal Quotations]—45

Straw—
  he delights to balance, 177
  he'll go to law for the wagging
    of a straw, 412

Streams, devise of, 565

Streams of justice kept clear and
  pure, 545

Streets—
  highways and streets, supra
  the man in, 491

Strength, bequest of confidence in
  their own strength, 566

Stretching of power, 452

Strict statutes and most biting laws,
  367

Strife—
  all the law in the world has
    been obtained by, 360
  welcome strife, 469

Strike, 532

Stringent execution, 365

Stronger, justice is but the interest
  of, 326

Struggle, life to the law is, 360

Strumpet, libel against, 397

Stubborn strength of constitution,
  107

Study of law—
  commendation of self for suc-
    cessful study, 94
  judges, 272
  law as a jealous mistress, 353
  objection to legal studies is the
    amount of detail they in-
    volve, 472

Study renders men acute, inquisitive, dexterous, prompt in attack, ready in defense, full of
  resources, 185

Stupidity, jury system putting
  premium upon, 322

Style of legal decisions, 145
  Supreme Court, 407

Styx, wait on the other bank of,
  559

Sub judice whether it be a libel or
  not, 397

Subsistence, a power over a man's
  subsistence amounts to a
  power over his will, 309

　　　　　　　　　　　　[Legal Quotations]

Swiss troops fighting on both sides, 84

Switch in time saves nine, 128

Switzers, law, logic and Switzers may be hired to fight for anybody, 347

Sword, pen is mightier than, 540

Sword of the community, 308

Syllables govern the word, 575

Symbolic law, 362, 363

Symbols—
flag, 217
overspeaking judge is no well tuned symbol, 291

Sympathetic and imaginative construction, 260

Sympathy before jury, 545

Syntactical correctness, 536

Synthesis, 21

T

Taft, things go happily in the conference room with, 549

Talk, 534
gobbledygook, 340
if the present Congress errs in too much talking, how can it be otherwise, 392

Talkative, let your speech be with gravity and not talkative, 291

Tape recordings, argument by use of, 36

Tapestry, man's life, like a piece of tapestry, is made up of many strands which interwoven make a pattern, 405

Tarantula of opposition, one bit by, 222

Tattoo on the epidermis, prejudice as clinging to the mind like, 464

Tautologies to be cut off, 497

Taxation—
generally, 534–539
court must be blind not to see that the so called tax is imposed to stop the employment of children, 290
king being in great want of money, called upon Parliament, 395

Taxation—Cont'd
legislature must not raise taxes on the property of the people without the consent of the people, 392
nothing certain but death and taxes, 106
Parliament, acts of, 394
private property, right of, 87

Tea, jury trial is not an afternoon tea, 545

Teacher—
government as, 229
the event is always a great teacher, 236

Teachers of the law when they understand neither what they say nor the things about which they make assertion, 337

Teaching reverence for the laws, 360

Tears as legitimate argument before a jury, 545

Technical details, the worst enemy of the law is the man who knows only, 338

Technical standpoint, fair play in criminal case from, 366

Technique of justice, law is, 350

Teeth of both law and facts, power of jury, 319

Telegraph company, source of law, 361

Telemarque's mother, 561

Telescope and microscope, Mr. Justice Brandeis as master of, 148

Television, 540

Temper—
between two blades, which bears the better temper, 338
change in tempers of men and society, 75
discretion of judge as depending upon, 163
Hocus was an old cunning attorney, 368
kindly and patient man who is not a profound lawyer will make a far better judge than an ill-tempered genius, 306

Temperament, I have the judicial temperament. I hate work, 272

Verdict—Cont'd
  not proven, 555, 556
  sentence, verdict after, 134
  the jury has the power to bring
    in a verdict in the teeth of
    both law and facts, 319
Verse, law cases in, 64
Verses were invented for the help
  of memory, 420
Vesper-time, agreement of jury at,
  321
Vessels—
  ships, supra
  words a judge must construe are
    empty vessels into which he
    can pour nearly anything he
    will, 259
Vested rights, judges are the final
  seat of authority, 288
Veto of judges wrapped up in protective veil of adjectives, 286
Vexatious cause of action, 61
Vexatious prosecutions, 328
Vice—
  craft is the vice, not the spirit
    of the profession, 477
  human laws do not forbid all
    vices, 352
  idleness is mother of all vices
    and weakness, 245
  reasonable man, 492
Victim of spirit of injustice tomorrow, 281
Victor's garland at thy door, 16
Vigilance, liberty, condition to,
  401
Vindication of policy of the law,
  288
Vinegar, slang as, 340
Violation of a right, negligence,
  431
Violence, revolution, 506
Virgin state of law, 25
Virtue—
  diligence, 161
  fraud as paying sort of homage
    to, 220
  human law is framed for a
    number of human beings,
    the majority of whom are
    not perfect in virtue, 352
  "if," 47

Virtue—Cont'd
  integrity is their portion and
    proper virtue, 291
  justice as the pontifical virtue,
    323
  law productive of virtue in those
    that live under it, 385
  liberty or happiness without any
    virtue in the people, 404
  mysterious view of wax and
    parchment, 440
  persecution is a very easy form
    of, 443
Vision. Sight, supra
Vitality of constitution, 551
Vital not formal, significance of
  constitution as, 265
Vitriol, profanity as, 340
Vituperative epithet, 432
Voice—
  constitution, Supreme Court as
    voice of, 550
  harmony of the world, voice of
    the law is, 363
  representative body as, 268
Void, human laws as becoming,
  428
Voila! the nonsuit of cow beef,
  213
Voluntary acts, insanity, 253
Voting. Elections, supra

W

Wagering. Gambling, supra
Wages—
  judicial selection, 305
  maximum wage, 422
  occupation, 438
Wagging of a straw, he'll go to
  law for, 412
Walk within the purlieus of the
  law, 344
Wall of separation between church
  and state, 79–82
Wall Street lawyer, 372
Wall to you or me would look like
  a triumphal arch to the experienced eye of a lawyer, 334
War, 557, 558
  constitution in time of, 106
  crimes, 558, 559

715

Words—Cont'd
many words have no legal meaning, 399
the fellow takes down my very words, 498
twisting of words by lawyers, 371
usage as one of the great master keys which unlocks the meaning of words, 141

Word was their bond, 471

Work—
I have the judicial temperament. I hate work, 272
is done, 405

Workman standing hard by saw the vase as it cracked, 170

Works do follow him, 472

World—
no man can be a knowing lawyer in any nation, who hath not well pondered the common law of the world, 338
stars of flag as our world, 217

Worms, the jury found as how certain slugs had sent him to the worms, 320

Wormwood, view that turned judgment into, 323

Worship. Religion, supra

Worst cause making most noise, 35

Would you be surprised to hear that—?, 139

Write that down, the king said to the jury, 315

Writings, 576
language, 338–341

Writ of habeas corpus, 234, 235

Writs of summons, 395

Written law, equity as that idea of justice which contravenes, 196

Written word, spoken word dissolves, but the written one abides and perpetuates a scandal, 397

Wrong—
abandonment of client upon perceiving wrongdoing, 435
act of Parliament can do no wrong, though it may do several things that look pretty odd, 388
authorities as, 45

Wrong—Cont'd
certainty, wrong as following, 69
directions which are wrong but do not put the traveler out of his way furnish no reasons for repeating the journey, 199
extreme right with wiseness is extreme wrong, 355
he did not dare to do right for fear of doing wrong, 177
I may be wrong, and often am, but I never doubt, 178
it is disheartening to find so much that is right in an opinion which seems to me fundamentally wrong, 172
it is never the law itself that is in the wrong, 256
judge courageous and not to give the devil his due, 281
king is incapable of doing or thinking wrong, 521
law is a rule of civil conduct commanding what is right and prohibiting what is wrong, 349
public wrongs are the public rights in embryo, 487
reversal, supra

Y

Yale College, a whale-ship was my, 184

Yearbooks, 56
decisions, seriatim, 151

Years, character of words as changing with, 572

Yesterday, law is what it is today because of what the law was yesterday, 240

Young or old—
bequest to, 565, 566
judge should not be young, 275
lawyers, 378–381
an old physician and a young lawyer, 469
do grow old in lawsuits, 369
judge as kind to, 51
relying too much on speech making, 188
there is nothing does a lawyer so much good as to be half starved, 187